FORMULA 1
CAR BY CAR 2000-09

Published in March 2024

ISBN 978-1-910505-86-1

Published by Evro Publishing
Westrow House, Holwell, Sherborne, Dorset DT9 5LF, UK

Edited by Mark Hughes
Designed by Richard Parsons

Printed and bound in China by 1010 Printing International Ltd

www.evropublishing.com

The author

Peter Higham is a freelance writer who has worked in the motor racing media for over 30 years.
A motor racing enthusiast since watching the 1973 Silverstone International Trophy on television,
Higham joined Haymarket Publishing in 1986 to work in Autosport's advertising department and remained
with the company for nearly 30 years. Part of the launch publishing team for football monthly magazine
FourFourTwo, he was involved with the LAT Photographic business for 17 years and Publishing Director of
Haymarket Consumer Media's motor racing publications during the 2000s. He has written nine previous
books, including the first five titles in the *Formula 1 Car by Car* series covering the 1950s, 1960s, 1970s, 1980s
and 1990s. He has been a columnist for *Autosport* and *Motor Sport* and was instrumental in running the
prestigious *Autosport* Awards for over 25 years.

The photographs

All of the photographs in this book have been sourced from Motorsport Images (www.motorsportimages.
com). This London-based archive is the largest motoring and motorsport picture collection in the world
with over 23 million colour images and black and white negatives dating back to 1895. It includes the
collections of LAT Images and Sutton Images as well as the work of Rainer Schlegelmilch, Ercole Colombo
and Giorgio Piola. Motorsport Images also photographs today's Formula 1 World Championship, with
full-time photographers and digital technicians at every race. Other events covered include the WRC, World
Endurance Championship, Le Mans 24 Hours, IndyCar, NASCAR, ALMS, GP2 Series, GP3 Series, World Series
by Renault, DTM and National Championships including BTCC and British F3. As part of Motorsport Network,
Motorsport Images supplies all of the company's leading media, including Autosport and GP Racing.

The cover

The main image on the front shows Michael Schumacher's Ferrari F2002 during the 2002 Brazilian GP. The
cars in the inset photos on the front are (from left) 2005 Renault R25 (Fernando Alonso, Brazilian GP), 2007
Ferrari F2007 (Kimi Räikkönen, British GP), 2008 McLaren MP4-23-Mercedes-Benz (Lewis Hamilton, German
GP) and 2009 Brawn BGP001-Mercedes-Benz (Jenson Button, Singapore GP). The photos on the back depict
(from top left to bottom right) 2001 McLaren MP4-16-Mercedes-Benz (David Coulthard, Brazilian GP), 2002
Ferrari F2002 (Rubens Barrichello, Japanese GP), 2008 Ferrari F2008 (Felipe Massa, Brazilian GP) and 2009 Red
Bull RB5-Renault (Sebastian Vettel, Italian GP).

FORMULA 1
CAR BY CAR **2000-09**

EVRO
PUBLISHING

Peter Higham

CONTENTS

INTRODUCTION

The first decade of the new millennium was characterised by the most prolonged era of Formula 1 dominance by a single team and driver thus far, followed by a bright new Spanish star, the most impressive rookie in history, a record fine for one of F1's grandee teams and, finally, the most unexpected of world championship successes.

Michael Schumacher and Ferrari won five successive drivers' and constructors' titles from 2000 in an awesome and sometimes dismissive display. That dynasty was finally toppled by the raw talent of Fernando Alonso allied to the engineering and strategic nous of Renault. The Spanish double champion then moved to McLaren but F1 and the team were rocked by the damaging 'Spygate' affair that overshadowed 2007. Lewis Hamilton, Alonso's team-mate, almost won that 2007 crown in his debut year before snatching his maiden title in the most dramatic circumstances 12 months later.

The major motor manufacturers had taken an increasing interest in F1 for several years, but economic recession and falling global car sales resulted in an exodus as the sport's financial viability was placed in question. One such to withdraw was Honda in December 2008, and the team only survived as an independent following a last-ditch management buyout for £1. That the renamed Brawn Grand Prix won the 2009 World Championship was the stuff of fairytale fuelled by its controversial 'double-diffuser' interpretation of new rules.

That was an exception in a period of incremental technical gains. Regulations were ever more restrictive with 3-litre V10 engines mandatory from 2000, reduced to 2.4-litre V8s in 2006, and longitudinal seven-speed semi-automatic gearboxes soon the norm, with a single tyre supplier from 2007. These were the years in which the FIA tried to implement cost controls. Testing was curtailed although that coincided with investment in wind tunnels, simulators and computational fluid dynamics.

The World Championship expanded to the east with well-funded new venues in Bahrain, China, Singapore and Abu Dhabi. The latest attempt to establish F1 in the United States occurred at the Indianapolis Motor Speedway but the 2005 event was marred when the Michelin-shod teams pulled out after the formation lap on safety grounds, and the race disappeared from the calendar once more by the end of the decade.

Michael Schumacher's narrow defeat by Fernando Alonso at Imola in 2005 represented the power shift from Ferrari to Renault

KEY TO 'DRIVER PERFORMANCE' CHARTS

Qualifying positions are included in superscript next to the race result. When a driver has led a Grand Prix across the line is indicated by that result being underlined and in bold.

R	Retired
NC	Not classified
DSQ	Disqualified
DNS	Did not start
DNP	Did not take part in qualifying
DNQ	Did not qualify
NPQ	Did not pre-qualify
FL	Fastest lap
NT	No time recorded in qualifying
T	Friday test driver

THE GRAND PRIX KEY IS AS FOLLOWS:

A	Austria
AUS	Australia
B	Belgium
BR	Brazil
BRN	Bahrain
CDN	Canada
D	Germany
E	Spain
EU	Europe
F	France
GB	Britain
H	Hungary
I	Italy
J	Japan
MAL	Malaysia
MC	Monaco
PRC	China
RSM	San Marino
SGP	Singapore
TR	Turkey
UAE	Abu Dhabi
USA	United States

ACKNOWLEDGEMENTS

Many thanks to Mark Hughes and Richard Parsons for their patient editing and design of *Formula 1 Car by Car 2000–09*, and to Eric Verdon-Roe of Evro Publishing for commissioning the series. The photographs all come from the vast archives of Motorsport Images, which includes collections such as LAT Photographic, Sutton Images and Rainer Schlegelmilch. Thanks to Steven Tee and all the photographers whose images are included on these pages. Thanks also to Tim Clarke, and to Kevin Wood, Tim Wright, Catherine Benham, Jade Gallagher and Paul Duncan for making so much of the pre-digital material available online. Finally, thanks to Françoise, Joe, Luc, Sofia and Florence as always.

SELECTED BIBLIOGRAPHY

MAGAZINES AND ANNUALS
Autocourse (Icon Publishing, Cheltenham, UK)
Autosport (Autosport Media UK, Isleworth, UK)
   F1 Racing (now GP Racing) (Autosport Media UK, Isleworth, UK)
Motor Sport (Motor Sport Magazine, London, UK)
Motorsport News (Kelsey Media, Yalding, UK)

BOOKS
Autocourse Grand Prix Who's Who Fourth Edition
   by Steve Small (Icon Publishing, Malvern, UK, 2012)

Driven To Crime by Crispian Besley (Evro Publishing, Sherborne, UK, 2022)

Ferrari: Men From Maranello by Anthony Pritchard (Haynes, Sparkford, UK, 2009)

Grand Prix Databook by David Hayhoe and David Holland (Haynes, Sparkford, UK, 2006)

How To Build A Car by Adrian Newey (HarperCollins, London, UK, 2017)

Survive. Drive. Win. by Nick Fry with Ed Gorman (Atlantic Books, London, UK, 2019)

Total Competition by Ross Brawn and Adam Parr (Simon & Schuster, London, UK, 2016)

WEBSITES
www.autosport.com
www.bbc.co.uk
www.f1technical.net
www.formula1.com
www.grandprix.com
www.historicracing.com
www.motorsportmagazine.com
www.oldracingcars.com
www.the-race.com
www.youtube.com

Corinna and Michael Schumacher celebrate the German driver's third world title with his Ferrari team

2000
SCHUMACHER ENDS FERRARI'S 21-YEAR WAIT

Mika Häkkinen takes the German Grand Prix lead as Michael Schumacher and Giancarlo Fisichella crash out

Michael Schumacher finally delivered Ferrari's first drivers' title since 1979 thanks to a record-equalling nine victories. It was the first time since 1988 that only two teams won races, with outgoing double champion Mika Häkkinen runner-up for McLaren-Mercedes.

There was increasing interest in F1 from motor manufacturers at the start of the new millennium. Fiat had owned a stake in Ferrari since 1969 but Ford now acquired Stewart Grand Prix, DaimlerChrysler took a 40 percent shareholding in McLaren and Renault bought Benetton. BMW and Honda were interested in buying their client teams while Toyota confirmed its entry for 2002. Eddie Jordan was

Bernd Mayländer's career driving the safety car began in 2000

circumspect: 'I'd like to caution that while we welcome you [the manufacturers] with open arms, when F1 stops fitting with your marketing mix, then leave the individuality of teams sacrosanct.'

Commercial ringmaster Bernie Ecclestone sold 50 percent in his holding company SLEC to German media group EM.TV in February. There was pressure to change the way that F1 was run for most of the decade, and the team principals met with Ecclestone and Max Mosley, President of the FIA, at Heathrow on 30 August. Mosley withstood pressure to stand down and accused Ron Dennis of wanting to run F1, which the McLaren boss denied. An open letter from Mosley to Dennis at the Malaysian GP only increased tensions between the two.

Normally aspirated 3-litre V10 engines became mandatory and a longitudinal gearbox was *de rigueur* to optimise airflow to the diffuser. In-cockpit warning lights supplemented traditional marshals' flags following two years of trials. Traction control remained outlawed despite all 11 teams wanting it legalised.

The Brazilian organisers were fined $100,000 after qualifying was halted three times due to an advertising board on the pit straight twice falling onto the track before another did likewise at Turn 1, hitting Jean Alesi's Prost-Peugeot. The British GP was switched to Easter only for pre-event rain to turn the car parks into a quagmire. Spectators were prohibited from parking in the waterlogged fields on Saturday and many missed the race due to traffic jams approaching Silverstone. In Monaco, a first-lap pile-up at the Loews hairpin blocked the track and forced a restart. The German GP was disrupted by a

The Monaco Grand Prix was stopped when the track was blocked following an opening-lap fracas

protester who walked along the track before the first chicane. The Italian GP was marred by the death of 33-year-old marshal Paolo Gislimberti following first-lap accidents at the Variante della Roggia.

United States returned to the calendar for the first time in nine years. Three months before the announcement on 2 December 1998 of a long-term deal for a road course at the Indianapolis Motor Speedway, Tommy Baker's proposed 2.7-mile semi-permanent circuit in Las Vegas, with the start/finish line on the Strip, had been rejected by local government, and Dallas, Road Atlanta and San Francisco had all been mentioned.

Malaysia was originally scheduled for 20 February but circuit boss Philippe Gurdjian negotiated its postponement to October. Cigarette branding was allowed at the German GP for the first time in 25 years and Belgium only went ahead when its tobacco sponsorship ban was reversed for international events. Circuits that extended their contracts were the Nürburgring (to 2004), Interlagos (2005), Barcelona, Hungaroring (both 2006) and Melbourne (2010). As in 1999, Zhuhai did not secure a date for an inaugural Chinese GP.

Honda had indicated that it would fill the 12th and final team franchise until the death of technical director Harvey Postlethwaite on 15 April 1999. Canadian businessman Marc Bourdeau planned to establish a new team with former Onyx Grand Prix owner Mike Earle with premises near Montréal. David Hunt, who owned the Team Lotus brand, also expressed an interest, but Toyota paid the required $48m bond to the FIA as well as a fine to defer its entry to 2002.

German GT driver Bernd Mayländer replaced Oliver Gavin as safety car driver and there was an embarrassing incident involving the medical car in Monaco. Professor Sid Watkins broke three ribs when former F1 driver Alex Ribeiro crashed the Mercedes-Benz C55 AMG at Tabac before Saturday practice. The FIA vowed to replace gravel traps with tarmac run-off areas by the end of the decade following analysis of on-car data recorders. Stirling Moss was knighted in the New Year's honours list. Championship-winning team owner John Cooper and Walter Hayes, who was the executive behind the Ford Cosworth DFV, died on 24 and 26 December 2000 respectively.

Mika Häkkinen and Michael Schumacher discuss their dice in Belgium

Michael Schumacher, Ferrari F1-2000 (Canadian GP)

SCUDERIA FERRARI MARLBORO

Constructors' champions in 1999, Ferrari ended its 21-year wait for the drivers' title courtesy of Michael Schumacher. The German was under contract until 2002 while Rubens Barrichello, whose two-year deal (plus an option for 2002) was confirmed before the 1999 Italian GP, replaced Jaguar-bound Eddie Irvine. Any thoughts of equal status disappeared when Barrichello qualified on pole at Silverstone but was denied use of the spare car. As *Scuderia* president Luca di Montezemolo said: 'The top driver remains Schumacher. There is a number one and a number one 'A'.' Luca Badoer concentrated on his Ferrari testing duties after his disappointing race campaign in 1999 with Minardi.

Launch of the Ferrari F1-2000 was delayed until 7 February so that Ross Brawn's design team, led by Rory Byrne, could maximise time in the new wind tunnel at Maranello to refine its aerodynamics. The vee angle of the lighter V10 engine (the 049) was widened to 90 degrees, lowering its centre of gravity, and periscope exhausts were retained. The engine was mated to the latest seven-speed longitudinal gearbox, which was more compact than its predecessor. The oil tank was the smallest in the field and a secondary tank on the bellhousing was introduced at the second race. Carbon-fibre was liberally used in the torsion bar/pushrod suspension and revised front suspension with pushrods attached to the bottom of the uprights was introduced in Monaco. A new carbon-fibre floor and diffuser were among a raft of upgrades at the French GP. The raised nose was retained and the sidepods were extended further forward.

Brembo carbon-ceramic discs were standard for the first time. Shell agreed a five-year extension to its fuel partnership.

Schumacher's shakedown at Fiorano was abandoned after just six laps due to a stiff neck, so Barrichello and Badoer took over. Reliable running and record pace at Mugello prompted Schumacher to declare: 'For the first time in many years I have a car capable of winning right from the first race.'

Qualifying in Australia was compromised by a red flag (Schumacher on a quick lap when David Coulthard crashed) and a yellow one (Barrichello). McLaren-Mercedes locked out the front row but suffered engine failures in the race, after which Schumacher dominated. Barrichello switched to a two-stop strategy to take second from Heinz-Harald Frentzen in the pitstops. Ferrari again filled row two at Interlagos where the two-stopping Schumacher passed Mika Häkkinen on lap two and cruised to victory; Barrichello was fourth when his hydraulics failed.

An impressive middle stint delivered another Schumacher victory at Imola, where Barrichello was a distant fourth. The roles were reversed at Silverstone. Barrichello qualified on pole position and was on course for victory when sidelined by falling hydraulic pressure. Fifth on the grid following a scrappy qualifying, Schumacher dropped to eighth at the start before benefitting from retirements and strategy to take third.

Schumacher claimed his first pole of 2000 in Spain but finished fifth after a calamitous race. Refueller Nigel Stepney broke his ankle at Schumacher's first pitstop when the driver was signalled to leave prematurely. A tardy second stop was followed by a slow puncture and Schumacher hit his brother's Williams-BMW as he defended robustly, before making another tyre stop. Barrichello qualified and finished third. Stepney did not resume refuelling duties when he returned at Monaco.

Rivals had criticised Schumacher's aggressive moves at the starts at Imola, Silverstone and Barcelona, but Häkkinen was the aggressor at the first corner of the European GP at the Nürburgring. Angered by contact as the Finn barged his way past, Schumacher shadowed the McLaren-Mercedes for ten laps before taking the lead into the chicane as rain began to fall and easing to victory. Schumacher dominated from pole in Monaco until a broken exhaust overheated his left-rear carbon-fibre pushrod and caused it to fail on lap 55. A lapped fourth at the Nürburgring, Barrichello inherited second in Monte Carlo.

The exhausts were strengthened for Canada, where a new front wing was introduced. Schumacher led a qualifying 1–3 but ran across the Turn 1 gravel during a deluge and was slowed by an issue with a front wheel bearing. Barrichello closed on the leader but heeded team orders so followed Schumacher home in a decisive 1–2. On pole at Magny-Cours, Schumacher chopped Coulthard at the start but was no match for the McLaren-Mercedes. Having forced the Scot wide at the Adelaide hairpin as he defended his lead on lap 34, the German could not deny Coulthard five laps later; Schumacher was running second when his engine failed.

Third in France, Barrichello outqualified his team-mate as they annexed the second row in Austria. They tried to swap positions on the run to the first corner, surprising their pursuers. Hit by Ricardo Zonta and Jarno Trulli respectively, Schumacher suffered terminal suspension failure and Barrichello damaged his car's floor as he bounced across the gravel trap. The Brazilian salvaged third as Coulthard reduced Schumacher's championship lead to six points.

'What goes around comes around,' was Coulthard's reaction when Giancarlo Fisichella's Benetton-Playlife hit Schumacher at the start at Hockenheim. Only 18th on the grid following an electrical failure in qualifying, the light-fuelled Barrichello cut his way through the field to run third by lap 15, and went on to score an emotional maiden victory by staying on dry tyres as rivals changed to wets when it rained in the stadium.

Momentum swung towards McLaren-Mercedes at the next two races with Häkkinen beating Schumacher into second both times. The Finn got the better of his rival into the first corner at the Hungaroring, while at Spa-Francorchamps he made a sensational move on the climb to Les Combes to take the lead with four laps to go, the pair passing Zonta's BAR-Honda on either side. Ferrari had a major upgrade in Belgium that featured another new front wing with revised endplates. A new diffuser with curved central channel was discarded after practice. Barrichello was fourth in Hungary and retired in Belgium.

Without a win since June, Schumacher converted pole into victory at the last four races. He out-ran Häkkinen at Monza, where his erratic driving at the end of a safety-car period caused

Rubens Barrichello, Ferrari F1-2000 (Japanese GP)

consternation behind, then regained the points advantage at Indianapolis by wheel-banging his way past Coulthard. Barrichello was involved in a first-lap accident at Monza's Variante della Roggia and finished second in America. Schumacher made a poor start at Suzuka before winning a race-long duel with Häkkinen that clinched his third drivers' title. Schumacher and Häkkinen lined up on the front row in Malaysia and both appeared to move and then stop before the lights. Schumacher, unlike his rival, escaped punishment and recovered from another slow start to beat Coulthard by less than a second. That equalled the record nine victories in a season, previously achieved by Nigel Mansell (1992) and Schumacher himself (1995). Fourth at Suzuka, 'flu-ridden Barrichello was a distant third in Malaysia to claim fourth in the drivers' standings.

WEST McLAREN MERCEDES

McLaren-Mercedes went head-to-head with Ferrari once more but fell just short in both championships. Mika Häkkinen and David Coulthard were retained for another season with an option on BAR's Ricardo Zonta's services not exercised. As reserve driver, the experienced Olivier Panis replaced Nick Heidfeld, the man who took his seat at Prost. DaimlerChrysler used the McLaren MP4-15-Mercedes launch at Jerez on 3 February to announce its 40 percent acquisition of the TAG McLaren Group. Ron Dennis and Mansour Ojjeh both retained 30 percent of the company. The engine partnership was extended until the end of 2004. Team principal and CEO Dennis was named Commander of the British Empire (CBE) in The Queen's birthday honours list.

Adrian Newey's evolutionary MP4-15 had a shorter nose and lower sidepods than its predecessor with fins ahead of the cockpit retained to comply with height regulations. The bargeboards were large with curved appendages at their base from the Brazilian GP. The exhausts now exited through the diffuser to produce a unique and shrill wail. A revised, more angular diffuser was used during practice at Magny-Cours and raced from the Austrian GP. Cooling was via radiator chimneys on each sidepod although these were removed on colder days. The 'Coke bottle' rear was narrower still, the steering rack was repositioned and pushrod/torsion bar suspension was retained. The size and weight of the Ilmor-built Mercedes-Benz V10 was further reduced in its latest iteration, the FO110J. Early fears that it was less powerful than before were dismissed by Ilmor's Mario Illien. Power steering was fitted from the Canadian GP.

McLaren-Mercedes initially edged Ferrari for single-lap pace and Häkkinen led qualifying 1–2s in Australia and Brazil, although the drivers left both events empty-handed. Häkkinen led his team-mate from the start in Melbourne's Albert Park only for double pneumatic valve failures to repeat their DNFs at the 1999 Australian GP. They chose one-stop strategies in Brazil so Häkkinen could not resist the light-fuelled Michael Schumacher in the early laps. He retook the lead when the Ferraris stopped but lost oil pressure after 30 laps. Coulthard was a hard-fought second on the road after losing third gear but was disqualified due to his front wing being 7mm too low.

At Imola, Häkkinen converted his third successive pole position into the lead only for debris to damage his undertray. Schumacher Sr's longer middle stint proved decisive and he led by the time second-placed Häkkinen rejoined, the Finn finishing just over

Mika Häkkinen, McLaren MP4-15-Mercedes-Benz (Monaco GP)

a second behind. Coulthard was third after jumping Rubens Barrichello's Ferrari in the pits. There was a major aero upgrade for the British GP where the McLaren-Mercedes pair occupied row two. The quicker driver on race day, Coulthard passed Barrichello around the outside of Stowe corner to seal his second successive British GP victory, while Häkkinen overcame understeer to complete a much-needed McLaren-Mercedes 1–2.

Nine days after that victory, Coulthard was *en route* to Monaco when his Learjet crash-landed at Lyon-Satolas airport with both pilots killed. Ferrari had the edge at that week's Spanish GP but Häkkinen took advantage of Michael Schumacher's problems in the pits to register his first victory of the year. In pain due to three cracked ribs sustained in the aircraft accident, Coulthard passed both Schumacher brothers during a brave race into second place.

Third on the grid for the European GP, Häkkinen barged passed Schumacher's Ferrari and into the lead at the start. That angered the German despite previous criticisms of his robust tactics, but he took control when rain arrived, with Häkkinen second and Coulthard, who had started from his first pole position since 1998, a lapped third due to his dry set-up. Coulthard shadowed second-placed Jarno Trulli at Monaco and inherited victory when the Jordan-Mugen and Schumacher's Ferrari retired. Only fifth on the grid, Häkkinen spent the first half of the race stuck behind the other Jordan-Mugen of Heinz-Harald Frentzen. He stopped to remove debris jammed behind his pedals and recovered from 14th to sixth despite subsequent gearbox issues.

Coulthard qualified second in Canada but stalled on the grid, so his crew were still restarting his car 15 seconds before the start.

Tenth after the ensuing 10sec stop-go penalty, he changed to dry tyres just as rain arrived and finished a frustrated seventh. Häkkinen qualified and finished fourth. Coulthard was in top form in France where he qualified on the front row but lost out to both Ferraris at the start when forced to lift by another crude Schumacher chop. He passed Barrichello before being pushed wide by Schumacher as he tried to take the lead around the outside of the Adelaide hairpin. Coulthard regrouped over the next six laps and forced his way inside the leading Ferrari at the same corner to score the finest win of his career. McLaren's day was complete when Schumacher's engine failure handed Häkkinen second place.

Improved engine mapping and a new aero package gave McLaren-Mercedes the advantage in Austria. Fresh from a holiday to clear his mind after a mini mid-season slump, the resurgent Häkkinen led a dominant McLaren-Mercedes 1–2 in qualifying and the race, but the victory was placed in doubt due to a missing seal on the electronic control unit. The stewards accepted that this was a team error at a meeting in London on 25 July so confirmed Häkkinen's win while fining McLaren and docking constructors' points. His return to form seemed destined to continue in Germany where he jumped from fourth to first at the start. On pole by 1.366sec, Coulthard followed his team-mate during the opening stint only for strategy calls as conditions changed and a protester on the track restricted the Silver Arrows to second (Häkkinen) and third (Coulthard). 'Our strategy was flexible,' Dennis said afterwards. 'But not flexible enough to allow for a deranged spectator.'

The Hungarian GP was the 77th for Häkkinen and Coulthard as team-mates, equalling the previous record of Gerhard Berger

David Coulthard, McLaren MP4-15-Mercedes-Benz (British GP)

and Jean Alesi. The Finn made another great start from third to dominate throughout despite suffering dehydration in the heat. Unhurt in a 180mph testing accident at Valencia, Coulthard was third when baulked by backmarkers at a crucial moment. Leading the standings for the first time, Häkkinen qualified on pole in Belgium but lost track position when he spun. He snatched victory from Schumacher with a dramatic late overtake into Les Combes as they passed either side of a bewildered Zonta.

The MP4-15s lacked balance at Monza where second-placed Häkkinen finished 3.810sec behind Schumacher. A distant fourth in Belgium, Coulthard was eliminated at Monza's second chicane on the opening lap as his title hopes all but ended. At Indianapolis, Coulthard qualified on the front row and led the opening laps following a jump-start. He held up Schumacher before serving his stop-go penalty and finished fifth. Häkkinen was closing on the Ferrari by a second a lap when his engine burst into flames. Needing victory at Suzuka to prolong his title challenge, Häkkinen was second after losing time in traffic and unable to get life into his dry tyres when drizzle intensified after his second pitstop. Third in Japan, Coulthard was second in Malaysia after losing the lead to Schumacher when he pitted early to clear his radiators after running wide. Häkkinen was fourth following a stop-go penalty for jumping the start (Schumacher's similar misdemeanour went unpunished).

The McLaren MP4-15-Mercedes had been the class of the field for much of the year so seven wins and runner-up status in both championships was below par by the team's expectations.

BMW WILLIAMS F1

Williams had been courting BMW for two years when their collaboration was announced at the Frankfurt Motor Show on 8 September 1997. This was initially for a sports car programme with their five-year F1 partnership beginning in 2000. BMW entered Le Mans in 1998 and 1999 with an open-cockpit V12-powered car designed by Williams engineer John Russell and assembled at Grove. With Gerhard Berger named as BMW motorsport director and Mario Theissen technical director, Yannick Dalmas, Pierluigi Martini and Joachim Winkelhock delivered victory in the 1999 Le Mans 24 Hours. Legendary BMW engineer Paul Rosche retired at the end of 1999 and was replaced by Audi's Werner Laurenz, while Cosworth project leader Andy Cowell joined with responsibility for the 2001 engine. Russell returned to the F1 operation after the Le Mans victory but moved to Jaguar Racing at the end of the year.

Munich-based test driver Jörg Müller gave the prototype 72-degree V10 its first run in a converted Williams FW20 at Miramas on 27 April 1999. The Step 3 version ran on the dyno on 19 August and made its track debut in front of the press at the A1-Ring on 4 October. BMW also replaced Winfield as title sponsor but the FIA turned down a request for the car to be officially called a BMW Williams. Compaq computers and Allianz insurance joined the commercial partners in a tobacco-free portfolio.

Ralf Schumacher signed a lucrative three-year contract extension with Alex Zanardi named as his team-mate again on the original

F1 entry list for 2000, although terms for the Italian's release were being negotiated and his departure was confirmed in the New Year. Choosing a replacement was not straightforward. Under long-term contract with Williams, Juan Pablo Montoya had won the 1999 Champ Car title at the start of a two-year secondment to Chip Ganassi Racing and remained in America. Formula 3000 race winner Bruno Junqueira tested a Williams FW21-Supertec at Monza on 3 September 1999 and proved quicker than Japanese Formula 3 Champion Darren Manning during a two-day pre-Christmas Jerez test in the BMW-powered FW21B.

It was a surprise when Promatecme Formula 3 driver Jenson Button, with just two years' post-karting experience and too young to drive a hire car, was offered a testing showdown with Junqueira at Jerez on 14–15 January. Poor reliability and weather prevented Junqueira getting a meaningful run there, so they reconvened at Barcelona on the eve of the 24 January car launch. Four days after his 20th birthday and getting to grips with left-foot braking, Button edged his rival. The ceremony was delayed by 45 minutes while Sir Frank Williams and Patrick Head deliberated. Informed that he had the drive just minutes before the press announcement, Button signed a five-year contract, although Montoya's likely return for 2001 remained a persistent threat. Junqueira was named as test driver.

Gavin Fisher (chief designer) and Geoff Willis (aerodynamicist) sought to improve the high-downforce aerodynamics on the evolutionary Williams FW22-BMW although that initially remained a problem, especially during qualifying in Monaco. The engine was large and heavy by modern standards and BMW's initial focus was on reliability. Conservative in design, it was more powerful than rumours had suggested and the rate of development throughout 2000 was impressive. Its size and cooling requirements meant the FW22's wheelbase was extended by 7cm and sidepods raised. The oil tank was between the engine and monocoque while the exhausts continued to blow into the diffuser. Front and rear torsion bars had horizontal inboard dampers while Williams switched to a seven-speed gearbox for the first time. Titanium uprights were introduced at the British GP.

An early issue with the oil system limited test mileage at Barcelona while the hot weather session at Kyalami was disrupted by rain and Button's 160mph bird strike. However, Button completed two successive 300km days to satisfy the watching Charlie Whiting that he warranted a super licence, which was endorsed by the F1 Commission's permanent council.

Williams and BMW management both downplayed expectations before a most promising first season together. Schumacher scored three podium finishes and was fifth in the World Championship. However, there were more mistakes than during his stellar 1999 campaign and being outqualified by his inexperienced team-mate at Spa-Francorchamps and Suzuka knocked his confidence. Button emerged as a future star despite having to learn many of the circuits and the pressures of new-found fame.

In Australia, Schumacher finished third after the McLaren-Mercedes and Jordan-Mugens had retired while ahead of him. Button crashed on Saturday morning before falling fuel pressure

Ralf Schumacher, Williams FW22-BMW (Hungarian GP)

rendered qualifying a disaster. He made a great start from the last row and was sixth when his engine failed with 12 laps to go. That promise continued in Brazil where Button outqualified his team-mate and both scored points, sixth-placed Button succeeding Ricardo Rodríguez as the youngest points scorer to date, Schumacher fifth.

Neither finished at Imola where Schumacher qualified fifth and challenged Jacques Villeneuve's BAR-Honda for that position until sidelined by a fuel pick-up issue before his second stop. Button struggled to learn the track and his engine blew after just five laps of the race. He starred on more familiar territory, at Silverstone, by outqualifying his team-mate, sixth versus seventh. Button snatched fourth at the start and initially led Michael Schumacher, who aggressively 'shut the door' on his brother into Bridge corner on the opening lap. At the first pitstops, Schumacher Jr leapfrogged Button to head a fine Williams-BMW finish, fourth and fifth.

Fifth on the grid at the next two races, Ralf was incensed when he clashed with Michael as they disputed third in Spain. Disappointed with fourth that day, he was involved in an accident between Eddie Irvine and Jos Verstappen at the Nürburgring. Button retired in the closing stages of both races, losing sixth at Barcelona when his engine failed with four laps to go.

Additional wings were fitted to the airbox and sidepods at Monaco but the team suffered a frustrating mid-season dip. The previously well-balanced FW22 now understeered in slow corners and was twitchy in fast ones. That said, Schumacher would have finished second had he not crashed at Ste-Dévote, needing stiches in his badly cut left leg. Button was involved in the first-lap Loews hairpin pile-up, took the restart from the pitlane and retired after 16 laps. With Junqueira on standby, Schumacher was declared fit for the Canadian GP although neither Williams-BMW qualified in the

top ten. He was challenging for sixth when eliminated by Jacques Villeneuve's optimistic pass and Button needed a new front wing after hitting a kerb.

Testing paid dividends and Schumacher ended the team's three-race pointless streak at Magny-Cours. He qualified and finished fifth despite a poor start and overheating caused by a visor tear-off lodged in his radiator. Button was eighth after stopping early to help Schumacher's strategy. The French race then looked like a false dawn when both qualified in the lower reaches of the top 20 at the A1-Ring but Button came from the back to score points at that race and the next. He gained 11 places amid the first-lap chaos in Austria before passing Mika Salo and Johnny Herbert in the pits to claim fifth. Although forced to start from the back of the German GP grid when his engine died on the parade lap, Williams timed his change to wets perfectly and he overtook Salo to take fourth. Damage delayed Schumacher at both events although he recovered to finish seventh at Hockenheim.

Schumacher used a major engine upgrade and refined high-downforce set-up (including a modified diffuser) to qualify a season-best fourth at the Hungaroring, then lost out to Rubens Barrichello in the pitstops and finished fifth. Third in Belgium and Italy confirmed the German as 'best of the rest' behind the Ferrari and McLaren-Mercedes drivers. Button responded to speculation about Montoya's arrival for 2001 in impressive fashion, by challenging for points in Hungary before his old-spec V10 lost power, then using the upgraded unit to qualify a superb third at Spa-Francorchamps, ahead of his team-mate. There he finished fifth after an early clash with Jarno Trulli's heavily fuelled Jordan-Mugen lost him track position to Schumacher and David Coulthard's recovering McLaren-Mercedes. Running sixth after the first-lap

Jenson Button, Williams FW22-BMW (Japanese GP)

accident at Monza, Button crashed behind the safety car when surprised by the sudden deceleration of the cars ahead of him.

Both drivers challenged during the United States GP at Indianapolis but left empty-handed. Sixth on the grid, Button punctured a tyre following another collision with Trulli before his engine failed. Schumacher was second until halted by a hydraulic leak. Button enjoyed his first visit to Suzuka where he qualified and finished fifth. Schumacher made a good start from sixth but was passed by his team-mate and spun out of the race to avoid hitting Marc Gené's Minardi-Fondmetal under heavy braking. The year came to a disappointing end in Malaysia with scruffy qualifying performances and engine failures in the race.

Williams's winless streak may have continued but third in the constructors' standings far outweighed the modest pre-season expectations of team and engine manufacturer alike.

MILD SEVEN BENETTON PLAYLIFE

Benetton narrowly clinched fourth in the constructors' standings after an inconsistent and winless campaign. It was 'all change' in the technical department when Tim Densham (chief designer), Ben Agathangelou (aerodynamicist) and Chris Radage (chassis) arrived from the stillborn Honda project in September 1999. Deposed chief designer Nick Wirth, head of composites Sergio Rinland and operations director Joan Villadelprat all left during the winter. With Giancarlo Fisichella under contract, talks were held with Pedro Diniz before Benetton exercised its option on Alexander Wurz after the

summer break. Original test driver Hidetoshi Mitsusada was dropped after failing to qualify for three successive F3000 races. Giorgio Pantano, Antônio Pizzonia and Mark Webber all tested during 2000.

The Benetton B200-Playlife was unveiled on 17 January at Barcelona's Museu Nacional d'Art de Catalunya. Chief executive Rocco Benetton did not hide from the recent disappointments: '1999 was a tough season. Benetton Formula is a team with a top capability, but we did not deliver the results we had targeted.' Densham and his team started the new car's aero concept afresh while retaining the monocoque inherited from the previous regime. They went back to basics by abandoning complex systems such as the twin-clutch gearbox and Front Torque Transfer. The wheelbase was reduced and aerodynamics improved, with large McLaren-like bargeboards ahead of longer sidepods that bucked prevailing design trends. The nose was lowered with the front wing attached by two curved supports. With 40kg shed, ballast could be used to optimise weight distribution from circuit to circuit. Pushrod suspension with front torsion bars and rear coil springs was retained, with the suspension arms now carbon-fibre. The Playlife-badged Supertec FB02 engine was already improved, and Renault Sport was increasingly influential during the season.

Benetton had wanted to renew its partnership with Renault since the French manufacturer's withdrawal in 1997 and now the family wanted to sell the team. Renault president Louis Schweitzer approved a new V10 engine programme in the autumn of 1999 and the $120m purchase of Benetton Formula was announced on 17 March 2000. The cars would remain known as Benettons for two

Alexander Wurz, Benetton B200-Playlife (Belgian GP)

years, with the constructors' title the stated aim when they became Renaults in 2002. Flavio Briatore returned as managing director with Renault Sport's Patrick Faure and Christian Contzen appointed to the new board of directors. Briatore immediately looked to augment Enstone's engineering talent and Jordan's Mike Gascoyne agreed a contract to the end of 2004 as technical director. Gascoyne vowed to respect his Jordan contract, which expired in July 2001, but was placed on gardening leave a year early before starting at Benetton in October 2000. Pat Symonds assumed the new role of executive director of engineering.

The B200 ran reliably during the winter and the season began with a double finish in Australia. Starting ninth, Fisichella experienced oversteer after a first-lap impact, so his fifth-place finish was a welcome result. Renault's takeover was announced before the Brazilian GP, where Fisichella started fifth and recorded the fastest pitstop on the way to second place (after David Coulthard's disqualification). Benetton's true midfield pace emerged at Imola as Fisichella bettered only the Minardi-Fondmetals and a Prost-Peugeot in qualifying, and the race brought the first of his three successive finishes outside the points. Eager to get the campaign back on track, further weight was saved before the Nürburgring, where Fisichella lined up seventh. He survived ramming Jarno Trulli's Jordan at the first corner to claim a morale-boosting fifth. Four days later, Fisichella hit Trulli again during testing at Valencia and this time the Benetton was launched into a double barrel-roll.

Fisichella continued his good record at Monaco and Montréal by finishing third in both races, benefitting from a race of attrition in

the Principality and gaining five places with a well-timed change to wet tyres in Canada. That briefly gave Benetton third in the constructors' standings, but Fisichella would not score another point. Back among the also-rans at Magny-Cours, he finished ninth that day and was eliminated from the next two races at the first corner. Hit by Pedro Diniz in Austria, he qualified an excellent third at Hockenheim only to run into the back of Michael Schumacher's Ferrari. Seventh on the grid in Hungary despite being baulked by Schumacher, Fisichella blamed his brakes for a couple of spins before giving up. He was an early retirement after a weekend to forget in Belgium that included rolling his car at Blanchimont during the warm-up. Four days later he injured his right ankle in another high-speed accident at Monza's Ascari chicane but was cleared to race in the Italian GP, where he challenged Ralf Schumacher for the final podium place only to lose a lap in the pits when unable to select first gear. Strangely disinterested at the last three races as his season petered out, Fisichella finished sixth in the drivers' standings as Benetton-Playlife edged BAR-Honda for fourth on countback.

Wurz struggled all-season and was soon under pressure. Seventh in Melbourne, he started from the pitlane in Brazil and was last when his engine failed. He was quicker than Fisichella at Imola but finished ninth on a bad day for Enstone. After he qualified only 20th and 18th for the British and Spanish GPs respectively, rumours intensified that he was about to be dropped. Symonds replaced Christian Silk as Wurz's race engineer at the Nürburgring, where the Austrian endured another dispiriting qualifying performance, but matters improved in the race until he crashed into Johnny Herbert's

Giancarlo Fisichella, Benetton B200-Playlife (Monaco GP)

Jaguar when trying to take seventh in the closing stages.

Engine failure on the formation lap forced Wurz to start the Monaco GP in the spare car and from the pitlane. Ninth in Montréal, he crashed out of the Monaco and French GPs as Briatore's criticism grew more vocal. After finishing tenth in Austria (failing to take eighth on the last lap), gearbox failure at the German GP resulted in a spin on the pit straight and another DNF. A testing crash at Valencia on 5 August caused a wishbone to puncture the monocoque, inflicting leg injuries. Outside the top ten at the next two races, Wurz scored his only points of the year with a steady drive to fifth at Monza. He outqualified Fisichella at the last three races without adding to his points tally. He spun out of the Japanese GP before achieving a surprise fifth on the grid in Malaysia after using Fisichella's qualifying chassis for once. He ran third during the pitstops before brake trouble restricted him to seventh in his last race for the team.

BRITISH AMERICAN RACING HONDA

British American Racing rebounded from its torrid F1 baptism in 1999 with a works engine deal and fifth position in the standings. Honda had investigated entering its own team but decided not to sanction the £125m budget required. Instead, it signed a three-year engine partnership with BAR in May 1999 while the team negotiated release from its 2000 commitment to Supertec. BAR's Honda deal included exclusive chassis development between the two companies.

Touted at the time as among the best three drivers in F1, Jacques Villeneuve remained under contract with the team that had been formed around him. Its option on Ricardo Zonta's services expired on 15 September but he was confirmed as Villeneuve's team-mate after subsequent negotiations. The fast-starting Villeneuve starred as he exceeded the car's capabilities, but Zonta struggled, especially in qualifying. Japanese F3 champion Darren Manning was named as reserve driver in the New Year with Patrick Lemarié continuing as development driver.

Majority shareholder British American Tobacco raised its budget in return for an increased stake in the team. The power struggle between Craig Pollock (chairman and team principal) and Adrian Reynard (vice chairman) was temporarily put on hold when they were named as joint managing directors in December, responsible for business and technical matters respectively. Behind-the-scenes tension was stoked by speculation that Barry Green, who had entered Villeneuve in Champ Cars, would join. BAT's Don Brown arrived as non-executive chairman on 1 January, Malcolm Oastler remained as technical director and motorsport development director Rick Gorne left Reynard Cars to concentrate on BAR. The team gave up its attempt to have different tobacco brands on each car with Lucky Strike now the predominant logo.

The BAR 002-Honda was the first new car to run when Villeneuve gave it its shakedown at Silverstone on 7 December and during subsequent testing the reliability so lacking during 1999 appeared sorted. The car was officially launched at an understated ceremony at London's Queen Elizabeth II conference centre on 24 January, where Pollock admitted 'we made mistakes last year, but we learned, and we hope not to repeat them.'

This was a conservative evolution with improved reliability crucial. That led to a heavy car, so weight saving continued throughout 2000. The wheelbase was shortened and aerodynamicist Willem Toet improved airflow to the rear wing with double flip-ups added on the sidepods by the first race. Conventional rear exhausts were preferred to the periscope arrangement pioneered by Ferrari since 1998. The all-new 72-degree Honda RA000E V10 engine, designed and built under the leadership of Takefumi Hosaka, was lighter and smaller than previous Mugen-badged units. Reduced revs were imposed at first, but it was increasingly powerful and smooth in comparison with the vibration-prone Supertec. The updated six-speed Xtrac/BAR semi-automatic gearbox had new internals at the Nürburgring to rectify earlier problems. Inboard torsion-bar front suspension was retained while a curved wishbone design allowed the pushrods to be mounted further forward. Torsion bars replaced coil springs at the rear. Although a distinct improvement, the 002 suffered at slow-speed circuits due to lack of mechanical grip.

Qualifying for the Australian GP confirmed that the car was 'slow but reliable' as Villeneuve started eighth and used a low-drag set-up to hold off a train of cars and finish fourth. Out of sorts during qualifying, Zonta completed a confidence-boosting double points score when he inherited sixth following Mika Salo's disqualification. Already under pressure to perform, Zonta outqualified Villeneuve when eighth on the Brazilian GP grid, although a loose wheel nut and gearbox trouble dropped him to ninth by the finish. After the promise of Australia, Villeneuve retired with a gearbox full of neutrals on a sobering day for the team.

Villeneuve described his start at Imola as 'one of the best of my career, if not the best' and held off quicker cars to finish fifth, while Zonta was delayed by an engine problem. The Brazilian escaped with a cut finger in a 190mph testing crash at Silverstone when his front-right suspension failed under braking for Stowe and the car cartwheeled over the barrier before landing upside down by a marshals' post. The shunt prompted carbon wishbones to be replaced by steel at the British GP, where Honda also introduced an Evo 4 version of its V10. Tenth on the grid following ill-timed yellow flags at Silverstone, Villeneuve made another lightning getaway but lost sixth when his gearbox failed with four laps to go. A new aero package for the Spanish GP included very light McLaren-inspired bargeboards with a pronounced 'V' at the top of the rear-wing endplates. Villeneuve qualified sixth and maintained that position during the first stint only for his engine to burst into flames shortly after he pitted. Zonta completed a character-building British GP week by spinning at Stowe and then finished eighth in Spain.

At the Nürburgring, Villeneuve leapt from ninth to fifth at the start before another engine blow-up. Lacking downforce in Monaco, he started 17th after troublesome qualifying and was lapped before finishing seventh. Zonta crashed out of both races and walked away from a 180mph testing shunt at Monza as his woes continued. It was a case of what might have been at Montréal where BAR's power steering system was tried. The BAR-Honda was better suited to the circuit and Villeneuve was set for a deserved podium before rain arrived. Dry tyres were fitted to both cars at the wrong moment and this forced an unscheduled extra stop. Villeneuve crashed into Ralf Schumacher while trying to pass David Coulthard for ninth with five laps to go, while Zonta, who lost use of his radio, finished eighth.

An aero upgrade with lower engine cover and revised wings generated much-needed extra downforce at Magny-Cours and the A1-Ring. Villeneuve converted seventh on the grid into fourth-place finishes at both races while Zonta started from a career-best sixth in Austria. However, he crashed in France and hit Michael Schumacher at the first corner two weeks later. Relegated to the back as a consequence, a day that began with such promise was ruined by a stop-go penalty and eventual engine failure.

Zonta's future prospects dimmed further at Hockenheim when he was blamed by Villeneuve for the collision that cost both drivers points. Villeneuve finished eighth after that spin while Zonta received another stop-go for causing the accident, only to spin out before he could serve the penalty. The lack of grip was apparent in Hungary where Villeneuve, his car fitted with Honda's own power-steering system for the first time, lost his front wing when he hit Pedro de la Rosa's Arrows on the opening lap. His recovery to 12th

Ricardo Zonta, BAR 002-Honda (European GP)

Jacques Villeneuve, BAR 002-Honda (Austrian GP)

included the sixth-fastest lap and passing Zonta.

Armed with yet another engine upgrade and revised front suspension, Villeneuve qualified and finished seventh at Spa-Francorchamps. Zonta was the bit-part player as Mika Häkkinen passed Michael Schumacher for the race lead into Les Combes in one of the most memorable overtaking manoeuvres in recent F1 history. Honda celebrated its 200th grand prix in Italy with a new qualifying engine that Villeneuve used to claim fourth on the grid. He was third when his ECU cut out. Set for an aggressive two-stop strategy after hydraulics failure had ruined qualifying, Zonta was quickest in the warm-up and finished sixth. Villeneuve completed a personally impressive campaign with three successive points scores. He recovered from a spin to challenge Heinz-Harald Frentzen for a podium at the United States GP. Villeneuve ran wide when he attempted to overtake into Turn 1 and so had to settle for fourth. Sixth in front of Honda's home crowd at Suzuka, Villeneuve again hoped for a podium place in Malaysia but finished fifth after going wheel-to-wheel with the recovering Häkkinen. Zonta was sixth at Indianapolis, ninth in Japan and suffered a spin and engine failure in Malaysia.

BENSON & HEDGES JORDAN MUGEN HONDA

Jordan extended its engine deal with Mugen for two years in May 1999 after being overlooked for the works partnership with parent company Honda. Benson & Hedges continued as title sponsor and Deutsche Post agreed a lucrative three-year deal. The impressive Heinz-Harald Frentzen re-signed but Damon Hill retired from F1. Jarno Trulli exercised a performance clause in his Prost contract although Jordan's preference for a two-year deal was complicated by a pre-existing commitment to Renault for 2001. Negotiations proved successful as Trulli was announced for 2000–01 after the summer break, with Renault's option deferred to 2002.

Frentzen gave the Jordan EJ10-Mugen (the designation chosen to celebrate EJ's tenth F1 season) its shakedown at a cold and damp Silverstone National Circuit on 17 January. With Trulli 'flu-ridden, Frentzen tested all that week but problems with the new electronic system prevailed throughout the winter.

Technical director Mike Gascoyne led a team that included

designers Mark Smith and John McQuilliam, chief aerodynamicist John Iley and head of engineering Tim Holloway. The EJ10 was well under the weight limit so ballast could be distributed as needed. Centre of gravity was lowered and the cockpit surround was as low as height regulations allowed, with fins on either side that rival designers questioned with the FIA. The EJ10 had a longer nose and distinctive triangular airbox profile. The pushrod suspension had torsion bars all round, with titanium used for the top-rear wishbones. The latest Mugen V10 (MF-301 HE) was said to produce 810bhp but was heavy and lacked development. Weight was saved in the six-speed longitudinal gearbox, which proved a weakness and had to be beefed up by the Spanish GP. Periscope exhausts were used for the first time following pre-Christmas tests on a year-old car.

Tomáš Enge tested on 12 December and was named as test driver at the launch on 31 January. That event at London's Theatre Royal, complete with Irish song and dance, concluded with Michael Aspel waylaying Eddie Jordan for an episode of television's *This Is Your Life*.

Best of the rest behind McLaren-Mercedes and Ferrari in Australia, the Jordan drivers challenged for the podium but retired. With a new aero package in Brazil that included revised winglets ahead of the sidepods, they finished third (Frentzen) and fourth (Trulli), the one-stopping German setting the race's second-fastest lap last time around. After gearbox issues accounted for both cars at Imola, Frentzen was denied pole position at Silverstone by just 0.003sec and was on course for another strong finish until an electronic glitch left him stuck in sixth gear. Trulli and Frentzen were sixth in Britain and Spain respectively, but both retired within three laps at the Nürburgring, Trulli eliminated at the first corner by Giancarlo Fisichella's Benetton. The Italians collided again during testing at Valencia with Fisichella launched into a barrel roll over the slow-moving Trulli.

It was a case of what might have been in Monaco, where Trulli qualified second and Frentzen fourth. Using Brembo's CCR (Carbon Clincher Rim) brake discs for the first time, Trulli maintained his position from the start and held off eventual winner David Coulthard until his gearbox failed again. Frentzen inherited second but crashed at Ste-Dévote with eight laps remaining. Trulli was sixth in Canada and France while Frentzen retired with fading brakes at the former and finished seventh at the latter.

Jarno Trulli, Jordan EJ10-Mugen (Canadian GP)

'As a result of our success in recent years it's inevitable that our key personnel are being approached by other teams,' was Eddie Jordan's reaction to news that Gascoyne would join Benetton when his contract expired in July 2001. Gascoyne, who crashed a Jordan 199-Mugen at the Goodwood Festival of Speed, was eventually placed on gardening leave at the behest of 2001 engine partner Honda. Holloway was placed in temporary charge of Jordan's technical department.

In Austria, Trulli qualified fifth but hit both Ferraris at the first corner and Frentzen followed him into retirement when he spun on his own oil after a pipe burst. An aero overhaul at Hockenheim included unusual rounded sidepods that curved inwards at the bottom; the front wing endplates, bargeboards and diffuser were also revised. The German GP was particularly galling. Trulli lost a second-place finish or better when handed a harsh 10sec stop-go penalty for passing eventual winner Rubens Barrichello behind the safety car as the Ferrari left the pits. Only 17th on the grid after having his fastest time deleted for gaining track position by missing the first chicane, Frentzen climbed through the field and was poised to take second with six laps to go when his electronics cut out.

Frentzen was sixth in the Hungarian and Belgian GPs while Trulli again started from the front row at the latter race. Fuelled heavy for a long opening stint, Trulli lasted just four laps before he was knocked into a spin at La Source by Jenson Button's Williams-BMW. Both Jordan-Mugens were eliminated in the Italian GP first-lap shunt. Fifth on the grid at Indianapolis, Trulli collided with Button

Heinz-Harald Frentzen, Jordan EJ10-Mugen (Monaco GP)

for the second time in three races, puncturing a tyre before he lost another engine. Deeply affected by the death of marshal Paolo Gislimberti at Monza, Frentzen withstood Jacques Villeneuve's late challenge to finish third. Judging the season 'the worst of my whole career', Trulli finished outside the top ten in Japan and Malaysia, where Frentzen retired.

From the heady heights of 1999, Jordan-Mugen scored just 17 points and slipped from third to sixth in the standings, a performance that led Eddie Jordan to cancel the team's Christmas party. Three front-row starts and a couple of podium finishes showed that the car could be quick on occasions, but uneven tyre wear and mediocre reliability were drawbacks.

ORANGE ARROWS F1 TEAM

Tom Walkinshaw abandoned Arrows's eponymous engine programme after two years as he attempted to propel the Leafield-based midfielders up the grid. A one-year agreement was reached with Supertec for its Renault-based V10. Development of the 1999 car stopped in May so the technical department could concentrate on the new Arrows A21.

Although Mark Webber and Tom Coronel tested at Barcelona in December, Arrows confirmed its drivers in the New Year as Jos Verstappen (after a year's absence) and Pedro de la Rosa (with Repsol sponsorship). Others in the frame had been Olivier Panis and Toranosuke Takagi, but that latter accepted Satoru Nakajima's Formula Nippon offer rather than wait for a decision. Steve Nielsen joined as team manager.

De la Rosa and Verstappen tested the unpainted Arrows A21-Supertec at Silverstone and Barcelona with promising results. They were first (de la Rosa) and third (Verstappen) after low-fuel runs during February's group test in Spain, prompting talk of running under the weight limit. The team launch was delayed until 3 March so that a shock three-year title sponsorship deal with Orange mobile phone network could be confirmed. That was so late that the new cars were already *en route* to Melbourne when the covers came off an old car at London's Planit 2000, where secondary deals with Eurobet and Chello were also announced.

The responsibility of technical director Mike Coughlan and chief designer Eghbal Hamidy, the A21 followed McLaren trends with a relatively low nose and fins on the monocoque to satisfy chassis height regulations. Hamidy stressed that vertical fins on either side of the driver's helmet 'adhered to the letter and spirit of the rules' but FIA technical delegate Charlie Whiting advised that they should be altered rather than risk disqualification. Unique for 2000, the front suspension was via pullrods and low-mounted inboard dampers. Pre-season optimism led to hopes that fifth in the standings could be achieved. Quick in a straight line, the A21 lacked low-speed traction, reliability was an issue and its small fuel tank compromised strategic options.

The A21s qualified midfield from the start of the campaign. Both retired in Australia when overheating front brakes led to carbon-fibre steering-arm breakages, with de la Rosa crashing heavily enough for Verstappen to be withdrawn as a precaution. The front suspension was modified and cooling improved for Brazil, where the pair finished in the top ten, Verstappen seventh after an aggressive opening stint that saw him as high as third before his pitstop. Off the pace at Imola, Verstappen served a stop-go penalty for ignoring blue flags and de la Rosa spun out. The Dutchman judged Silverstone's changeable conditions well to qualify eighth, but both had electronic failures in the race.

Ninth quickest in Spain before his qualifying times were deleted due to an irregular fuel sample, de la Rosa crashed into Jean Alesi's Prost on the second lap of the race and Verstappen's gearbox failed at his pitstop. The Spaniard finished sixth at the Nürburgring, his strongest performance of the season, but his team-mate posted another DNF with suspension damage after contact with Eddie Irvine's Jaguar. In Monaco, de la Rosa crashed in qualifying and the warm-up before causing the race to be stopped on the opening lap by colliding with Jenson Button at the Loews hairpin; Verstappen also crashed out, at Tabac.

The A21s suited Montréal, where de la Rosa qualified ninth and ran in the top ten before another crash, while Verstappen used a wet-weather setting to finish fifth. Gearbox failures caused a double DNF in France and a similar problem denied de la Rosa a podium in Austria after he avoided the first-lap pile-up to run third. A season-best fifth on the grid at Hockenheim, the Spaniard held fourth in the dry before dropping to sixth after running wide when it began

Jos Verstappen, Arrows A21-Supertec (United States GP)

Pedro de la Rosa, Arrows A21-Supertec (Italian GP)

to rain. Delayed by changing his front wing during both races, Verstappen had an engine failure in Austria and spun out of seventh with six laps to go at Hockenheim.

Uncompetitive in Hungary and Belgium, the A21s displayed impressive straight-line speed at Monza to qualify tenth (de la Rosa) and 11th (Verstappen). The Spaniard was lucky to escape a violent barrel roll on the opening lap when he hit Ricardo Zonta and Johnny Herbert on the approach to the second chicane. Verstappen avoided the chaos to drive a strong one-stop race into fourth. They challenged for points at Indianapolis before Verstappen crashed out of fourth and de la Rosa's gearbox failed – the first of three non-scores that completed Arrows's campaign. Twelfth at Suzuka, de la Rosa crashed in Malaysia when hit by Pedro Diniz at the second corner. Verstappen was the first retirement in Japan (gearbox) and lost a possible sixth-place finish at Sepang when stuck in fifth gear.

RED BULL SAUBER PETRONAS

Sauber extended its deal with Ferrari for year-old V10 engines for another year in July 1999. Negotiations with Jean Alesi for a new two-year contract ended when he accepted Prost Grand Prix's offer in the wake of Sauber's disastrous 1999 Hungarian GP. Parmalat-backed Pedro Diniz renewed on 27 August for what was a crash-strewn final F1 season. Ferrari 'super-sub' Mika Salo was announced as his team-mate following advice from the *Scuderia*'s sporting director Jean Todt. Petronas was in its final year of its sponsorship and engine-badging contract while Red Bull retained a 51 percent stake in the team.

Salo gave the Sauber C19-Petronas its shakedown at Fiorano before Christmas ahead of its first Barcelona test on 9 January. While the C18 had been on the minimum limit, Leo Ress, Sauber's technical director since the team's graduation to F1 in 1993, pared almost

Mika Salo, Sauber C19-Petronas (Monaco GP)

Pedro Diniz, Sauber C19-Petronas (Italian GP)

30kg from the new design so that ballast could be used to optimise weight distribution. Ferrari supplied 1999 Italian GP-specification engines at the start of the year with a lighter and more powerful upgrade in Montréal. There were cooling issues so additional ducts on the engine cover were required but they increased drag. A Sauber seven-speed longitudinal gearbox was preferred to Ferrari's titanium alternative due to cost. Seamus Mullarkey revised the aerodynamics along McLaren lines with flat nose, new wings and sidepods that waisted to a narrower 'Coke bottle' rear. Pushrod suspension was employed with the lower-front wishbones mounted on two pylons under the nose. Carbon-fibre rather than steel suspension wishbones were tried during the season, but the team's new hydraulic differential was not raced.

Chief designer Sergio Rinland joined from Benetton in the winter of 1999/2000 and Willy Rampf returned from BMW as head of vehicle engineering. He was promoted to technical director when Ress switched to a research and development role in March. A Lapland-themed launch, complete with reindeer and huskies, at Zürich's Hallenstadion on 2 February attracted 7,000 paying fans. Erratic F3000 driver Enrique Bernoldi was confirmed as reserve driver.

Sauber's perennial hopes of breaking out of the midfield were hit by early rear-wing failures, cooling issues, and its customary lack of in-season development. Both drivers suffered heavy pre-season testing crashes, Salo breaking a bone in his hand at Barcelona and Diniz losing his rear wing at 180mph at Jerez.

Salo scored a convincing sixth place in Melbourne only to be disqualified for a front-wing infringement; Diniz spun early before his transmission failed. Worse came in Brazil when both had rear-wing failures on Saturday, forcing Sauber to withdraw from the race. Outqualified by Diniz at the next two races, Salo opened the team's account with sixth at Imola but neither scored at Silverstone. Diniz spun on the opening lap in Spain, where Salo beat Ricardo Zonta's BAR-Honda into seventh.

A new diffuser introduced at the European GP did not resolve the C19's lack of traction but Diniz recovered from another spin to salvage a season-best seventh after a race of attrition. They again qualified outside the top ten at Monaco but Salo withstood Mika Häkkinen's late advances to claim fifth – his fourth points score in the Principality in five years. Having ended his Monaco GP in the Ste-Dévote barriers, Diniz was penalised and placed on probation by the Canadian GP stewards for colliding with Pedro de la Rosa's Arrows. Uncompetitive at Magny-Cours, the C19s were better suited to the A1-Ring. Salo qualified ninth and took advantage of the first-corner mayhem to run third in the early stages before losing out to de la Rosa and the recovering Rubens Barrichello, and eventually finishing sixth despite fading brakes and oversteer. In contrast, Diniz's wild campaign continued with a stop-go penalty in Austria for easing Giancarlo Fisichella off the road at the start, followed by criticism at Hockenheim for a high-speed collision with Jean Alesi's Prost at the first chicane. Salo took fifth in the Hockenheim rain and qualified ninth in Hungary, where the team-mates ran together before Diniz's transmission failed while ahead for once.

With Peter Sauber absent following a shoulder operation and both drivers looking to leave, they qualified poorly but finished in

Belgium. The lack of single-lap pace continued at Monza, where Salo sustained a left-rear puncture and bodywork damage when eliminating Eddie Irvine's Jaguar at the first corner and Diniz damaged his suspension avoiding the pile-up further round the lap, but both drivers finished, seventh (Salo) and eighth (Diniz). Indianapolis brought Diniz's best qualifying performance (ninth) and he ran as high as third during the first pitstops, but then his C19's handling deteriorated so much that he stopped to check for a loose wheel and dropped from sixth to eighth. Salo's lacklustre race ended with a spin. Slow but reliable in Japan, they finished a dispiriting campaign at Sepang in customary fashion – Salo eighth and Diniz the cause of another first-lap accident.

JAGUAR RACING

The Ford Motor Company had ambitious goals when it acquired Stewart Grand Prix in 1999. Race wins were expected during its first season before a challenge for the World Championship in 2001, so just four points and ninth overall was a bitterly disappointing return. Wolfgang Reitzle arrived from BMW in March 1999 to oversee Ford's new Premier Automotive Group, which also included Cosworth Engineering. Plans to build a new 'super' factory to house both companies at Silverstone and then Gaydon were finally abandoned in 2001. That facility would have included a wind tunnel for Jaguar Racing, which was handicapped by its use of the Swift Race Cars company's tunnel 5,250 miles away in Sacramento, California.

Rubens Barrichello moved to Ferrari at the end of his three-year Stewart contract and $10m per annum was set aside to lure a star replacement. But Jordan exercised its option on Heinz-Harald Frentzen, Ralf Schumacher earned an extension at Williams, Mika Häkkinen and David Coulthard remained at McLaren and Michael Schumacher's manager Willi Weber reported that they had turned down a tentative approach. Ford used the official announcement of its rebranding to Jaguar Racing at the Frankfurt Motor Show on 14 September 1999 to confirm long-standing rumours that Eddie Irvine had signed a three-year deal and that Johnny Herbert, constantly under pressure despite having a firm contract for 2000, would remain. British F3 runner-up Luciano Burti was reserve driver and was joined in test duties by Tomas Scheckter and André Lotterer.

Ford's corporate culture replaced Stewart family management, squandering direct F1 experience and saddling the team with layers of bureaucracy inappropriate to the sport. Ford's chief technical officer Neil Ressler replaced Jackie Stewart as chairman in January although the three-time champion remained as a consultant. Paul Stewart stepped down from his role as chief operating officer in the spring when diagnosed with cancer. John Russell arrived from Williams as chief designer in November 1999, reporting to technical director Gary Anderson.

Irvine first drove a Stewart SF3-Ford on 14 December during a group test at Jerez and Herbert completed the week with the fastest time. Burti gave the plain-green Jaguar R1-Cosworth its shakedown at Silverstone on 5 January before the race drivers took over at Barcelona. Herbert set the fastest time on two days that month before the car and definitive team colours were revealed on 25 January at a lavish function at Lord's Cricket Ground in London. The R1 was an evolution of the race-winning Stewart SF3-Ford, with a new version of the compact and powerful 72-degree Cosworth V10 (CR-2). Anderson aimed to make the R1's systems easier to work on when he began the design process in June. The hydraulics and electronics were revised, and nose lowered still further. The bargeboards, fins on the chassis and 'Coke bottle' rear resembled the McLaren MP4-14, while fuel capacity was increased to facilitate flexible race strategies. Unconventional multi-link suspension was employed at the rear. Irvine initially struggled without the power steering he had enjoyed at Ferrari and Jaguar's own system was introduced by the end of winter testing.

Crucial mileage during winter testing was lost by Irvine's 125mph crash when a water pipe worked loose and issues with the oil system that lubricated both the engine and gearbox. A temporary fix was introduced at the final Jerez test where they topped the timesheets once more, albeit on low fuel and in cool conditions. Those quick times masked the R1's pronounced oversteer, lack of downforce and high-speed instability. Irvine regularly qualified in the top ten, but a clutch-mapping issue caused a succession of slow starts and poor reliability compromised results.

The Australian GP set the tone. Oil-circulation problems persisted throughout practice and Herbert described his weekend as 'the worst three days I've ever had'. Irvine started seventh but both

Johnny Herbert, Jaguar R1-Cosworth (Japanese GP)

Eddie Irvine, Jaguar R1-Cosworth (Monaco GP)

drivers were out by lap seven, Herbert's clutch having failed on the opening lap and Irvine after a spin while trying to avoid Pedro de la Rosa's errant Arrows. An extra oil tank was fitted for Brazil where Herbert's gearbox broke and Irvine crashed out of sixth. An aero upgrade at Imola improved the nervous rear-end handling and both cars finished, Irvine a misfiring seventh and Herbert tenth. At Silverstone, both drivers stalled at their second pitstops due to clutch problems and finished outside the top ten. Oversteer and poor starts ruined the Spanish GP so Ressler abandoned his wider Ford responsibilities to concentrate on sorting the troubled team.

Both drivers crashed out of the European GP, Irvine having lost

Luciano Burti, Jaguar R1-Cosworth (Austrian GP)

his rear wing following contact with Jos Verstappen's Arrows while disputing sixth. Herbert had made an early switch to wet tyres and was seventh in the closing stages when hit by Alexander Wurz's Benetton. Irvine's fourth place after a race of attrition in Monaco finally delivered Jaguar's first F1 points; Herbert had led his team-mate but a pitstop to fix the power steering dropped him to last by the finish. The grip-less R1s were off the pace in Canada, where Herbert outqualified his team-mate for the first time only to suffer the first of two successive gearbox failures, and Irvine finished last after stalling. At Magny-Cours, Irvine qualified sixth but made another poor start and finished 13th thanks to a faulty refuelling rig necessitating four replenishment stops, but his third-fastest race lap at least showed potential.

Irvine missed the Austrian GP through illness so Burti made his F1 debut. Both cars finished outside the points with Herbert seventh after earlier running fifth. Smaller bargeboards and a revised version of the 1999 engine, developing an additional 30bhp, were introduced at Hockenheim. Herbert qualified a season-best eighth only for gearbox issues to end that race and the next in Hungary, where he spun twice. Irvine's German GP was ruined by a qualifying spin and ill-timed safety car in the race, but he finished eighth in Hungary despite carrying extra fuel to counter a pressure issue.

With his position in the team under threat, Herbert was the quicker driver at Spa-Francorchamps, qualifying ninth and finishing eighth. Tenth in Belgium, Irvine was eliminated at the first corner of the Italian GP while Herbert lasted to the Variante della Roggia before being hit by de la Rosa. They qualified at the back at Indianapolis where Herbert was the only driver to gamble on slick tyres at the start. He charged into fifth only to lose control in the wet

Marc Gené, Minardi M02-Fondmetal (British GP)

pitlane and damage his R1's nose against a wheel gun, relegating him to the back; Irvine was seventh despite understeer.

A new undertray improved the cars in Japan, where both qualified and finished inside the top ten, Herbert having passed Irvine for seventh at his second pitstop. 'There's nothing like ending your career with a bang,' was Herbert's reaction when right-rear suspension failure in the closing stages of his final F1 race in Malaysia caused a 150mph accident. He had to be carried away from the wreckage and hospital checks revealed a badly bruised left knee. Buoyed by improved traction, Irvine started seventh for the second successive race and finished sixth to score Jaguar's first point since June.

TELEFÓNICA MINARDI FONDMETAL

Minardi faced an engine crisis in April 1999 when Ford announced that it would not supply customer versions of its old 72-degree Zetec-R. Talks with Supertec failed before Bernie Ecclestone helped reverse Ford's decision with contracts signed in December. Rebadged as Fondmetal V10s in deference to majority shareholder Gabriele Rumi's company, the engines remained heavy and underpowered and there was just one upgrade when new cylinder heads were introduced at the Spanish GP.

Title sponsor Telefónica wanted a South American as partner for Marc Gené, who was in the final year of his contract. Bruno Junqueira was considered before Norberto Fontana and Max Wilson tested at Jerez in December, with Giorgio Vinella, Peter Sundberg and 18-year-old Fernando Alonso given the prize test at that time for respectively winning the Italian F3000, F3 and Euro Open by

Nissan titles. Vinella and Alonso were rewarded with test contracts although it was mid-summer before either ran again. Sporting director Cesare Fiorio was replaced by former team manager Frédéric Dhainaut in August following a disagreement with Rumi.

The Minardi M02-Fordmetal was launched on 16 February at the Guggenheim Museum in Bilbao, where former test driver Gastón Mazzacane was the surprise choice as Gené's team-mate. His inclusion coincided with additional backing from the Miami-based Pan-American Sports Network (PSN). Technical director Gustav Brunner developed his 1999 car with 85 percent new parts, an angular and lower nose with both driver and engine moved back. The casing for the new six-speed longitudinal gearbox was initially magnesium although that was replaced by cast titanium following developments by CRP Technology in Modena. Lighter and stiffer than before, it was introduced on Mazzacane's car in Spanish practice. He raced the new gearbox at the Nürburgring, and both cars used it from Monaco onwards. The suspension was via torsion bars and carbon pushrods as before and exhausts exited through the top of the rear bodywork. Brembo carbon-ceramic disc brakes were introduced mid-season and an active differential was raced at Monza. The M02 handled well and was generally reliable, but the old engine, restricted testing and lack of wind-tunnel time led to another campaign among the backmarkers.

Gené hit Nick Heidfeld's Prost at the start of the Australian GP and lost a lap while a broken steering arm was replaced, going on to set the ninth-fastest race lap and finish eighth. Sidelined by engine failure in Brazil, he spun out of qualifying and the race at Imola and lacked the horsepower to trouble rivals at Silverstone. An unscheduled stop restricted Gené to 14th in Spain before he

Gastón Mazzacane, Minardi M02-Fondmetal (Italian GP)

accused of blocking third-placed David Coulthard in Hungary. The infield was wet at the start of the United States GP and Mazzacane climbed into a remarkable third position by delaying his change to dry tyres. However, he hit two mechanics at his second stop and was last when his engine failed. His was the final car to be classified at Suzuka and Sepang (where his engine failed with five laps to go) as Minardi-Fondmetal failed to score a point all season.

Rumi was now terminally ill with cancer and 2000 was overshadowed by takeover rumours as he looked to sell his 70 percent stake. Negotiations with Telefónica, for whom former Benetton operations director Joan Villadelprat worked as a consultant, broke down in May. PSN agreed to buy the shares in September but that deal also collapsed in November. There would be another uncertain winter in Faenza.

GAULOISES PROST PEUGEOT
Having spent 1999 blaming each other for another uncompetitive season, Prost Grand Prix and Peugeot staggered into the third and final year of their contract. It was a disastrous campaign and Peugeot confirmed season-long rumours that it was quitting F1 on 25 July.

Alain Prost fell out with his drivers during 1999 so it was no surprise when an all-new line-up was announced. Olivier Panis was released and Jarno Trulli exercised a performance clause to end his commitments for 2000. Prost's former team-mate and close friend Jean Alesi signed as team leader. F3000 champion-elect Nick Heidfeld, who was under contract to McLaren-Mercedes, tested a Prost AP02-Peugeot at Silverstone on 19 August 1999 and signed a one-year deal later that month. British F3 star Jenson Button impressed at Barcelona on 17 December and was expected to be named as reserve before his surprise Williams-BMW call-up, so Stéphane Sarrazin was retained in that role. Gauloises cigarettes remained as title partner while Yahoo! agreed a three-year deal as F1's first major internet sponsor. Ex-Jordan/Arrows team manager John Walton joined as sporting director in January 2000.

The latest A20 version of Peugeot's V10 engine was smaller and lighter than the old-fashioned A18, but it was overweight (10 percent heavier than the latest offerings from Mercedes-Benz and Cosworth), unreliable and lacked power (especially in hot conditions). Having

retired from the next two races. He crashed with three laps to go in Montréal and finished last at Magny-Cours. He benefitted from the first corner mêlée at the A1-Ring to run in the top ten throughout and finish a creditable eighth. Denied another top-ten finish by engine failure in Germany, Gené received a stop-go penalty for baulking Eddie Irvine in Hungary. Having celebrated Minardi's 250th GP at Spa-Francorchamps with a lowly double finish, both drivers avoided Monza's opening-lap accidents to finish ninth (Gené) and tenth (Mazzacane). At Indianapolis, Gené briefly led David Coulthard's delayed McLaren before finishing last following a pitlane incident. He retired from the last two races of an increasingly frustrating season.

Mazzacane was the perennial tailender throughout his rookie season, qualifying on the last row at every race bar San Marino, where he started 20th. He finished last in Brazil before four successive finishes culminated with a career-best eighth at the Nürburgring. He crashed at Ste-Dévote during the Monaco GP and spun out of last place at Magny-Cours, after Minardi-Fondmetal's preparations had been disrupted by a transport strike in Italy. He spun in the rain at Hockenheim and both Minardi drivers were

Nick Heidfeld, Prost AP03-Peugeot (Australian GP)

run on the dyno since June 1999, its track debut at Barcelona in October lasted just two laps before it failed with Heidfeld behind the wheel. Variable trumpets due from the start of the season were delayed until Imola.

Former Stewart Grand Prix technical director Alan Jenkins completed six months' gardening leave before arriving in June 1999, although his appointment proved short-lived. Jenkins declared that 'fifth in the championship is up for grabs' at the launch of the Prost AP03-Peugeot on 1 February at Circuit de Barcelona-Catalunya. *Autosport* noted that the new car owed more to Jenkins's Stewart SF3 than the AP02. Chief designer Loïc Bigois was responsible for the AP03's aerodynamic performance and this was questioned all year. The car's wheelbase was reduced with driver and sidepods moved rearward. McLaren-inspired fins ahead of the cockpit satisfied chassis-height regulations. There were large bargeboards, twin flip-ups ahead of the rear wheels and a new diffuser. John Barnard's Surrey-based B3 Technologies designed the front end, which included new torsion-bar suspension. The rear suspension was carbon-fibre for the first time with periscope exhausts to direct heat away from this area. However, a left-rear wishbone fractured after three laps of Barcelona testing, so steel was substituted. A new seven-speed longitudinal gearbox was developed with Xtrac.

Alesi's suspension failure at that first test forced the team to return to base and his gearbox broke next time out at Barcelona. Persistent problems with the Electronic Control Unit included random downshifts, which Prost blamed on the late delivery of the engine. With poor rear-end grip and initial chassis flex, the AP03 vied with the Minardi M02 as the slowest car in the field. Alesi was not impressed. 'Give me a few bits of wool to stick on the car, a good gust of Mistral wind and I could come up with a better aerodynamic package on the bridge at Avignon than the team has managed,' he declared in June.

The unsorted AP03s were a handful in Australia, where Heidfeld outqualified his team-mate and finished ninth and last. 'Alesi's debut with Prost proved fruitless,' read *Autosport*'s photo caption. 'The car was slow, handled badly, then broke.' The problems persisted in Brazil where Alesi hit a rival cigarette brand's advertising board that had fallen onto the track at Turn 1 during qualifying. Having lost its rear wing during the warm-up, his light-fuelled AP03 passed five cars in the opening 11 laps before another electronic failure, moments after Heidfeld's engine had blown up.

Hydraulic failures accounted for both cars at Imola. Heidfeld suffered engine failures at Silverstone in qualifying and the race while his team-mate's tenth was hardly reason for cheer. Alesi tangled with Pedro de la Rosa on lap two in Spain, where Heidfeld struggled home 16th after being lapped three times. The German was not allowed to start the European GP after his car was found to be 2kg underweight in qualifying, but Alesi drove a spirited race in the rain until more gearbox issues and a stop-go penalty for speeding in the pitlane restricted him to ninth.

With the team in freefall, Jenkins left before the Monaco GP amid rumours of discontent among the French workforce, with Jean-Paul Gousset named as acting technical director. Alesi used a new front

Jean Alesi, Prost AP03-Peugeot (Monaco GP)

wing and diffuser to qualify a surprise seventh in Monaco and held that position until the transmission failed. Heidfeld finished eighth in the spare car after crashing on Thursday, spinning on Saturday and getting involved in the Loews hairpin shunt. They were back among the tailenders in Montréal qualifying but Alesi climbed into the top ten by half distance before both cars retired once again.

An upgraded V10 at Magny-Cours did not satisfy Alesi, who criticised the engine live on French television after qualifying 18th, prompting angry Peugeot engineers to initially refuse to start his engine before the warm-up. If matters could hardly get worse, the team-mates collided at that race and the next. During the French GP, Heidfeld nudged Alesi into a spin at the Adelaide hairpin as he tried to pass Giancarlo Fisichella. They collided on lap 41 in Austria with both drivers eliminated and blaming each other. In Germany, Heidfeld qualified 13th for the second race in a row (his best starting position of the year) but another lacklustre race ended in alternator failure with five laps to go. Alesi hit Pedro Diniz with such force (10G) as he attempted to pass into the first chicane that he vomited after climbing out of the wreckage.

The calamities continued after the summer break. Passed fit and having considered his F1 future, Alesi crashed in the Hungarian pitlane during a second stop to check for suspension damage and Heidfeld's engine cut at his scheduled pitstop. A well-timed switch to dry tyres saw Alesi run fourth at Spa-Francorchamps although both retired once more. Only the Minardi-Fondmetals were slower at Monza, where Alesi lost a lap when he stalled on the grid. Last that day, he threatened to score points at Indianapolis before the engine failed. Heidfeld spun out of the Italian GP and finished a lapped ninth in the USA. A double DNF in Japan was followed by another rout at the Malaysian finale. Both were involved in another first-lap accident, with Heidfeld eliminated, but Alesi was able to continue and finished 11th. Last in the constructors' championship due to Minardi's greater number of eighth-place finishes, Prost GP lost the vital FOCA travel money awarded to F1's top ten teams.

DRIVER PERFORMANCE

DRIVER	CAR-ENGINE	AUS	BR	RSM	GB	E	EU	MC	CDN	F	A	D	H	B	I	USA	J	MAL
Jean Alesi	Prost AP03-Peugeot	17 R	15 R	15 R	15 10	17 R	17 9	7 R	17 R	18 14	17 R	20 R	14 R	17 R	19 12	20 R	17 R	18 11
Rubens Barrichello	Ferrari F1-2000	4 2 FL	4 R	4 4	1 R	3 3	4 4	6 2	3 2	3 3	3 3	18 1 FL	5 4	10 R FL	2 R	4 2	4 4	4 3
Luciano Burti	Jaguar R1-Cosworth	–	–	–	–	–	–	–	–	21 11	–	–	–	–	–	–	–	–
Jenson Button	Williams FW22-BMW	21 R	9 6	18 R	6 5	10 17	11 10	14 R	18 11	10 8	18 5	16 4	8 9	3 5	12 R	6 R	5 5	16 R
David Coulthard	McLaren MP4-15-Mercedes-Benz	2 R	2 DSQ	3 3	4 1	4 2	1 3	3 1	2 7	2 1 FL	2 2 FL	1 3	2 3	5 4	5 R	2 5 FL	3 3	3 2
Pedro de la Rosa	Arrows A21-Supertec	12 R	16 8	13 R	19 R	22 R	12 6	16 R	9 R	13 R	12 R	5 6	15 16	16 16	10 R	18 R	13 12	14 R
Pedro Diniz	Sauber C19-Petronas	19 R	20 DNS	10 8	13 11	15 R	15 7	19 R	19 10	15 11	11 9	19 R	13 R	15 11	16 8	9 8	20 11	20 R
Giancarlo Fisichella	Benetton B200-Playlife	9 5	5 2	19 11	12 7	13 9	7 5	8 3	10 3	14 9	8 R	3 R	7 R	11 R	9 11	15 R	12 14	13 9
Heinz-Harald Frentzen	Jordan EJ10-Mugen	5 R	7 3	6 R	2 17	8 6	10 R	4 10	5 R	8 7	15 R	17 R	6 6	8 6	8 R	7 3	8 R	10 R
Marc Gené	Minardi M02-Fondmetal	18 8	18 R	21 R	21 14	21 14	20 14	20 R	21 R	20 16	21 15	20 8	22 R	21 15	21 14	21 9	22 12	21 R
Mika Häkkinen	McLaren MP4-15-Mercedes-Benz	1 R	1 R	1 2 FL	3 2 FL	2 1 FL	3 2	5 6 FL	4 4 FL	4 2	1 1	4 2	3 1 FL	1 1	3 2 FL	3 R	2 2 FL	2 4 FL
Nick Heidfeld	Prost AP03-Peugeot	15 9	19 R	22 R	17 R	19 16	22 DNQ	18 8	21 R	16 12	13 R	13 12	19 R	14 R	20 R	16 9	16 R	19 R
Johnny Herbert	Jaguar R1-Cosworth	20 R	17 R	17 10	14 12	14 13	16 11	11 9	11 R	11 R	16 7	8 R	17 R	9 8	18 R	19 11	10 7	12 R
Eddie Irvine	Jaguar R1-Cosworth	7 R	6 R	7 7	9 13	9 11	8 R	10 4	16 13	6 13	NT DNP	10 10	10 8	12 10	14 R	17 7	7 8	7 6
Gastón Mazzacane	Minardi M02-Fondmetal	22 R	21 10	20 13	22 15	21 15	21 8	22 R	22 12	22 R	22 12	21 11	22 R	22 17	22 10	21 R	22 15	22 13
Mika Salo	Sauber C19-Petronas	10 DSQ	22 DNS	12 6	18 8	12 7	19 R	13 5	15 R	12 10	9 6	15 5	9 10	18 9	15 7	14 R	19 10	17 8
Michael Schumacher	Ferrari F1-2000	3 1	3 1 FL	2 1	5 3	1 5	2 1 FL	1 R	1 1	1 R	4 R	2 R	1 2	4 2	1 1	1 1	1 1	1 1
Ralf Schumacher	Williams FW22-BMW	11 3	11 5	5 R	7 4	5 4	5 R	9 R	12 14	5 5	19 R	14 7	4 5	6 3	7 3	10 R	6 R	8 R
Jarno Trulli	Jordan EJ10-Mugen	6 R	12 4	8 15	11 6	7 12	6 R	2 R	7 6	9 6	5 R	6 9	12 7	2 R	6 R	5 R	15 13	9 12
Jos Verstappen	Arrows A21-Supertec	13 R	14 7	16 14	8 R	11 R	13 R	15 R	13 5	20 R	10 R	11 R	20 13	20 15	11 4	13 R	14 R	15 10
Jacques Villeneuve	BAR 002-Honda	8 4	10 R	9 5	10 16	6 R	9 R	17 7	6 15	7 4	7 4	9 8	16 12	7 7	4 R	8 4	9 6	6 5
Alexander Wurz	Benetton B200-Playlife	14 7	13 R	11 9	20 9	18 10	14 12	12 R	14 9	17 R	14 10	7 R	11 11	19 13	13 5	11 10	11 R	5 7
Ricardo Zonta	BAR 002-Honda	16 6	8 9	14 12	16 R	16 8	18 R	20 R	8 8	19 R	6 R	12 R	18 14	13 12	17 6	12 6	18 9	11 R

FORMULA 1 RACE WINNERS

ROUND	RACE (CIRCUIT)	DATE	WINNER
1	Qantas Australian Grand Prix (Albert Park)	Mar 12	Michael Schumacher (Ferrari F1-2000)
2	Grande Prêmio Marlboro do Brasil (Interlagos)	Mar 26	Michael Schumacher (Ferrari F1-2000)
3	Gran Premio Warsteiner di San Marino (Imola)	Apr 9	Michael Schumacher (Ferrari F1-2000)
4	Foster's British Grand Prix (Silverstone)	Apr 23	David Coulthard (McLaren MP4-15-Mercedes-Benz)
5	Gran Premio Marlboro de España (Catalunya)	May 7	Mika Häkkinen (McLaren MP4-15-Mercedes-Benz)
6	Warsteiner Grand Prix of Europe (Nürburgring)	May 21	Michael Schumacher (Ferrari F1-2000)
7	Grand Prix de Monaco (Monte Carlo)	Jun 4	David Coulthard (McLaren MP4-15-Mercedes-Benz)
8	Grand Prix Air Canada (Montréal)	Jun 18	Michael Schumacher (Ferrari F1-2000)
9	Mobil 1 Grand Prix de France (Magny-Cours)	Jul 2	David Coulthard (McLaren MP4-15-Mercedes-Benz)
10	Grosser A1 Preis von Österreich (Spielberg)	Jul 16	Mika Häkkinen (McLaren MP4-15-Mercedes-Benz)
11	Grosser Mobil 1 Preis von Deutschland (Hockenheim)	Jul 30	Rubens Barrichello (Ferrari F1-2000)
12	Marlboro Magyar Nagydíj (Hungaroring)	Aug 13	Mika Häkkinen (McLaren MP4-15-Mercedes-Benz)
13	Foster's Belgian Grand Prix (Spa-Francorchamps)	Aug 27	Mika Häkkinen (McLaren MP4-15-Mercedes-Benz)
14	Gran Premio Campari d'Italia (Monza)	Sep 10	Michael Schumacher (Ferrari F1-2000)
15	SAP United States Grand Prix (Indianapolis)	Sep 24	Michael Schumacher (Ferrari F1-2000)
16	Fuji Television Japanese Grand Prix (Suzuka)	Oct 8	Michael Schumacher (Ferrari F1-2000)
17	Petronas Malaysian Grand Prix (Sepang)	Oct 22	Michael Schumacher (Ferrari F1-2000)

DRIVERS' CHAMPIONSHIP

	DRIVERS	POINTS
1	Michael Schumacher	108
2	Mika Häkkinen	89
3	David Coulthard	73
4	Rubens Barrichello	62
5	Ralf Schumacher	24
6	Giancarlo Fisichella	18
7	Jacques Villeneuve	17
8	Jenson Button	12
9	Heinz-Harald Frentzen	11
10=	Mika Salo	6
	Jarno Trulli	6
12	Jos Verstappen	5
13	Eddie Irvine	4
14	Ricardo Zonta	3
15=	Pedro de la Rosa	2
	Alexander Wurz	2

CONSTRUCTORS' CHAMPIONSHIP

	CONSTRUCTORS	POINTS
1	Ferrari	170
2	McLaren-Mercedes-Benz	152
3	Williams-BMW	36
4=	Benetton-Playlife	20
	BAR-Honda	20
6	Jordan-Mugen	17
7	Arrows-Supertec	7
8	Sauber-Petronas	6
9	Jaguar-Cosworth	4

David Coulthard leads at the start of the United States Grand Prix

Michael Schumacher's victory in Hungary equalled Alain Prost's record 51 wins and confirmed back-to-back world titles

2001
MORE MARANELLO RECORD-BREAKING

Prost Grand Prix's Luciano Burti barrel-rolled out of the German Grand Prix after hitting Michael Schumacher's slow-starting Ferrari

The FIA's World Motor Sport Council approved new rules in June 2000 intended to make following another car easier. The front wing was raised by 50mm while the rear wing could only contain three elements. Chassis dimensions were tightened to outlaw the ancillary twin fins on top of the chassis. Safety measures included larger cockpits, wheel tethers and more rigorous crash tests with side-impact and roll-hoop loads increased. Electronic driver aids such as traction control were reallowed from the Spanish GP although automatic start systems remained illegal. Exotic metals such as beryllium were outlawed on health and cost grounds. The three-week summer break was introduced with testing banned in August and at any GP venue for 28 days before the event. A 10-second stop-go

David Coulthard gives Mika Häkkinen a lift after the Spanish Grand Prix

penalty was now imposed on any driver who ignored more than three blue flags before being lapped.

The Ferrari F2001 was the class of the field. Michael Schumacher clinched his fourth world title at the Hungarian GP in August and passed Alain Prost's long-standing record of 51 wins next time out in Belgium. Michelin returned to F1 to challenge Bridgestone. Tyre preparation was crucial for those using the French rubber and they often found it preferable to start on scrubbed tyres.

The Concorde Agreement limited the calendar to 17 events although there was a push to expand outside F1's traditional European races. Zhuhai's attempt to hold the Chinese GP was again denied and Kyalami failed to activate its option to revive the South African GP. Further rumours and releases suggested potential projects in Dubai, Beirut, Moscow, Seoul, Cairo, Tunis, Istanbul and Auckland.

A two-year battle over the British GP was resolved by a 15-year lease deal between Octagon Motorsports (which had a six-year contract to stage the race from 2002) and the British Racing Drivers' Club (owners of Silverstone). The 2001 event went ahead despite the foot-and-mouth epidemic but severe traffic congestion threatened its future. Spa-Francorchamps was the first circuit to replace gravel with tarmac run-off areas with Eau Rouge and Blanchimont modified. The Australian GP was marred by the death of marshal Graham Beveridge when he was hit by a wheel; he was the second marshal to be killed in the space of five races.

The Italian GP was run in the aftermath of the terrorist

Mika Häkkinen, Ralf Schumacher and Michael Schumacher celebrate in Canada

attacks on New York and following Alex Zanardi's serious accident during the Lausitzring Champ Car race. Monza's first two chicanes had been criticised following the tragic 2000 race with some demanding that the race be started behind the safety car. Michael Schumacher's suggestion that they agree not overtake at those chicanes on the opening lap collapsed when Jacques Villeneuve refused.

This was a period of commercial upheaval. The FIA reached agreement with the European Union regarding the governance of the sport after a confrontational six-year investigation. As part of that agreement, Bernie Ecclestone gave up his role as FIA vice president for promotional affairs, while selling a controlling stake in his SLEC holding company with Kirch Gruppe eventually owning 58.3 percent when former partner EM.TV collapsed. SLEC extended its contract for F1's commercial rights for another 100 years from 2011. Fiat, DaimlerChrysler, BMW, Renault and Ford formed the Association des Constructeurs Européens d'Automobiles as they sought to protect free-to-air television coverage and receive a greater revenue share. That included a threat to form a rival breakaway championship once the current Concorde Agreement expired in 2008. FIA president Max Mosley was re-elected unopposed for a third term in October.

Triple World Champion Jackie Stewart was knighted in The Queen's Birthday Honour's list, but his championship-winning team owner Ken Tyrrell succumbed to cancer in August. British broadcasting legend Murray Walker retired at the United States GP aged 76.

Tarmac replaced gravel for the run-off at Spa's Eau Rouge

Michael Schumacher, Ferrari F2001 (Hungarian GP)

SCUDERIA FERRARI MARLBORO

There was a confident air at Ferrari when the F2001 was unveiled at Fiorano on 29 January, with stability in the cockpit and on the pitwall. Michael Schumacher and Rubens Barrichello were contracted until the end of 2002 and '01 respectively. Entering the final year of their contracts, sporting director Jean Todt, technical director Ross Brawn and chief designer Rory Byrne all extended for another three years. The impressive technical department was augmented by Aldo Costa, James Allison and aerodynamicist Nikolas Tombazis. Electronics expert Ted Czapski returned to Benetton while chief mechanic Nigel Stepney was promoted to technical manager to stave off interest from Jaguar. Bridgestone tyres were retained and Philip Morris International extended its Marlboro sponsorship to the end of 2006.

Schumacher spent much of the winter recuperating with his family in Norway after removal of the pins in the leg he had broken during the 1999 British GP. Winter testing was interrupted on 21 January when Luca Badoer crashed a Ferrari F1-2000 over Barcelona's Turn 1 barrier following left-rear suspension failure; Fabrizio Giovanardi was his temporary replacement.

The new Ferrari F2001 and type 050 engine were evolutions of the successful 2000 package. The nose was lower than rival designs while the front wing drooped at the centre. The monocoque and sidepods were tall with small bargeboards and periscope exhausts. The airbox intake was now oval while the smaller 90-degree V10 allowed for lower rear bodywork. The pushrod/torsion-bar suspension configuration was unchanged although its manufacture was altered to improve tyre management. The F2001 was fast out of

the box but niggling issues prevented Schumacher from completing a race simulation before Australia. However, it proved bullet-proof when it mattered, posting only three mechanical retirements all year.

Schumacher recovered from a barrel roll in Albert Park's Turn 6 gravel during Friday practice to dominate the opening two races from pole position. Barrichello completed Ferrari front-row lock-outs on both occasions and finished third in Australia despite contact with Heinz-Harald Frentzen's Jordan and being passed by David Coulthard's McLaren when he was baulked by Fernando Alonso's Minardi. Sepang was eventful for Ferrari. Barrichello's hit Ralf Schumacher's Williams at the start and both Ferraris ran wide as the monsoon arrived on lap three. They spent a chaotic minute changing to intermediate tyres but were up to six seconds a lap quicker than the wet-shod McLarens once released from behind the safety car. They finished 1–2, although Barrichello was miffed by his team leader's risky passing manoeuvre in the rain.

Now winner of six consecutive GPs, Schumacher qualified on pole in Brazil with his younger brother alongside – a championship first. A set-up error caused oversteer and on the third lap the other Williams of Juan Pablo Montoya passed Schumacher Sr, who then spun when it rained and finished a well-beaten second behind Coulthard. Barrichello struggled all weekend and was eliminated in another collision with Schumacher Jr.

Fourth on the grid at Imola after using hard tyres, Schumacher retired after gearshift problems, a front-left puncture and damage caused by a brake issue. Barrichello snatched third from Mika Häkkinen in the San Marino pitstops and retired from that position in Spain following another suspension failure. Schumacher bounced

Rubens Barrichello, Ferrari F2001 (British GP)

back at that latter race by qualifying on pole. Tyre vibrations during his final stint handed the advantage to Häkkinen but Schumacher inherited victory when the Finn retired on the last lap.

Slow away from pole when his launch control failed in Austria, Schumacher was forced wide by Montoya as he tried to take the lead, with Barrichello the beneficiary. The Brazilian lost out to Coulthard in the pitstops and was ordered to hand Schumacher second place at the final corner of the race, prompting much criticism of Ferrari. Schumacher led a straightforward 1–2 in Monaco after the McLarens had problems.

Schumacher used a new-specification engine to lead qualifying 1–2s at Montréal and the Nürburgring. Beaten into second in Canada due to high fuel consumption and low grip, he sparked a family row when he edged Ralf towards the pitwall at the start of the European GP, then held off Montoya to earn a hard-fought victory. Barrichello crashed during qualifying and the race in Canada and was fifth at the 'Ring.

Bridgestone brought a new compound to the French GP in response to a disappointing test at Magny-Cours. That proved crucial as Schumacher eased to victory once his pole-winning brother was delayed in the pits. Switching to a three-stop strategy, Barrichello recovered from only eighth on the grid to finish third. Schumacher and Barrichello could not match Häkkinen at Silverstone so they finished second and third respectively.

Schumacher's heavy testing crash at Monza's second chicane resulted in the floor of the F2001s being strengthened for the German GP. Fourth on the grid as Williams dominated, Schumacher missed a gear on the run to the first corner and was hit by Luciano Burti, whose Prost barrel-rolled spectacularly. The World Champion took the spare car for the restart but retired with fuel-pressure problems; Barrichello finished a distant second. Schumacher dominated in Hungary to clinch his fourth drivers' crown with his record-equalling 51st GP victory. Barrichello completed Maranello's day by finishing second as Ferrari retained the constructors' title.

Uninjured when his rear wing failed while testing at Mugello, Schumacher came from third on the grid in Belgium to lead throughout the restarted race, despite a momentary 'off' at Stavelot on lap 17; Barrichello was fifth. Schumacher was deeply affected by the New York terrorist attacks and the Ferraris sported black nose sections at the Italian GP out of respect for the victims. With another new qualifying engine and aero upgrade, Barrichello qualified and finished second after a fuel-rig problem denied his best chance of victory. Outqualified by his team-mate for the only time that season, an out-of-sorts Schumacher finished fourth. At Indianapolis, the two-stopping Barrichello was closing on race leader Häkkinen with two laps to go when his engine failed. On pole for the last two races, Schumacher inherited second in the United States and dominated the Japanese GP to match his record nine victories in a season. Barrichello was fifth at Suzuka and third in the World Championship.

WEST McLAREN MERCEDES

McLaren-Mercedes lost further ground to Ferrari with a disappointing technical package and the distraction of a 'tug-of-war' for its highly rated technical director. Adrian Newey's contract was due to expire on 31 July 2002 and Jaguar Racing made a very public approach for his services. The Ford-owned team claimed his signature on the morning of 1 June 2001 only for Newey later that day to sign McLaren's three-year contract extension, which included the promise of non-F1 projects in the future. Jaguar's legal action was settled out of court later that month. There had already been departures from Woking before the 2001 season with Steve Nichols and Henri Durand named as technical directors for Jaguar and Prost respectively. McLaren's veteran team co-ordinator Jo Ramirez retired after the United States GP. Jaguar's pursuit of Newey prompted McLaren to introduce a 'matrix' structure to its engineering department that cross-referenced key engineers and disciplines to reduce over-reliance on a single person.

An unchanged driver pairing was named for the sixth successive season despite winter whispers of Mika Häkkinen's retirement and Jacques Villeneuve replacing David Coulthard. Team principal Ron Dennis opted for experience when choosing the reserve driver once more. Olivier Panis accepted British American Racing's offer of a race seat with Alexander Wurz confirmed as his replacement at the 2000 Malaysian GP.

The launch of the compact McLaren MP4-16-Mercedes was delayed until 7 February so that Newey could optimise its radical design following three years of gradual evolution. The front-wing rules led to the nose being raised by 50mm, affecting airflow to the engine, lower rear bodywork and sculpted 'Coke bottle'. Longer sidepods housed the strengthened side-impact structures with the extra weight saved elsewhere. With tighter height regulations, the distinctive twin fins on the chassis were absent for the first time since 1998. Pushrod suspension was retained with inboard torsion bars and dampers. Ilmor Engineering's latest 72-degree Mercedes-Benz V10 (designated FO110K) lacked the outright power developed by Ferrari or BMW with the ban on beryllium having disadvantaged Mercedes more than its rivals. A late rule clarification on mechanical torque-steer gearboxes forced retention of the old unit. Like Ferrari, the tyre contract with Bridgestone was renewed.

Wurz joined Coulthard for his test debut at Jerez on 4 December

as they worked on the revised engine's reliability in an interim MP4-15K chassis. Häkkinen took an extended winter break and spent much of a disappointing (by his standards) season fielding speculation about his future. There was winter optimism when the Finn was quickest at Valencia on his return in January and Coulthard then topped the timing sheets at Barcelona. When the new MP4-16 was unveiled at Valencia's Circuito Ricardo Tormo, 7,000 miles had already been covered. Coulthard immediately lapped at record pace despite teething troubles but gearbox issues curtailed the subsequent Barcelona test. Furthermore, wind-tunnel expectations concerning front-end behaviour initially did not translate to the track with understeer the consequence.

McLaren-Mercedes was second best to the year-old Ferraris in Australia, where Häkkinen chased Michael Schumacher until right-front suspension failure caused him to crash heavily. Sixth on the grid, Coulthard banged wheels with Heinz-Harald Frentzen at the start before passing three cars to claim second. Poor balance blighted qualifying for the Malaysian GP, where the switch to full wets during the early downpour proved overly conservative. Coulthard led behind the safety car after that pitstop but could not hold off the intermediate-shod Ferraris when the race went green. He finished third with Häkkinen sixth after a frustrating day.

The front-wing issues were solved by round three in Brazil, where Häkkinen qualified third only to stall on the grid. Coulthard chose a semi-wet set-up and benefitted when heavy rain arrived on lap 46; a late change to intermediates handed Schumacher the lead but as they started lap 50 he repassed the Ferrari to take the win. Coulthard led a McLaren qualifying 1–2 at Imola – the team's first front-row starts of the year – and finished second to equal Schumacher in the standings, with Häkkinen only fourth after initially being delayed behind Jarno Trulli's Jordan. Häkkinen started second at Barcelona but lost a fourth successive Spanish victory on the last lap due to hydraulics-induced clutch failure. Coulthard was relegated to the back when the relegalised launch control failed before the parade lap and then lost his front wing in a first-lap

David Coulthard, McLaren MP4-16-Mercedes-Benz (Japanese GP)

Mika Häkkinen, McLaren MP4-16-Mercedes-Benz (Belgian GP)

contretemps with Giancarlo Fisichella's Benetton before storming through the field to finish fifth.

The Austrian GP weekend was overshadowed by the death of Ilmor co-founder Paul Morgan when his Sea Fury vintage aircraft overturned on landing at Sywell, Northamptonshire. Although the class of the field during free practice, the McLarens languished on row four after wrong set-up choices for qualifying. At the start 'flu-ridden Häkkinen stalled due to another launch-control glitch but Coulthard had a great day. Second when Schumacher's Ferrari and Montoya's Williams ran wide and the light-fuelled Jos Verstappen (Arrows) pitted, the Scotsman produced two stellar laps to jump Rubens Barrichello in the pitstops and claim ten more points. He did not spray the victory champagne out of respect for Morgan.

Coulthard snatched pole position for the Monaco GP in the final seconds only for another electronics-induced stall before the parade lap. Stuck behind Enrique Bernoldi until the Arrows pitted after 42 laps, the fired-up McLaren driver then broke the lap record as he finished fifth. Second when his front suspension failed in Monaco, Häkkinen finally scored his first podium of the year when third in Canada, where Coulthard persevered despite a loose front-suspension linkage before a spectacular engine blow-out further eroded his title hopes.

McLaren's least competitive race followed at the Nürburgring, where understeer in qualifying and oversteer during the race ensured that both Ferrari and Williams outgunned them. Coulthard held off the recovering Ralf Schumacher for third with Häkkinen sixth. Balance improved at Magny-Cours, where Häkkinen did not start again (gearbox) and a 10sec stop-go penalty for speeding in the pitlane denied fourth-placed Coulthard another podium.

With reports of imminent retirement in *Auto Bild* magazine denied and having walked away from a 180mph testing accident at Monza, Häkkinen passed Michael Schumacher to dominate the British GP. Coulthard qualified third but suffered terminal suspension damage in his first-corner collision with Jarno Trulli. Engine failures ruined their German GP and Coulthard's mathematical title chances evaporated when third behind the Ferraris in Hungary. They failed to exploit drying conditions in qualifying for the Belgian GP, where Coulthard passed Häkkinen and Fisichella to take second. Häkkinen finished fifth in Hungary and fourth at Spa-Francorchamps.

Since Monaco, Häkkinen had discussed with his team principal the possibility of taking an F1 sabbatical and this was confirmed at Monza. On McLaren's least competitive weekend due to nervous handling and a straight-line speed deficit, the Finn crashed heavily at the second Lesmo during qualifying and neither driver made an impression before retiring from the race. Häkkinen was happier with his car's handling at Indianapolis, where his quickest qualifying time was deleted for ignoring the pitlane red light during the warm-up. Demoted from second to fourth on the grid as a result, superior strategy and some scintillating laps gave him the lead at the pitstops for the last of his 20 career wins. Coulthard finished third in America despite oversteer and Häkkinen handed him that position during the closing laps at Suzuka in a generous appreciation of their long and successful partnership at McLaren.

Although he had been just four points behind Michael Schumacher after winning in Austria, the sixth race, Coulthard did not stand on the top step again. Both team and driver finished distant runners-up as their challenge waned.

BMW WILLIAMS F1

Williams enjoyed a resurgence during 2001 with its first victories since 1997 helping to retain third in the constructors' championship. Key to that momentum was BMW power and the switch to Michelin rubber upon the French tyre company's return to F1 after almost two decades away. In preparation, Michelin acquired a year-old Williams FW21B-BMW that Tom Kristensen first drove at Miramas in April 2000.

Ralf Schumacher was in the middle of a three-year contract while Jenson Button was loaned to Benetton to make way for much-hyped Juan Pablo Montoya from Champ Cars. Marc Gené quit Minardi to sign as reserve while F3000 drivers Antônio Pizzonia and Ricardo Sperafico tested at Estoril in September as they auditioned for a future role. Jordan's Sam Michael was reunited with Schumacher when he replaced James Robinson as chief operations engineer on 1 January 2001. Although Montoya immediately engaged in a war of words in the press with his new team-mate, it was Schumacher who delivered victory and finished fourth in the drivers' standings, even if Montoya completed his rookie campaign on the ascendency. A disappointing retirement rate included four accidents for each driver (self-inflicted or otherwise).

The Williams FW23-BMW was unveiled at Silverstone on 27 January with Sir Frank Williams looking to 'win a race if the red and silver cars make a mistake'. BMW produced a compact new version of its V10 that Bruno Junqueira track tested at Magny-Cours in October 2000. Chief engineer Werner Laurenz widened the vee angle to 90 degrees to lower the centre of gravity. Williams chief designer Gavin Fisher and aerodynamicist Geoff Willis evolved the FW22 with pronounced flick-ups in front of the rear wheels. The front wing beneath its raised nose was flat rather than having a lowered central section as preferred by rivals. The rear diffuser was redesigned following a rules clarification after the Spanish GP. The BMW V10 was the most powerful engine on the grid although poor early reliability and those accidents thwarted a title challenge.

Quickest of the Michelin runners in Australia, Schumacher was running sixth when he was rear-ended by Jacques Villeneuve at high speed. A loose wheel from the Canadian's BAR-Honda caused fatal injuries to track marshal Graham Beveridge. Having already clashed with Villeneuve in qualifying, Montoya hit Eddie Irvine's Jaguar on the opening lap before climbing into the top six only for his engine to let go. Schumacher qualified third in Malaysia despite lacking downforce and recovered from contact with Rubens Barrichello at the start to finish fifth and score Michelin's first points for 17 years. Forced to start from the pitlane in the spare car when his engine cut on the grid, Montoya spun out of the race in the early downpour.

Schumacher qualified alongside his brother on the front row in Brazil only for his race to be ruined by another clash with Barrichello. He lost three laps replacing his rear wing and set the fastest lap before spinning out. Montoya passed Michael Schumacher for the lead in an audacious manoeuvre as they started lap three, but a deserved breakthrough victory was denied when he was hit by the lapped Arrows of Jos Verstappen. Williams-BMW's first win followed at Imola where Schumacher made a great getaway from third to lead from start to finish.

Williams was no match for the leading two teams in Spain, where relegalised traction control was set aside due to reliability concerns. Montoya ended a run of four successive retirements by finishing second after a race of attrition while Schumacher spun out of fourth. They were back on the pace in Austria where Montoya and Schumacher lined up second and third respectively. The Colombian initially led a Williams 1–2 before his tyres degraded and he was robust in his defence of the lead when challenged by Michael Schumacher. That included locking up and forcing the Ferrari off the road at the Remus-kurve (now Turn 3) on lap 16. Neither Williams finished after Montoya's hydraulics leaked and Schumacher suffered a braking issue.

Ralf Schumacher, Williams FW23-BMW (San Marino GP)

Juan Pablo Montoya, Williams FW23-BMW (Italian GP)

Both also retired from the Monaco GP. Having crashed at the exit to the Swimming Pool on Thursday, Schumacher qualified fifth and was on course to finish third when his hydraulics failed; Montoya crashed out. BMW power suited Montréal's long straights and Schumacher challenged his brother in qualifying and the race. He started second, took the lead at the pitstops and went on to head the first fraternal 1–2 in GP history. Montoya, who had a confrontation with Jacques Villeneuve following incidents in practice, crashed out again, trying too hard to impress. There was another all-Schumacher front row at the Nürburgring, where Michael ruthlessly muscled Ralf towards the pitwall at the start. The younger sibling lost the chance of victory when he crossed the pit exit line and dropped to fourth when handed a 10sec stop-go penalty. Montoya finished second to ease mounting pressure following seven DNFs from eight races.

Schumacher recorded his first pole position in France but was beaten into second by his brother following a slow pitstop. Choosing harder tyres, Montoya challenged for victory until his engine failed. Both were off the pace at Silverstone, where Montoya adopted an aggressive two-stop strategy. He was held up for seven crucial laps by his one-stopping team-mate and finished fourth, with Patrick Head claiming 'Juan Pablo would have finished third if Ralf had let him through as we asked'; Schumacher's engine failed after 36 laps. While testing at Monza, the German suffered a high-speed puncture that prompted Michelin to introduce a new batch of tyres. Montoya headed an all-Williams front row at Hockenheim and dominated until his pitstop, when an electronic fault with the fuel rig resulted in a 30-second stop and caused his engine to overheat and expire two laps later. Schumacher could not keep up with Montoya during the opening stint but inherited victory due to his team-mate's problems.

The FW23s struggled at the twisty Hungaroring where Schumacher was happy to salvage fourth. Montoya led another qualifying 1–2 at Spa-Francorchamps when they timed late dry-tyre runs to perfection. However, they were relegated to the back for the restart after Montoya stalled on the dummy grid and the mechanics had insufficient time to complete repairs to Schumacher's rear wing. Montoya suffered an early engine failure and Schumacher's seventh-place finish was scant reward for the team's qualifying endeavours.

It was finally Montoya's day at Monza as he began to impose himself within the team. On pole for the third time in four races, he fought Barrichello for the lead of the Italian GP until the Brazilian was delayed at his first pitstop. Montoya then withstood his team-mate's challenge until blistered tyres and braking issues dropped Schumacher to third by the finish. At Indianapolis, where both drivers qualified in the top three, Montoya passed Michael Schumacher for the lead only for another hydraulics failure to deny back-to-back victories, while Ralf Schumacher spun out. Montoya qualified and finished second in Japan with Schumacher dropping from third on the grid to sixth at the finish after serving a stop-go penalty for missing the chicane.

RED BULL SAUBER PETRONAS

That Sauber finished fourth in the constructors' championship was one of the major surprises of 2001. The Swiss outfit entered the season with a reduced budget, inexperienced drivers and an ominous warning from majority shareholder Dietrich Mateschitz following eight largely mediocre campaigns. 'You cannot be a constant winner, but at least you must shine,' the Red Bull owner told the press. 'I am not very good with the Olympic Spirit. I am not involved in Formula 1 just to be there.' Red Bull remained as title sponsor but patience was running thin. Sauber exercised its option for Ferrari V10 engines with Petronas extending its badging deal. An engine upgrade was used in qualifying in Canada and raced from the French GP.

An all-new driver line-up was required when Mika Salo exercised a performance clause to join Toyota and Pedro Diniz retired, taking his Parmalat backing with him. Enrique Bernoldi, Olivier Panis, Alexander Wurz, Jos Verstappen, Ricardo Zonta and Jenson Button were all mentioned as possibilities before Nick Heidfeld signed a three-year deal after his Prost option expired on 27 August 2000. Sauber's accent on youth was reinforced by the choice of team-mate. British Formula Renault champion Kimi Räikkönen impressed at two three-day Mugello tests in September 2000 and was quicker than Bernoldi during the second one, but it was still a surprise when the 21-year-old Finn was announced as Heidfeld's team-mate having started just 23 car races. Bernoldi, who was preferred by Red Bull, was placed on standby until Räikkönen's super licence was confirmed in December.

Heidfeld and Räikkönen were quick in the old car before shaking down the Sauber C20-Petronas at Fiorano on 11 January. It was formally unveiled 13 days later at the team's Hinwil base when new Crédit Suisse backing was announced. Chief designer Sergio Rinland's C20 was a light and well-balanced car with downforce to spare and the strongest customer engine in the business.

Broadly conventional in design, the C20 was 47kg lighter than its predecessor with the nose raised above the 'spoon-shaped' front wing. Aerodynamicist Seamus Mullarkey redesigned the sidepods to incorporate the new side-impact structures. There was an oval air intake and particular care was taken to cool the engine and brakes. Sauber's seven-speed longitudinal gearbox was revised with

the oil tank moved in front of the 90-degree V10 engine. Pushrod suspension was retained with Sachs shock absorbers mounted inboard while Rinland further developed the C19's lower-front suspension pylons, replacing them with two longitudinal keels under the nose. This innovative twin keel improved airflow and was soon followed by others, despite being heavier and compromising set-up flexibility. The front toe link was moved in line with the top wishbones. Magneti Marelli traction control was used on its relegalisation at the Spanish GP and Bridgestone tyres were retained.

There was a surprise when Rinland was released before the launch. McLaren composites specialist Stephen Taylor was named as his replacement but soon returned to England. Jost Capito was transferred to the engine department and moved to Ford Special Vehicle Engineering in May.

Sauber's season began in fine fashion in Australia, where Heidfeld qualified tenth and finished fifth on the road, which became fourth when Olivier Panis was penalised for passing Heidfeld under yellow flags. With four races to confirm he deserved a super licence, Räikkönen dispelled any lingering doubts by claiming sixth on debut. There was controversy when Jordan's Heinz-Harald Frentzen wrote on his website that Sauber had used traction control during the race, an accusation that was denied by Sauber and FIA president Max Mosley. After non-scoring in Malaysia when Räikkönen's transmission failed at the start and Heidfeld spun in the rain, they filled the fifth row in Brazil and were nose-to-tail in the top six when rain arrived. Räikkönen's second spin proved terminal but Heidfeld stayed out of trouble to claim third and his first podium.

Räikkönen outqualified his more experienced team-mate at Imola although a mistake restricted him to tenth on the grid. His impressive weekend ended in the barriers on lap 17 when the steering wheel came away in his hands on the climb out of Tosa. Heidfeld finished seventh. Restricted to eighth in Spain due to understeer, Räikkönen rebounded from a testing accident at Silverstone to finish fourth in Austria despite BAR-Honda's protests that he had passed a backmarker under yellow flags. Heidfeld finished a competitive sixth in Spain and qualified in that position at the A1-Ring only to lose a lap when his launch control failed at the start.

The C20 was expected to suit Monaco but proved unbalanced and twitchy throughout. Heidfeld was punted off by Jos Verstappen

Nick Heidfeld, Sauber C20-Petronas (French GP)

Kimi Räikkönen, Sauber C20-Petronas (German GP)

on the opening lap while Räikkönen finished last after losing five laps in the pits. In Canada, Räikkönen battled compatriot Mika Häkkinen for the final podium place before finishing fourth, while Heidfeld crashed at the final chicane during qualifying and was the innocent victim of Eddie Irvine's second-lap overtaking attempt. Blistering tyres ruined their European GP before Sauber returned to form. Heidfeld was sixth at three of the next four races and Räikkönen claimed fifth at Silverstone. They filled row four at Hockenheim but were out of luck in the race, with Heidfeld hit by Pedro de la Rosa's Jaguar on lap one. Denied points by driveshaft failure in Germany, Räkkönen finished seventh in France and Hungary.

Gearbox issues plagued their Belgian GP weekend where both were out by the end of lap one of the restarted race. Räikkönen suffered a 120mph testing accident at Magny-Cours and both drivers crashed during Friday practice at Monza. More gearbox issues stymied progress and Heidfeld was forced to start from the pitlane in Italy following a hydraulics failure on his race car. Räikkönen finished seventh as neither scored.

As Heidfeld had been a McLaren-Mercedes junior since 1997, many were surprised when he was overlooked as Häkkinen's replacement for 2002 and responded by qualifying and finishing sixth at Indianapolis despite losing gears during the race. Preferred by McLaren, Räikkönen was off form in America and collected Jean Alesi as he spun during the Japanese finale. Having survived a huge 'off' during practice at Suzuka's Esses, Heidfeld finished in a subdued ninth position. That was a downbeat conclusion but Peter Sauber hailed finishing fourth overall as akin to winning the World Championship – 'the maximum'.

BENSON & HEDGES JORDAN HONDA

Jordan Grand Prix secured a major boost when Honda agreed to supply the team with works engines in 2001 in addition to British American Racing, prompting Honda subsidiary Mugen to withdraw. Jarno Trulli was in the second year of his contract and Heinz-Harald Frentzen ignored interest from Jaguar and Sauber to sign a two-year extension before the German GP. Ricardo Zonta returned to the test/reserve role he had fulfilled in 1997.

Technical director Mike Gascoyne moved to Benetton and was eventually replaced by Arrows's Eghbal Hamidy in January. Gascoyne was followed to Enstone by Jordan's joint chief designer Mark Smith, leaving John McQuilliam to take sole responsibility for that role. David Brown replaced Williams-bound Sam Michael as Frentzen's race engineer. Trulli banned his new engineer Gabriele delli Colli from speaking Italian to him. Jordan agreed a three-year contract with Bridgestone.

Trulli gave the Jordan EJ11-Honda its shakedown at Silverstone on 15 January, the day before its public launch at the factory. The front wing with lowered central section was mounted beneath the EJ11's long nose, which featured dramatic shark's head artwork. The compact Honda V10 allowed the rear bodywork to be lowered and Jordan's recalcitrant six-speed gearbox was replaced by a new seven-speed unit. Carbon-fibre pushrods and torsion bars were fitted front and rear. Often blindingly quick over a single lap but less convincing come race day, Trulli grew frustrated with lack of development and poor reliability. Frentzen finished in the top six at three of the first four races but suffered a couple of heavy crashes and was eventually replaced without scoring again.

Jarno Trulli, Jordan EJ11-Honda (Brazilian GP)

Overheating issues restricted winter mileage while tyre wear was a problem in races. Frentzen raised hopes with a new unofficial lap record at Silverstone before the cars were sent to Australia. A promising fourth on the grid in Melbourne, Frentzen banged wheels with David Coulthard at the start and was spun down the field by Rubens Barrichello on lap three before recovering to claim fifth. Trulli lost fourth when his engine began to misfire and was soon forced to retire. In Malaysia, Trulli qualified fifth and led a lap when the rain was at its heaviest only to damage his car in a spin and finish a disappointing eighth. Fourth at Sepang following a one-stop strategy, Frentzen was on course for third in Brazil thanks to a well-timed switch to intermediate tyres when his engine failed eight laps from home. Trulli had already changed tyres when the rain arrived and his subsequent choice of full wets proved an error, so fifth was something of a save. Both scored at Imola, where Trulli jumped from fifth to third at the start before losing two places at the first pitstops and finishing fifth, one place ahead of his team-mate.

Trulli was a strong fourth in Spain despite severe tyre wear. Frentzen stalled at the start when his launch control failed and crashed into Pedro de la Rosa's Jaguar as he recovered. Those electronic issues continued in Austria where both drivers were left stranded on the grid. Having qualified fifth, Trulli started from the pitlane but was black-flagged for pulling away while the red light at the pit exit was showing. Trulli's Monaco GP came to a fiery

Heinz-Harald Frentzen, Jordan EJ11-Honda (Monaco GP)

Ricardo Zonta, Jordan EJ11-Honda (German GP)

end while Frentzen crashed heavily exiting the tunnel. The after-effects of that 160mph shunt forced Frentzen to abandon testing at Magny-Cours and he withdrew from the Canadian GP following another crash there during Friday practice. Late stand-in Zonta finished seventh despite hitting Kimi Räikkönen's Sauber and losing his brakes. Trulli started fourth and held that position until six laps from the finish when the brake hydraulics failed.

Frentzen returned at the Nürburgring where both cars spun out following mechanical failures. Trulli qualified and finished fifth in France as he continued to eclipse Frentzen, who spun on his way to eighth. Having criticised Jordan's lack of development in *Gazzetta dello Sport*, Trulli wasted another fine qualifying effort at Silverstone (fourth) by colliding with Coulthard at the first corner. Frentzen made a slow start and lost his battle for sixth with Nick Heidfeld.

Tensions within the team were now surfacing and Frentzen was dropped before his home race following an exchange of views with Eddie Jordan at Silverstone. Successive Monza tests were marred by failures at the Ascari chicane, Zonta going into the barriers following suspension failure and Trulli avoiding contact when he lost his rear wing. For the German GP, Zonta was drafted in for another one-off appearance that ended in a collision with Jos Verstappen's Arrows. The off-form Trulli spun out of contention before hydraulics failure ended his race.

For the last five races, Jean Alesi, 1989 F3000 Champion with Eddie Jordan Racing, replaced Frentzen but struggled in Hungary. Trulli started that race from fifth and held up a queue of quicker cars until a slow pitstop and terminal hydraulic failure. Alesi withstood Ralf Schumacher's late pressure to claim sixth in Belgium and finished eighth in Italy. Trulli had another engine failure at Spa-Francorchamps and was knocked out of the Italian GP by Jenson Button at the first corner.

Fourth-placed Trulli was disqualified from the United States GP with wear on his car's titanium plank beyond the acceptable tolerance. Alesi qualified just 0.002sec slower than his team-mate and finished seventh in his 200th and penultimate GP. Vainly attempting to become the first driver since Richie Ginther in 1964 to finish every race in a season, Alesi hit Kimi Räkkönen's spinning Sauber on lap 6 of the Japanese GP while Trulli completed his Jordan career with a lacklustre eighth. Jordan took fifth overall from Honda rival BAR when it successfully appealed Trulli's disqualification at Indianapolis on 26 October.

Jean Alesi, Jordan EJ11-Honda (Japanese GP)

LUCKY STRIKE BRITISH AMERICAN RACING HONDA

Team principal Craig Pollock admitted to 'a certain amount of disappointment' when Honda chose to also supply works engines to Jordan, a move that was interpreted as criticism of British American Racing. With rumours that Honda would only supply one team in 2002, the rivalry between BAR and Jordan to be its top team was a major storyline in 2001.

This was another disappointing campaign as the team regressed. The BAR 003-Honda was not stiff enough and technical director Malcolm Oastler admitted to *Autocourse* that it was 'slow and difficult to drive'. The BAR-Hondas slipped down the grid as the season unfolded although Jacques Villeneuve did score two podium finishes. The Canadian pulled no punches when assessing the team's position after the British GP: 'This year has been a step backwards. We're not as competitive as last year and not as reliable.'

Speculation that the former champion would move to Benetton, Jaguar or McLaren had been rife as he negotiated with British American Racing during 2000. His move to Enstone seemed certain until a new three-year contract with BAR was agreed in July of that year, albeit with performance clauses. Ricardo Zonta was released to make way for highly rated McLaren test driver Olivier Panis. Darren Manning remained as reserve and was joined in testing duties by Anthony Davidson, Takuma Satō and Marc Hynes. Having worked with Villeneuve at Williams, James Robinson arrived as chief race engineer while BAR co-founder Rick Gorne left in the New Year. Former Chancellor of the Exchequer Kenneth Clarke replaced Don Brown as non-executive chairman.

The conservative design approach of 2000 was abandoned as the new BAR 003 took shape, with 30kg saved to allow more use of ballast to adjust weight distribution. Longer sidepods enclosed the enlarged mandatory side-impact structures. The Honda RA001E V10

engine was also lighter than its predecessor with 840bhp claimed. BAR developed a more compact version of its six-speed gearbox and power steering was standard. The front wing was flat with a shallow vee-shaped central section. Suspension was an evolution of the 002's pushrod arrangement and Bridgestone tyres were retained.

Panis gave the BAR 003-Honda its systems check at Silverstone on 10 January with Villeneuve taking over at Jerez the following week. Initially 2.255sec slower than Panis's times in the old car, Villeneuve crashed the 003 when its suspension failed on the second day. That forced an old car to be used to reveal the new Lucky Strike livery on 26 January in London, where Pollock was bullish: 'Our aim in 2001 has to be to finish at least third overall and to win some races.' Panis requested number nine for his car because that was his number when he won the 1996 Monaco GP for Ligier. Brake failure caused Panis to crash at Barcelona and the BAR-Hondas were outpaced by Williams during warm-weather testing at Kyalami.

They qualified in the top ten at the first two races but failed to score. Villeneuve was challenging for sixth in Australia when he ran into the back of Ralf Schumacher's Williams as they approached Turn 3 for the fifth time. That launched the BAR-Honda into a violent accident in which track marshal Graham Beveridge was struck by a loose wheel and fatally injured. Panis lost fourth when penalised 25 seconds for overtaking Nick Heidfeld under yellow flags, dropping him to seventh. Both cars were out by the end of lap three in Malaysia, Panis with an oil fire and Villeneuve having spun in the rain.

Progress was made in back-to-back tests between the 002 and 003 at Barcelona where only Michael Schumacher was quicker than Panis. The Frenchman outqualified his team-mate in Brazil and recovered from a slow start to challenge for the podium. A minute was lost when both BAR-Hondas were called into the pits at the same time following a radio error, after which Panis charged

Jacques Villeneuve, BAR 003-Honda (Monaco GP)

Olivier Panis, BAR 003-Honda (San Marino GP)

back to snatch fourth from Jarno Trulli's Jordan with four laps to go; Villeneuve was seventh after a further issue with his differential. With the 003 proving a handful over Imola's kerbs, eighth-placed Panis was hampered by oversteer and a gearbox problem while Villeneuve's lacklustre midfield run ended with engine failure.

Outpaced by Jordan thus far, BAR got back on terms thanks to new exhausts and revised aerodynamics at the Spanish GP. Seventh on the grid despite lacking rear brakes for one run and carrying too much fuel on another, Villeneuve inherited third when Mika Häkkinen retired on the last lap to take BAR's first podium, while Panis was seventh after stalling at his pitstop. Panis scored his first points of the season with fifth in Austria, where Villeneuve, suffering from back pain, finished only eighth after spinning as he passed Eddie Irvine's Jaguar.

Villeneuve was a solid fourth in Monaco – his best result in the Principality – and Panis qualified sixth in Montréal where both cars retired. Practice for the Canadian GP had included an ugly spat after Villeneuve was blocked by Juan Pablo Montoya on Friday and was later accused of brake testing the Colombian in retaliation. Tempers flared on the way to the drivers' briefing and they had to be separated during the subsequent confrontation.

High temperatures compromised traction during qualifying for the European GP, where Villeneuve finished ninth after stopping once and Panis spun due to an electronics glitch. Another aero upgrade was introduced at Magny-Cours but lack of power and grip remained. Villeneuve ran seventh after a good start before coasting to a halt on lap six while Panis was an uncompetitive ninth. Villeneuve caused a collision that eliminated a furious Panis at the start of the British GP and finished a lapped eighth that day, apologising afterwards for his error. He came home third at Hockenheim after a race of attrition.

BAR now led Jordan by a point, but another frustrating campaign saw form fade further as midfield rivals made better progress. After a lacklustre ninth in Hungary, Villeneuve qualified a noteworthy sixth at Spa-Francorchamps and finished a fuel-saving sixth at Monza. However, he was criticised by journalists and team members alike in the United States. Only 18th on the grid with an 'undriveable' car, he crashed into Pedro de la Rosa's Jaguar before parking because 'the left rear of the car could have been damaged and it would have been

dangerous to continue'. Villeneuve's season concluded with a lowly tenth in the Japanese GP. Panis finished the last four races but never in the points.

BAR seemed to have done enough to edge Jordan for fifth overall. However, those positions were reversed when Jarno Trulli's disqualification from the United States GP was overturned by the FIA Court of Appeal on 26 October. Sixth in the constructors' standings was a far cry from pre-season expectations.

MILD SEVEN BENETTON RENAULT

Now owned by Renault, the Enstone-based concern completed its final campaign as Benetton before becoming a fully fledged works outfit in 2002. Giancarlo Fisichella's fourth successive season was confirmed at the 2000 Hungarian GP but Alexander Wurz was released. A lucrative deal with Jacques Villeneuve had seemed a certainty throughout the summer of 2000 until he appeared to change his mind and remained with BAR. F3 star Antônio Pizzonia impressed in testing but managing director Flavio Briatore agreed to a two-year loan for Jenson Button with Williams. F3000 aspirant Mark Webber signed as test driver.

Mike Gascoyne arrived from Jordan as technical director – albeit too late to influence the latest design – and was followed by key colleagues. Designer Mark Smith joined in the spring to collaborate with Tim Densham on the 2002 car and former McLaren engineer Bob Bell was appointed as deputy technical director in September. Arrows team manager Steve Nielsen replaced Gordon Message. Electronics expert Ted Czapski, who had moved to Ferrari at the start of the Michael Schumacher era in 1996, returned to Benetton. Renowned engine guru Jean-Jacques His returned from the road car division as Renault Sport technical director.

St Mark's Square in Venice was chosen to launch the Benetton B201-Renault on 6 February. Its front wing curved downwards at the centre while extended sidepods enclosed the side-impact structures. The radical 111-degree RS21 V10 engine had the widest vee angle on the grid, dramatically lowering the centre of gravity and aiding chassis aerodynamics. The aluminium six-speed longitudinal gearbox was new. Torsion bars replaced coil springs in the pushrod rear suspension, matching the front arrangement, and

Jenson Button, Benetton B201-Renault (Japanese GP)

carbon-fibre was used for all wishbones bar the lower rear where steel was retained. Power steering was only introduced mid-season. Excellent electronics meant that the Benetton-Renaults were among the fastest off the starting line by the end of 2001. The team switched to Michelin tyres.

The B201 lacked aerodynamic efficiency in its original guise and engines proved both unreliable and underpowered, so a character-building campaign ensued with top-ten starts and points a rarity. Now living in Monte Carlo with the trappings of stardom, 21-year-old Button was outqualified 13–4 and Briatore was among those to question his commitment and lifestyle. The lack of power steering

was blamed for Button's shoulder injury in the spring, although he did not miss a race.

The Benetton-Renaults circulated at the back in Australia following exhaust failures. Fisichella caused the Malaysian GP start to be aborted by taking the wrong grid position and then retired while Button finished 11th. A new aero package taken to Brazil was abandoned for qualifying and the race. Button was slower in a straight line than the Minardis and Michelin's wet tyres were uncompetitive. However, Fisichella benefitted from high attrition to finish sixth after passing Jean Alesi with five laps to go. Button was last in Brazil and at Imola following problems with his engine and

Giancarlo Fisichella, Benetton B201-Renault (Australian GP)

fuel rig respectively. Fisichella retired at Imola with a misfire.

Beaten by Fernando Alonso's Minardi in Spain, both suffered terminal engine failures in Austria. Monte Carlo's tight confines masked the B201's inadequacies with Fisichella able to qualify tenth and challenge Jacques Villeneuve for fifth before crashing at Ste-Dévote; Button finished seventh. They were back among the tailenders in Canada where they collided on lap one and eventually retired. They were also-rans at the next three races as their dismal form continued. A new aero package and engine upgrade at Magny-Cours made little discernible difference and they were 3.5sec off the pace at Silverstone. Only quicker than the Arrows and Minardis in qualifying for the German GP, Fisichella and Button stayed out of trouble and took advantage of retirements ahead to finish a surprising fourth and fifth respectively.

Another upgrade taken to Hungary included a Ferrari-inspired front wing that would eventually transform the B201. That was not immediately apparent, but progress was made at the next Barcelona test and the Belgian GP proved a major step forward. An impressive eighth on the grid, Fisichella made a great restart and ran second for much of the race before claiming a shock third. Button ran in the top six before crashing at the Bus Stop chicane.

Neither scored in Italy and blistering tyres restricted them to eighth (Fisichella) and ninth (Button) in America. Another engine upgrade at Suzuka delivered their best qualifying of the season – Fisichella sixth and Button ninth. Fisichella made a good start but spun on lap three and stopped when he lost fourth gear late in the race. Button finished seventh as Benetton-Renault beat Jaguar into seventh overall by one point.

JAGUAR RACING

It was another year of on-track disappointment and boardroom intrigue for Jaguar Racing. The team entered its second season under new management with Bobby Rahal signing a three-year contract as team principal and chief executive officer on 20 September 2000. The American Champ Car team owner's arrival on 1 December coincided with Gary Anderson's replacement by McLaren's Steve Nichols as technical director. Chairman Neil Ressler, who had appointed Rahal, stepped aside in the New Year for personal reasons. The top-heavy structure was further complicated on 6 February when Wolfgang Reitzle, president of Ford's Premier Automotive Group, appointed Niki Lauda to oversee its Premier Performance Division and Formula 1 interests (Jaguar Racing, Cosworth Engineering and Pi Research).

John Russell remained as chief designer and aerodynamicist Mark Handford arrived from Lola's Champ Car programme in October 2000. Continued use of Swift's wind tunnel in California was augmented by a limited deal with Southampton University. Race engineers Robin Gearing and Andy Le Fleming were replaced by Gerry Hughes and Humphrey Corbett, both of whom reported to Mark Ellis when he was poached from BAR in May. Rahal showed Jaguar's ambition with an offer to appoint close friend Adrian Newey after his McLaren contract ended on 31 July 2002. Newey's signature was announced on the morning of 1 June 2001 but by the end of the day F1's most respected designer had extended his McLaren stay.

In the middle of his three-year deal as lead driver, Eddie Irvine was only too happy to share his thoughts with the press, at one

Eddie Irvine, Jaguar R2-Cosworth (Monaco GP)

Pedro de la Rosa, Jaguar R2-Cosworth (Italian GP)

stage telling *Autosport* that 'this year's car is the slowest I've had in my career'. Johnny Herbert was released but talk of Jacques Villeneuve, Giancarlo Fisichella or Heinz-Harald Frentzen as his replacement proved false. Dario Franchitti tested a Jaguar R1-Cosworth at Silverstone on 18 July 2000 only to remain in Champ Cars. Test driver Luciano Burti was eventually confirmed as Irvine's team-mate at the 2000 Italian GP. Just two weeks after committing to Prost Grand Prix, Pedro de la Rosa was named as Jaguar's test driver on 20 February, with a race seat assured for 2002. The French team's consequent legal action was settled out of court. Tomas Scheckter had been appointed as test driver on 28 September 2000 but was released in May, after which Jaguar juniors André Lotterer and James Courtney shared those duties. Narain Karthikeyan became the first Indian to test an F1 car when he completed 23 laps of Silverstone on 14 June.

Nichols's arrival was too late to influence the Jaguar R2-Cosworth, which was unveiled on 9 January at the car company's Whitley Engineering Centre. Russell and his team concentrated on improving the rear traction and aerodynamic stability that had blighted the unloved R1. Conventional pushrod suspension was activated by torsion bars with rear uprights now cast in titanium. The previous year's front wing was fitted at launch but a new iteration with lowered centre section was raced. The latest Cosworth CR-3 engine was track-tested in a modified R1B during December and drove through a new seven-speed gearbox. A conventional oil system was fitted after the unsuccessful experiments on the R1. Jaguar was the second team to confirm its switch to Michelin tyres for 2001. The search for reliability led to an overly conservative and overweight design that lacked aerodynamic efficiency. The high-speed instability

remained, and qualifying was a particular weakness.

Irvine's first run in the R2 at Valencia ended when he crashed due to a stuck throttle. His view that the car was 'too slow' irked management but was proven when both qualified outside the top ten at the first four GPs. Involved in first-lap incidents at the opening two races, Irvine was further delayed by a fuel-pressure problem in Australia and spun during the Malaysian downpour. Possible points were lost when he crashed in Brazil and his engine failed during the San Marino GP. Burti inherited eighth in Australia and was tenth in Malaysia. Less than two tenths slower than Irvine in qualifying at the next two rounds, Burti retired in Brazil and was 11th at Imola despite losing three gears.

Rahal had publicly denied that hiring de la Rosa placed any extra pressure on his race drivers, but the Spaniard now replaced the underperforming Burti. De la Rosa's debut weekend in Barcelona was a nightmare. He crashed on Saturday when his steering failed and was victim of Heinz-Harald Frentzen's optimistic lunge after five laps of the race. Eighth when his engine failed in Spain, Irvine made a great start in Austria but faded to seventh when passed by quicker cars. An aero upgrade featuring new undertray, rear wing and diffuser in Monaco improved downforce although aerodynamic efficiency remained an issue. Irvine used the package to qualify sixth and claim third behind the Ferraris, while de la Rosa retired again.

Irvine's Monaco form proved an anomaly for Jaguar slipped back to midfield in Canada, where de la Rosa edged his team-mate in qualifying (by 0.001sec) and finished sixth while Irvine crashed into Nick Heidfeld on the opening lap. Irvine led a Jaguar 7–8 at the Nürburgring and eyed the top six at Magny-Cours before his engine

Luciano Burti, Jaguar R2-Cosworth (San Marino GP)

failed. Neither scored at Silverstone and both retired from the German GP, de la Rosa when he crashed into Heidfeld on lap one after qualifying ninth. As Irvine had a neck strain at Hockenheim, Lotterer was on standby to step in but missed out on his F1 debut – and then had to wait 13 years for that to finally happen. The high-downforce Hungaroring proved no better as Irvine crashed at the first corner and de la Rosa blistered his tyres.

Mounting friction between Lauda and Rahal came to a head in the summer. Lauda agreed to supply Arrows with engines in 2002 while there were suggestions that Rahal was brokering a deal to swap Irvine with Jordan's Heinz-Harald Frentzen without the Austrian's knowledge. Rahal left the team following a meeting with Reitzle on 23 August, with Lauda taking on his duties as well as his own. Another casualty of Rahal's departure was former BAR-Honda operations director Otmar Szafnauer, whose offer to become chief operating officer was withdrawn.

Lauda's first race in direct charge of the team, the Belgian GP, was a self-acknowledged disaster: both drivers crashed out within two laps of the start, Irvine after getting involved in Burti's high-speed accident at Blanchimont. Tenth on the grid for a successive race, de la Rosa adopted a one-stop strategy at Monza to finish fifth in his strongest performance of 2001. Irvine's Italian GP was blighted by a brake-bias problem during practice and a sick engine in the race.

Slowed by understeer on Saturday at Indianapolis, Irvine used a long first stint to finish fifth and score his first points since May. De la Rosa made a poor start and was further delayed by contact with Jacques Villeneuve. It was a similar story at Suzuka where Irvine's challenge for points evaporated with fuelling issues on successive laps and de la Rosa succumbed to an oil leak. Jaguar-Cosworth failed to snatch seventh in the constructors' standings from Benetton-Renault by a single point.

PROST GRAND PRIX

Alain Prost faced a bleak summer in 2000 as he tried to secure engines and finance for his beleaguered team. Société d'Exploitation Industrielle des Tabacs et des Allumettes (SEITA) had provided backing with its Gitanes and Gauloises cigarette brands since Ligier's F1 arrival in 1976. SEITA merged with the Spanish Tabacalera concern in 1999 and announced its withdrawal from F1 on 26 September 2000. Prost's brave assertion that the team would have an increased budget for 2001 was laid bare by the further loss of PlayStation, Bic, Yahoo!, Total and Agfa. The shortfall was exacerbated by the lack of travel money due to finishing 11th in 2000 and having to pay for engines.

Peugeot ended its seven-year F1 sojourn when it announced its withdrawal on 25 July 2000, with the rights to the engine sold to Asia Motor Technologies (Asiatech). Prost's hopes of securing Mercedes-Benz engines were dashed when the German manufacturer opted to maintain McLaren's exclusivity. With choice limited by the departures of Mugen and Supertec, Prost agreed a three-year deal for year-old Ferrari engines that further stretched finances by $28m in 2001. Maranello also supplied the titanium longitudinal seven-speed gearbox, differential and rear suspension.

Needing to sell or restructure, Prost sold a 10 percent stake in the team to media giant Bertelsmann CLT but rumoured interest from

Jean Alesi, Prost AP04-Acer (Brazilian GP)

Marc Bourdeau's Ontario-based Vector Motorsport Group came to naught. Joan Villadelprat was appointed as managing director so that Prost could concentrate on securing much-needed new backing. The Diniz family acquired 38 percent of the team with Pedro retiring from driving to take a management role. That secured backing from Parmalat and the Pan-American Sports Network (PSN) was lured from Minardi. An engine-badging deal was agreed with Acer computers in February. Ex-Ferrari/McLaren aerodynamicist Henri Durand arrived as technical director in January, too late to influence design of the new car.

Jean Alesi confirmed in the autumn that he was staying but the identity of his team-mate remained unresolved after the option to retain Nick Heidfeld expired on 27 August 2000. Enrique Bernoldi was quicker than Oriol Servià when they drove a Prost AP03-

Peugeot at Barcelona on 13 and 14 December respectively. However, it was Gastón Mazzacane who was announced as number two driver with Prost stressing that it was his 'real potential' rather than PSN sponsorship that was the deciding factor. Pedro de la Rosa was engaged as reserve driver and tested at Estoril on 11–13 February only to defect to Jaguar a fortnight later, prompting Prost to sue with the dispute settled out of court. Jonathan Cochet eventually joined as test driver in April with Jaroslav Janiš added in September.

The new car was another to be designed by committee. Loïc Bigois was responsible for the aerodynamics, although he left in the spring. John Barnard's B3 Technologies designed the front suspension with carbon-fibre wishbones while steel was retained at the rear. Torsion bars were employed at all four corners. A three-year tyre deal with Michelin was agreed in December. The AP04 lacked

Gastón Mazzacane, Prost AP04-Acer (San Marino GP)

power steering, downforce and balance with understeer a particular vice. The conservative rear diffuser had to be replaced and a new front wing and floor were introduced in Monaco.

Alesi gave the Ferrari-powered Prost AP04 a trouble-free shakedown at Magny-Cours as scheduled on 15 January. He set impressive low-fuel testing times although cynics believed these to be nothing more than underweight headline-grabbing tactics to attract new sponsorship. With no team launch, the definitive livery was revealed in the Melbourne pitlane before the Australian GP. The financial void was partly filled by global recruitment firm Adecco and Dark Dog energy drink although the large Prost logo on each sidepod was testament to the lack of a title sponsor. Insufficient budget delayed new parts and restricted testing, and soon left the team unable to meet Ferrari's payment schedule.

Those winter times did not translate in race conditions and the relationship with Alesi soon deteriorated. At least he had a reliable car for he finished the first six races, albeit without scoring. He was eighth after a race of attrition in Brazil when the team claimed that a faulty fuel rig denied a top-six finish. Alesi then used the new aero package at Monaco to qualify 11th and finish sixth – Prost's first point since the 1999 European GP – despite a late puncture and blistered hands. Forced to miss testing at Magny-Cours as a consequence, he returned in Montréal and repeated his 1995 act of throwing his helmet into the crowd when he finished fifth. He spun on the last lap at the Nürburgring in a desperate attempt to take tenth from Kimi Räikkönen.

With his commitment open to public debate, Alesi languished outside the top ten at Magny-Cours and Silverstone before finishing sixth at Hockenheim when narrowly beaten by Jenson

Tomáš Enge, Prost AP04-Acer (United States GP)

Button's Benetton. Alesi had not been receiving his full salary and his contract was terminated by mutual consent so that he could replace Heinz-Harald Frentzen at Jordan. A furious Prost labelled Alesi as 'childish' following criticism in a subsequent radio interview. Frentzen replaced Alesi for the last five races with renumeration for each point scored. Among the backmarkers before he spun in Hungary, Frentzen was the last driver to start his qualifying lap at Spa-Francorchamps and used the drying track to snatch a stunning fourth on the grid. Forced to start from the back after he stalled on the original grid, Frentzen finished ninth after a collision with Juan Pablo Montoya damaged his floor. His single-lap pace continued to impress at Monza where he lined up 12th only to retire without making an impression. Tenth at Indianapolis, he was delayed in Japan by losing his nosecone when he hit Pedro de la Rosa's Jaguar.

Luciano Burti, Prost AP04-Acer (Belgian GP)

Heinz-Harald Frentzen, Prost AP04-Acer (Belgian GP)

Mazzacane did only four races before Prost fired him after Imola, where he had qualified 2.339sec slower than Alesi. A loose brake pedal forced him to withdraw from the Australian GP without completing a lap, he was delayed by a faulty fuel rig in Malaysia, and he retired in Brazil and San Marino. As pressure mounted on Mazzacane, Servià and Stéphane Sarrazin tested at Barcelona. After Jordan test driver Ricardo Zonta turned down an approach, Jaguar refugee Luciano Burti replaced Mazzacane for the rest of 2001.

Burti outqualified his experienced new team-mate at the first two attempts but finished 11th on both occasions. He was forced to race the old aero package at Monaco when brake failure at Ste-Dévote caused him to crash on Saturday. Delayed in the race by a broken front wing when he hit Jos Verstappen, Burti retired with another brake issue. A pointless finisher at the next three races, his engine broke after six laps at Silverstone. His F1 career finished with two massive crashes in three races. First, heavy contact with Michael Schumacher's slow-moving Ferrari at the start of the German GP launched Burti into a sickening barrel roll; he took the spare for the restart but spun out. After another spin ended his race in Hungary, he crashed at Spa-Francorchamps when he lost control on the grass at the 180mph Blanchimont curve as he tried to pass Eddie Irvine's Jaguar; he was fortunate to escape with facial lacerations and concussion that ended his season.

Tomáš Enge became the first Czech driver to start a World Championship GP when he replaced Burti at Monza. The penultimate classified finisher there and at Indianapolis, Enge walked away from a 170mph crash at Suzuka's 130R during Friday practice for the Japanese GP. In the race, he pitted early after mistakenly responding to Minardi's pit board before terminal brake issues intervened.

The team's financial plight overshadowed the campaign with mounting debts and rumours of unpaid bills. Talk of a new title sponsor – Camel, Stella Artois, Telefónica and La Caixa were all mentioned – went unfulfilled. The Diniz family walked away when advances to buy the team were rebuffed and negotiations with Khaled al Waleed broke down. Prost Grand Prix entered administration in November 2001 owing more than 200m francs (£19.1m) with liquidation confirmed on 28 January 2002. The factory at Guyancourt closed for the final time on 8 March 2002, ending Alain Prost's ambitions of establishing a French national F1 team.

ORANGE ARROWS ASIATECH

Peugeot confirmed its F1 withdrawal on 25 July 2000. Rights to its V10 were sold to Asia Motor Technologies (Asiatech) with an exclusive one-year deal with Arrows for free engines also announced that day. Asiatech appointed Enrique Scalabroni as technical director and staffing at Peugeot's former factory at Vélizy expanded over the winter. Pedro de la Rosa and Jos Verstappen first tried the 72-degree V10 at Valencia on 11–13 October 2000 in a modified plain white Arrows A21B.

Those drivers were expected to be retained and de la Rosa had a seat fitting at Leafield on 26 January 2001. Enrique Bernoldi had tested at Barcelona, but it was a shock when he was announced as Verstappen's team-mate just five days later. Bernoldi's long-term backers Red Bull replaced Repsol as an associate sponsor. The relationship between the team-mates was not helped by Verstappen judging Bernoldi 'the worst team-mate I have had in F1'. Outgoing Jaguar driver Johnny Herbert was the experienced choice for test driver.

Orange remained as title sponsor but associate partner Eurobet, which was owned by Arrows shareholder Morgan Grenfell at the time, announced before the season that it would not continue, leading to to a budget shortfall and legal action.

The concept of F1 passenger rides was taken to another level when the three-seat Arrows AX3 was unveiled during the *Autosport* International show at Birmingham's National Exhibition Centre on 11 January. Chief designer Eghbal Hamidy moved to Jordan and was eventually replaced by Sergio Rinland in September. Benetton-bound Steve Nielsen was replaced by Mick Ainsley-Cowlishaw as team manager. Nicolò Petrucci, who had worked with technical director Mike Coughlan at Ferrari's Guildford Technical Office, was recruited as head of aerodynamics.

The Arrows A22-Asiatech was a conventional evolution of the fast but fragile A21, although Verstappen's 2 February shakedown at Silverstone lasted a single lap. Bridgestone-equipped Arrows anticipated that the tyre war would lead to high degradation and two-stop races, so the compact A22 was designed around a small fuel tank. That proved a mistake for one-stop proved preferable and the team was unable to switch strategy. However, the light-fuelled Verstappen was an early star at several races. Carbon-fibre

Jos Verstappen, Arrows A22-Asiatech (Monaco GP)

pullrods were retained at the front with pushrods to the rear. A nose-mounted high wing fitted at Monaco was banned by the stewards. The Arrows A22 lacked downforce and team owner Tom Walkinshaw described the traction control as 'relatively crude'. The Asiatech 001 was underpowered and thirsty, and its operating temperature necessitated larger radiators that increased drag. Limited budget and development resulted in Arrows becoming less competitive as the season progressed. That neither driver qualified inside the top ten reflected the team's fading fortunes. The acquisition from the Ministry of Defence of the half-scale DERA wind tunnel in Bedford was completed in May.

Tenth in Australia, Verstappen used a low-downforce set-up to run as high as second in Malaysia before dropping to seventh at his final stop. He was fined £10,000 for knocking race leader Juan Pablo Montoya out of the Brazilian GP when he misjudged his braking after being lapped. An early retirement at Imola and 12th in Spain, Verstappen starred in Austria. Two-stopping once more, he made a lightning getaway and was second when Montoya ran Michael Schumacher off the road. He then held off Eddie Irvine in the closing stages to finish sixth and score the team's only point of 2001.

Eighth in Monaco despite stalling at his pitstop, Verstappen lost another score when his brakes failed with three laps to go in Canada. His engine broke at the Nürburgring and a faulty fuel rig ruined his French GP. Low finishes at the next four races included a damaged ninth at Hockenheim following contact with Ricardo Zonta. Last in Hungary and tenth in Belgium, Verstappen delivered

Enrique Bernoldi, Arrows A22-Asiatech (Monaco GP)

more light-fuel fireworks at Monza (where he stormed into the top six) and Indianapolis, but engine failure ended his challenge on both occasions. Starting near the back of the grid for the championship finale at Suzuka, quicker than only one Minardi, both cars went out with power-steering failures.

Bernoldi outqualified Verstappen 10–7 but did not score a point. He crashed on debut after a couple of laps of the Australian GP and lasted only one lap longer in Malaysia before spinning in the heavy rain. He was lapped twice on his way to tenth at Imola and retired from the Brazilian, Spanish and Austrian GPs. The highlight of his season was holding off David Coulthard's McLaren-Mercedes for lap after lap in Monaco and eventually claiming ninth. Bernoldi retired from the next three races before finishing 14th in England and a career-best eighth in Germany. He spun out of the Hungarian GP, made no impression in Belgium and suffered engine failure in Italy. Finishes outside the top ten at Indianapolis and Suzuka (having started from the pitlane when he stalled on the parade lap) concluded an underwhelming rookie campaign.

EUROPEAN MINARDI F1

That Minardi survived 2001 was success in itself. The team entered the New Year with takeover talks unresolved and without engines, tyres or drivers confirmed. Title sponsor Telefónica withdrew from F1 on 16 October 2000 and negotiations with Pan-American Sports Network (PSN) broke down in November. Test driver Fernando Alonso's five-year contract with Minardi was acquired by Flavio Briatore as majority shareholder Gabriele Rumi fought to secure the team's future amid serious illness. Australian aviation entrepreneur Paul Stoddart visited Faenza on 23 January 2001 and confirmed his acquisition from Rumi and Giancarlo Minardi seven days later, with Minardi remaining as a director. The race team continued to be based at Faenza with Stoddart's European Aviation facility at Ledbury in England responsible for research and development and the test team.

Having tested a Benetton B200 at Barcelona on 13–14 December 2000 to gain the mileage required to qualify for his super licence, Alonso was confirmed as Minardi's lead driver in February. The returning Tarso Marques was preferred to Gianni Morbidelli to partner Alonso in the second car with Christijan Albers and Andrea Piccini assuming testing duties.

Engine talks with Supertec broke down in January so designs for the Minardi PS01 were converted back to the old 72-degree Ford Zetec-R. This 1998-specification V10, which was rebadged 'European' in deference to the new owner, was underpowered (by 150bhp) and overweight (by 30kg). Langford & Peck handled the rebuilds. Michelin agreed to supply tyres in February and the new car was shaken down at the Varano test track on 21 February, 24 hours before departure for Melbourne and just six weeks after Stoddart's takeover.

The Minardi PS01-European was conventional by necessity and had just 150 hours in Fondmetal's wind tunnel. The distinctive flat needle-nose supported a front wing that curved downwards at the centre. Suspension was pullrod front and pushrod rear, with carbon-wrapped titanium wishbones and torsion springs. The B-spec version introduced at Spa-Francorchamps had an extended wheelbase with revised rear suspension and CRP's more compact titanium gearbox. The elderly engine normally consigned Minardi to the back of the grid although the PS01 handled well and Alonso enjoyed an impressive maiden campaign.

Fernando Alonso, Minardi PS01-European (Australian GP)

Alex Yoong, Minardi PS01B-European (Italian GP)

Prost's Loïc Bigois was announced as chief aerodynamicist on 29 March. Technical director Gustav Brunner had vowed to remain with Minardi in the autumn so his shock move to Toyota despite having three years left on his contract angered Stoddart when it was announced on 7 May. Gabriele Tredozi was promoted to replace Brunner while ex-Arrows engineer John Davis arrived as deputy technical director in October 2001, with George Ryton remaining as chief designer. Rupert Manwaring joined as commercial director.

The Minardi PS01-European was presented to the press on 28 February at the parliament building in Melbourne, Stoddart's home city. Four days later, Alonso was 12th on debut despite baulking Rubens Barrichello's Ferrari and a penalty for speeding in the pitlane. The Minardis finished at the back in Malaysia and a throttle issue sidelined Alonso in Brazil. Impressively outqualifying the Benettons at the next three races, Alonso crashed at Imola following brake failure and beat the blue cars in Spain. Minardi introduced traction control at the Austrian GP and problems with the system were blamed for double retirements at that race and the next. Alonso started behind his team-mate when his qualifying times were deleted in Canada on a technicality. He passed Marques and Luciano Burti (Prost) before a driveshaft failed and his car was the last still circulating at the Nürburgring. Both Minardis were classified outside the top ten at Magny-Cours with Alonso withdrawn to save his engine. Last at Silverstone and Hockenheim after losing a wheel and catching fire in the pits respectively, Alonso spun out of the Hungarian GP when his brakes locked.

Marques struggled in Alonso's shadow. The Australian GP stewards allowed him to start despite qualifying outside the 107 percent limit. Last in Malaysia, he was the slowest qualifier for the next 12 races. Ninth in Brazil and Canada (when lapped three times on each occasion) were the best results of his F1 career. Marques continued on a race-by-race basis as Stoddart admitted that 'we are looking for a driver but no decision has been made'. Tomáš Enge turned down the chance to replace Marques before Formula Nippon driver Alex Yoong tested at Mugello and Monza in July. With Yoong finalising sponsorship and his super licence, Marques became the first non-qualifier since 1998 when more than 107 percent outside the British GP pole time. He retired from the next two races.

Both Minardis were allowed to start the Belgian GP despite failing the 107 percent rule due to the changeable conditions. Alonso destroyed his car at Blanchimont during the warm-up and retired the spare before the race was stopped so did not take the restart. Making his last start for the team, Marques was 13th after six pitstops to sort his suspension.

Granted a provisional super licence, Yoong replaced Marques at the Italian GP thanks to backing from Malaysian lottery company Magnum. After gearbox issues stranded both drivers during qualifying, Alonso finished a distant 13th and Yoong's debut ended in the Lesmo gravel. Alonso lined up a season-best 17th at Indianapolis where both cars retired by half distance. They were classified at Suzuka with Alonso beating better-funded rivals into 11th.

European Minardi launched a two-seater F1 programme at Donington Park in June with the first such race held there in August. That was red-flagged when 1992 World Champion Nigel Mansell crashed into race leader Alonso as they started their last lap.

Tarso Marques, Minardi PS01-European (French GP)

2001 RESULTS

DRIVER PERFORMANCE

DRIVER	CAR-ENGINE	AUS	MAL	BR	RSM	E	A	MC	CDN	EU	F	GB	D	H	B	I	USA	J
Jean Alesi	Prost AP04-Acer	14 9	13 9	15 8	14 9	15 10	20 10	11 6	16 5	14 15	19 12	14 11	14 6	–	–	–	–	–
	Jordan EJ11-Honda	–	–	–	–	–	–	–	–	–	–	–	–	12 10	13 6	16 8	9 7	11 R
Fernando Alonso	Minardi PS01-European	19 12	21 13	19 R	18 R	18 13	18 R	18 R	22 R	21 14	21 17	21 16	21 10	18 R	–	–	–	–
	Minardi PS01B-European	–	–	–	–	–	–	–	–	–	–	–	–	–	20 R	21 13	17 R	18 11
Rubens Barrichello	Ferrari F2001	2 3	2 2	6 R	6 3	4 R	4 3	4 2	5 R	4 5	8 3	6 3	6 2	3 2	5 5	2 2	5 15	4 5
Enrique Bernoldi	Arrows A22-Asiatech	18 R	22 R	16 R	16 10	16 R	15 R	20 9	17 R	18 R	20 R	20 14	19 8	20 R	21 12	18 R	19 13	20 14
Luciano Burti	Jaguar R2-Cosworth	21 8	15 10	14 R	15 11	–	–	–	–	–	–	–	–	–	–	–	–	–
	Prost AP04-Acer	–	–	–	–	14 11	17 11	21 R	19 8	17 12	15 10	16 R	16 R	19 R	18 R	–	–	–
Jenson Button	Benetton B201-Renault	16 14	17 11	20 10	21 12	21 15	21 R	17 7	20 R	20 13	17 16	18 15	18 5	17 R	15 R	11 R	10 9	9 7
David Coulthard	McLaren MP4-16-Mercedes-Benz	6 2	8 3	5 1	1 2	3 5	7 1 FL	1 5 FL	3 R	5 3	3 4 FL	3 R	5 R	2 3	9 2	6 R	7 3	7 3
Pedro de la Rosa	Jaguar R2-Cosworth	–	–	–	–	20 R	14 R	14 R	14 6	16 8	14 14	13 12	9 R	13 11	10 R	10 5	16 12	16 R
Tomáš Enge	Prost AP04-Acer	–	–	–	–	–	–	–	–	–	–	–	–	–	–	20 12	21 14	19 R
Giancarlo Fisichella	Benetton B201-Renault	17 13	16 R	18 6	19 R	19 14	19 R	10 R	18 R	15 11	16 11	19 13	17 4	15 R	8 3	14 10	12 8	6 17
Heinz-Harald Frentzen	Jordan EJ11-Honda	4 5	9 4	8 11	9 6	8 R	11 R	13 R	NT DNP	8 R	7 8	5 7	–	–	–	–	–	–
	Prost AP04-Acer	–	–	–	–	–	–	–	–	–	–	–	–	16 R	4 9	12 R	15 10	15 12
Mika Häkkinen	McLaren MP4-16-Mercedes-Benz	3 R	4 6 FL	3 R	2 4	2 9	8 R	3 R	8 3	6 6	4 DNS	2 1 FL	3 R	6 5 FL	7 4	7 R	4 1	5 4
Nick Heidfeld	Sauber C20-Petronas	10 4	11 R	9 3	12 7	10 6	6 9	16 R	11 R	10 R	9 6	9 6	7 R	7 6	14 R	8 11	6 6	10 9
Eddie Irvine	Jaguar R2-Cosworth	12 11	12 R	13 R	13 R	13 R	13 7	6 3	15 R	12 7	12 R	15 9	11 R	14 R	17 R	13 R	14 5	13 R
Tarso Marques	Minardi PS01-European	22 R	20 14	22 9	22 R	22 16	22 R	22 R	21 9	22 R	22 15	22 DNQ	22 R	22 R	22 13	–	–	–
Gastón Mazzacane	Prost AP04-Acer	20 R	19 12	21 R	20 R	–	–	–	–	–	–	–	–	–	–	–	–	–
Juan Pablo Montoya	Williams FW23-BMW	11 R	6 R	4 R	7 R	12 2	2 R	7 R	10 R	3 2 FL	6 R	8 4	1 R FL	8 8	1 R	1 1	3 R FL	2 2
Olivier Panis	BAR 003-Honda	9 7	10 R	11 4	8 8	11 7	10 5	12 R	6 R	13 R	11 9	11 R	13 7	11 R	11 11	17 9	13 11	17 13
Kimi Räikkönen	Sauber C20-Petronas	13 6	14 R	10 R	10 R	9 8	9 4	15 10	7 4	9 10	13 7	7 5	8 R	9 7	12 R	9 7	11 R	12 R
Michael Schumacher	Ferrari F2001	1 1 FL	1 1	1 2	4 R	1 1 FL	1 2	2 1	1 2	1 1	2 1	1 2	4 R	1 1	3 1 FL	3 4	1 2	1 1
Ralf Schumacher	Williams FW23-BMW	5 R	3 5	2 R FL	3 1 FL	5 R	3 R	5 R	2 1 FL	2 4	1 2	10 R	2 1	4 4	2 7	4 3 FL	2 R	3 6 FL
Jarno Trulli	Jordan EJ11-Honda	7 R	5 8	7 5	5 5	6 4	5 DSQ	8 R	4 11	7 R	5 5	4 R	10 R	5 R	16 R	5 R	8 4	8 8
Jos Verstappen	Arrows A22-Asiatech	15 10	18 7	17 R	17 R	17 12	16 6	19 8	13 10	19 R	18 13	17 10	20 9	21 12	19 10	19 R	20 R	21 15
Jacques Villeneuve	BAR 003-Honda	8 R	7 R	12 7	11 R	7 3	12 8	9 4	9 R	11 9	10 R	12 8	12 3	10 9	6 8	15 6	18 R	14 10
Alex Yoong	Minardi PS01B-European	–	–	–	–	–	–	–	–	–	–	–	–	–	22 R	22 R	22 16
Ricardo Zonta	Jordan EJ11-Honda	–	–	–	–	–	–	–	12 7	–	–	–	15 R	–	–	–	–	–

FORMULA 1 RACE WINNERS

ROUND	RACE (CIRCUIT)	DATE	WINNER
1	Qantas Australian Grand Prix (Albert Park)	Mar 4	Michael Schumacher (Ferrari F2001)
2	Petronas Malaysian Grand Prix (Sepang)	Mar 18	Michael Schumacher (Ferrari F2001)
3	Grande Prêmio Marlboro do Brasil (Interlagos)	Apr 1	David Coulthard (McLaren MP4-16-Mercedes-Benz)
4	Gran Premio Warsteiner di San Marino (Imola)	Apr 15	Ralf Schumacher (Williams FW23-BMW)
5	Gran Premio Marlboro de España (Catalunya)	Apr 29	Michael Schumacher (Ferrari F2001)
6	Grosser A1 Preis von Österreich (Spielberg)	May 13	David Coulthard (McLaren MP4-16-Mercedes-Benz)
7	Grand Prix de Monaco (Monte Carlo)	May 27	Michael Schumacher (Ferrari F2001)
8	Grand Prix Air Canada (Montréal)	Jun 10	Ralf Schumacher (Williams FW23-BMW)
9	Warsteiner Grand Prix of Europe (Nürburgring)	Jun 24	Michael Schumacher (Ferrari F2001)
10	Mobil 1 Grand Prix de France (Magny-Cours)	Jul 1	Michael Schumacher (Ferrari F2001)
11	Foster's British Grand Prix (Silverstone)	Jul 15	Mika Häkkinen (McLaren MP4-16-Mercedes-Benz)
12	Grosser Mobil 1 Preis von Deutschland (Hockenheim)	Jul 29	Ralf Schumacher (Williams FW23-BMW)
13	Marlboro Magyar Nagydíj (Hungaroring)	Aug 19	Michael Schumacher (Ferrari F2001)
14	Foster's Belgian Grand Prix (Spa-Francorchamps)	Sep 2	Michael Schumacher (Ferrari F2001)
15	Gran Premio Campari d'Italia (Monza)	Sep 16	Juan Pablo Montoya (Williams FW23-BMW)
16	SAP United States Grand Prix (Indianapolis)	Sep 30	Mika Häkkinen (McLaren MP4-16-Mercedes-Benz)
17	Fuji Television Japanese Grand Prix (Suzuka)	Oct 14	Michael Schumacher (Ferrari F2001)

Chaos reigns at the start of the Italian Grand Prix

DRIVERS' CHAMPIONSHIP

	DRIVERS	POINTS
1	Michael Schumacher	123
2	David Coulthard	65
3	Rubens Barrichello	56
4	Ralf Schumacher	49
5	Mika Häkkinen	37
6	Juan Pablo Montoya	31
7=	Jacques Villeneuve	12
	Jarno Trulli	12
	Nick Heidfeld	12
10	Kimi Räikkönen	9
11	Giancarlo Fisichella	8
12=	Heinz-Harald Frentzen	6
	Eddie Irvine	6
14=	Olivier Panis	5
	Jean Alesi	5
16	Pedro de la Rosa	3
17	Jenson Button	2
18	Jos Verstappen	1

CONSTRUCTORS' CHAMPIONSHIP

	CONSTRUCTORS	POINTS
1	Ferrari	179
2	McLaren-Mercedes-Benz	102
3	Williams-BMW	80
4	Sauber-Petronas	21
5	Jordan-Honda	19
6	BAR-Honda	17
7	Benetton-Renault	10
8	Jaguar-Cosworth	9
9	Prost-Acer	4
10	Arrows-Asiatech	1

Rubens Barrichello sheds a tear after handing victory in Austria to Michael Schumacher

2002

TEAM ORDERS AND TEARS AMID THE SCARLET TIDE

F1 faced several threats during 2002. Ferrari's continued domination – more extreme than at any previous time in the sport's history – was blamed for falling television audiences. The economic recession threatened teams up and down the pitlane, with cost-cutting measures becoming urgent. Prost and Arrows folded. Talk of a manufacturer-led breakaway Grand Prix World Championship strengthened with BMW, DaimlerChrysler, Fiat, Ford and Renault to the fore. There was ongoing uncertainty regarding ownership of Bernie Ecclestone's SLEC holding company when majority shareholder Kirch was declared bankrupt on 8 April, with its creditor banks (Bayerische Landesbank, Lehman Brothers and JPMorgan Chase) taking on its 75 percent stake. Among the companies said to be in talks to acquire Kirch during the winter of 2001/02 had been Liberty Media.

The Australian GP was only confirmed when the coroner's report into marshal Graham Beveridge's death in 2001 was published just weeks before the season opener. Capacity for the British GP was reduced with a new traffic plan that included a dual-carriage approach road to Silverstone. Hockenheim secured the German GP for 2002–08 by agreeing to rebuild with a shorter layout and increased grandstand seating.

There was a furore in Melbourne when it was revealed that Tom Walkinshaw Racing planned to provide engineering assistance to former TWR saloon car driver Charles Nickerson (*aka* Chuck Nicholson). Nickerson's Phoenix Finance acquired a pair of Prost AP04s, fitted them with three-year-old TWR

Tom Walkinshaw faces the media in Australia after prompting uproar

engines, and claimed the television/travel money that would have gone to the defunct French team. The cars were sent to Sepang but did not make it through customs because the FIA said they did not have a valid F1 entry, leaving drivers Tarso Marques and Gastón Mazzacane unemployed. Phoenix's claims were dismissed in London's High Court on 21 May.

Red Bull wanted to establish an 'All-American F1 team' with acquisition of Arrows, Jordan or Jaguar discussed. Its search for the next American star was launched in 2002 with 1985 Indianapolis 500 winner Danny Sullivan as its figurehead.

The class of 2002 face the assembled press before the opening race in Australia

The early dice between Juan Pablo Montoya and Kimi Räikkönen was a highlight of the German Grand Prix

The 16 finalists, including future F1 driver Scott Speed, were evaluated at Paul Ricard before four were offered sponsored drives in Europe's junior categories. The energy-drink giant was still three years from team ownership.

The FIA introduced new rules to improve safety following recent marshal fatalities. Side impact structures and wheel tethers were strengthened and wing mirrors had to be 20 percent larger. New SAFER (Steel and Foam Energy Reduction) barriers were installed at Indianapolis. Automatic-start detection systems and electronic power steering were outlawed. Due to Ferrari switching its drivers on the last lap of the Austrian GP, team orders were banned. Pelé, the world's greatest footballer, waved the chequered flag in Brazil but missed the leaders and signalled ninth-placed Takuma Satō instead. F1 lost one of its greatest privateers when Rob Walker died on 29 April.

Testing was banned from the end of the 2001 season until 7 January 2002 to cut costs, although this led to an increase in the use of simulators and second test drivers. From Monaco onwards, teams were not allowed to use screens to conceal their cars in the pitlane. F1 experimented with advertising logos on the track itself, although this was abandoned after the season following complaints from drivers. From Brazil onwards, stewards were given the power to impose grid penalties for bad driving.

Indianapolis saw Michael Schumacher attempt to orchestrate a Ferrari photo finish

Michael Schumacher, Ferrari F2001 (Malaysian GP)

SCUDERIA FERRARI MARLBORO

This was a year of total domination. Ferrari's points tally was double that of the rest of the field combined. The team won 15 of the 17 races and scored nine 1–2s. Michael Schumacher claimed a record 11 victories, became the first driver to finish every race on the podium, and equalled Juan Manuel Fangio's five World Championships. At the launch of the Ferrari F2002, company president Luca di Montezemolo said: 'It was not easy to improve a car that was already perfect' — but that is exactly what Ferrari did.

On 22 May 2001, Ferrari announced that Schumacher had extended his contract for another three seasons with Rubens Barrichello confirmed for 2002. Luca Badoer was retained as test driver with Luciano Burti the surprise choice as his colleague. Ferrari's close working relationship with Bridgestone, extended until 2004, was key to continued success. Di Montezemolo considered his position before extending his contract until the end of 2006. Luca Baldisserri continued as Schumacher's race engineer while Gabriele delli Colli arrived from Jordan to work with Barrichello. Vodafone, the mobile phone network, agreed a three-year deal as associate sponsor.

Accidents interrupted testing with the old car during January, with Barrichello launched airborne at Valencia and a subsequent Barcelona test curtailed when both race drivers crashed. The F2002's launch at the new road-car factory in Maranello on 6 February revealed a strong family resemblance to the previous design, although much had changed under the bodywork. Early plans to evolve the dominant F2001 were shelved because

technical director Ross Brawn feared incremental gains would be insufficient to stay ahead. A compact seven-speed gearbox, its titanium casing integral with the engine, gave a 15 percent improvement in gearchange speed thanks to having hydraulic shifting rather than dog rings. Paolo Martinelli's team introduced a smaller, lighter derivative (051) of the successful 90-degree V10 with lowered centre of gravity and optimised weight distribution. The aerodynamics were overhauled with exhausts exiting diminutive sidepods from backward-facing periscopes ahead of its svelte 'Coke bottle' rear. Bridgestone engineers contributed to new pushrod/torsion spring suspension that helped to maximise traction and roadholding.

Early testing was promising but the old cars were sent to Australia following gearbox issues. Schumacher's view on this – 'the F2001 has been quick in testing this winter, so there is no reason to take unnecessary risks' – was born out when Barrichello led a Ferrari qualifying 1–2. After Ralf Schumacher's Williams hit the Brazilian at the first corner, triggering an eight-car pile-up, Michael Schumacher avoided the carnage to win after a duel with Williams's Juan Pablo Montoya. In Malaysia, still with the F2001, pole winner Schumacher clashed with Montoya at the first corner but salvaged third behind the dominant Williams-BMWs. Barrichello led until his pitstop only to suffer a rare engine failure.

That defeat prompted Ferrari to give Schumacher a F2002 in Brazil, where rivals questioned whether the rear wing was flexing to reduce drag. After leading from second on the grid, he chopped across Montoya's front wing as he defended on the back straight,

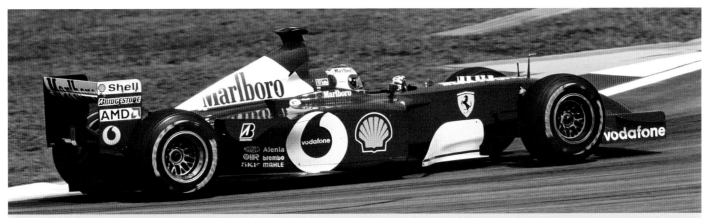

Rubens Barrichello, Ferrari F2001 (Malaysian GP)

causing damage that ruined the Colombian's race, but the Ferrari driver survived the contact to beat his brother to victory after stopping once. Barrichello, who qualified only eighth after deletion of his best lap for ignoring the pitlane red light, started the race with his F2001 light-fuelled and took the lead on lap 14 only for the hydraulics to fail.

Both drivers had F2002s for Imola, where Schumacher led an emphatic 1–2 in qualifying and the race. The rear wing was revised for that outing following the Brazilian controversy and then the bargeboards were modified for Spain after they had also been called into question. Having crashed while testing at Mugello

following front-suspension failure, Schumacher's domination continued with a pole-to-chequered-flag victory in Spain. Second on the grid, Barrichello did not start the race due to a gearbox electronics malfunction on the dummy grid.

Barrichello was the quicker Ferrari driver in Austria, where he started from pole and dominated before being ordered to let Schumacher take the lead on the last lap. As well as denying the Brazilian a deserved victory, this prompted booing at the podium ceremony – where an embarrassed Schumacher insisted that his team-mate take the top step – and angered fans around the world. The FIA summoned Ferrari to the FIA World Council on 26 June

Michael Schumacher, Ferrari F2002 (San Marino GP)

and issued a $1m fine for breaching podium protocol – the only punishment that the rules permitted.

Michelin had the advantage in Monaco, where Schumacher claimed a close second behind David Coulthard's McLaren and Barrichello came home seventh after an eventful afternoon. The Brazilian ran into Kimi Räikkönen's McLaren at the chicane and had to stop for a new nosecone, then received a 10sec stop-go for causing an accident followed by a drive-through penalty for speeding in the pitlane. In Canada, the one-stopping Schumacher nursed a blistered left-rear tyre to score Ferrari's 150th GP victory. Barrichello finished third after leading in the early stages until a safety car ruined his two-stop strategy, then losing out to Coulthard in a feisty dice that saw both straight-line the final chicane on lap 60.

Ferrari was second best to Williams-BMW during qualifying for the European GP at the Nürburgring but emerged from the race with another 1–2. Barrichello took the lead on the opening lap with an uncharacteristic Schumacher spin helping to extend that advantage – and this time, with the FIA hearing into team orders just days away, there was no call to switch positions. In changeable conditions at Silverstone, Schumacher scored his 60th GP victory while Barrichello, who had been stranded in neutral before the parade lap, charged through the field to finish second despite a spin.

Armed with a new aero upgrade, Ferrari appeared to lose out at Magny-Cours when Barrichello's engine refused to fire before the start and Schumacher received a drive-through penalty for crossing the pit exit line. However, the German recovered and snatched victory when Räikkönen ran wide at the hairpin with four laps to go, thereby clinching the title with six races remaining.

After Schumacher won the German GP with Barrichello fourth, the last five races of the season brought Ferrari 1–2s, Barrichello the winner three times, at the Hungaroring (where Ferrari retained the constructors' title), Monza and Indianapolis. There was further indignation when the world champion tried to engineer a photo-finish at Indy (prompting more boos on the podium), although Barrichello was 0.011sec ahead as they crossed the famous strip of bricks and sealed his position as championship runner-up. Schumacher, who had won in Belgium, extended his own record for victories in a season when he led Barrichello home in Japan.

BMW WILLIAMS F1

BMW Williams F1's aim for the new campaign was to add consistency and reliability to the race-winning speed shown in glimpses during 2001. Ralf Schumacher extended his contract until the end of 2004 and Juan Pablo Montoya was in the second year of his original deal. The simmering feud between the two men remained and both were publicly criticised by technical director Patrick Head. Reserve driver Marc Gené re-signed and Antônio Pizzonia was preferred to Ricardo Sperafico as test driver.

Recent progress made it inevitable that key staff would be approached by ambitious rivals. Chief designer Gavin Fisher eschewed advances but head of aerodynamics Geoff Willis moved to British American Racing as technical director, a transfer that coincided with a critical phase of the FW24's design process. Aerodynamicists Jason Somerville and Nick Alcock were promoted from within with Antonia Terzi recruited from Ferrari.

There was title talk when the new FW24 was revealed at a windy Silverstone on 25 January. 'We expect to be competitive… and need to be serious championship contenders,' said Sir Frank Williams. Fisher chose a ground-up evolution with the main changes beneath the FW24's shapely bodywork, particularly on the layout and systems. The longest car on the grid, it retained a flat front wing. Traditional front-suspension mounting points were preferred to the twin-keel concept pioneered by Sauber in 2001. The rear end was repackaged and the pushrod suspension developed, with torsion bars at the front and coil springs to the rear. The latest version of BMW's 90-degree V10 (P82), the most powerful engine in the business and said to deliver 900bhp at 19,000rpm, impressed Montoya: 'It is a big step forward in every meaning of the word.' The seven-speed gearbox was new.

The FW24 was a conservative design and Schumacher bemoaned the lack of rear downforce at the first major Barcelona test while Gené suffered four engine failures as he put miles on the new unit. Schumacher injured his neck in a high-speed crash at Estoril, but Montoya's record pace at Valencia raised hopes before the season. However, the gap to Ferrari was now a chasm.

Third on the grid in Australia, Schumacher was launched over the back of Rubens Barrichello's year-old Ferrari at the start, triggering an eight-car pile-up. Montoya avoided trouble to battle the older

Rubens Barrichello, Ferrari F2002 (European GP)

Juan Pablo Montoya, Williams FW24-BMW (Australian GP)

Schumacher's Ferrari before having to settle for second. Those two rivals qualified on the front row at Sepang and neither gave way into Turn 1 with contact inevitable. Ralf Schumacher beat Barrichello to score Williams-BMW's only win of the year on a rare day when Michelin held sway. Angered by a drive-through penalty for causing an accident, Montoya raced back through the field and inherited second when Barrichello retired.

Montoya failed to make the most of pole at Interlagos when beaten away by Michael Schumacher. They ran side-by-side for two corners before the Ferrari sliced across the Williams's front wing. That necessitated a change and the furious Colombian set the fastest lap as he charged back into fifth. Ralf finished a close second without attempting to pass his brother. The true scale of Williams-BMW's task was evident at Imola where Ferrari had new F2002s for its drivers, who outclassed the field with Ralf Schumacher and Montoya third and fourth on the grid and at the finish. That pattern continued in Spain where Ralf's race was compromised by damage sustained in a run through the Turn 9 gravel trap, an unscheduled pitstop and engine failure on the penultimate lap. Montoya was a distant second despite hitting chief mechanic Carl Gaden at his second pitstop, breaking a bone in Gaden's foot.

In Austria, Ralf Schumacher outqualified his brother to split the Ferraris although there was no denying the red cars on Sunday. Montoya, who was narrowly missed by Nick Heidfeld's out-of-control Sauber before it collected Takuma Satō's Jordan, used a longer opening stint to jump his team-mate in the pitstops and head another Williams 3–4.

That Williams and Michelin made single-lap progress was evidenced by Montoya's five consecutive pole positions starting in Monaco. However, his engine failed when running second in that race and in Montréal, where he was closing on leader Michael Schumacher. The Williams drivers locked out the front row at the Nürburgring only to collide at the first corner. With damaged steering, Montoya disputed fourth with David Coulthard's McLaren until he spun into it. He led the opening laps at Silverstone before it rained, at which point Bridgestone's superior intermediate tyres restored Ferrari's advantage. Third that day, Montoya headed a Williams 4–5 in France as the FW24s were eclipsed once more. The younger Schumacher finished the Monaco GP for the first time in six attempts, in third place despite a precautionary stop to change a cut tyre. A faulty fuel rig denied points in Canada and Britain while excessive rear-tyre wear, a recurring complaint, restricted him to fourth at the European GP.

A major aero upgrade and improved traction control software worked at Hockenheim. Ralf Schumacher joined his brother on the front row and was on course to finish second before a hydraulic leak forced an extra stop that dropped him to third. Montoya duelled with Kimi Räikkönen's McLaren in the early stages and inherited second when his team-mate and Barrichello were delayed. Ralf was 'best of the rest' in Hungary, starting and finishing third. Montoya made a slow start and damaged his front wing by running wide while defending seventh.

The Ferrari steamroller continued in Belgium, where Montoya made a good start from fifth and passed Räikkönen to take third despite Coulthard's pressure; Ralf Schumacher spun on his way to fifth. Using a new high-revving qualifying engine, Montoya's

Ralf Schumacher, Williams FW24-BMW (Brazilian GP)

161.467mph pole at Monza was the fastest F1 lap since Keke Rosberg at Silverstone in 1985. Ralf cut the chicane at the start to lead but his engine blew up before he could relinquish the position. Montoya was passed by both Ferraris before retiring from third due to chassis damage.

Patrick Head called it 'totally unacceptable' when Schumacher crashed into Montoya as his team-mate overtook him into Turn 1 on the second lap of the United States GP. Schumacher lost a lap while changing his rear wing. Montoya, pitting early in error, recovered from the positions lost to finish fourth. That incident precipitated another spat between the team-mates and their season ended with further disappointment in Japan. The FW24s were a handful during practice, unable to generate tyre temperature. With handling improved for the race, Schumacher was denied third by a late engine failure that promoted Montoya to fourth.

Williams-BMW finished runner-up behind Ferrari, but a single victory and 129-point deficit were testament to the task ahead.

WEST McLAREN MERCEDES

Ron Dennis reflected on a 'shortfall in reliability and performance' as he looked back on 2001. 'We've gone way beyond just the engineering issues and looked at the relationship between Ilmor, Mercedes and McLaren… we intend to be one.' The team looked to safeguard its future engineering strength following Jaguar's unsuccessful pursuit of technical director Adrian Newey. It adopted a 'matrix' of specialists in each area of design and engineering to retain knowledge within the company irrespective of personnel changes. With Newey continuing in his role, Neil Oatley became the executive director of engineering, Ferrari head of transmission design John Sutton was recruited in July and Mike Coughlan arrived from Arrows as chief designer on 2 September.

There was a driver change for the first time since 1996 when Mika Häkkinen's sabbatical was confirmed at the 2001 Italian GP. Dennis looked to Sauber for his replacement, although the choice surprised Nick Heidfeld and others. Heidfeld had been a McLaren-Mercedes junior since 1997 but rookie team-mate Kimi Räikkönen was selected on a long-term deal. There were high-profile appearances for Jean Alesi at Mugello on 16 April and 21-year-old IndyCar driver

Sarah Fisher during the United States GP weekend, although her run lasted just three demonstration laps.

A switch from Bridgestone to Michelin was confirmed on 30 October 2001. The Bridgestone-shod Ferraris dominated once more, but the good wear rate and temperature-generating characteristics of the McLarens were crucial in the fight with Michelin rival Williams-BMW. The high-tech new McLaren Communications Centre replaced regular hospitality units from the San Marino GP. Mercedes increased its shareholding in Ilmor Engineering to 55 percent in September.

Räikkönen knew he would be judged against the experienced David Coulthard. After driving a McLaren MP4-16B-Mercedes for the first time at a wet Barcelona on 8 January, the Finn said: 'We will work together in the tests, and in the races we will work against each other… every team-mate always tries to beat the other one.' Räikkönen outqualified Coulthard 10-7 although the Scot finished higher in the standings, fifth, and scored the team's only victory.

Twelve days after Räikkönen's public debut, test driver Alexander Wurz completed 45 trouble-free laps of Barcelona in the new McLaren MP4-17-Mercedes. Ilmor responded to the previous season's disappointment with its lightest and most compact V10 to date. The vee angle of the all-new Mercedes-Benz FO110M was widened from 72 to 90 degrees, allowing the car's rear bodywork to be lowered further still. The new engine matched BMW for revs but was not as powerful as its main rivals. McLaren opted for a 'radical' front end with suspension that incorporated an intricate twin keel and aerodynamic lower wishbones mounted within the brake ducts and bargeboards. The revised engine requirements meant the exhausts were moved from the diffuser to the top of the sidepods, eradicating the shrill note of the previous two seasons. The new aluminium gearbox casing reduced weight while multi-element wing mirrors were introduced at the drivers' behest. The late switch of tyre supplier meant the suspension was only finalised in the wind tunnel following eleventh-hour provision of data from Michelin, and Newey admitted that 'it was the least understood area of the car in terms of correlation between predicted and actual track performance.'

A rear puncture was suspected when Coulthard rolled at Barcelona's Turn 1 during testing and the MP4-17 initially lacked

David Coulthard, McLaren MP4-17-Mercedes-Benz (San Marino GP)

grip, with an unwelcome tendency to oversteer. The Michelins degraded more than Bridgestone's equivalent rubber and the French manufacturer's efforts were compromised by having to satisfy two top teams. Furthermore, lack of power and straight-line speed were consistent themes for McLaren-Mercedes during 2002.

Australia's first-corner chaos had contrasting outcomes for the drivers: Coulthard jumped into the lead from fourth and Räikkönen dropped nearly to the back with a damaged nosecone. Coulthard led for ten laps until gearbox maladies caused repeated 'offs' and eventually proved terminal. Räikkönen recorded the fastest race lap as he recovered to finish third. A low-downforce set-up reduced the straight-line deficit in Malaysia, where engine failures denied both a possible podium. They ran 3–4 in the closing stages at Interlagos before Räikkönen lost fourth place when the right-rear wheel hub failed. Outqualified at the next three races, Coulthard scored on each occasion, with sixth at Imola (when lapped), third at Barcelona (where Dennis admitted to being 'light years away

from Ferrari') and sixth again at the A1-Ring (despite running wide on oil). Räikkönen meanwhile had frustrating setbacks, including a high-speed rear-wing failure on lap four in Spain.

Monaco masked the straight-line shortcomings of the MP4-17 and Coulthard was a factor all weekend. He qualified second, used fine-tuned launch control to beat Juan Pablo Montoya into Ste-Dévote and held off Michael Schumacher to score a fine victory. In contrast, Räikkönen crashed twice during practice and retired from the race after being hit by Rubens Barrichello at the chicane. Canada saw both McLarens finish in the points for the first time: Coulthard prevailed in a late battle with Barrichello's Ferrari to finish second after a timely full-course yellow helped his one-stop strategy, with Räikkönen fourth after a faulty rig left him tight on fuel. The quicker McLaren driver at the Nürburgring, Coulthard was eliminated when collected by Montoya's spinning Williams as they disputed fourth but Räikkönen passed Ralf Schumacher's Williams to finish third.

Kimi Räikkönen, McLaren MP4-17-Mercedes-Benz (United States GP)

Interference from F1's digital television feed was blamed for radio issues that turned the British GP into a disaster with both drivers making four pitstops in the changeable conditions. Engine failure finally ended Räikkönen's misery while Coulthard was lapped twice in tenth. An engine upgrade for French GP qualifying brought more pace and Räikkönen appeared on course for his breakthrough victory when Michael Schumacher served a penalty. Kimi defended stoically before running wide on oil at the hairpin with four laps to go. Disconsolate to only finish second, he remarked: 'This was my best-ever finishing position and my worst-ever race.' Coulthard completed McLaren's only double podium of 2002 in third despite his own drive-through penalty for crossing the pit exit line.

That fillip proved short-lived for the MP4-17s lacked grunt at Hockenheim, where Räikkönen three-wheeled back to the pits following a puncture before spinning into retirement, and Coulthard finished fifth. Hopes that the Hungaroring would replicate the cars' Monaco form were dashed when they qualified 10th and 11th, although both drivers scored points. A surprise second in qualifying at Spa-Francorchamps, Räikkönen had engine failures at that race and the next. Coulthard finished fourth in Belgium and was seventh in Italy despite losing his front wing when he ran into the back of his team-mate at the start.

Crucial chassis and engine developments saw McLaren edge ahead of Williams by the end of the season. Coulthard excelled at Indianapolis by qualifying and finishing third but lost that position in Japan due to an early throttle issue. Räikkönen's third successive engine failure ended his United States GP but he inherited third in Japan following his team-mate's demise.

MILD SEVEN RENAULT SPORT

Renault completed its return to F1 as a full works team in 2002. The progress from the depths experienced during its final season as Benetton Formula in 2001 to becoming the fourth-best team was impressive.

Jenson Button remained for the second year of his Williams-BMW loan despite Flavio Briatore's close-season criticism. Renault's flamboyant managing director told *Gazzetta dello Sport*: 'After an excellent 2000, he spent a winter as a superstar and was then distracted by new toys. He has to pull himself together.' Briatore exercised his option on Jarno Trulli during the 2001 summer break to replace the out-of-contract Giancarlo Fisichella in what amounted to a swap. Fernando Alonso's return from Minardi as reserve driver only intensified pressure on Button. Oliver Gavin was drafted in to assist the test team later in the season. Jordan's technical brain drain continued when John Iley arrived as head of aerodynamics in December 2001.

Winter testing at Barcelona with a yellow-and-white Benetton B201 was followed by the Renault R202 reveal at Viry-Châtillon on 27 January. Finished in the blue of title sponsor Mild Seven and Renault's corporate yellow, this was the first complete car led by technical director Mike Gascoyne alongside long-time director of engineering Pat Symonds. Renault alternated its chief designer role with Mark Smith responsible for the R202 while Tim Densham concentrated on 2003. This was an evolutionary process with improved aerodynamics and engine reliability the focus. Jean-Jacques His, who succeeded Christian Contzen as managing director of Renault Sport in February, persevered with

Jenson Button, Renault R202 (Brazilian GP)

Jarno Trulli, Renault R202 (Italian GP)

the wide-angle concept in the new RS22 V10. That was quoted as 111 degrees at the time although later reports claimed the vee to be five degrees narrower. Engine vibration was an issue, and its power deficit only grew as rival manufacturers pursued more development. However, the R202 chassis proved well balanced and easy to set up. Naoki Takunaga and Ted Czapski were named head of control systems and research and development respectively and the R202's electronics were credited for impressive traction and the fastest starts in the field. Renault was the leading team to retain a six-speed gearbox, mounted longitudinally as was the norm. Suspension was via pushrod-activated torsion bars.

In Australia, Trulli jumped from seventh on the grid to second, where he withstood pressure from Juan Pablo Montoya and Michael Schumacher for seven laps before crashing out at Turn 1, with oil or mechanical failure blamed; Button was a casualty of the first-corner pile-up. The Englishman started eighth in Malaysia and only lost a podium finish through a rear-suspension breakage on the last lap, leaving him fourth, while Trulli went out with an overheating engine. Trulli led a qualifying 6–7 at Interlagos and the Renaults made lightning starts to run in the top four. Trulli was leading his team-mate and heading for fourth when his engine expired with 11 laps to go, leaving Button to claim that fourth place.

Button beat David Coulthard into fifth at Imola, describing it at the time as 'the best race of my F1 career… particularly on a

circuit where I have had a nightmare for the past two years', but ninth-placed Trulli was slowed by an overheating gearbox. Button shone in Spain, duelling with Coulthard for third before late hydraulics failure denied another score, while Trulli was sidelined by a throttle issue. The R202 was uncompetitive in Austria, where Button salvaged seventh, but better suited to Monaco, where Trulli was quickest in both practice sessions although traffic restricted them to the fourth row of the grid. Button jumped the start and crashed into Olivier Panis's BAR-Honda at Ste-Dévote as he recovered from the resulting penalty. Trulli was initially disqualified from fourth because his electronic control box lacked the required FIA seal but was reinstated.

Renault's horsepower shortage was evident in Montréal although Trulli adopted a low-downforce set-up to take sixth. 'Best of the rest' behind the 'big three' teams once more at the Nürburgring, Button finished fifth with the misfiring Trulli eighth after his alternative two-stop strategy did not work. At Silverstone, Trulli used an aero upgrade with new sidepods and rear wing to qualify seventh but engine failure forced Button to race the old-specification spare; both retired from the race, albeit with Button classified. After announcing that he was moving to British American Racing in 2003, Button claimed a point in France. Both retired from an uncompetitive German GP, Trulli having led a train of faster cars before spinning off.

In Hungary, Button wasted another quick getaway by spinning out of fifth while Trulli slipped back in the opening laps and finished a dispirited and lapped eighth. Little was expected of the power tracks that followed, and engine failures accounted for both cars at the Belgian GP. Relegated to the back of the Italian GP grid after stalling before the parade lap, Trulli led a surprise Renault 4–5 by the finish. He beat BAR-Honda's Jacques Villeneuve into fifth at Indianapolis and Button completed his career at Enstone with sixth position in Japan.

Trulli won the internal qualifying battle 12–5 but Button was often the more convincing on race day and shaded his team-mate with seventh in the drivers' standings. There was no podium finish during 2002, but Renault claimed fourth overall as Renault F1 president Patrick Faure had demanded before the season.

SAUBER PETRONAS

There was a change of majority shareholder when Peter Sauber brokered the sale of Dietrich Mateschitz's shares to Crédit Suisse at the start of 2002. Frustrated for over a year with the lack of satisfactory results, Mateschitz remained a major sponsor with his Red Bull brand, albeit at a reduced level. Sauber extended its deal for Petronas-badged Ferrari V10s until the end of 2004.

Sauber bowed to the inevitable and released Kimi Räikkönen from his contract when compensation was agreed with McLaren. The team searched for another rough diamond by testing Euro 3000 champion Felipe Massa at Mugello on 18–19 September and 2–4 October 2001 with impressive results. Fastest overall at that latter session, Massa was quickly confirmed as Nick Heidfeld's new team-mate. There was no reserve driver once more although Jos Verstappen visited Hinwil in February but proved too tall to be considered for the role.

Heidfeld was entrusted with the Sauber C21-Petronas's shakedown at Fiorano on 15 January and declared: 'Of all the cars I have driven, none has given me such a thrill.' Unveiled to the press ten days later at Dübendorf military airfield near Zürich, this evolution of the successful C20 was 10kg lighter and featured a new monocoque. The front wing at the start of 2002 was angular while the lower-front wishbones were mounted on twin-keel

flanges under the nose. A triangular air intake was preferred to the previous oval to aid cooling and increase power. The cockpit surround was lowered and mirrors moved from chassis to sidepods. Chief aerodynamicist Seamus Mullarkey and his team relied on the venerable wind tunnel at Emmen with a new facility in Hinwil still two years from completion. The seven-speed gearbox was redesigned to fit the lower 90-degree engine (designated Petronas 02A) that was initially of September 2001 specification. The more compact engine/gearbox package helped lower the centre of gravity but the design was overly conservative and prone to oversteer in high-speed corners.

Willy Rampf remained as technical director while test team manager Jacky Eeckelaert was promoted to head of track engineering. Eeckelaert had also been Räikkönen's race engineer in 2001 and was now responsible for Massa's rookie campaign. Peter Sauber warned Massa 'to keep under control' after several incidents during Barcelona testing and his wild, erratic driving style was a feature of 2002. Hopes were raised when Heidfeld traded quick times during that Barcelona test, although both crashed heavily in changeable conditions at Mugello.

Massa achieved his aim of qualifying in the top ten for his debut in Melbourne's Albert Park – ninth and 0.260sec ahead of Heidfeld. Sauber's hopes of scoring points were dashed at the first corner when Heidfeld hit Giancarlo Fisichella, whose Jordan cannoned into the hapless Massa. In contrast, both finished in the points in Malaysia, fifth (Heidfeld) and sixth (Massa). They left Brazil empty-handed after challenging once more: Heidfeld hit the medical car's open door during the warm-up and suffered a brake issue in the race, while Massa crashed. The Brazilian finished eighth at Imola but Heidfeld's race was ruined by a drive-through penalty after a pitstop mix-up. The German was impressive in Spain when he led a strong Sauber 4–5 after the pair battled their way past the Renault drivers.

In Austria, a new floor and upgraded Petronas Ferrari engines (now 2001 Japanese GP-specification) helped Heidfeld qualify fifth and Massa seventh. The German claimed third on the opening lap but could not hold off the faster Williams-BMWs. He was duelling with David Coulthard's McLaren-Mercedes when he lost control as they approached Turn 3 and crashed violently into the

Nick Heidfeld, Sauber C21-Petronas (British GP)

Felipe Massa, Sauber C21-Petronas (British GP)

Heinz-Harald Frentzen, Sauber C21-Petronas (United States GP)

unsuspecting Takuma Satō. Massa was forced wide at the start and eventually retired with suspension failure.

The C21s were a handful over Monaco's bumps and lacked grip. Nursing an injured knee from his Austrian accident, Heidfeld finished eighth despite degraded tyres. Massa endured a tough weekend: he crashed on Thursday, rivals accused him of blocking on Saturday, and he had two race dramas at Ste-Dévote, the first a clash with Enrique Bernoldi's Arrows that brought a 10sec stop-go, the second a 100mph impact with the barriers following rear-brake failure.

Problematic pitlane speed limiters ruined their Canadian GP before Massa edged his team-mate for the final point at the Nürburgring. Heidfeld preserved his Bridgestone intermediate tyres for sixth place at Silverstone, finished seventh at Magny-Cours despite haywire electronics, and scored another point at Hockenheim. Massa, who had escaped unharmed from a heavy testing shunt at Barcelona, spun five times during his wild British GP, retired from a penalty-strewn French race, and was angered in Germany when team orders denied him sixth. The Brazilian was the quicker Sauber driver at the next three races and only lost a hard-earned fifth place in Hungary when he was passed by both McLarens at the final pitstops.

As was so often the case, Sauber lost its edge as the season progressed. Tyre warm-up was an issue during qualifying for the Belgian and Italian GPs with both drivers mired on the penultimate row at Spa-Francorchamps. Heidfeld finished tenth on both occasions while Massa was penalised for causing an accident with Pedro de la Rosa at Monza's Variante della Roggia. That resulted in a ten-place grid drop at the United States GP, so Sauber placed Heinz-Harald Frentzen, who had already signed to replace the Brazilian in 2003, in Massa's car as a one-off. Frentzen crashed while testing at Silverstone and could only finish 13th. Massa was reinstated for the Japanese GP following a positive test at Mugello. However, the C21 lacked balance at Suzuka and Massa crashed after just three laps of his final race before taking an enforced sabbatical. Heidfeld finished ninth in the USA and seventh at Suzuka as Sauber-Petronas narrowly held onto fifth overall.

DHL JORDAN HONDA

Jordan Grand Prix's season was compromised by a technical exodus, mounting financial worries, poor reliability and troublesome handling. That it beat rival Honda-powered British American Racing into sixth place was a small triumph. Honda had considered supplying just one team before Jordan's two-year extension was announced in the summer of 2001. It was all-change in the cockpit and technical office. Eddie Jordan moved quickly when he could not agree terms with Jarno Trulli by rehiring Giancarlo Fisichella on a three-year deal. Justin Wilson impressed during autumn tests at Silverstone and Mugello but Honda protégé and new British F3 champion Takuma Satō was confirmed as second driver.

After Mike Gascoyne's defection to Renault, key technical staff followed, including Bob Bell, John Iley and Mark Smith. Part of Jordan's response was a surprise recall for Gary Anderson as director of race and test engineering. Jordan's original technical director had briefly worked with the 2002 incumbent, Eghbal Hamidy, at Stewart GP during the 1998/99 close season and conflict was predicted. Henri Durand (ex-Ferrari/McLaren) also arrived from Prost as director of development and design. Rob Smedley and James Key were promoted from within to race engineer for Fisichella and Satō respectively. Team manager Jim Vale moved to the V8 Supercar series in his native Australia and was replaced by Tim Edwards.

Testing with the 2001 car and engine began with quick times at Barcelona and a near miss at Valencia where Fisichella spun to avoid Satō's stricken machine. Fisichella gave the new Jordan EJ12-Honda its shakedown at Silverstone on 22 January but teething troubles and a lack of power scuppered progress. A difficult winter continued when Fisichella crashed at Valencia's Turn 3 in February, injuring his knees. German Formula Renault champion Marcel Lasée stood in for the Italian on day one of the next Barcelona test.

With reduced support from Benson & Hedges, DHL (Deutsche Post's courier arm) was named as the new title partner at the launch in a Brussels aircraft hangar on 22 February. Hamidy had

Giancarlo Fisichella, Jordan EJ12-Honda (Canadian GP)

Takuma Satō, Jordan EJ12-Honda (Monaco GP)

adopted a back-to-basics approach to what turned out to be his only Jordan in charge. The EJ12's pushrod/torsion bar suspension was heavily revised with twin-keel front that required a horizontal lower brace, which disturbed airflow under the car. Mountings for the rear dampers were moved from gearbox to chassis. Honda introduced a completely new 90-degree V10 engine, the RA002E, which was mated to Jordan's existing seven-speed longitudinal gearbox. Engine/gearbox weight, which was said to be at least 30kg more than for the front-runners, induced snap oversteer and excessive rear-tyre wear. It was feared that Bridgestone's concentration on Ferrari would compromise service to other teams. Launch-control glitches repeatedly caused the yellow cars to make slow getaways.

The consequences of a negative winter were soon felt. Hamidy was reported to be 'on holiday' when he was absent from the Australian GP with his departure confirmed by the end of April. Budgetary shortfall forced testing to be cut and 15 percent of the workforce were laid off in the spring, including managing director Trevor Foster plus engineers David Brown and Tim Holloway.

With late upgrades having improved the EJ12's balance in Australia, Fisichella qualified eighth despite running lower revs to improve reliability but was eliminated in the first-corner fracas. A crash during Saturday practice and hydraulics failure on the spare

left Satō without a representative qualifying time. That said, the debutant briefly ran in the top six before retiring after 12 laps. Satō apologised after he rammed his team-mate on lap two of the Malaysian GP, forcing both to pit. Satō finished ninth and repeated that result at Interlagos where the notorious bumps accentuated the EJ12's handling deficiencies. 'Fisi' was last in Malaysia and first to retire when his engine failed in Brazil. Hydraulic issues ruined the San Marino GP weekend, and both were out by lap 10 in Spain, Fisichella with more hydraulics woes, Satō another spin.

A revised front wing and hydraulics system were fitted for the Austrian GP and new suspension for Monaco. Fisichella finally delivered the season's first points for both Jordan and Honda with successive fifth places in Austria, Monaco and Canada. In contrast, Satō continued his incident-filled rookie campaign. First, he injured his legs when T-boned by Nick Heidfeld's Sauber in a frightening accident at the A1-Ring's Remus-kurve (now Turn 3) and required a precautionary overnight stay in Graz hospital. He made it three accidents in three GPs when attempting to let Fisichella past as they approached Monaco's harbourside chicane. Tenth in Montréal at least saw the Japanese driver reach the chequered flag for the first time in five races.

Honda introduced its full 2002-spec unit at the Nürburgring, but it did not deliver the performance step required. Fisichella ran into the back of his team-mate on the opening lap, terminally damage his steering, while Satō lost a lap and finished last. Seventh at Silverstone, Fisichella sat out the French GP on doctor's orders after front-wing failure caused a 170mph crash during Saturday practice. An attempt to hire Heinz-Harald Frentzen for the race, just a year after Jordan had sacked him, was prevented by 'contractual obstacles'. Sidelined by engine failure at Silverstone, Satō sustained damage when forced across the gravel trap at the start of the French GP following contact with Olivier Panis's BAR-Honda and he spun out 23 lap later.

With Anthony Davidson an unused stand-by at the German GP, Fisichella returned and used a higher-revving Honda engine to qualify a surprise sixth, but made another slow start and lost further places from running wide and a slow pitstop before his engine eventually let go. The EJ12 handled well in Hungary, where the Italian started fifth, ran fourth for the first two-thirds of the race and was disappointed to only finish sixth. Honda introduced another upgrade in Belgium where a problem in the oil system was blamed for failures during the weekend – Fisichella's fiery exit denying him seventh – and in testing. Eighth in Italy, Fisichella ran in the top ten throughout the United States GP, but tyre degradation accentuated by his one-stop strategy restricted him to seventh. He suffered engine failures on the way to the Japanese GP grid and in the race after switching to the spare car.

Having spent as much time in the gravel as on track so far, Satō began a run of six successive finishes with eighth place in Germany. Tenth or worse at the next four races, the Japanese was the home hero at the Suzuka finale and led the Honda challenge all weekend to the delight of the partisan crowd, qualifying seventh

and finishing a superb fifth. 'The crowds were unbelievable, waving at me on every single lap,' Satō enthused. 'This is one of the best feelings in my life.' That result proved crucial as Jordan snatched sixth in the constructors' standings from Jaguar and BAR-Honda.

JAGUAR RACING

Jaguar Racing entered its third season with a stable design team by default. High-profile advances to McLaren's Adrian Newey eventually came to naught and rumoured offers to Williams duo Gavin Fisher and Geoff Willis went unheeded. So, the Jaguar R3-Cosworth was the work of a team led by technical director Steve Nichols, chief designer John Russell and aerodynamicist Mark Handford. General wisdom was that the new car had to be an improvement on its disappointing predecessors when it broke cover as scheduled on 4 January during an understated function at the team's factory.

There had been change at the very top of parent company Ford by that time, for chief executive officer Jacques Nasser, who had originally sanctioned the purchase of Stewart Grand Prix, was replaced by Sir Nick Scheele in October 2001, with Bill 'Clay' Ford installed as president. There was speculation about the future of team principal Niki Lauda. That intensified when key ally Wolfgang Reitzle left the Premier Automotive Group on 1 May 2002, to be replaced by Richard Parry-Jones.

Eddie Irvine and Pedro de la Rosa remained under contract while André Lotterer was confirmed as reserve despite rumoured interest from Arrows. Comingmen Mark Webber, Fernando Alonso and Antônio Pizzonia all tested during 2002 as Jaguar looked to

Eddie Irvine, Jaguar R3-Cosworth (Brazilian GP)

Pedro de la Rosa, Jaguar R3B-Cosworth (Italian GP)

the future. Deficiencies in the new car were soon evident and the depressing mood in Milton Keynes was hardly improved by antipathy between its race drivers. 'Working with Irvine has been the worst part of the year,' de la Rosa said after the season. 'We hardly talked at the start of the season, and as the races went by, we stopped talking altogether.'

Establishing a wind tunnel near the factory rather than using the Swift Race Cars facility in Sacramento, California was a key objective. Plans to acquire Arrows's Bedford tunnel were shelved with an alternative in Brackley opened on 1 April 2002, under the management of David Pitchforth (ex-Reynard North America).

The design team was briefed to prioritise outright performance over reliability and 33kg was reportedly saved. The R3 was higher at the front bulkhead, ahead of which the nose drooped to twin supports and a distinctive front wing. The suspension was via pushrods and torsion bars with Michelin tyres retained. The Cosworth CR-3 V10 engine was used initially with a major upgrade for the San Marino GP delayed until Canada. The resulting CR-4 was among the most powerful engines by the end of the season. The seven-speed longitudinal gearbox had a magnesium casing. BP Castrol replaced Texaco as fuel partner.

Jaguar did not make the step forward it required and the R3 was slower than its predecessor when it first turned a wheel at Barcelona on 8 January. Correlation errors between track and wind tunnel were blamed when an expected eight percent front downforce gain translated into a two percent loss. Engine issues prevented long runs, the monocoque flexed at the front-suspension mounts, and the rear suspension needed strengthening to improve stability under braking. Lotterer conducted back-to-back tests with the R2C test hack at Lurcy-Lévis and Handford was despatched to Sacramento to devise a new front wing before the next test. Lauda, who had spun twice while trying an R2 at Valencia, denied that there was a crisis when Nichols resigned on 4 February. Having transferred from Ford's rally programme on 3 December 2001 as managing director, Guenther Steiner became acting technical director for the season while a permanent replacement was found. Aerodynamicists Ben

Agathangelou, Mark Gillan and Peter Matchin joined in the spring from Renault, McLaren and Arrows respectively, Agathangelou working alongside Handford as head of aero.

A new aerodynamic package and uprights were ready for the opening race in Australia but dire lack of grip and mid-corner understeer consigned the green cars to the penultimate row. That was far enough back to avoid the first-corner carnage, so they completed lap one in an unrepresentative fifth and sixth. Irvine's fourth-place finish could not mask Jaguar's uncompetitive plight; de la Rosa was last of the eight finishers after losing four laps fixing electrical issues. Slower than the R2 a year earlier in Malaysia, where both drivers required new front wings following incidents, Jaguar persevered with the new car despite another underwhelming back-to-back test at the Circuit de Barcelona-Catalunya.

Seventh (Irvine) and eighth (de la Rosa) in Brazil provided temporary hope before they returned to the tailenders at Imola. Unable to generate sufficient tyre temperature, the Jaguars were slower than the similarly powered Arrows A23s and retired with driveshaft failures. With Irvine sent to the back of the Spanish GP grid because his fuel did not match the FIA's approved sample, both cars retired at Barcelona. The A1-Ring also brought non-finishes and both drivers were lapped twice during the Monaco GP.

Only quicker than the Minardis so far, hopes rested on much anticipated upgrades to both car and engine. Irvine and de la Rosa used the revised CR-4 engine to qualify an improved 14th and 16th in Canada but retired, the Spaniard after surviving a high-speed brush with Allan McNish's Toyota and the concrete wall on the opening lap. De la Rosa was 11th at the Nürburgring but Irvine had a spin in the pitlane before hydraulic failure. Agathangelou and Handford reworked the recalcitrant R3 in the new wind tunnel with revised front wing, floor and sidepods.

Designated R3B, this version ran at Barcelona on 27–28 June and was taken to the British GP. That was a crushing disappointment for the car lacked mechanical grip and the understeer remained, although progress would eventually be made. Irvine spun in the Silverstone rain and de la Rosa was a lapped 11th. British F3 leader James Courtney was knocked out in an 180mph accident at

Monza's Variante Ascari when the suspension on his standard R3 failed in what was his last test for the team.

There was improvement at Magny-Cours with Irvine qualifying ninth – Jaguar's first top-ten start of the season – and challenging for points before his rear wing failed, while de la Rosa finished ninth. 'At least our car showed performance,' reflected the under-pressure Lauda. 'But the wing failure pisses me off like you wouldn't believe… wing failures should not happen.' Both drivers retired at Hockenheim and were off the pace in Hungary, which 13th-placed de la Rosa described as 'probably the most boring race I have ever driven'. Chief designer Russell then became the latest casualty with Arrows's Rob Taylor effectively his replacement when appointed head of vehicle design. Ex-BAR technical chief Malcolm Oastler arrived as director of engineering.

Cosworth power suited the high-speed demands of Spa-Francorchamps and Monza with new front suspension and revised aero, plus sticky Michelins, allowing both drivers to challenge for the top ten. Sixth in Belgium delivered Irvine's first point since Australia while de la Rosa was denied eighth when his left-rear suspension failed in the closing stages. Buoyed when the Spaniard topped the time sheets at the pre-Monza test, Jaguar was the surprise package of the Italian GP. Irvine qualified fifth and inherited third when Kimi Räikkönen and both Williams-BMWs retired. Having started eighth, de la Rosa was eliminated on lap one when he was hit by Felipe Massa's Sauber after missing a gear.

Ford's decision to supply Cosworth engines to Jordan in 2003 heightened speculation about Jaguar's future and Parry-Jones spent three months compiling a report for presentation to Ford's board in September. That supported Jaguar as Ford's works future while suggesting that the Premier Performance Division needed better technical leadership. Ford publicly reiterated its commitment to the team before the United States GP at Indianapolis, where Irvine was quick in morning practice before rising ambient temperatures adversely affected traction. Tenth in America, Irvine completed his F1 career by finishing ninth at Suzuka after another uncompetitive race for Jaguar. De la Rosa retired from both races with transmission failures.

LUCKY STRIKE BRITISH AMERICAN RACING HONDA

There were management and engineering changes at British American Racing after three years of under-achievement. Team principal Craig Pollock left on the eve of the 18 December launch of the BAR 004-Honda with Prodrive founder David Richards named as his replacement. BAR technical director since 1999, Malcolm Oastler led the design of the new car before being moved sideways before the season. 'If the BAR 004 is the best our design team can do,' Richards told *Autocar*, 'we will have to make fundamental changes.' His three-month company review led to redundancies in March, with Oastler and head of design Andy Green both relieved of their duties. The new technical director was already in place by then as Geoff Willis, who had turned down Jaguar's advances, had been poached from Williams and began work on 1 March 2002 following five months on 'gardening leave'.

BAR extended its Honda contract to the end of 2004 although the Japanese manufacturer renewed its agreement with Jordan as well. An unchanged driver pairing of Jacques Villeneuve and Olivier Panis was announced at the 2001 German GP, but Pollock's departure angered Villeneuve: 'If I could physically walk out I would, but I have a contract.' Relations between Richards and his star driver worsened when the new boss questioned if the Canadian's sizeable retainer could be better used for technical development. Anthony Davidson signed a one-year contract as reserve driver while Ryo Fukuda joined Darren Manning on the test team. Patrick Lemarié remained as development driver.

The bulky BAR 004-Honda was another evolutionary design although Oastler claimed it to be 90 percent new. The front wing followed contemporary thinking with curved lower central section, suspended beneath the high raised nose via two supports. The 004's transmission was developed in cooperation with Honda with a seven-speed longitudinal gearbox used for the first time. Talks were held with Michelin before BAR extended its Bridgestone deal. The 004 was too heavy, lacked downforce and was nervous on corner entry, so Willis oversaw a major upgrade in time for the Canadian GP with a new gearbox, rear suspension and revised aerodynamics.

Jacques Villeneuve, BAR 004-Honda (European GP)

Olivier Panis, BAR 004-Honda (Monaco GP)

Honda widened the vee angle of its latest V10 to 90 degrees to lower the centre of gravity but the RA002E was heavy and underpowered in comparison to leading rivals. Reliability was an issue with reduced revs used at first to protect the valve system. The definitive 2002 engine did not appear until the European GP, where Panis expressed reservations: 'I respect Honda a lot, but this new engine is not really a big step.' However, slow progress was made and a problem with the oil system was finally solved before the Italian GP so performance gains followed.

Former BAR operations director Otmar Szafnauer joined Honda as vice president of Honda Racing Development in Bracknell, reporting to president Shoichi Tanaka. There was closer integration between BAR and Honda with a dedicated test team established under former Jaguar engineer Mark Ellis.

Panis gave the 004 its shakedown at Barcelona on 7 January with Villeneuve taking over two days later. Initial optimism proved short-lived for Villeneuve was mystified by a loss of performance at the second test and the deficiencies were all too evident in Australia. It was the end of the season before he regularly broke into the qualifying top ten and he only scored points on two occasions. A crash through rear-wing failure cost him points in Australia and he languished outside the top six at the next five races. Seventh at Imola and Barcelona, he received a drive-through penalty for causing an accident with Heinz-Harald Frentzen in Austria before his engine failed on the last lap, the first of three successive failures. Panis retired from the first seven races. Victim of the first-corner chaos in Australia, he crashed into Jenson Button in

Monaco and suffered mechanical gremlins elsewhere. Panis finally finished when eighth in Canada and ninth at the Nürburgring.

It was Silverstone before BAR-Honda scored points when information from Richards's helicopter pilot stationed a couple of miles away helped predict changing weather. Villeneuve and Panis finished fourth and fifth to the obvious relief of the team. They retired from the French and German GPs although Panis used the new engine and soft Bridgestones to qualify seventh at Hockenheim. Gearbox electronic glitches ruined Hungary while Honda's Shuhei Nakamoto described Spa-Francorchamps as 'the weekend from hell for us'. With Villeneuve outside the points in Belgium and Italy, Panis made the most of a fine opening lap and his two-stop strategy at Monza to climb from 16th to sixth.

A year on from his lacklustre 2001 United States GP, Villeneuve enjoyed his most competitive weekend of 2002 at Indianapolis, converting seventh on the grid into a strong sixth by the finish. Another upgraded qualifying engine at Suzuka helped Villeneuve to his third successive top-ten start although both drivers retired following mechanical failures as BAR-Honda slumped to an unsatisfactory eighth in the standings.

GO KL MINARDI ASIATECH

Paul Stoddart's second season in charge of Minardi proved to be another year-long struggle to stay afloat. Having finished 11th in 2001, Minardi claimed the prize money previously owing to the now defunct Prost Grand Prix. That was challenged by four

Mark Webber, Minardi PS02-Asiatech (Australian GP)

rival teams and by Phoenix Finance's assertion that it had bought Prost's championship entry. That dispute, plus the economic recession, forced lay-offs in Minardi's research and development department in the spring as Stoddart warned of closure. Phoenix's case was rejected in London's High Court on 21 May, the FIA issued support for Minardi on 18 June and the money was finally paid on the proviso it would be returned if the unhappy teams won their case in arbitration, which was finally settled after the season.

Budget aside, Minardi enjoyed a settled winter in 2001/02 with its new engine partner already announced at the Belgian GP.

Having used the venerable Ford Zetec-R for four seasons, Minardi agreed a one-year free supply with Asiatech financial director John Gano for its Peugeot-based V10s. Malaysian backing from Kuala Lumpur's tourist board (Go KL) and lottery (Magnum) assured Alex Yoong's place in the team despite three lacklustre appearances in 2001. An experienced team-mate such as Heinz-Harald Frentzen or Jos Verstappen was mooted before F3000 runner-up Mark Webber was confirmed following impressive tests at Valencia and Misano in January. The addition of petrochemical giant Gazprom as associate sponsor during the season led to Sergey Zlobin

Alex Yoong, Minardi PS02-Asiatech (Italian GP)

becoming the first Russian to test an F1 car when he drove a PS01 at Fiorano and Mugello in September. Bryan Herta and David Saelens were among those to test during the season.

Yoong gave the evolutionary Minardi PS02-Asiatech its shakedown at Imola on 1 February. Under technical director Gabriele Tredozi's guidance, chief designer George Ryton and aerodynamicist Loïc Bigois opted for a higher nose and taller sidepods, while the more modern engine allowed the centre of gravity and rear bodywork to be lowered. The main change was pushrod/torsion bar front suspension in place of pullrods. With new cylinder heads and internals, the reliable Asiatech AT02 was coupled with the latest version of CRP's titanium six-speed gearbox. Minardi used Michelin tyres. Prost sporting director John Walton was hired in that role.

Stoddart's pre-season target of two championship points was immediately achieved with Webber a joyous fifth in Australia. The newcomer started 18th, avoided the first-corner pile-up and withstood Mika Salo's late pressure to earn the appreciation of the local crowd and an impromptu champagne moment with Stoddart on the podium. Yoong also stayed out of trouble to finish a career-best seventh. Minardi's true level was clear two weeks later in Malaysia when the cars qualified on the back row and retired. Webber scored 11th places at Interlagos and Imola while the struggling Yoong respectively finished 13th and missed the 107 percent qualifying cut.

Both lost front wings during qualifying in Spain and were forced to withdraw from the race when Webber's rear wing failed during the warm-up. The supports were strengthened for Austria where they occupied the final row once more. Yoong's engine broke while Webber finished last after his launch control failed at the start and he received a drive-through penalty for ignoring blue flags when mistakenly racing Mika Salo, who was actually a lap ahead. In Monaco, a puncture denied Webber a top-ten finish and Yoong crashed at Massenet.

Both finished in Canada with Webber 11th again. Penalised for speeding in the pitlane at that race and for jumping the start at the Nürburgring, Yoong failed to qualify for the British GP. Lapped twice during the European GP, Webber made early progress at Silverstone before clutch failure caused him to spin out at Stowe. The Australian passed Toyota and Jaguar rivals to snatch eighth in France with Yoong two seconds a lap slower and tenth. Yoong again failed to qualify at Hockenheim so was rested for the next two races with British American Racing reserve Anthony Davidson his surprise replacement. Justin Wilson had a seat fitting but was too tall (6ft 3in) and Jos Verstappen declined a short-term return. Davidson was fined $1,000 for speeding as he left the garages during FP1 in Hungary and spun out on both appearances for the team. Webber hit a mechanic at his first pitstop in Hungary and his gearbox failed after four laps of the Belgian GP.

Yoong admitted that he had 'a point to prove' during Monza

Anthony Davidson, Minardi PS02-Asiatech (Belgian GP)

testing and qualified last when he returned for the final three races of the season. Delayed by stalling at his pitstop in Italy, he retired in America and exited the Japanese GP following his second spin of the race. Worsening reliability accounted for Webber at Monza and Indianapolis, but he finished tenth (and last) at Suzuka where financial constraints forced Minardi to disable its power steering. By now a distant memory, Webber's Australian performance delivered ninth in the constructors' standings.

PANASONIC TOYOTA RACING

Toyota made its highly anticipated F1 entry in 2002. The third largest car company in the world originally announced its intention on 21 January 1999 with car and engine to be built at an expanded Toyota Motorsport GmbH facility in Cologne. Tsutomu Tomita was appointed team chairman to work with existing president Ove Andersson. The need to buy an existing team (Jordan, Arrows, Sauber, Minardi and Benetton were all touted) disappeared when Honda did not take up the 12th and final franchise. Toyota deposited the $48m bond with the FIA and incurred a further $12m penalty to defer entry until 2002. Technical director André de Cortanze, head of aerodynamics René Hilhorst and team manager Ange Pasquali all transferred from Toyota's sports car programme in 1999.

Allan McNish was named as test driver on 14 April 2000 and was confirmed as a race driver 18 months later. Mika Salo extricated himself from his Sauber contract to sign a three-year deal with Toyota on 24 August 2000.

Toyota Motorsport's general manager (engines), Norbert Kreyer, recruited project leader Luca Marmorini from Ferrari with Ilmor's Axel Wendorff named as head of design. The original V12 design was shelved when ten-cylinder engines became mandatory and the first 90-degree V10 was bench-tested on 18 September 2000. Minardi's Gianfranco Fantuzzi was appointed as team co-ordinator, while race engineers Humphrey Corbett and Dieter Gass arrived from Jaguar and Audi respectively. The Fuji circuit was acquired from Mitsubishi Estate Company in 2000 with plans to host the Japanese GP after the expiry of Honda-owned Suzuka's contract.

The Toyota TF101 test chassis was revealed at Paul Ricard, Toyota's designated European test track, on 23 March 2001. De Cortanze and chassis designer Jean-Claude Martens penned a conventional carbon-fibre/honeycomb monocoque with pushrod/torsion bar suspension all round. The 90-degree V10 (RVX-01) drove through a six-speed semi-automatic longitudinal gearbox. Toyota renewed its long and fruitful association with Michelin, Esso supplied fuel and lubricants and Panasonic became title sponsor during the summer.

Salo completed six exploratory laps after the launch but was sidelined for three weeks with a back injury when he crashed head-on at Signes a day later following a mechanical failure. After de Cortanze's departure following a disagreement with Andersson, Minardi's Gustav Brunner was poached as chief designer on 7 May 2001. An extensive test programme at 11 F1 circuits from Imola to Suzuka did not yield competitive times. Toyota believed that a new team was exempt from the winter testing ban but agreed to stop once it formally entered the World

Mika Salo, Toyota TF102 (Austrian GP)

Allan McNish, Toyota TF102 (Spanish GP)

Championship on 15 November following pressure from rivals.

Brunner began design of the Toyota TF102 on 1 June 2001 and claimed that 'every bolt and every nut is new' when the car was revealed in Cologne on 17 December. The first 2002 challenger to be launched, this was a lighter but overly conservative design with driver further reclined to lower the centre of gravity. The revised RVX-02 engine's 850bhp was the third most powerful in F1 and the TF102s were quickest in the speed trap in Australia. A six-speed gearbox was retained, redesigned to be lighter and smaller than before, while twin-keel mounting for the front suspension was investigated but not pursued. The car lacked rear downforce and traction, while chassis flex was an issue with kerbs such as those at Imola, Montréal and the Hungaroring upsetting the handling. A new half-scale wind tunnel at the Cologne factory became operational in July 2002.

The experienced Stéphane Sarrazin and Ryan Briscoe joined as test drivers and the latter was an unused standby in Australia after Salo was laid low with 'flu. Champ Car stars Cristiano da Matta and Toranosuke Takagi tested at Paul Ricard in May and Hélio Castroneves ran in September.

Toyota scored points at two of the first three races before tumbling down the order when it switched development focus. Andersson described the engine as 'reasonably good' but played down expectations when respectable times were achieved during Barcelona's first group test of 2002. The cars qualified midfield in Melbourne and suffered contrasting fortunes in the race. McNish was eliminated at the first corner while Salo survived a late spin to finish sixth, two laps down after changing a damaged track rod. McNish would have finished sixth in Malaysia had the team been ready for his second pitstop. Salo qualified a promising tenth at that race and the next. He was sixth in Brazil, where McNish picked up a puncture on the first lap and spun out after half distance.

Off the pace before retiring at Imola, both finished in the top ten in Spain and Austria, where Salo was delayed respectively by a puncture and by a late decision to make a pitstop behind the safety car. Ninth (Salo) and tenth (McNish) in Monaco was Toyota's best qualifying performance of the season and both drivers eyed the top six before McNish crashed at Ste-Dévote and Salo's tyres degraded, causing him to fade to ninth before crashing heavily in Casino Square after losing his brakes – the first of Salo's five successive retirements.

An aero upgrade was taken to Montréal but still the drivers struggled, McNish spinning out after a troubled run. He finished 14th at the Nürburgring despite severe shoulder pain caused by a new seat. Salo started a season-best eighth on the grid at Silverstone but McNish stalled at the start. With traction lacking at Magny-Cours, both had major engine failures. At Hockenheim, Salo finally finished again, albeit ninth and last, and McNish's race came to a fiery end. Another uncompetitive weekend brought a lowly double finish in Hungary, Salo having had a 25sec penalty for an unsafe release.

With both drivers informed that they would not be retained in 2003, Salo used brute power to qualify ninth and finish seventh at Spa-Francorchamps, just 0.439sec from scoring another point. Ninth in Belgium despite errant traction control, McNish made a good start to the Italian GP and lost sixth due to a suspension issue. Tenth on the grid at Monza, Salo ran as high as fourth before serving a stop-go penalty for crossing the pit exit line. The TF102s lacked balance and speed in the Indiana heat. McNish was unable to start at Suzuka after a huge qualifying accident at the 130R corner left him with a badly bruised knee, but Salo finished eighth on his final F1 appearance.

ORANGE ARROWS F1 TEAM

It was a sad irony that Arrows produced its best car in years but was unable to exploit it. 'It was an opportunity lost,' chief designer Sergio Rinland told *Autocourse*. 'The car was good, the engine was decent, the tyres were winners. It was a case of what might have been.' But F1's great underachievers spent more time in the High Court than on the track and slid into oblivion during the team's 25th and final F1 season.

Arrows owner Tom Walkinshaw informed Asiatech on 23 June

2001 that he would not renew its engine contract and a Cosworth deal was soon confirmed at the German GP. These engines were to be of the same specification as Jaguar's from mid-season with electronics supplied by Pi Research. Arrows renewed its tyre contract with Bridgestone. Jos Verstappen was announced as lead driver in June 2001 but doubts emerged by the end of the season due to his qualifying form against Enrique Bernoldi and the availability of Heinz-Harald Frentzen. Bernoldi was retained in the New Year and Frentzen's arrival in February prompted Verstappen to consult his lawyers. Furthermore, Arrows lost its case in London's Court of Appeal regarding Pedro Diniz's departure to Sauber in 1999 and the dispute with former sponsor Eurobet rumbled on.

Title sponsor Orange was in its final year and associate partner Red Bull re-signed, but 2002 was a story of financial peril. A potential £10m sale to Jaguar of the recently acquired DERA wind tunnel in Bedford fell through. That was suggested as the reason for late payment to Cosworth for its CR-3 engines and therefore delayed delivery. Arrows missed the start of testing as a consequence and the new A23's shakedown at Silverstone did not happen until 2 February. Design work was begun by technical director Mike Coughlan's team that included head of aerodynamics Nicolò Petrucci before the arrival of chief designer Sergio Rinland in September 2001. They evolved the A22 concept around a full-size fuel tank to allow strategic flexibility. The A23

Heinz-Harald Frentzen, Arrows A23-Cosworth (Canadian GP)

Enrique Bernoldi, Arrows A23-Cosworth (German GP)

had a twin-keel mount for the lower front suspension as seen on Rinland's Sauber C20 while aerodynamic efficiency was preferred to the low-drag emphasis of the previous car. The pushrod suspension had carbon-fibre wishbones and shock absorbers were mounted inboard. There were intermittent problems with the power steering when it was introduced at the San Marino GP. The A23 was a well-balanced car with useable downforce and good straight-line speed although the team's dire straits and consequent lack of development limited results.

Frentzen crashed twice following rear-wing failures at Valencia during the truncated winter programme. A 'solvable' fault in the little-tested traction control was blamed when both drivers stalled before the start of the Australian GP. They eventually emerged from the pitlane but were black-flagged for separate procedural offences: Frentzen received a stop-go penalty for ignoring yellow flags and then failed to stop at a red pit exit light; Bernoldi joined in the spare car but was excluded for switching cars after the race had started. A promising 11th in qualifying in Malaysia, Frentzen lost two laps when he stalled on the grid again. He got away at Interlagos and challenged for ninth but both A23s suffered track-rod failures. Loss of power blighted their Imola race.

A new floor and front wing were taken to Barcelona with an upgraded engine used in qualifying. An impressive tenth on the grid, Frentzen inherited sixth when the Renaults were delayed. The Austrian GP saw Bernoldi put himself out when he hit Frentzen at the start, after which the German hit Jacques Villeneuve's BAR-Honda at the next corner and could only finish 11th. Frentzen hinted at the A23's potential pace by topping the times in the Monaco GP warm-up and finished sixth despite a refuelling error necessitating an extra stop. Bernoldi was 12th after being forced up the Ste-Dévote escape road by Felipe Massa's lunge and serving a drive-through penalty for missing the chicane.

With budget running out, Walkinshaw called Bernie Ecclestone's claims that Arrows and Minardi were in danger of folding as 'irresponsible'. Volkswagen's Bernd Pischetsrieder was a visitor to the Austrian GP while American investors led by former BAR boss Craig Pollock and Red Bull's Dietrich Mateschitz were

among interested parties as Walkinshaw searched for new finance. There were staff departures at this time with Coughlan placed on 'gardening leave' before taking up an offer to join McLaren. A switch of brake supplier compromised driver confidence and overall performance in Montréal, where Bernoldi, 17th on the grid, outqualified Frentzen for the only time all year. The Brazilian finished tenth at the Nürburgring, with the German placed outside the top ten, as he had been in Canada.

Arrows's precarious position emerged in the High Court on 4 July when Justice Lightman described its finances as 'dire'. Morgan Grenfell Private Equity (45 percent stakeholders) won a court injunction that day to prevent an immediate sale to Red Bull. The deal did not include repayment of a 2001 loan and the bank considered the company undervalued. The cars did not run at Silverstone on Friday because Walkinshaw had to address debts to Cosworth and reschedule payments for the rest of the year. They qualified on Saturday and Frentzen ran eighth in the race after making an early pitstop but hopes of a morale-boosting result were lost to engine failure; Bernoldi's transmission failed.

Agreement with Morgan Grenfell was not forthcoming before the French GP, so the drivers were instructed to abort their session and not qualify to save money. They completed a full weekend at Hockenheim where Frentzen was stranded on the grid once more and both retired. Having missed the Hungarian GP, an eleventh-hour decision was taken to send the cars to Spa-Francorchamps as 'heads of agreement have been signed regarding the purchase of the team by an American investor'. However, the sale was not concluded before the weekend and they returned to Leafield after remaining idle on Friday. Arrows missed the rest of the season but confirmed that Olivier Behring of Asset Trust & Partners (ATP) had taken a controlling interest on 12 November, three days before the deadline to enter the 2003 World Championship.

However, patience had run out and the entry was rejected. ATP's takeover collapsed and the job losses extended to the wider TWR Group. Arrows entered liquidation on 13 January 2003 having competed in 382 world championship events in 25 years, without ever winning a race.

2002 RESULTS

DRIVER PERFORMANCE

DRIVER	CAR-ENGINE	AUS	MAL	BR	RSM	E	A	MC	CDN	EU	GB	F	D	H	B	I	USA	J
Rubens Barrichello	Ferrari F2001	[1] R	[3] R	[8] R	–	–	–	–	–	–	–	–	–	–	–	–	–	–
	Ferrari F2002	–	–	–	[2] 2 FL	[2] DNS	[1] 2	[5] 7 FL	[3] 3	[4] 1	[2] 2 FL	[3] DNS	[3] 4	[1] 1	[3] 2	[4] 1 FL	[2] 1 FL	[2] 2
Enrique Bernoldi	Arrows A23-Cosworth	[17] DSQ	[16] R	[21] R	[20] R	[14] R	[12] R	[15] 12	[17] R	[21] 10	[18] R	[21] DNQ	[18] R	–	NT DNP	–	–	–
Jenson Button	Renault R202	[11] R	[8] 4	[7] 4	[9] 5	[6] 12	[13] 7	[8] R	[13] 15	[8] 5	[12] 12	[7] 6	[13] R	[9] R	[10] R	[17] 5	[14] 8	[10] 6
David Coulthard	McLaren MP4-17-Mercedes-Benz	[4] R	[6] R	[4] 3	[6] 6	[7] 3	[8] 6	[2] 1	[8] 2	[5] R	[6] 10	[6] 3 FL	[9] 5	[10] 5	[6] 4	[7] 7	[3] 3	[3] R
Anthony Davidson	Minardi PS02-Asiatech	–	–	–	–	–	–	–	–	–	–	–	–	[20] R	[20] R	–	–	–
Pedro de la Rosa	Jaguar R3-Cosworth	[20] 8	[17] 10	[11] 8	[21] R	[16] R	[19] R	[20] 10	[16] R	[16] 11	–	–	–	–	–	–	–	–
	Jaguar R3B-Cosworth	–	–	–	–	–	–	–	–	–	[21] 11	[15] 9	[20] R	[15] 13	[11] R	[8] R	[17] R	[17] R
Giancarlo Fisichella	Jordan EJ12-Honda	[8] R	[9] 13	[14] R	[15] R	[12] R	[15] 5	[11] 5	[6] 5	[18] R	[17] 7	NT DNP	[6] R	[5] 6	[14] R	[12] 8	[9] 7	[8] R
Heinz-Harald Frentzen	Arrows A23-Cosworth	[15] DSQ	[11] 11	[18] R	[13] R	[10] 6	[11] 11	[12] 6	[19] 13	[15] 13	[16] R	[20] DNQ	[15] R	–	NT DNP	–	–	–
	Sauber C21-Petronas	–	–	–	–	–	–	–	–	–	–	–	–	–	–	[11] 13	–	–
Nick Heidfeld	Sauber C21-Petronas	[10] R	[7] 5	[9] R	[7] 10	[8] 4	[5] R	[17] 8	[7] 12	[9] 7	[10] 6	[10] 7	[10] 6	[8] 9	[18] 10	[15] 10	[10] 9	[12] 7
Eddie Irvine	Jaguar R3-Cosworth	[19] 4	[20] R	[13] 7	[18] R	[22] R	[20] R	[21] 9	[14] R	[17] R	–	–	–	–	–	–	–	–
	Jaguar R3B-Cosworth	–	–	–	–	–	–	–	–	–	[19] R	[9] R	[16] R	[16] R	[8] 6	[5] 3	[13] 10	[14] 9
Felipe Massa	Sauber C21-Petronas	[9] R	[14] 6	[12] R	[11] 8	[11] 5	[7] R	[13] R	[12] 9	[11] 6	[11] 9	[12] R	[14] 7	[7] 7	[17] R	[14] R	–	[15] R
Allan McNish	Toyota TF102	[16] R	[19] 7	[16] R	[17] R	[19] 8	[14] 9	[10] R	[20] R	[13] 14	[15] R	[17] 11	[17] R	[18] 14	[13] 9	[13] R	[16] 15	[18] DNS
Juan Pablo Montoya	Williams FW24-BMW	[6] 2	[2] 2 FL	[1] 5 FL	[4] 4	[4] 2	[4] 3	[1] R	[1] R FL	[1] R	[1] 3	[1] 4	[4] 2	[4] 11	[5] 3	[1] R	[4] 4	[6] 4
Olivier Panis	BAR 004-Honda	[12] R	[18] R	[17] R	[12] R	[13] R	[9] R	[18] R	[11] 8	[12] 9	[13] 5	[11] R	[7] R	[12] 12	[15] 12	[16] 6	[12] 12	[16] R
Kimi Räikkönen	McLaren MP4-17-Mercedes-Benz	[5] 3 FL	[5] R	[5] 12	[5] R	[5] R	[6] R	[6] R	[5] 4	[6] 3	[5] R	[4] 2	[5] R	[11] 4	[2] R	[6] R	[6] R	[4] 3
Mika Salo	Toyota TF102	[14] 6	[10] 12	[10] 6	[16] R	[17] 9	[10] 8	[9] R	[18] R	[10] R	[8] R	[16] R	[19] 9	[17] 15	[9] 7	[10] 11	[19] 14	[13] 8
Takuma Satō	Jordan EJ12-Honda	[22] R	[15] 9	[19] 9	[14] R	[18] R	[18] R	[16] R	[15] 10	[14] 16	[14] R	[14] R	[12] 8	[14] 10	[16] 11	[18] 12	[15] 11	[7] 5
Michael Schumacher	Ferrari F2001	[2] 1	[1] 3	–	–	–	–	–	–	–	–	–	–	–	–	–	–	–
	Ferrari F2002	–	–	[2] 1	[1] 1	[1] 1 FL	[3] 1 FL	[3] 2	[1] 1	[3] 2 FL	[3] 1	[2] 1	[1] 1 FL	[2] 2 FL	[1] 1 FL	[2] 2	[1] 2	[1] 1 FL
Ralf Schumacher	Williams FW24-BMW	[3] R	[4] 1	[3] 2	[3] 3	[3] 11	[2] 4	[4] 3	[4] 7	[2] 4	[4] 8	[5] 5	[2] 3	[3] 3	[4] 5	[3] R	[5] 16	[5] 11
Jarno Trulli	Renault R202	[7] R	[12] R	[6] R	[8] 9	[9] 10	[16] R	[7] 4	[10] 6	[7] 8	[7] R	[8] R	[8] R	[6] 8	[7] R	[11] 4	[8] 5	[11] R
Jacques Villeneuve	BAR 004-Honda	[13] R	[13] 8	[15] 10	[10] 7	[15] 7	[17] 10	[14] R	[9] R	[19] 12	[9] 4	[13] R	[11] R	[13] R	[12] 8	[9] 9	[7] 6	[9] R
Mark Webber	Minardi PS02-Asiatech	[18] 5	[21] R	[20] 11	[19] 11	[20] DNS	[21] 12	[19] 11	[21] 11	[20] 15	[20] R	[18] 8	[21] R	[19] 16	[19] R	[19] R	[18] R	[19] 10
Alex Yoong	Minardi PS02-Asiatech	[21] 7	[22] R	[22] 13	[22] DNQ	[21] DNS	[22] R	[22] R	[22] 14	[22] R	[22] DNQ	[19] 10	[22] DNQ	–	–	[20] 13	[20] R	[20] R

FORMULA 1 RACE WINNERS

ROUND	RACE (CIRCUIT)	DATE	WINNER
1	Foster's Australian Grand Prix (Albert Park)	Mar 3	Michael Schumacher (Ferrari F2001)
2	Petronas Malaysian Grand Prix (Sepang)	Mar 17	Ralf Schumacher (Williams FW24-BMW)
3	Grande Prêmio do Brasil (Interlagos)	Mar 31	Michael Schumacher (Ferrari F2002)
4	Gran Premio di San Marino (Imola)	Apr 14	Michael Schumacher (Ferrari F2002)
5	Gran Premio Marlboro de España (Catalunya)	Apr 28	Michael Schumacher (Ferrari F2002)
6	Grosser A1 Preis von Österreich (Spielberg)	May 12	Michael Schumacher (Ferrari F2002)
7	Grand Prix de Monaco (Monte Carlo)	May 26	David Coulthard (McLaren MP4-17-Mercedes-Benz)
8	Grand Prix Air Canada (Montréal)	Jun 9	Michael Schumacher (Ferrari F2002)
9	Allianz Grand Prix of Europe (Nürburgring)	Jun 23	Rubens Barrichello (Ferrari F2002)
10	Foster's British Grand Prix (Silverstone)	Jul 7	Michael Schumacher (Ferrari F2002)
11	Mobil 1 Grand Prix de France (Magny-Cours)	Jul 21	Michael Schumacher (Ferrari F2002)
12	Grosser Mobil 1 Preis von Deutschland (Hockenheim)	Jul 28	Michael Schumacher (Ferrari F2002)
13	Marlboro Magyar Nagydíj (Hungaroring)	Aug 18	Rubens Barrichello (Ferrari F2002)
14	Foster's Belgian Grand Prix (Spa-Francorchamps)	Sep 1	Michael Schumacher (Ferrari F2002)
15	Gran Premio Vodafone d'Italia (Monza)	Sep 15	Rubens Barrichello (Ferrari F2002)
16	SAP United States Grand Prix (Indianapolis)	Sep 29	Rubens Barrichello (Ferrari F2002)
17	Fuji Television Japanese Grand Prix (Suzuka)	Oct 13	Michael Schumacher (Ferrari F2002)

DRIVERS' CHAMPIONSHIP

	DRIVERS	POINTS
1	Michael Schumacher	144
2	Rubens Barrichello	77
3	Juan Pablo Montoya	50
4	Ralf Schumacher	42
5	David Coulthard	41
6	Kimi Räikkönen	24
7	Jenson Button	14
8	Jarno Trulli	9
9	Eddie Irvine	8
10=	Nick Heidfeld	7
	Giancarlo Fisichella	7
12=	Jacques Villeneuve	4
	Felipe Massa	4
14	Olivier Panis	3
15=	Mark Webber	2
	Mika Salo	2
	Heinz-Harald Frentzen	2
	Takuma Satō	2

Michael Schumacher's Ferrari F2002 takes control of the San Marino Grand Prix

CONSTRUCTORS' CHAMPIONSHIP

	CONSTRUCTORS	POINTS
1	Ferrari	221
2	Williams-BMW	92
3	McLaren-Mercedes-Benz	65
4	Renault	23
5	Sauber-Petronas	11
6	Jordan-Honda	9
7	Jaguar-Cosworth	8
8	BAR-Honda	7
9=	Toyota	2
	Arrows-Cosworth	2
	Minardi-Asiatech	2

Kimi Räikkönen went wheel-to-wheel with Michael Schumacher in Australia and challenged him until the final race of the season

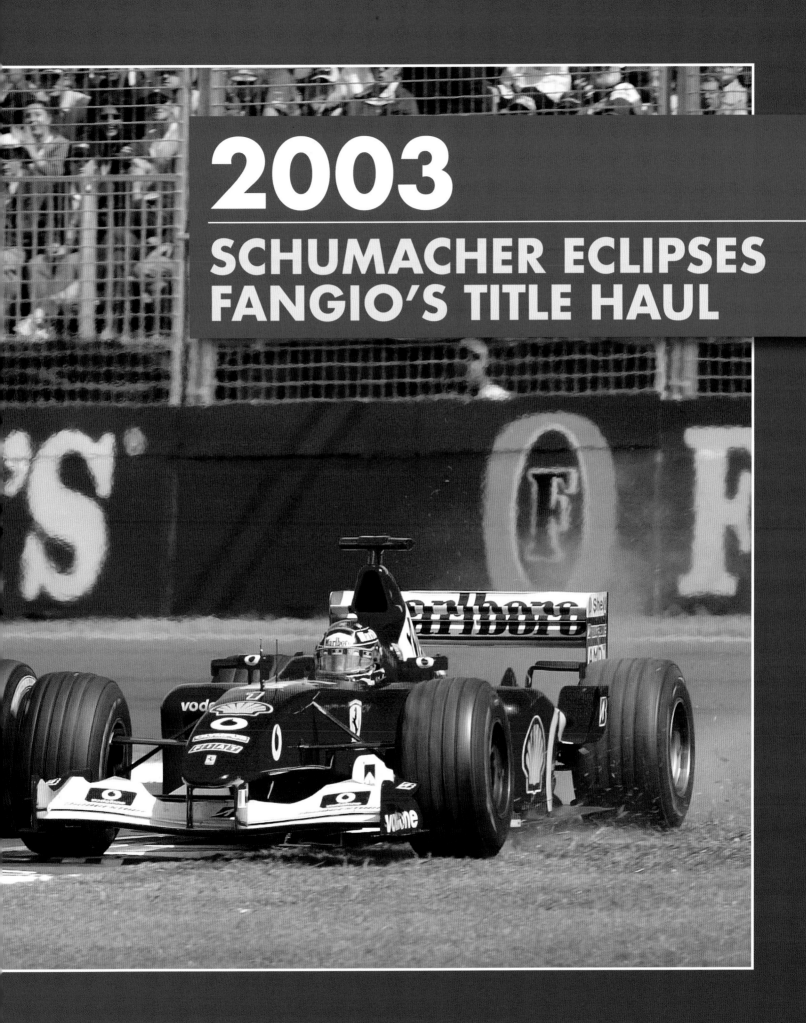

2003
SCHUMACHER ECLIPSES FANGIO'S TITLE HAUL

Fernando Alonso became the youngest grand prix winner to date with victory in Hungary

With costs spiralling and television audiences diminishing, FIA president Max Mosley presented the team principals with changes to the sporting regulations on 28 October 2002. Points were to be awarded to the top eight finishers on the scale 10–8–6–5–4–3–2–1, which Ferrari argued would reward consistency rather than outright speed. Bernie Ecclestone dismissed F1's new single-car qualifying as 'horrible' in an interview with *Agencia Estado*. Drivers set times one by one in reverse championship order on Friday to determine the running order for Saturday's single flying laps to decide grid positions. Refuelling and set-up changes were not allowed

Giancarlo Fisichella received his Brazilian GP trophy on the grid at Imola

between qualifying and the start, so competitors traded grid position for optimum race fuel strategy. Sunday warm-up was replaced by a 15-minute session before Saturday qualifying.

Teams outside the previous year's top three had until 28 February to accept two hours' free running for a third car on grand prix Fridays if in-season testing elsewhere was cut to 20 days. McLaren's Ron Dennis described Renault, Jaguar, Jordan and Minardi as 'Friday track cleaners' when they accepted, which drew a sharp retort from Eddie Jordan.

With Prost and Arrows having recently closed, it was vital that the ten remaining teams were kept solvent and on the grid. Dennis suggested a fighting fund for impoverished independents in return for rules stability, a possibility that was discussed at a meeting of team principals on 15 January. When that stability was not forthcoming, McLaren and Williams challenged the FIA in the International Chamber of Commerce in Lausanne. A renewed ban on traction control due from the British GP did not happen. Eddie Jordan and particularly Minardi's Paul Stoddart waged a vocal campaign for the manufacturer-backed teams to stand by the fighting fund. That dominated the Canadian GP weekend although Stoddart's threat to protest anyone using electronic driver aids at Silverstone was subsequently averted.

The Head And Neck Support (HANS) device was mandatory in 2003 despite initial resistance from some drivers. There was a deep soul-searching within F1 regarding improving 'The Show' and how to police track-limit infringements now that

A one-man track invasion threw the British Grand Prix into chaos

tarmac run-offs were replacing gravel traps at most circuits.

The future of traditional circuits in the sport's European heartland was placed at risk as F1 looked East for lucrative new hosts and to get around increasing restrictions on cigarette promotion. Spa-Francorchamps was dropped despite Belgium's 1 August 2003 tobacco advertising ban being rescinded. Plans for a Russian GP on Moscow's Nagatino Island failed when contracts could not be agreed. A 45mm downpour made a lottery of the 2003 Brazilian GP, where there were four safety-car periods before Fernando Alonso's Renault hit a wheel from Mark Webber's crashed Jaguar, forcing the race to be stopped. David Coulthard pitted from the lead a lap before that incident and Giancarlo Fisichella had just passed Kimi Räikkönen when the red flag flew. The results were initially declared after 53 laps with Räikkönen the winner but the stewards eventually changed that decision and Fisichella received the winner's trophy two weeks later at Imola. There was chaos after 11 laps of the British GP when protestor Neil Horan ran along Hangar Straight and oncoming cars narrowly missed him.

Tyres were key to the outcome of the World Championship. With Michelin in the ascendency and Michael Schumacher's Bridgestone-shod Ferrari having been lapped in Hungary, the FIA redefined how tyre widths were measured, forcing Michelin to reprofile its front tyres and diverting momentum to the *Scuderia*. Schumacher won his record sixth World Championship, eclipsing Juan Manuel Fangio, but this was a more competitive contest. Eight drivers from five teams won

a race and Kimi Räikkönen (McLaren-Mercedes) took the title battle to the final race. That was more due to consistency than winning pace, and McLaren-Mercedes was distracted by the saga of the unraced MP4-18. Dan Gurney was the public face of an unnamed new American team announced at the 2002 United States GP. The ambitious timescale to enter F1 in less than six months and lack of funding proved insurmountable.

Two ex-Ferrari engineers were accused of using data from their former employer while working on the 2003 Toyota. That prompted long-running legal proceedings although the Japanese team was not implicated.

The Head And Neck Support device became mandatory in 2003

Michael Schumacher, Ferrari F2002 (Australian GP)

SCUDERIA FERRARI MARLBORO

With no reason to change a winning team, Rubens Barrichello signed a two-year extension to remain as Michael Schumacher's team-mate. Furthermore, an announcement of 9 June 2002 confirmed that Schumacher, sporting director Jean Todt, technical director Ross Brawn, chief designer Rory Byrne, engine director Paolo Martinelli and his assistant Gilles Simon had all committed until the end of 2006. One important departure that month was Nikolas Tombazis, head of aerodynamics since 1998, who was placed on 'gardening leave' before a move to McLaren. Luca Baldisserri transferred to a factory role with Chris Dyer now Schumacher's race engineer. Gabriele delli Colli continued to be responsible for Barrichello's car.

Ferrari began 2003 with its old F2002 to help early reliability, although Schumacher crashed one of the old chassis on his first lap of Barcelona testing on 21 January and made his worst start to an F1 season to date. With both 2002 titles all but clinched, Ferrari had switched its attention to the new car in June 2002. The resulting F2003-GA was launched on 7 February, with the 'GA' referring to Fiat chairman Giovanni Agnelli, who died two weeks before the ceremony. At launch, Brawn promised that the F2003-GA was 'the biggest single step of improvement we have made… bigger than we made from 2001 to 2002'. This was an evolution of the F2002 with a slightly longer wheelbase, although the ban on refuelling between qualifying and the race compromised set-up options. There were twin-element bargeboards and distinctive

Rubens Barrichello, Ferrari F2002 (Malaysian GP)

Michael Schumacher, Ferrari F2003-GA (French GP)

sidepods, which had the option of cooling gills for hotter venues. The rounded diffuser had two vertical vanes on either side rather than one. Pushrod/torsion spring suspension was retained, with compact Sachs rotary rear shock absorbers fitted from Austria to aid packaging and improve tyre wear. The latest 90-degree type 052 V10 engine was integral with the seven-speed gearbox, which was slimmer than ever. Todt reiterated the mood of optimism around Maranello: 'The figures from the wind tunnel, from the stiffness, from the centre of gravity, from weight distribution, from the engine and the torque of the engine are all very encouraging.'

Ferrari's relationship with Bridgestone continued to be crucial. The team tested tyres more than any rival, *Autocourse* describing the commitment as 'some 120 days and around 200 different compound/construction combinations'. Felipe Massa, who was already being touted as a future Ferrari driver, joined Luca Badoer in the test team after being dropped by Sauber. Luciano Burti was released but did test at Fiorano on 2 September 2003.

The season began with a front-row lock-out in Australia but the race ended with no Ferrari driver on the podium for the first time

this millennium. Pole winner Schumacher only finished fourth after sustaining damage when forced across the grass by Kimi Räikkönen's McLaren. Barrichello jumped the start and crashed before he could serve his penalty. Having missed some tests in February due to back pain caused by the HANS device, Barrichello blamed it for his early Australian exit: 'It was really hurting me, and I lost concentration… The pain was unbearable.'

Barrichello was given dispensation to race without HANS in Malaysia, where he finished second. Schumacher needed a new front wing and received a drive-through penalty after colliding with Jarno Trulli on the opening lap but recovered to take sixth. Barrichello claimed pole position for his home race at Interlagos only for a fuel-feed issue to deny certain victory; Schumacher crashed at Turn 3 in the rain.

Early testing of the F2003-GA was beset by mechanical difficulties that caused Badoer to crash twice while the race drivers each had an engine failure at Mugello. This prompted postponement of the new car's scheduled debut at Imola, where family sadness overshadowed the Schumacher brothers' weekend.

Rubens Barrichello, Ferrari F2003-GA (Austrian GP)

Having qualified first and second, Michael and Ralf flew to Cologne to be with their mother Elisabeth, who died that evening. Michael's F2002 took the lead at the first of three pitstops and he ended premature talk of a Ferrari crisis with an emotional victory; Barrichello finished third.

With Brawn stating that the F2002 had 'reached the end of its development cycle', the F2003-GA was pressed into service at the Spanish GP following successful race runs during another Mugello test. 'We finally know that it is even faster than our old car and now there are no question marks about its reliability,' warned Schumacher. The result was instantaneous with Schumacher and Barrichello first and second in both qualifying sessions, and 1–3 in the race. The German closed to within two points of championship leader Räikkönen in Austria by converting another pole position into victory despite a flash fire at his first pitstop. Barrichello finished third after being delayed by a slow first fuel stop. Michelin's supremacy during Monaco qualifying condemned the Ferraris to racing in the pack on Sunday, with Schumacher third and Barrichello a frustrated eighth.

Outpaced by the Williams-BMWs in Canadian GP qualifying, Schumacher got ahead at the first pitstops and looked after fading brakes to win and move into the championship lead. Barrichello changed his front wing following an opening-lap altercation with Fernando Alonso's Renault and finished fifth. The deficit to Williams-BMW and Michelin continued at the next two races. Barrichello was an unobtrusive third at the Nürburgring and, troubled by understeer, spun on the opening lap of the French GP. Schumacher had his own spin at the 'Ring (when challenged by Juan Pablo Montoya) so could only manage fifth, but in France he passed both McLarens to take third. Ferrari received a $10,000 fine for an unsafe release during Friday practice at Magny-Cours when Schumacher ran into Mark Webber's Jaguar.

Barrichello used 'a car you dream of' to claim pole position at Silverstone. He dropped as low as eighth after the one-man track invasion triggered a second safety car but then made a series of on-track passes and took advantage of Kimi Räikkönen's error at Bridge corner to snatch a fine victory. Criticised for running Alonso off the road on the Hangar Straight on the opening lap, Schumacher recovered from 15th at the first pitstops to finish fourth. His championship advantage was reduced to a single point after he was lapped in Germany (following a puncture) and Hungary. Barrichello left those races without adding to his score, hit by Ralf Schumacher at the Hockenheim start and due to high-speed rear-suspension failure during the Hungarian GP.

Ferrari protested Michelin's tyres following its sobering defeat at the Hungaroring and this was upheld. That ruling forced Michelin to modify its construction and handed the initiative back to Maranello, as confirmed in testing and by Schumacher's pole position for the Italian GP. He emerged from an opening-lap dice with Montoya at the Roggia chicane with the lead and was unchallenged thereafter. His race average of 153.842mph eclipsed the 1971 Italian GP at a pre-chicane Monza as the fastest GP in history. Only seventh on the grid at Indianapolis, Schumacher scored a resounding victory in changeable conditions to stand on the verge of a sixth title. Barrichello qualified and finished third in Italy before Montoya ran into him after two laps of the United States GP.

With Räikkönen needing victory in Japan to stand any chance of denying Schumacher, formalities were completed when Barrichello converted pole and beat the Finn by 11.085sec to confirm his fourth position in the final drivers' standings. After a damp track hampered his qualifying efforts, Schumacher started 14th (his worst starting position since Belgium in 1995) and his race to the title was anything but straightforward. He needed a new front wing when he ran into the back of Takuma Satō's BAR-Honda during the early laps and then collided with his brother before recovering to finish eighth, which would have been enough even if Räikkönen had won.

Ferrari won the constructors' championship for the fifth successive year after a hard-fought campaign on and off the track.

BMW WILLIAMS F1

BMW produced the most powerful engine in F1 but there was growing frustration as another title challenge stuttered before it had started. Senior management in Munich sought increased influence over chassis development as Williams were too slow to hone the all-new FW25 and its revised philosophy. Negotiations between the two companies to extend their partnership beyond 2004 rumbled on until June when a new five-year deal was agreed.

Ralf Schumacher was under contract to the end of 2004 and a two-year extension was agreed with Juan Pablo Montoya to cover that period. However, their relationship was uneasy at best, and both men had tensions with team personnel as well. They wanted better machinery, and the team wanted them to work harder. As chief operations engineer Sam Michael said at launch of the new car: 'Both our drivers are certainly capable of being world champions, but they're the same as everyone else in the team in that they need to work harder.' Montoya responded: 'You hear it every five minutes that you need to do the things the way Michael [Schumacher] does... but Michael wins because he has got the car with which to win, and we haven't.'

Marc Gené was confirmed as reserve driver in the autumn while Williams looked to replace Jaguar-bound Antônio Pizzonia as test driver. Giorgio Pantano and Vitantonio Liuzzi were tried at Valencia during a 26–29 November 2002 session without obtaining a role. Olivier Beretta ran at Barcelona and Valencia in January and Estonian Formula Ford driver Marko Asmer tested at the Catalan venue in July before being confirmed. As part of the prize for winning the Formula BMW Championship, 17-year-old Nico Rosberg drove a Williams FW24-BMW at Barcelona on 3 December 2002. A long-awaited driver swap took place at Indianapolis on the Wednesday before the Canadian GP. Four-time NASCAR champion Jeff Gordon sampled a Williams FW24-BMW before Montoya tried the American's Chevrolet Monte Carlo. BMW lost its F1 development director Werner Laurenz to Mercedes-Benz at the end of 2002.

The latest 90-degree BMW V10 (P83) was fired on the dyno on 31 July 2002 and track tested in a modified FW24B from September. A back injury forced Schumacher to withdraw from the first Barcelona test of 2003 after just five laps on 13 January, although he was fit to return to the Spanish circuit for the FW25's launch 18 days later.

Gone was the evolutionary approach to the FW24 as Williams-BMW sought to overthrow Ferrari. When the FW25 was revealed, technical director Patrick Head admitted that 2002 had been 'pretty uncomfortable for all of us because we were down on expectations, so we're pretty much on tenterhooks... about this car'. Gavin Fisher's design team adopted a clean sheet of paper once the full extent of Ferrari's advantage became obvious at the 2002 Spanish GP. The overall dimensions were much reduced with lower centre of gravity, shorter wheelbase (to make handling more responsive) and tightly packaged 'Coke bottle' rear. The flat front wing at launch was replaced by a contoured version by round three. Fisher did not follow the fashion for twin-keel front-suspension mounting because 'we've gone with what the wind tunnel tells us'. The BMW V10 nestled under an angular airbox that sported a dorsal fin from Silverstone. The small, lightweight six-speed gearbox was designed with BMW's input.

Initial Barcelona tests were underwhelming before the full aero kit with new front wing and turning vanes (rather than larger bargeboards) was added at Valencia. With the drivers struggling for balance and downforce on their return to Barcelona and at Jerez, the Williams FW25-BMW was initially difficult to set up

Ralf Schumacher, Williams FW25-BMW (Monaco GP)

Juan Pablo Montoya, Williams FW25-BMW (Austrian GP)

but eventually emerged as the class of the field. However, that slow initial development prevented a title challenge and aerodynamicists Jason Somerville and Nick Alcock had already left in the spring. Under pressure to sort its chassis, Williams turned to the past. Frank Dernie rejoined the team he had left in 1988 as special projects engineer in May and worked alongside Montoya's race engineer Tony Ross from the British GP.

Criticised by drivers and engine partner alike before the Australian GP, Williams began the season with the rear suspension and interim gearbox from the FW24B test chassis. They improved during the weekend with Montoya claiming a morale-boosting third on the grid. He took advantage of Ferrari problems to take the lead by not changing tyres at his final stop. However, that worn rubber caused him to spin in Turn 1 with ten laps to go although his second-place finish was 'a positive surprise' according to Ralf Schumacher. Eighth in Australia following a slow pitstop and a couple of off-track excursions, Schumacher recovered from poor qualifying to finish fourth in Malaysia. Montoya's chances at Sepang ended on the opening lap when he lost his rear wing after being hit by Pizzonia's Jaguar.

The FW25s had the *pukka* 2003 rear end and gearbox for the 25–28 March Barcelona test, where Ralf Schumacher was quickest. They qualified in the top ten for the subsequent Brazilian GP despite choosing a heavy fuel load. Montoya was fifth when he crashed while Schumacher was denied points by the timing of the red flag. Both Schumacher brothers qualified on the front row at Imola before flying home to be with their mother Elisabeth, who had fallen into a coma. Mourning her death on Saturday evening, Ralf led the opening stint of the race from the Ferraris and Montoya only for pitstop errors to drop the Williams pair to fourth and seventh by the finish.

Montoya survived a 180mph testing accident at Silverstone's Becketts corner and was banned from driving in France when caught doing 204kph on a 130kph road. With BMW thought to be considering its options after 2004 and criticism from BMW motorsport director Gerhard Berger widely reported, both drivers scored points in Spain despite struggling for set-up. Montoya qualified third in Austria and took the lead when Michael Schumacher's Ferrari caught fire in the pits. Troubled by a water

leak throughout, he was pulling away when BMW suffered its only failure of the season. That later prompted BMW technical director Mario Theissen to say: 'Even the best engine cannot run without water.' Schumacher finished sixth in Austria.

The resurgence continued in Monaco, prompting Berger, who was to leave BMW after the European season, to declare that 'the championship is not a lost cause'. Schumacher qualified on pole, with Montoya third, and led a Williams-BMW 1–2 for the first 20 laps. Montoya made the better pitstop and secured his second F1 victory by fending off Kimi Räikkönen and Michael Schumacher to the chequered flag. Ralf finished only fourth after locking up at Rascasse and losing time as he reversed away from the barrier.

Schumacher led a Williams-BMW front-row lock-out in Montréal but they suffered excessive brake wear in the race and were beaten by the similarly affected Michael Schumacher. The Ferrari assumed a decisive lead at the first pitstops and was shadowed to the finish by the brakeless Williams-BMWs. After the race, Patrick Head questioned whether second-placed Ralf Schumacher could have tried harder to pass his brother. Montoya recovered from an early spin to finish third with just 1.355sec covering the top three.

With the engine deal confirmed to the end of 2009, Williams-BMW was the team to beat on the return to Europe, where Ralf Schumacher led successive 1–2 finishes at the Nürburgring and Magny-Cours. A new aero package at the European GP included revised sidepods with exhausts that exited through chimneys in front of simplified flick-ups. Schumacher used an extended first stint at that former race to wrestle the lead from Räikkönen at the pitstops and was unchallenged once the Finn retired. In France, he secured his third pole in four races and led throughout, sealing his victory after responding strongly to Montoya's early third stop. Having survived a feisty battle with Michael Schumacher at the Nürburgring that ended with the Ferrari in a spin, Montoya tried to undercut his team-mate in France and was furious when Ralf covered that move. The colourful radio messages that followed caused such dismay that Sir Frank Williams wrote to Montoya telling him that he would need to look for an alternative employer after the 2004 season.

Momentum within the team swung towards the Colombian at the next two races. Second at Silverstone despite being delayed

Marc Gené, Williams FW25-BMW (Italian GP)

when double-stacked in the pits, Montoya qualified on pole position at Hockenheim (0.018sec ahead of Ralf) and beat David Coulthard to victory by 65.459sec – the largest winning margin since 1995. After Schumacher damaged a turning vane on the Silverstone kerbs, soaring temperatures forced an extra pitstop to have it removed. In Germany he was adjudged to have caused the start-line accident that also accounted for Kimi Räikkönen and Rubens Barrichello.

With the resulting ten-place grid penalty for the Hungarian GP replaced by a $50,000 fine on appeal, Schumacher qualified second only to spin down to 18th at the second corner of the race. Montoya also made a poor start before both staged fine comeback drives to finish third (Montoya, despite a late spin of his own) and fourth (Schumacher). Williams-BMW now led the constructors' championship with Montoya just a point adrift in the drivers' standings, but their challenge was derailed by the FIA's ruling on how tyre widths were measured.

Then Schumacher suffered concussion in a high-speed testing accident at Monza's first Lesmo corner, his car pitched into a barrel roll when the rear suspension failed. He was passed fit to race in the Italian GP but withdrew on Saturday morning. Montoya qualified and finished second with stand-in Gené a noteworthy fifth on his race return.

Williams-BMW's title challenge evaporated during disastrous races at Indianapolis and Suzuka. Montoya made a slow start in America from fourth and received a drive-through penalty for causing an avoidable accident with Barrichello on lap three. His sixth-place finish was not enough to prolong lingering title hopes. Schumacher ran second on his return from injury only to crash when it rained with team and driver blaming each other for not changing to wet-weather tyres. Williams-BMW entered the final race just three points behind Ferrari but left Japan empty-handed – the only time Williams-BMW failed to score all season. Second on the grid, Montoya led the opening nine laps until his hydraulics failed. Starting last after rain ruined his qualifying lap, Schumacher spun twice and lost his front wing against his brother's rear wheel, leaving him 12th despite setting the fastest race lap.

Williams-BMW was championship runner-up once more with Montoya third in the drivers' standings.

WEST McLAREN MERCEDES

McLaren-Mercedes confirmed an unchanged line-up of David Coulthard and Kimi Räikkönen when Mika Häkkinen announced in a video press conference at the 2002 German GP that he was not returning from his sabbatical. Reserve driver Alexander Wurz was handed a three-year contract to deflect interest from Toyota with Pedro de la Rosa added to the testing strength on the eve of the season. Mercedes-Benz restructured the newly renamed Mercedes-Ilmor to fill the void created by the death of co-founder Paul Morgan. Mario Illien remained as the engine manufacturer's technical director with Hans-Ulrich Maik appointed managing director. Werner Laurenz, Gerhard Holy and Mike Wilson were all lured from BMW.

An early decision was taken to start the season with an updated MP4-17 so that Adrian Newey and the technical department could formulate radical ideas for the MP4-18. 'It is hard to think of a Formula 1 car in recent times that has excited more interest and speculation than the McLaren MP4-18,' enthused *Autosport* when it was finally tested on 21 May. Newey's brief had been to make a step-change to overtake Ferrari rather than evolving the existing car. The MP4-18 was a super-light, slender design with a long needle nose, curved front wing, wide channel between the twin-keel front-suspension mountings, and 'size zero' packaging to its waisted 'Coke bottle' rear. The rounded sidepods were shorter and fell away to an extremely low rear with side winglets and flick-ups ahead of the back wheels. The inboard torsion bar/pushrod suspension benefited from a year's data with Michelin tyres.

However, impressive wind-tunnel results could not be replicated on track with interaction between the chassis and the leading edge of the sidepods causing an aerodynamic imbalance. The drivers reported that the MP4-18 was unstable and struggled to make the tyres work. The low-slung Mercedes FO110P V10 engine was also difficult to work on and slow to change. Its exhausts were initially blown into the diffuser although these were soon repositioned. The seven-speed gearbox was a revised version of the existing aluminium unit rather than the rumoured titanium/carbon-fibre double-clutch development. The brake callipers were mounted vertically instead of horizontally, and this arrangement was also used on the MP4-17D at heavy-braking circuits from Canada onwards.

Once the season was under way, testing of the MP4-18 continued

Kimi Räikkönen, McLaren MP4-17D-Mercedes-Benz (Italian GP)

to be problematical and its race debut was postponed time and again. On the first day of a Paul Ricard test, Wurz had to protect the gearbox by short-shifting and avoiding seventh, restricting him to a tenth of the mileage achieved by Coulthard's MP4-17D. A hydraulic issue was solved but overheating and excessive engine vibration persisted. There were crashes at Barcelona and Jerez, for Räikkönen and Wurz respectively, and the new car twice failed its side-impact test. The MP4-18 was just too ambitious and set the team back 18 months because it compromised 2004 as well. McLaren finally abandoned it in September.

The updated MP4-17D was already dominating pre-season testing by the time the MP4-18's layout was finalised in February. The existing car was substantially reworked around the original monocoque by a team led by Neil Oatley. Its new front suspension and gearbox were introduced in the autumn of 2002 with a revised aerodynamic package, including different wings, added during the winter. McLaren's twin-prong approach appeared vindicated with victories for the MP4-17D in the opening two races, although it did not win again.

Qualifying positions outside the top ten in Australia did not

bode well but pre-race rain upset the weekend's form book with McLaren-Mercedes's fortunes transformed by early stops for wet tyres and extra fuel. Räikkönen did this after the formation lap and came from the pitlane to finish third. He forced Michael Schumacher onto the grass as they went wheel-to-wheel and would have won but for a drive-through penalty for speeding in the pitlane. Coulthard pitted during the first safety car and benefitted from the misfortune of others to score an unexpected win.

Coulthard was second when his electrics failed on the third lap of the Malaysian GP, leaving Räikkönen to take the lead at the first pitstops and ease to his maiden victory by 39.286sec. The Finn was originally declared winner of the Brazilian GP although he was demoted to second in the appeal court. Coulthard had started that race from the front row and pitted from the lead just a lap before the race was red-flagged while he was running fourth.

McLaren-Mercedes qualified with a heavy fuel load at Imola where a two-stop strategy brought second place (Räikkönen) and fifth (Coulthard). Spain was a disaster with both drivers involved in opening-lap accidents. Last on the grid after aborting his qualifying lap following an 'off' at Turn 7, Räikkönen crashed into Antônio

David Coulthard, McLaren MP4-17D-Mercedes-Benz (Japanese GP)

Pizzonia's stalled Jaguar on the start line. Coulthard collided with Jarno Trulli's Renault at the first corner and was hit by Jenson Button (BAR) as he climbed back through the field. With Coulthard struggling to adapt to single-lap qualifying, Räikkönen started and finished second in Austria as Schumacher's Ferrari F2003-GA won again, with the downbeat Scot fifth.

Räikkönen qualified second in Monaco and maintained his narrow title lead by finishing in that position when 1.720sec covered the top three, but seventh-placed Coulthard struggled again. In Montréal, where the MP4-17Ds had revised front suspension but suffered overheating brakes all weekend, McLaren-Mercedes surrendered the points lead it had held all year. Coulthard was fifth when forced to retire with loss of gears. Having hurt his knee in his MP4-18 shunt at Barcelona, Räikkönen spun during his qualifying run and so started from the pitlane with a heavy fuel load. After a puncture ruined his one-stop strategy, he could only finish sixth.

Räikkönen proved that the MP4-17D was still competitive at the European GP by snatching his first pole position and dominating until his engine failed. Coulthard's qualifying travails continued but in the race he challenged Fernando Alonso for fourth until he spun at the chicane with four laps to go when surprised by the heavy-braking Renault. Slower than Ferrari and Williams-BMW in France, Räikkönen and Coulthard finished fourth and fifth despite the Finn having a rear brake disc shatter with three laps to go and Coulthard upending two mechanics without injury at a pitstop. At Silverstone, Räikkönen emerged from the final pitstops with the lead but both Rubens Barrichello and Juan Pablo Montoya then passed him. Coulthard was fifth after losing time when his headrest came adrift.

Räikkönen made a fast start to the German GP only to be eliminated in the Barrichello/Ralf Schumacher first-corner shunt. Coulthard inherited second – his first podium finish since Australia – following Michael Schumacher's late puncture. Kimi's distant second in Hungary maintained his title hopes before a much-needed upgrade at Monza, including revised electronics, brakes

Alexander Wurz, McLaren MP4-18-Mercedes-Benz (Paul Ricard testing)

Fernando Alonso, Renault R23 (Hungarian GP)

and exhaust chimneys from the MP4-18. Fourth in Italy, Räikkönen qualified on pole at Indianapolis only for heavy rain to turn the race in Bridgestone's favour, handing Michael Schumacher a victory that left him needing a single point at the last race, with Räikkönen second after switching back to dry Michelins. Coulthard was fifth in Hungary after switching to a two-stop strategy and retired from the Italian and United States GPs.

Needing a miracle to steal the title at the Japanese finale, Räikkönen's chances were knocked by a heavy crash during Saturday free practice. Starting eighth and without the race pace to threaten the victory he required, Räikkönen finished second – and championship runner-up. Coulthard was third having dutifully shadowed his team-mate while the pair hoped for an unlikely double Ferrari retirement.

McLaren-Mercedes finished third in the constructors' championship, two points behind Williams-BMW.

MILD SEVEN RENAULT F1

Managing director of the British operation at Enstone, Flavio Briatore extended his power base to Viry-Châtillon when he replaced Jean-Jacques His as head of the engine facility. Amid mounting criticism of Renault's wide-angle engine philosophy, His was initially given a development role before joining Maserati

in May. Bernard Dudot, engine guru from the 1990s, had already returned from Nissan's IndyCar programme by that time as deputy managing director at Viry-Châtillon. His remit also included management of a small engine team established at Enstone with staff from defunct Tom Walkinshaw Racing.

Talks were held with Jenson Button before the promotion of reserve driver Fernando Alonso was confirmed in July 2002. Button had outraced Jarno Trulli thus far, but the Italian was already contracted so was retained for 2003. Renault F1 president Patrick Faure echoed Briatore's faith in the youngster: 'We believe we have in Alonso somebody who is going to be one of the very best drivers in the future.' Faure set a target of multiple podium finishes and retaining fourth overall as Renault entered the second of its five-year quest to finally win the constructors' title.

Renault was the highest-ranked team to opt for reduced in-season testing in return for two hours' free running on GP Fridays. Romain Dumas, Tiago Monteiro, Sébastien Bourdais and Franck Montagny tested in December before Renault chose experience for its Friday man. Allan McNish signed in January and his contribution was crucial to the development Renault achieved during 2003. Montagny was also named as a test driver and replaced McNish at the French GP, although rain and engine issues limited his mileage.

The Renault R23 with full Mild Seven branding was unveiled in

Jarno Trulli, Renault R23 (European GP)

Lucerne on 20 January. The shakedown followed three days later at Paul Ricard where French law demanded removal of tobacco logos.

Technical director Mike Gascoyne's contract ran until 2005 but he was placed on 'gardening leave' in the summer when he accepted Toyota's advances for 2004. Bob Bell, Gascoyne's deputy since 2001, was promoted by the end of the season. Starting in October 2001, Tim Densham headed the creative process for the R23, evolving the Mark Smith-led Renault R202. Its pushrod/ torsion bar suspension was revised but Michelin's variable-camber Optimal Patch de Contact (OPC) system, which always maximised tyre contact with the track surface, was not raced. The R23 featured a drooping nose section and wind-tunnel data suggested that aerodynamic efficiency improved by 15 percent. Better reliability and reduced engine vibration were key objectives for Renault's

latest wide-angle V10, which had a more rigid new block but was heavier than its predecessor. Power output at the start of the season was still adrift of BMW and Ferrari, by at least 80bhp, and torque was lacking in slow and medium corners. The periscope exhausts were integrated into the sidepod-mounted rear winglets.

A new front wing at Imola had revised channels on the outside of the endplates and downforce in Monaco was augmented by an additional wing over the rear axle. There were double bargeboards and a new rear wing for that race with the endplates detached from the upper element to the back. New bodywork was introduced for the British GP at Silverstone.

The prototype engine first ran at the 26–29 November Valencia test in a modified R202B chassis that featured 2002 bodywork around the R23's monocoque and six-speed titanium/carbon

Allan McNish, Renault R23 (Hungarian GP)

gearbox. The R23 was a nimble and well-balanced chassis with great traction and aerodynamics and was easy on its tyres. The launch electronics normally ensured fast starts and director of engineering Pat Symonds was quick to optimise strategy following the new qualifying rules, with his preference for a low-fuel qualifying run and short opening stint becoming standard.

The engine had not completed a race distance on the dyno or in testing before the Australian GP, so Renault's double finish was a welcome surprise. Starting on dry tyres, the cars ran second and third before the early safety car. Alonso refuelled at that time and came from the back of the field to finish seventh, while Trulli's stop when the safety car was deployed for a second time vaulted him to fifth. Malaysia confirmed both Renault's upward trajectory and the arrival of a new star. Alonso became the youngest pole winner to date when he headed a Renault qualifying 1–2 (its first since France in 1983), led the opening laps and finished a competitive third. Trulli recovered from being spun around by Michael Schumacher's opening-lap assault and a self-induced error to pass Button on the last lap for fifth.

Alonso was running third on lap 54 of the wet Brazilian GP when Mark Webber crashed at the final corner. The Spaniard hit a loose wheel from the Jaguar at unabated speed despite yellow flags and crashed into both barriers in a heavy accident that forced the race to be abandoned. Alonso escaped with a cut left leg and was classified third once results had been confirmed. Trulli qualified fifth and finished eighth to register Renault's third successive double score. After sixth place at Imola, Alonso's growing reputation was further enhanced at his home race, where he qualified third and used the undercut to finish second and split the

Ferraris. Trulli started fourth but was eliminated at the first corner.

A new-specification engine was introduced at the Austrian GP for what was an ultimately disappointing weekend. Last but one on the grid after running wide at Turn 5 during his qualifying attempt, Alonso was forced to start from the pitlane in the spare car due to a problem with his intended race engine. Fuelled 'long' for a one-stop strategy, he was fifth when he finally pitted although another engine failure soon ended his day; Trulli finished eighth. Renault was fancied for success in Monaco, where the Italian qualified fourth in both sessions and led a couple of laps during the first pitstops before slipping to sixth. Alonso, who only started eighth after various 'offs', passed his team-mate at the second stops and finished fifth. Alonso's impressive campaign continued with fourth places in Canada and at the Nürburgring while Trulli was a non-finisher. They retired within a lap of each other at Magny-Cours, Alonso after a spectacular blow-up.

With the new aero package a success, Trulli snatched a surprise front-row start at Silverstone, led until the first pitstops and finished sixth. Alonso only qualified eighth after struggling for grip and was forced onto the grass by Michael Schumacher's robust defence on the opening lap as he attempted to pass on the high-speed approach to Stowe. Engine failure again ended his race.

After third (Trulli) and fourth (Alonso) in Germany, Hungary's low-speed layout was ideal for the R23 and Michelin rubber. Alonso started from pole and led every lap bar one to score Renault's first victory since its return as a works team. The youngest GP winner to date, ending Bruce McLaren's 44-year record, he received a congratulatory phone call from King Juan Carlos I. Trulli finished seventh after a wild qualifying lap and

Franck Montagny, Renault R23 (French GP)

concern about the balance of his car during the race.

The Michelin teams were all affected by the FIA's tyre ruling before the Italian GP and Renault had a weekend to forget. Last on the grid after a traction-control glitch caused him to spin, Alonso hit Jos Verstappen's Minardi at the start but after pitting for repairs drove a forceful race to claim eighth, while Trulli was sidelined by hydraulics failure on the opening lap. Trulli scored points at Indianapolis and Suzuka and completed the season with an 8–8 qualifying record against his highly rated young team-mate. Alonso's engine failed in both races, in Japan when he looked on course for another victory.

Fourth in the constructors' standings satisfied Renault's stated pre-season ambitions while sixth-placed Alonso was fêted as a future World Champion.

LUCKY STRIKE BRITISH AMERICAN RACING HONDA

An exclusive partnership between British American Racing and Honda was confirmed on 18 August 2002, with regular podium finishes the ambition. Jacques Villeneuve said the BAR 005-Honda looked like 'a proper F1 car' but suspect reliability and Bridgestone's focus on Ferrari were blamed when early promise faded. That said, BAR-Honda had its best season since 2000 with fifth in the constructor's standings.

Villeneuve remained for the final year of his lucrative contract, despite team principal David Richards questioning whether the money would be better spent by the engineering department. Olivier Panis was released after Jenson Button signed a two-year deal, with BAR holding a two-year option to extend, a day after

being informed that Renault would not retain him. The rivalry between the drivers as they competed for their F1 futures was a significant subplot. Button admitted that 'Jacques just doesn't speak to me' before the campaign started while Villeneuve knew he needed to impress: 'If I have a bad season, I will be skiing next year. If I have a good season, I will be racing.' Button bolstered his reputation as his team-mate's exit loomed.

BAR-Honda continued its private test programme rather than opting for extra running on grand prix Fridays. Ralph Firman and Kosuke Matsuura were tried in December before Takuma Satō signed a three-year contract, initially as reserve driver. Satō's F3 team-mate Anthony Davidson was rehired as test driver. Honda drafted in Toyoharu Tanabe and Yusuke Hasegawa to work directly with the drivers, hired ex-Sauber technical director Leo Ress as a consultant and poached transmission ace Jörg Zander from Toyota. This was Geoff Willis's first full season as technical director and Gary Savage was promoted to be his deputy in August.

The BAR 005-Honda was launched in Barcelona on 14 January with Villeneuve predicting that the team 'should be able to fight everyone, except Ferrari'. Willis described the BAR 004 as 'out-of-date, clunky and expensive to manufacture', so started the design process with a clean sheet of paper. The long wheelbase was retained with turn-in stability and lower centre of gravity key aims. The chassis was stiffer and lighter than before but the car was still too heavy and bulky. Davidson hailed the aerodynamics following a trouble-free test debut at Barcelona. The season brought an extensive development programme with five major upgrades. A new rear wing increased downforce at Monaco, then its lower element was modified for the French GP to twist and

Jenson Button, BAR 005-Honda (San Marino GP)

Jacques Villeneuve, BAR 005-Honda (Monaco GP)

widen towards its endplates. Another major upgrade at Silverstone featured a new diffuser and sidepods plus narrower 'Coke bottle' rear. rear. Pushrod/torsion bar suspension was retained.

Honda shed 15kg in its RA003E engine while claiming more power and an improved torque curve. An initial engine-installation issue caused failures and limited winter mileage. A B-specification engine appeared in Australia but was set aside after practice breakdowns. Marginally heavier than the original RA003E but with another 30bhp, it was raced from round two once a camshaft problem had been fixed.

'The chassis is really quite good, but the engine lacks punch,' was

Villeneuve's assessment before the Australian GP, where his sixth and Button's eighth on the grid gave cause for optimism. However, Villeneuve's error in pitting on the same lap as Button dropped them out of contention for points. Villeneuve apologised after the race but a public war of words followed in Malaysia. Button won the on-track battle by qualifying ninth and was set for fifth in the race before losing two places on the last lap. Villeneuve was stranded on the grid before the formation lap by a gearbox/electrical issue.

Button was among those to crash in Interlagos's Turn 3 during the chaotic Brazilian GP but Villeneuve avoided the carnage to claim sixth. Electrical fires ended the Canadian's San Marino and Spanish

Takuma Satō, BAR 005-Honda (Japanese GP)

GPs as his frustrations grew. Eighth at Imola, Button was fifth in qualifying at Barcelona only for his race to be compromised by his light initial fuel load and an extra pitstop after clashing with David Coulthard. The BARs were competitive in Austria, where Button qualified seventh despite a heavy fuel load and claimed fourth once his strategy unfolded; Villeneuve was running fifth (20sec behind Button) when he lost a lap by stalling in the pits.

Monaco was overshadowed by Button's concussion-inducing accident at the chicane during Saturday practice after setting the best non-Ferrari time. With the Englishman sidelined for the rest of the weekend, Villeneuve's race ended with another engine failure. Button was fit for the Canadian GP where both cars retired.

Now mired in a mid-season slump, the BARs lacked grip at the Nürburgring although Button salvaged seventh after a race-long battle with Mark Webber's Jaguar. Villeneuve lost second gear and retired following a scrappy race that included a bad start, a mid-race spin and a front-wing breakage after knocking a cone at the chicane. In France, where the drivers were forced to sit out opening practice due to legal action brought by a marketing company over unpaid commission (dismissed before first qualifying and settled by the end of the season), another chastening weekend saw them start outside the top ten and fail to score. Villeneuve's ninth was a rare finish while Button ran out of fuel following an issue with his rig. Button's suspension broke during his qualifying attempt at Silverstone, so he started last and lost further time during a safety-car period when double-stacked behind Villeneuve in the pits. They almost collided as Button recovered to claim eighth, two places ahead of his team-mate.

Button was the final points scorer again in Germany and finished tenth at the Hungaroring after delay on the opening lap. Villeneuve's German GP was compromised by first-corner contact with Justin Wilson's Jaguar and he lost hydraulic pressure in Hungary. In Italy, Button qualified seventh but lost gears in the race and retired, while the under-pressure Villeneuve had a steady

drive into sixth and only his second points score of the year.

Button returned from a 160mph testing accident at Jerez to challenge for the podium in the United States after set-up changes transformed his car on Saturday. He led for 15 laps following a well-timed switch to wet-weather tyres and was still second when his engine failed four laps later; Villeneuve's engine also broke on what turned out to be his last appearance for the team. After Satō's promotion for 2004 was announced in Tokyo on the Tuesday before the Japanese GP, Villeneuve pulled out of the race. Button led for a couple of laps and finished an excellent fourth, although the crowd was more interested in the driver who finished sixth, Satō having caused great excitement when running as high as second and dicing with Michael Schumacher. That double score was enough to snatch fifth in the constructors' standings from Sauber-Petronas.

RED BULL SAUBER PETRONAS
That Sauber finished sixth in the World Championship was thanks to early-season results and one wild weekend at Indianapolis in September. That apart, 2003 was a lacklustre disappointment for Peter Sauber's privateers, with a car that was blighted by aerodynamic deficiencies.

Sauber exercised its option on Nick Heidfeld's services before the 2002 Hungarian GP to foil Toyota's interest. In a reversal of its recent youth policy, the team reappointed Heinz-Harald Frentzen, whose first three F1 seasons had been with Sauber, on a one-year deal to replace Felipe Massa, although the Brazilian remained as a test driver (alongside similar Ferrari duties) after his hopes of a Jordan drive ended. Swiss teenager Neel Jani was added in a test role in April 2003 after making a winning start in the Formula Renault V6 championship.

Two years remained on Sauber's Ferrari customer engine deal and the team renewed with Bridgestone following exploratory talks with Michelin. Former technical director Leo Ress left his research

Heinz-Harald Frentzen, Sauber C22-Petronas (United States GP)

Nick Heidfeld, Sauber C22-Petronas (Canadian GP)

and development role in the New Year to join Honda. Rumours of an association with Audi proved premature by a decade or so. Sauber rued the decision to opt for unlimited testing instead of the new two-hour GP Friday alternative.

The Sauber C22-Petronas was a totally new design as technical director Willy Rampf and head of aerodynamics Seamus Mullarkey eschewed the evolutionary shackles of the C21. Its 9 January shakedown at Fiorano was cancelled due to snow and the C22 proved reliable if slow at the following week's Barcelona test. Times improved during subsequent outings at Valencia and back at Barcelona so there was a mood of quiet optimism by the time the 'blue Ferrari' was officially launched near Zurich airport on 9 February. The Ferrari 051 V10 engine was badged as the Petronas 03A. That was initially of 2002 Italian GP vintage with upgrades available for Canadian qualifying (03B) and at Monza (03C). Rampf was keen to stress that the super-slim seven-speed longitudinal

gearbox was designed and built by Sauber rather than supplied by the *Scuderia* as had been reported. Optimising tyre performance was a key objective, although Bridgestone's concentration on Ferrari compromised Sauber.

Peter Sauber was concerned that the C22's 'aerodynamic efficiency is not quite there'. With correlation errors at the six-decades-old Emmen wind tunnel blamed for overstated gains, the car lacked downforce and balance. A deal was agreed to use Lola's Huntingdon facility during the summer break, by which time Mullarkey and his 32-strong aero department had switched focus from the front wing, which had brought incremental gains at best, to the rear. New suspension and 'twisted' rear wing were introduced at the Nürburgring, while the airbox sported a dorsal fin from Hungary. A new floor for the Italian GP was among development parts destroyed in Heidfeld's high-speed crash at the first chicane while the new rear end worked so well it initially generated understeer.

Sauber-Petronas scored points at the first three races of the season, although its true midfield position in the F1 hierarchy became apparent once the circus returned to Europe. Having used light fuel loads to qualify fourth and seventh in Australia, Frentzen finished sixth while Heidfeld went out with a suspension failure blamed on an earlier collision. In Malaysia, Heidfeld qualified sixth and ran third before stalling at his pitstop, then recovered to eighth, one place ahead of Frentzen after his delay in the opening-lap fracas. Running non-stop in Brazil, Frentzen rescued fifth place despite starting from the pitlane and a mid-race spin.

Sauber's normal reliability now disappeared with a spate of valvetrain issues and engine failures. Tenth at Imola and Barcelona, Heidfeld was fuelled light to snatch a headline-grabbing fourth on the grid in Austria, although both cars retired. The bleak run continued in Monaco where Frentzen crashed at the Swimming Pool exit on the opening lap and Heidfeld finished 11th. After a double DNF in Montréal, the Nürburgring saw Heidfeld drive from the pitlane to eighth place with Frentzen ninth.

The Saubers were anonymous at Magny-Cours and Silverstone before Heidfeld achieved top-ten finishes at the last five races. Frentzen was eliminated at the first corner at Hockenheim and ran out of fuel in Hungary after not heeding pit signals. With both drivers informed that they would not be required in 2004, there was some progress at Monza where they were denied points in the dying moments. Frentzen was seventh when his transmission failed with two laps to go, elevating Heidfeld to eighth only to lose a position on the last lap.

Indianapolis brought a shock result when Bridgestone rubber suited the wet conditions. Second after his timely switch to full-wet tyres, Frentzen led lap 48 (the first time Sauber had led a GP) and finished third. With Heidfeld's fifth place also bringing points, Sauber-Petronas vaulted from ninth to fifth in the standings with a race to go. They were back among the also-rans at Suzuka where contact with rival cars delayed both drivers. Frentzen's engine failed and Heidfeld finished ninth for the third time in four races as Sauber-Petronas slipped to sixth overall.

JAGUAR RACING

There were wholesale changes at Jaguar Racing once more despite some signs of improvement during the latter months of 2002. Ford vice-president Richard Parry-Jones axed Niki Lauda from his role as team principal and head of the Premier Performance Division on 25 November and promoted from within the Ford empire. Pi Research's Tony Purnell replaced Lauda in that latter role with a brief to reduce expenditure and steady the ship. Lauda declined a New Year offer to remain as a consultant.

Purnell planned a revised management structure with engineering at its heart during his first fortnight in charge. An engineer with a background in the automotive sector, David Pitchforth replaced Lauda appointee Guenther Steiner as managing director on 5 December and implemented the restructure throughout the team. Malcolm Oastler moved sideways to the chief engineer role with Ian Pocock appointed as director of engineering in March. Redundancies included chief aerodynamicist Mark Handford, leaving Ben Agathangelou in sole charge of that department. Steiner, who turned down an alternative role and so spent 2003 on 'gardening leave', had also been acting technical director during 2002 and there was surprise when that position remained vacant. A team principal was not appointed after Martin Brundle reportedly turned down the job and talk of Craig Pollock was denied. One high-profile appointment from outside Ford was former Philip Morris marketeer John Hogan, who came out of retirement to spend a year as sporting director.

Jaguar was looking for an all-new driver line-up by the middle of 2002. Eddie Irvine and Pedro de la Rosa were released despite the latter having another year on his contract, with test driver James Courtney also surplus to requirements. Minardi rookie Mark Webber impressed on his single test day at Barcelona on 28 June by lapping just 0.035sec slower than de la Rosa. Fernando Alonso also tested but was Renault-bound while Jenson Button was mentioned before he chose BAR. Williams-BMW wanted its highly rated test driver Antônio Pizzonia to race in 2003, with Jaguar, Sauber and Toyota all possibilities. In one of Lauda's last acts for Jaguar, Webber and

Mark Webber, Jaguar R4-Cosworth (Austrian GP)

Antônio Pizzonia, Jaguar R4-Cosworth (Monaco GP)

Pizzonia were confirmed on 1 November once settlement with de la Rosa had been agreed. The Brazilian made an inauspicious start to life at Jaguar. He rolled a road car with journalists aboard at Barcelona's Turn 1 on 21 November before crashing the R3C test chassis (with 2003 engine and gearbox) at Turn 2 12 days later. Further mileage on the R3C was restricted by two engine failures and problems with its electronics.

The Jaguar R4-Cosworth completed straight-line systems tests at Belgium's Lommel airfield before being launched live on the internet on 17 January. Rob Taylor (head of vehicle design) and Agathangelou led the design of a conventional single-keel car, with stiffer chassis and improved aerodynamics. The relationship with Michelin was central to improving the R3's suspect handling characteristics. Rob White and the team at Cosworth produced a completely new V10 with vee angle widened to 90 degrees. Managing director Nick Hayes hailed the CR-5 as the 'highest-revving Cosworth engine ever'. Glimpses of single-lap pace for the R4 gave the team much-needed respectability but excessive rear-tyre temperature over a race distance affected performance and reliability left much to be desired.

Cost-saving measures included the late decision to join the GP Friday test sessions, with Jaguar alone in relying on its race drivers for that exercise. Although Purnell spoke of a new culture, 2003 began in familiar fashion with niggling issues and suspect handling during the R4's first Barcelona test from 21 January. However, Pizzonia was quickest a week later at Valencia – albeit on low fuel – and Webber starred as progress was finally made.

Jaguar did not score a point at the first four races with the fuel system a persistent problem. Both cars had driveshaft-induced suspension failures in Australia, Webber when running sixth

and Pizzonia after completing sufficient distance to be classified. They were delayed in the pits during the Malaysian GP before Pizzonia spun and Webber stopped to save his engine. Webber was sensational in Brazil, where he used changeable conditions to qualify first on Friday and third on Saturday, but both Jaguars crashed during the race with Webber classified ninth after debris from his hefty shunt forced the race to be red-flagged.

With Pizzonia struggling, Jaguar made very public attempts to woo McLaren-Mercedes tester Alexander Wurz to replace him. After stalling at the start of the San Marino GP and earning a rebuke for not acknowledging a radio message, Pizzonia finished 14th, the last still circulating. In contrast, Webber was fifth in both qualifying sessions but a launch-control malfunction and subsequent driveshaft failure ruined his race.

Webber delivered Jaguar's first points with hard-earned seventh places in Spain and Austria, where the third-fastest race lap was an additional fillip. That Austrian result was achieved despite a stop-go penalty for infringing *parc fermé* regulations in bizarre circumstances. Having opted to start from the pitlane after qualifying 17th, Webber's car was topped up with fuel as the field began the parade lap, but the aborted start then meant Jaguar was deemed to have refuelled between qualifying and the race. Pizzonia's torrid Spanish weekend began with an injured mechanic when he overshot his pit box and ended with launch-control failure on the starting grid and a ram from Kimi Räikkönen's McLaren-Mercedes. Given assurances about his future in an embarrassing climbdown by management, Pizzonia used low fuel in Austria to qualify eighth before a couple of 'offs' restricted him to ninth in the race.

Early retirees from the Monaco GP, the Jaguars finished in the top ten at the next three races. Sixth on the grid and seventh at the

Justin Wilson, Jaguar R4-Cosworth (United States GP)

finish in Canada, Webber then scored back-to-back sixth places at the Nürburgring and Magny-Cours. Pizzonia's trio of tenth places included a couple of unscheduled stops in Montréal and a stop-go penalty for speeding in the Nürburgring pitlane. Webber was fortunate to avoid the protester on Silverstone's Hangar Straight during a disappointing British GP while Pizzonia, who had been marginally quicker in qualifying, had an engine failure. That was Pizzonia's final contribution because Minardi's Justin Wilson replaced him for the last five races. The Brazilian turned down an offer to remain with the team as reserve driver.

Wilson completed a 50km acclimatation test on Silverstone's south circuit on the Monday before the German GP. Eager to secure the drive for 2004, he retired from his first three GPs for Jaguar, eliminated at Hockenheim when caught up in a first-lap accident and by mechanical failures at the Hungaroring (engine) and Monza (gearbox). Those travails were accentuated by Webber's continued form in the sister car. Fifth in the early laps of the German GP before his tyres blistered, the Australian crashed on the last lap while trying to snatch eighth from Jenson Button. Points at the next two races included sixth in Hungary, where he started third and ran second during the early laps.

Lacking traction at the United States GP, Webber led a couple of laps during the pitstops when rain arrived only to crash before changing to wets. Wilson ran as high as third after a timely switch and finished eighth to register the only point of his F1 career. Before the final race at Suzuka, Jaguar was within a point of Purnell's stated aim of finishing fifth overall. Prospects looked hopeful when Webber qualified sixth and Wilson tenth but their light fuel loads compromised race strategy and they faded to 11th and 13th respectively, and the team to seventh in the final table.

PANASONIC TOYOTA RACING

Toyota restructured its motor racing activities on 1 January 2003. John Howett replaced Ove Andersson as president of Toyota Motorsport with vice-president Toshiro Kurusu responsible for technical matters. That freed 65-year-old Andersson to concentrate on F1 as vice-chairman and team principal, while Tsutomu Tomita was named as chairman in July. Gustav Brunner was promoted to technical director with Keizo Takahashi now general manager of car design and development. Engine chief Norbert Kreyer took a new role on the race and test teams with Luca Marmorini his replacement. Former Williams aerodynamicist Jason Somerville was hired in June.

Andersson began formulating driver options for 2003 as soon as the team had made its debut at the 2002 Australian GP. Mika Salo was already under contract but both he and Allan McNish were released on 28 August 2002, with BAR-Honda refugee Olivier Panis announced as one driver for 2003. Cristiano da Matta impressed when tested at Paul Ricard in May but negotiations to release the new Champ Car champion from the final year of his Newman-Haas Racing contract were slow. Months of speculation were finally confirmed on 5 November when da Matta signed a two-year deal with Toyota. The experienced Ricardo Zonta replaced Ryan Briscoe as test and reserve driver.

Development of the Toyota TF102 stopped mid-season so the focus could switch to 2003. With the V10 engine already a strength, the compact, lighter RVX-03 version and new aluminium seven-speed gearbox were tested in a modified TF102B from September to gain data before the winter testing break. An upgrade taken to the Nürburgring developed over 900bhp and matched BMW so there was no problem in the power stakes. The TF103 was launched on 8 January at Paul Ricard, where its resemblance to the championship-

Cristiano da Matta, Toyota TF103 (British GP)

winning Ferrari F2002 was noted. This was another evolutionary design with extensive weight saving (20kg) that included carbon-fibre pushrod/torsion bar suspension with the wishbones raised. The chassis was stiffened, while René Hilhorst overhauled the aerodynamics in Toyota's new wind tunnel in search of the rear downforce its predecessor had lacked. The sidepods had periscope exhausts and shark-like cooling gills. Engine, gearbox and differential were all lowered to improve centre of gravity. Brunner continued to ignore the twin-keel fashion and redesigned the rear suspension to improve traction.

When Panis was quickest at the 17–21 February Barcelona test, Ralf Schumacher commented: 'They did a perfect copy of the 2002 Ferrari, and it seems to work.' Da Matta completed 7,000km in testing as he prepared for his debut although his pace and a heavy accident at Barcelona tempered expectations. The possibility of Toyota challenging the established top three was reinforced when Panis qualified fifth in Australia only to be denied points due to loss of fuel pressure. He lost out again in Malaysia because of a

Olivier Panis, Toyota TF103 (European GP)

problem with the fuel rig and he was the innocent victim of Ralph Firman's spinning Jordan in Brazil. Da Matta spun out in Australia and finished the next three races without scoring. The Toyotas were a handful over Imola's kerbs but Panis registered his first finish, a lapped ninth, with the TF103's promising initial pace now waning.

The car was better suited to Barcelona's smooth surface and Panis used minimal fuel to qualify sixth. He made a bad start but had recovered into the top eight when his gearbox failed at his second pitstop, while da Matta finished sixth on his best F1 weekend to date. Launch-control failures on da Matta's car twice forced the Austrian GP start to be aborted, consigning him to an afternoon at the back; Panis lasted just six laps before debris broke his front suspension.

Toyota responded to its lost pace by augmenting its technical team and questioning data from the new wind tunnel. An approach was made for Renault's Mike Gascoyne and Toyota hired the Fondmetal Technologies wind tunnel at Casumaro to improve the TF103. Slower than the Minardis on Thursday at Monaco, where da Matta finished ninth, an aero upgrade for the Canadian GP improved matters. Panis led Toyota's qualifying 7–9 and inherited eighth when da Matta had a suspension breakage with five laps to go. They retired from the European GP but both finished in France, Panis eighth, da Matta 11th.

Armed with another new aero package at Silverstone that featured a revised front wing and simplified sidepod-mounted winglets, Toyota was the main beneficiary of Neil Horan's track antics. Da Matta had qualified sixth and, having already stopped during the first safety-car period, emerged from the chaos at the head of a brief Toyota 1–2. He led for 17 laps before his second pitstop and finished seventh while Panis dropped out of the points. Toyota's improved form continued at Hockenheim where the TF103s qualified in the top ten and scored points, Panis fifth and da Matta sixth after three-stopping. They did not figure in Hungary and retired at Monza, da Matta with a spectacular right-rear puncture at Parabolica and Panis following brake failure.

Competitive all weekend at Indianapolis, Panis qualified third and claimed second at the start, but poor tyre decisions in the changing conditions ruined his race before he spun out after 27 laps. Da Matta started and finished ninth after receiving a drive-through penalty for speeding in the pitlane. Much was expected of the final race in Japan when the light-fuelled cars qualified an impressive third (da Matta) and fourth (Panis). However, their three-stop strategy did not work and by the end they were seventh and tenth. As Toyota's budget dwarfed most rivals, eighth overall with no podium results was a modest return.

JORDAN FORD

Four years after coming within an ace of stealing the drivers' title, Jordan Grand Prix fought a hand-to-mouth existence as it tumbled down the grid. There were redundancies and a significant budget cut following the withdrawal of Deutsche Post/DHL in November. That shortfall was only partly replenished by increased Benson & Hedges exposure and a new partnership with Chinese broadcaster CCTV from the Malaysian GP. Ill-fated legal action against Vodafone, claiming the mobile phone giant had reneged on a verbal agreement, was an expensive distraction.

Eddie Jordan was searching for a new engine partner from February 2002 following Honda's decision to concentrate on BAR. Talks with Cosworth continued throughout the summer before Jordan claimed at the 2002 Hungarian GP to have a three-year agreement for Ford RS-badged engines, with the split from Honda confirmed. Formally announced at the United States GP, the Cosworth tie-up amounted to a customer deal for the 72-degree CR-3 V10, subsidised by a three-year marketing agreement with Ford of Europe.

Whether or not this engine deal was a works arrangement had commercial and contractual consequences, particularly for Giancarlo Fisichella's continued tenure. Takuma Satō left after a single season although he had signed a two-year deal. Heinz-Harald

Giancarlo Fisichella, Jordan EJ13-Ford (Malaysian GP)

Zsolt Baumgartner, Jordan EJ13-Ford (Hungarian GP)

Frentzen's return was a possibility despite ongoing proceedings relating to his departure in 2001 but the German opted for Sauber.

Fisichella's team-mate remained uncertain until a month before the new campaign. The need for a 'commercially driven' decision eventually precluded Eddie Irvine or Anthony Davidson while Enrique Bernoldi and Bryan Herta were mentioned as Jordan unsuccessfully courted Red Bull backing. It became a choice between Sauber refugee Felipe Massa and Formula Nippon champion Ralph Firman. That latter name was well-known in racing circles because Ralph Sr's Van Diemen marque was the most successful Formula Ford manufacturer of all time. Massa was left disappointed when Firman finally signed a three-year deal subject to options on Jordan's side.

Jordan wanted to supplement its budget with a Friday test driver. Christijan Albers, Gianmaria Bruni, Narain Karthikeyan, Richard Lyons, Paolo Montin, Gary Paffett, Giorgio Pantano and Hayanari Shimoda were all mentioned without a deal being done. Zsolt Baumgartner was named for Germany and Hungary and was retained for the Italian GP after finding extra funds. This delayed newly crowned F3000 champion Björn Wirdheim's agreed appearance until the United States GP and Satoshi Motoyama drove the third car in Japan.

Gary Anderson continued to lead on-track engineering while Henri Durand was the factory-based director of design and development. Durand promised a 'brand-new design concept' for the Jordan EJ13-Ford, which was unpainted when Fisichella presided over a troubled shakedown at Barcelona on 20 January. Chief designer John McQuilliam and ex-Arrows aerodynamicist Nicolò Petrucci were tasked with creating a simple car that was easy

to work on. Its packaging benefitted from the compact 72-degree V10 and the proximity of Cosworth's Northampton headquarters eased communication. The twin keel for the lower-front wishbones was further refined to optimise airflow. The team's agreement with Bridgestone was extended into a fifth year. Anderson reckoned 'the car was reasonable when it first ran' but it lacked downforce and mechanical grip. Jordan's reduced circumstances precluded modifying a Cosworth-powered EJ12 test hack, so winter testing began late and there was no glitzy car launch.

An aero upgrade for the British GP was cancelled while the lack of development sapped Fisichella's motivation and led Anderson to question his own future. 'I'm not really interested in going to the factory for lots of meetings and paperwork,' the Ulsterman told *Autosport* in August, adding at season's end, 'I've decided to retire and let someone else take the pressure.' The cash-strapped team only registered one top-six finish, albeit a lucky victory, and slipped to last but one in the constructors' championship.

A refuelling issue cost Fisichella points in Australia and launch-control failure left him stranded on the Malaysian grid. He qualified eighth for Jordan's 200th GP start in Brazil and refuelled early as the team gambled on the race being stopped. When Kimi Räikkönen's McLaren-Mercedes ran wide moments before the red flag was shown, Fisichella took the lead, but the results were declared as the positions at the end of the previous lap (after 53 laps) and the Italian was disappointed to be handed the second-place trophy. However, that decision was reversed the following Thursday when Jordan proved that Fisichella had completed lap 54 just 0.06sec before the stoppage and he was finally declared an F1 race winner five days late and after 110 attempts, with the trophies handed over by

Ralph Firman, Jordan EJ13-Ford (European GP)

Räikkönen and Ron Dennis in a ceremony at Imola.

The rest of the season was a sharp contrast. Engine failures ended Fisichella's races in San Marino and Spain, then loss of fuel pressure after qualifying ninth caused his late elimination in Austria. Following low finishes in Monaco (10th) and at the Nürburgring (12th after a puncture), he retired in Canada (gearbox), France (engine), Britain (suspension), Germany (water leak/overheating but still classified in the results) and Hungary (one of four Jordan engine failures that weekend). Tenth after starting from the pitlane at Monza, Fisichella scored points for only the second time in 2003 when seventh at Indianapolis despite a couple of slow pitstops. His Jordan career ended with engine failure after a lacklustre Japanese GP.

Firman endured a crash-strewn single season at this level, with

Björn Wirdheim, Jordan EJ13-Ford (United States GP)

Satoshi Motoyama, Jordan EJ13-Ford (Japanese GP)

the added pressure of a team-mate who some believed was from the top echelon. Firman started the Australian GP on dry tyres and was up to eighth by lap seven when he crashed at Turn 5. Tenth in Malaysia after qualifying last due to his heavy fuel and one-stop strategy, he crashed into Olivier Panis's Toyota during the Brazilian GP after a front-suspension failure. Barcelona was the first track that Firman already knew and he capped an improved weekend by passing Fisichella on the way eighth. Classified outside the top ten at five of the next six races, he retired in Canada and was a victim of the first-corner mayhem at Hockenheim.

A 46G crash at the Hungaroring's Turn 5 on Saturday morning due to rear-wing failure ruled Firman out of the race, so Baumgartner took over his car and made a solid debut before his engine blew up, shortly after Fisichella's similar failure. The first Hungarian to race in the F1 World Championship, Baumgartner was retained for Monza with Firman still not fit to race and finished 11th on a rare occasion when both Jordans completed the race. Admitting to 'a tough day' on his return at Indianapolis, Firman lost his front wing in contact with Jos Verstappen's Minardi at the start, found Fisichella in his pit box when he stopped for wets, then spun out. He finished 14th on his final F1 appearance in Japan.

EUROPEAN MINARDI F1

Unwilling to pay for Asiatech engines following its free deal in 2002, Minardi considered an offer from Ferrari before reaching agreement with Cosworth in December to use the less expensive 72-degree

CR-3 V10 previously earmarked for Arrows. Asiatech had planned to launch its own team and displayed a wind-tunnel model of its Enrique Scalabroni-designed chassis at the 2002 Italian GP. However, Hideo Morita withdrew his backing and the venture closed in November. Minardi's own financial situation remained dire. Winter-long negotiations with title sponsor Go KL failed on the eve of the season. Paul Stoddart battled the grandee teams for the fighting fund and previous sponsor commitments went unpaid, resulting in one logo having 'Cheque Bounced' and 'Not Paid' superimposed over it at the Japanese GP.

Mark Webber moved to Jaguar while Alex Yoong explored a future in Champ Cars rather than accept the reserve-driver role at Minardi. Justin Wilson had been too tall to replace Yoong at the 2002 Hungarian GP but remained Stoddart's priority signing. The front wheels and wing of the new PS03 were moved forward to accommodate Wilson's 6ft 3in frame while maintaining the PS02's wheelbase. The Yorkshireman's signature was duly announced on 16 December 2002. Allied to Wilson's appointment was a unique scheme introduced by his manager Jonathan Palmer to sell shares in the driver on the London Stock Exchange. With Stoddart looking for 'the best driver/commercial combination' for the second seat, Christijan Albers failed to secure sufficient backing, so Jos Verstappen's return was confirmed in January.

Sergey Zlobin remained with the test team thanks to backing from Gazprom, although the Russian petrochemical giant's deal was terminated after six races. Verstappen was not impressed by Friday test driver Matteo Bobbi when he took part at Imola. 'Bobbi

Jos Verstappen, Minardi PS03-Cosworth (San Marino GP)

drives some Friday tests, but that is almost useless,' Verstappen told Dutch media. 'Bobbi is just too slow.' The Italian did not reappear. Bryan Herta's hopes of driving the third car in North America were thwarted and Gianmaria Bruni fulfilled that Friday role at the last five rounds. After two years with Minardi, Rupert Manwaring moved to Lola Cars as managing director.

There were no renewal negotiations with Michelin and agreement with Bridgestone was only reached in February. That forced Minardi to run its old PS01Bs on F3000 Avons for its first winter test at Valencia and Bridgestone only supplied 2002-specification rubber at the start of the campaign. Gabriele Tredozi, George Ryton and Loïc Bigois upgraded existing machinery into Cosworth-

powered PS03s with pushrod suspension and the upgraded cars had a delayed shakedown at Fiorano on 19–20 February. The original front wing with a dramatically lower central section was replaced by a more contoured upgrade at Imola and smaller bargeboards were fitted at the European GP. The PS03s sported an extra low-mounted wing above the rear suspension in Monaco.

The possibility of missing the Australian GP was averted with a week to go when Stoddart gave Cosworth the necessary financial guarantees to secure engines for the first four races. However, optimistic talk of challenging for a first podium finish was quickly dispelled with Minardi rooted to the back of the grid. Verstappen finished the first two races while Wilson made great starts to briefly

Justin Wilson, Minardi PS03-Cosworth (French GP)

Matteo Bobbi, Minardi PS03-Cosworth (San Marino GP)

Gianmaria Bruni, Minardi PS03-Cosworth (Hungarian GP)

Nicolas Kiesa, Minardi PS03-Cosworth (German GP)

feature in the top ten only to retire. His Malaysian demise was due to pain and loss of feeling in his arms that was blamed on his HANS device and prompted a post-race hospital visit. Both Minardis spun out of the Brazilian GP – heavily fuelled Verstappen was ahead of eventual race winner Giancarlo Fisichella at the time – and retired from the San Marino GP.

Wilson made another fast start to run ninth in Spain and finished for the first time, 11th with Verstappen 12th and last. The Dutchman's new launch control failed in Austria, where Wilson was 13th and last. Gazprom's departure coincided with increased support from Trust Computers and revised livery for Monaco, where simultaneous fuel-system faults accounted for both cars before one-stop strategies could unfold.

Stoddart's increasingly fractious relationship with rival team owners regarding the fighting fund came to a head in Canada. An incendiary press conference alongside the likes of Ron Dennis and Sir Frank Williams ended with Dennis telling Stoddart: 'This is a tough, competitive sport and if you can't take the heat, get out of the bloody kitchen.' With the concept of the fund all but dead, Minardi's immediate future was secured by Bernie Ecclestone's offer to invest £3m. Dennis called that 'a very elegant solution to a difficult situation. I am delighted for Paul and applaud Bernie for managing to do one of the things we rarely see him do, which is put his hand in his pocket.' On track, Verstappen finished a season-best ninth after a race of attrition. They finished the European GP at the

back before Verstappen led a shock Minardi 1–2 in first qualifying for the French GP thanks to a drying track but the optimism proved brief. Wilson's car was found to be underweight and both Minardis qualified and finished among the tailenders as usual.

Stoddart's threatened traction-control protest at the British GP was averted and his cars trailed home 15th (Verstappen) and 16th (Wilson). That proved to be Wilson's last appearance for his efforts had attracted Jaguar's attention. Nicolas Kiesa replaced him after the other teams agreed the Dane could complete a single day's running at Fiorano during the summer testing ban to complete sufficient mileage to qualify for a super licence.

When the assets of defunct Arrows were offered for sale on 17–18 June, Stoddart acquired five A23 chassis and spare parts. A back-to-back comparison between the PS03 and the PS04 (*née* Arrows A23) planned for 21 July at Rockingham was postponed until after the summer break. It went ahead at Mugello on 16 September with Verstappen marginally quicker in the PS03, although gearbox issues on the PS04 made the exercise inconclusive.

A non-finisher in Germany and Italy, Verstappen was 12th at the Hungaroring (Minardi's 300th GP) and 10th at Indianapolis. Kiesa took a considered approach to his GP baptism and finished all five races without setting things alight. His best result was 11th and last at Indianapolis. The Minardis occupied the last two finishing positions once more in Japan after Verstappen qualified with so little fuel that he needed to refill after the parade lap.

DRIVER PERFORMANCE

DRIVER	CAR-ENGINE	AUS	MAL	BR	RSM	E	A	MC	CDN	EU	F	GB	D	H	I	USA	J
Fernando Alonso	Renault R23	[10]7	[1]**3**	[10]3	[8]6	[3]2	[19]R	[8]5	[4]**4** FL	[8]4	[7]R	[8]R	[8]**4**	[1]**1**	[20]8	[6]R	[5]R
Rubens Barrichello	Ferrari F2002	[2]R	[5]2	[1]R FL	[3]**3**	–	–	–	–	–	–	–	–	–	–	–	–
	Ferrari F2003-GA	–	–	–	–	[2]**3** FL	[5]3	[7]8	[5]5	[5]3	[8]7	[1]**1** FL	[3]R	[5]R	[3]3	[2]R	[1]**1**
Zsolt Baumgartner	Jordan EJ13-Ford	–	–	–	–	–	–	–	–	–	–	–	T	[19]R	[18]11	–	–
Matteo Bobbi	Minardi PS03-Cosworth	–	–	–	T	–	–	–	–	–	–	–	–	–	–	–	–
Gianmaria Bruni	Minardi PS03-Cosworth	–	–	–	–	–	–	–	–	–	–	–	T	T	T	T	T
Jenson Button	BAR 005-Honda	[8]10	[9]7	[11]R	[9]8	[5]9	[7]4	[20]DNS	[17]R	[12]7	[14]R	[20]8	[17]8	[14]10	[7]R	[11]**R**	[9]**4**
David Coulthard	McLaren MP4-17D-Mercedes-Benz	[11]**1**	[4]R	[2]**4**	[12]5	[8]R	[14]5	[6]7	[11]R	[9]15	[5]5	[12]5	[10]2	[9]5	[8]R	[8]**R**	[7]3
Cristiano da Matta	Toyota TF103	[16]R	[11]11	[18]10	[13]12	[13]6	[13]10	[10]9	[9]11	[10]R	[13]11	[6]**7**	[9]6	[15]11	[12]R	[9]9	[3]7
Ralph Firman	Jordan EJ13-Ford	[17]R	[20]10	[16]R	[19]R	[15]8	[16]11	[16]12	[19]R	[14]11	[18]15	[17]13	[18]R	[NT]DNP	–	[18]R	[15]14
Giancarlo Fisichella	Jordan EJ13-Ford	[13]12	[14]R	[8]**1**	[17]15	[17]R	[9]R	[12]10	[16]R	[13]12	[17]R	[15]R	[12]13	[13]R	[13]10	[17]7	[16]R
Heinz-Harald Frentzen	Sauber C22-Petronas	[4]6	[13]9	[14]5	[14]11	[10]R	[15]R	[15]R	[10]R	[15]9	[16]12	[14]12	[14]R	[17]R	[14]13	[15]**3**	[12]R
Marc Gené	Williams FW25-BMW	–	–	–	–	–	–	–	–	–	–	–	–	–	[5]5	–	–
Nick Heidfeld	Sauber C22-Petronas	[7]R	[6]8	[12]R	[11]10	[14]10	[4]R	[14]11	[12]R	[20]8	[15]13	[16]17	[15]10	[11]9	[16]9	[13]5	[11]9
Nicolas Kiesa	Minardi PS03-Cosworth	–	–	–	–	–	–	–	–	–	–	–	[20]12	[20]13	[19]12	[20]11	[18]16
Allan McNish	Renault R23	T	T	T	T	T	T	T	T	T	–	T	T	T	T	T	T
Franck Montagny	Renault R23	–	–	–	–	–	–	–	–	–	T	–	–	–	–	–	–
Juan Pablo Montoya	Williams FW25-BMW	[3]2	[8]12	[9]R	[4]7	[9]4	[3]R	[3]1	[2]3	[4]2	[2]**2** FL	[7]2	[1]**1** FL	[4]**3** FL	[2]2	[4]6	[2]**R**
Satoshi Motoyama	Jordan EJ13-Ford	–	–	–	–	–	–	–	–	–	–	–	–	–	–	–	T
Olivier Panis	Toyota TF103	[5]R	[10]R	[15]R	[10]9	[6]R	[11]R	[17]13	[7]8	[7]R	[10]8	[13]11	[7]5	[10]R	[9]R	[3]R	[4]10
Antônio Pizzonia	Jaguar R4-Cosworth	[18]13	[15]R	[17]R	[15]14	[16]R	[8]9	[13]R	[13]10	[16]10	[11]10	[10]R	–	–	–	–	–
Kimi Räikkönen	McLaren MP4-17D-Mercedes-Benz	[15]**3** FL	[7]**1**	[4]**2**	[6]2	[20]R	[2]2	[2]**2** FL	[20]6	[1]**R** FL	[4]4	[3]**3**	[5]R	[7]**2**	[4]4	[1]**2**	[8]**2**
Takuma Satō	BAR 005-Honda	–	–	–	–	–	–	–	–	–	–	–	–	–	–	–	[13]6
Michael Schumacher	Ferrari F2002	[1]**4**	[3]6 FL	[7]R	[1]**1** FL	–	–	–	–	–	–	–	–	–	–	–	–
	Ferrari F2003-GA	–	–	–	–	[1]**1**	[1]**1** FL	[5]**3**	[3]**1**	[2]5	[3]3	[5]4	[6]7	[8]8	[1]**1** FL	[7]**1** FL	[14]8
Ralf Schumacher	Williams FW25-BMW	[9]8	[17]4	[6]7	[2]**4**	[7]5	[10]6	[1]**4**	[1]2	[3]1	[1]1	[4]9	[2]R	[2]4	[NT]DNP	[5]R	[20]12 FL
Jarno Trulli	Renault R23	[12]5	[2]5	[5]8	[16]13	[4]R	[6]8	[4]**6**	[8]R	[6]R	[6]R	[2]**6**	[4]3	[6]7	[6]R	[10]4	[19]5
Jos Verstappen	Minardi PS03-Cosworth	[19]11	[18]13	[19]R	[20]R	[19]12	[20]R	[18]R	[15]9	[18]14	[19]16	[19]15	[19]R	[18]12	[17]R	[19]10	[17]15
Jacques Villeneuve	BAR 005-Honda	[6]9	[12]DNS	[13]6	[7]R	[11]R	[12]12	[11]R	[14]R	[17]R	[12]9	[9]10	[13]9	[16]R	[10]6	[12]R	–
Mark Webber	Jaguar R4-Cosworth	[14]R	[16]R	[3]9	[5]R	[12]7	[17]7	[9]R	[6]7	[11]6	[9]6	[11]14	[11]11	[3]6	[11]7	[14]**R**	[6]11
Justin Wilson	Minardi PS03-Cosworth	[20]R	[19]R	[20]R	[18]R	[18]11	[18]13	[19]R	[18]R	[19]13	[20]14	[18]16	–	–	–	–	–
	Jaguar R4-Cosworth	–	–	–	–	–	–	–	–	–	–	–	[16]R	[12]R	[15]R	[16]8	[10]13
Björn Wirdheim	Jordan EJ13-Ford	–	–	–	–	–	–	–	–	–	–	–	–	–	–	T	–

FORMULA 1 RACE WINNERS

ROUND	RACE (CIRCUIT)	DATE	WINNER
1	Foster's Australian Grand Prix (Albert Park)	Mar 9	David Coulthard (McLaren MP4-17D-Mercedes-Benz)
2	Petronas Malaysian Grand Prix (Sepang)	Mar 23	Kimi Räikkönen (McLaren MP4-17D-Mercedes-Benz)
3	Grande Prêmio do Brasil (Interlagos)	Apr 6	Giancarlo Fisichella (Jordan EJ13-Ford)
4	Gran Premio Foster's di San Marino (Imola)	Apr 20	Michael Schumacher (Ferrari F2002)
5	Gran Premio Marlboro de España (Catalunya)	May 4	Michael Schumacher (Ferrari F2003-GA)
6	Grosser A1 Preis von Österreich (Spielberg)	May 18	Michael Schumacher (Ferrari F2003-GA)
7	Grand Prix de Monaco (Monte Carlo)	Jun 1	Juan Pablo Montoya (Williams FW25-BMW)
8	Grand Prix Air Canada (Montréal)	Jun 15	Michael Schumacher (Ferrari F2003-GA)
9	Allianz Grand Prix of Europe (Nürburgring)	Jun 29	Ralf Schumacher (Williams FW25-BMW)
10	Mobil 1 Grand Prix de France (Magny-Cours)	Jul 6	Ralf Schumacher (Williams FW25-BMW)
11	Foster's British Grand Prix (Silverstone)	Jul 20	Rubens Barrichello (Ferrari F2003-GA)
12	Grosser Mobil 1 Preis von Deutschland (Hockenheim)	Aug 3	Juan Pablo Montoya (Williams FW25-BMW)
13	Marlboro Magyar Nagydíj (Hungaroring)	Aug 24	Fernando Alonso (Renault R23)
14	Gran Premio Vodafone d'Italia (Monza)	Sep 14	Michael Schumacher (Ferrari F2003-GA)
15	United States Grand Prix (Indianapolis)	Sep 28	Michael Schumacher (Ferrari F2003-GA)
16	Fuji Television Japanese Grand Prix (Suzuka)	Oct 12	Rubens Barrichello (Ferrari F2003-GA)

Fernando Alonso converts pole position into victory at the Hungaroring

DRIVERS' CHAMPIONSHIP

	DRIVERS	POINTS
1	Michael Schumacher	93
2	Kimi Räikkönen	91
3	Juan Pablo Montoya	82
4	Rubens Barrichello	65
5	Ralf Schumacher	58
6	Fernando Alonso	55
7	David Coulthard	51
8	Jarno Trulli	33
9	Jenson Button	17
10	Mark Webber	17
11	Heinz-Harald Frentzen	13
12	Giancarlo Fisichella	12
13	Cristiano da Matta	10
14	Nick Heidfeld	6
15	Olivier Panis	6
16	Jacques Villeneuve	6
17	Marc Gené	4
18	Takuma Satō	3
19	Ralph Firman	1
20	Justin Wilson	1
21	Antônio Pizzonia	0
22	Jos Verstappen	0
23	Nicolas Kiesa	0
24	Zsolt Baumgartner	0

CONSTRUCTORS' CHAMPIONSHIP

	CONSTRUCTORS	POINTS
1	Ferrari	158
2	Williams-BMW	144
3	McLaren-Mercedes-Benz	142
4	Renault	88
5	BAR-Honda	26
6	Sauber-Petronas	19
7	Jaguar-Cosworth	18
8	Toyota	16
9	Jordan-Ford	13
10	Minardi-Cosworth	0

The Ferrari team acknowledge Michael Schumacher's achievement after he clinched his seventh world title at Spa-Francorchamps

2004

FERRARI'S ACE CARRIES ON SETTING THE STANDARD

Tyre chiefs Hiroshi Yasukawa and Pierre Dupasquier address the press

Michael Schumacher and Ferrari completed their fifth successive double championship with domination that seemed never-ending. His then record-breaking tally of 13 victories included 12 from the opening 13 races.

In this manufacturer-led era of F1, the FIA tried to address rising costs to ensure the viability of independent concerns. One new measure required an engine to last for a whole GP weekend (potentially a distance of 800km), with a ten-place grid drop for any breach. FIA president Max Mosley also advocated the use of common parts, but the return of buying 'off-the-shelf' customer cars was not agreed, with teams still obliged to design and build their own machinery.

The independents, most notably Jordan and Minardi, agitated for affordable engines. 'A solid commitment by the manufacturers was made on 29 April [2003],' railed Minardi's Paul Stoddart before the first race, 'to cut engine costs in return for myself and Jordan agreeing to the continued use of traction control, but so far nothing has happened.' His renewed threat to protest traction control did not go ahead. Launch control and fully automatic transmissions were banned while rear wings were limited to two upper elements.

Single-car qualifying remained despite being unpopular. The session that decided the running order, with cars despatched in their reverse finishing position from the previous race, was immediately followed by the one-by-one qualifying runs. That lengthy process prompted Bernie Ecclestone to say in Australia: 'The teams are unhappy, the journalists are unhappy, and the race organisers did an opinion poll of the public leaving the circuit here and they are unhappy.' The problem was highlighted at Silverstone when rain was expected later in the afternoon which turned the renamed pre-qualifying into farce. Drivers dawdled to gain an early qualifying slot: Michael Schumacher spun, Rubens Barrichello ran wide, and others slowed to a crawl although those tactics proved in vain for it did not rain. The controversial format was kept because the teams could not agree an alternative.

Teams outside the top four in the 2003 constructors' standings could run a third car in Friday practice for drivers who had started no more than six GPs in the past two years. Colour coding on the camera was introduced to help identify drivers –

Designed by Hermann Tilke, the Bahrain International Circuit was an impressive addition to the World Championship

fluorescent red for a team's leading driver, black for the second car and yellow for the Friday tester. The 2003 qualifying rules and increased pitlane speed limit led designers to reduce fuel capacity and plan for more stops. Qualifying for the Japanese GP was postponed to Sunday morning due to the forecasted arrival of Typhoon 22.

Expansion outside Europe continued with new races in Bahrain and China announced in the autumn of 2002. F1's architect of choice, Hermann Tilke, designed impressive new facilities in the desert outside Manama and in Shanghai. The Brazilian GP organisers signed a five-year extension and the date switched to the end of the season. With late reprieves for Montréal and Magny-Cours, a record 18 races were held. Harvey Goldsmith promoted an F1 parade on Regent Street that brought central London to a standstill on 6 July and prompted talk of a London GP. Despite ongoing sanctions, Libyan prime minister Shukri Ghanem visited the Bahrain GP as his country considered holding a GP for the first time since the 1939 *voiturette* race in Tripoli.

The banks that now owned 75 percent of F1's parent company – Bayerische Landesbank, Lehman Brothers and JPMorgan Chase – took Bernie Ecclestone to London's High Court on 22 November 2004 regarding composition of the board of directors. The court found in the banks' favour although Ecclestone insisted that 'the board has changed but nothing else has'. A new Concorde Agreement was delayed while the threat of the manufacturer-led Grand Prix World Championship breakaway in 2008 was reignited.

Michael Schumacher began 2004 with victory in Australia

Jarno Trulli held off Jenson Button to win the Monaco Grand Prix

Michael Schumacher, Ferrari F2004 (Belgian GP)

SCUDERIA FERRARI MARLBORO

If Ferrari had been dominant in 2002, then 2004 was even more so. The *Scuderia* won 15 of the 18 races to seal the constructors' title with Michael Schumacher champion once more. Indeed, he won 12 of the opening 13 rounds before easing off once title number seven was a formality.

Schumacher and Rubens Barrichello had signed contract extensions during 2003. Luca Badoer and Felipe Massa remained as test drivers, despite the Brazilian regaining his Sauber race seat, with Luciano Burti and Andrea Bertolini also used. Giancarlo Fisichella's hopes of a Ferrari test were denied due to Sauber's clashing oil sponsor even though Massa was also backed by Petronas.

Sporting director Jean Todt also became managing director of the road-car division on 1 June 2004. Renault's John Iley replaced McLaren-bound Nikolas Tombazis as head of aerodynamics in November 2003, reporting to chief designer Rory Byrne. As Byrne was planning to retire in 2007, Aldo Costa had already been identified as his successor. Mattia Binotto replaced Pino d'Agostino as manager of the engine department, while Luca Baldisserri was promoted to chief race engineer. Jordan race engineer Rob Smedley joined the test team.

There was an air of confident evolution as the conservative Ferrari F2004 was launched in Maranello on 26 January with aero package from the championship-winning F2003-GA. Schumacher stressed: 'What is important is what you see on the stopwatch…

not whether it is radical or not.' Byrne retained a single keel and lowered the nose with wing supports that curved outward. The wheelbase was reduced by 5cm with a smaller fuel tank in keeping with contemporary thinking. Weight was moved forward while the composite gearbox was more rigid and lighter than before. The taller sidepods were shorter, with cooling chimneys ahead of sculpted flick-ups that curved around the rear wheels and with smaller exhausts adjacent to the engine. Built to last a whole weekend as now required, the engine had greater cooling needs that meant it did not fit into the F2003-GA, so Ferrari raced the new car from the start of the season. The rear diffuser was a development of the 2003 version. Bridgestone continued its input into the suspension as technical director Ross Brawn conceded that 'we will succeed or fail on the strength of our tyres'.

When Schumacher completed F2004's shakedown at Fiorano four days after the launch, it had a new front wing that curved up at its extremities within complex endplates. The rear wing's lower element rose on either side of the centreline although a flat alternative was used later. Additional wings on the airbox were retained for the Australian GP. Badoer had already crashed a F2003-GA into Barcelona's pitwall on 27 November before poor weather and transmission issues curtailed the F2004's initial programme. However, Barrichello lapped Mugello at record pace as Ferrari initially tested away from its main opposition. Snow forced Ferrari to relocate to Imola where, armed with a new Bridgestone tyre,

Schumacher was 1.242sec quicker than David Coulthard's Michelin-shod McLaren-Mercedes. That dispelled concerns in the Italian press and installed Ferrari as clear title favourites once more.

That was confirmed in Australia where Schumacher and Barrichello were 0.5sec clear of the field in qualifying and ran 1–2 throughout in an utterly dominant race performance. Their advantage was marginally less marked in Malaysia, but Schumacher nonetheless converted pole position into victory at that race and the next. Fourth at Sepang after running wide on the opening lap, Barrichello qualified and finished second in Bahrain despite Ferrari being fined $10,000 for his unsafe release into Jarno Trulli's path during the first pitstops. Denied pole position for the San Marino GP when he ran wide at the Variante Alta, Schumacher angered Juan Pablo Montoya with his robust opening-lap defence of second place at Tosa. When race leader Jenson Button pitted, the German assumed control to win by 9.702sec. Barrichello finished sixth after failing to pass Trulli at Rivazza on the last lap. A broken exhaust and misfire in Barcelona did not prevent Schumacher's fifth successive victory with the two-stopping Barrichello second once more.

Schumacher's winning run came to an end in Monaco. Only fourth on the grid, he took the lead by not pitting under the second safety car only to hit Montoya's Williams-BMW and crash while warming his tyres in the tunnel; Barrichello finished third. Driving a replacement chassis at the European GP, Schumacher dominated from pole position (the 60th of his career) with Barrichello second despite handling affected by a damaged bargeboard following contact with Takuma Satō. Sixth and seventh on the Canadian

grid after troubled qualifying, Schumacher and Barrichello climbed through the field to finish 1–3 on the road. Barrichello was initially denied second by fading brakes that forced him to run wide but he inherited that position when Ralf Schumacher was disqualified. On pole at Indianapolis despite 17 extra litres of fuel, Barrichello lost out to Schumacher on the first safety-car restart before they eased to a third successive 1–2.

Schumacher lost pole position to Fernando Alonso in France and Kimi Räikkönen at Silverstone before adopting a radical four pitstops to overturn Alonso's advantage at Magny-Cours and a two-stop strategy to beat Räikkönen the following week. Barrichello's back-to-back third places included mugging Trulli on the last lap of the French GP. Schumacher converted another pole into victory at Hockenheim, where Barrichello ruined his race on the opening lap when he ran into David Coulthard at the hairpin. At the Hungaroring, Schumacher returned from the summer break to lead a Ferrari 1–2 in qualifying and the race, thereby sealing another constructors' title. His conservative drive to second place at Spa-Francorchamps clinched a record seventh drivers' crown. Barrichello was third that day after recovering from Mark Webber's first-corner assault.

Schumacher crashed four days later when a tyre punctured at 200mph on the main straight during Monza testing. Barrichello starred during the Italian GP by outperforming the new champion and finally scoring a win. He qualified on pole, led the short opening stint on intermediate tyres and took a decisive lead on lap 37. Starting on dry tyres, Schumacher spun down to 15th on the opening lap before storming back to second.

Rubens Barrichello, Ferrari F2004 (Monaco GP)

Barrichello's form continued in China where, starting from pole again, he withstood Button's pressure to win by 1.035sec. Last after a qualifying spin, Schumacher started from the pitlane with a new engine and full fuel load, but a puncture and another spin restricted him to 12th. Schumacher sealed his record 13th victory of 2004 by leading the Japanese GP from pole position to chequered flag. Having collided with Coulthard at Suzuka's chicane, Barrichello started his home race in São Paulo from pole but was outpaced by Michelin rivals on the drying track and finished third. Schumacher was seventh following poor qualifying, an engine change and an early spin in the race. Ferrari's drivers finished 1–2 in the standings and the team topped the constructors' table for the 14th time.

LUCKY STRIKE BRITISH AMERICAN RACING HONDA

Now in its sixth season, British American Racing finally produced a competitive F1 challenger and finished runner-up in the constructors' championship. Jenson Button was in the second year of his contract and there was little surprise when Honda protégé Takuma Satō replaced Jacques Villeneuve as his team-mate. Anthony Davidson was confirmed as reserve driver at the 2003 Japanese GP and contributed vital data during Friday practice at each event, enhancing his claims for a race drive in 2005 by being fastest in sessions at the Nürburgring, Hockenheim, Spa-Francorchamps and Shanghai (FP1 and FP2).

BAR-Honda ended its Bridgestone contract a year early to switch to Michelin despite Pierre Dupasquier's concerns that his company lacked the capacity to service six teams. The black-and-silver interim BAR 005 'concept car' – fitted with the 2004 engine, gearbox and

suspension to hone reliability – was immediately quick on the French rubber when testing resumed on 25 November, but optimism was tempered by three substantial engine failures during Jerez's first major test of the New Year.

On 2 February, Button lapped at record pace at Barcelona on his first day in the new BAR 006-Honda and was quickest on the first two days back at Jerez. Technical director Geoff Willis and a design team that included chief designers Jörg Zander (mechanical) and Kevin Taylor (composites) plus aerodynamicists Willem Toet and Simon Lacey evolved the promising if fragile 2003 car by maintaining its relatively long wheelbase. Overall dimensions were reduced thanks to a smaller fuel tank and the compact carbon-fibre gearbox that had been developed in cooperation by BAR and Honda. A single-keel front-suspension layout was retained with pushrods and torsion bars at both front and rear. Beginning the last year of its current F1 contract and with its future participation in doubt, Honda produced a smaller 90-degree V10 (RA004E) with the new long-life rules the focus, so its winter failures were a concern. However, Honda made strong progress with major engine upgrades at Imola, Monaco, Montréal, Monza and Shanghai offering more power and less weight. Andrew Shovlin engineered Button's car while long-time Villeneuve collaborator Jock Clear worked with Satō.

Button entered the opening race in positive mood: 'The car has been very strong during winter testing… I'm expecting us to be reliable and to be fighting for podiums.' McLaren-Mercedes rival David Coulthard noted the progress: 'BAR has made a step forward irrespective of whether they are showboating or not.'

Testing times were no mirage, for Button snatched fourth on the grid in Melbourne before an issue with his fuel rig and tyre

Jenson Button, BAR 006-Honda (San Marino GP)

Takuma Satō, BAR 006-Honda (Hungarian GP)

wear dropped him to sixth by the finish. Seventh on the grid, Satō hit Jarno Trulli's Renault in the first corner and the resulting nose damage affected handling, restricting him to ninth. Button finally scored his first podium finishes with thirds in Malaysia and Bahrain. Satō spun in qualifying and during the early laps at Sepang, then his race ended with a blown engine with three laps to go. He was fifth in Bahrain despite colliding with Ralf Schumacher and sustaining more damage on a kerb.

The 006s sported an airbox-mounted aerofoil at Imola, where controversial rear-wing vertical 'fences' had to be modified following clarification from the FIA. With an extra 20bhp from the upgraded engine, Button underlined BAR-Honda's position as Ferrari's closest challenger by claiming pole position and leading the opening stint. He was beaten by Michael Schumacher at the first pitstops and ran second thereafter. A qualifying mistake ruined Button's weekend in

Spain, where Satō started third and finished fifth.

Twelve months on from his Monaco accident, Button started second and shadowed Jarno Trulli's winning Renault, finishing just 0.497sec behind. Fourth-placed Satō's spectacular blow-up caused his demise on lap three and mayhem in the midfield as smoke engulfed the track. The Japanese comingman starred at the Nürburgring, where he qualified on the front row, hit Trulli on the opening lap, led briefly, then ran third. He challenged second-placed Rubens Barrichello until he lost his front wing in an impetuous Turn 1 move, then his engine burst into flames on the next lap, promoting Button to third.

In Canada, Satō spun in qualifying and the race before his fifth race-engine failure of 2004. Button qualified second and finished third despite oversteer and a slow pitstop. Accused of overdriving when he crashed into Felipe Massa during practice

Anthony Davidson, BAR 006-Honda (Chinese GP)

for the United States GP, Satō claimed third in qualifying and the race. Button held that position before gearbox failure caused his first retirement of the season.

BAR-Honda had a mini dip in form at Magny-Cours and Silverstone despite successive upgrades that included a new undertray and winglets. Button scored at both races, but Satō had engine failure number six in France and was outside the top ten at Silverstone. An electro-hydraulic Front Torque Transfer (FTT) differential was fitted for practice at Hockenheim although the system, which enhanced braking by altering torque between the front wheels, was removed when rival protests were upheld. Forced to take a ten-place grid penalty in Germany when his engine failed during practice, Button charged from 13th to second thanks to a combination of strategy and racecraft. Satō spun on his way to finishing in eighth place.

There were two ongoing distractions during the autumn, one personal, the other technical. Now third in the standings, Button shocked team principal David Richards by signing a two-year contract with Williams-BMW on 5 August, believing that BAR's option had expired. The Contracts Recognition Board finally met in Milan on 20 October when it ruled in BAR-Honda's favour for 2005. The FTT appeal was lost on 9 August, so BAR-Honda raced a mechanical (rather than electronic version) from the Italian GP, before agreeing for the system to be banned for 2005.

Satō led a qualifying 3–4 in Hungary only to lose ground at the first corner and finish behind fifth-placed Button. BAR-Honda endured a bruising Belgian GP. Off the qualifying pace when rain fell, both drivers were involved in the first-lap fracas at La Source with Satō eliminated. Button pitted for a new nosecone and was

back into the points when a high-speed puncture, Michelin's third of the race, sent him crashing into Zsolt Baumgartner while lapping the Minardi at Les Combes.

Button led 24 laps of the Italian GP before finishing third with Satō fourth as BAR-Honda passed Renault for second in the constructors' standings. British American Tobacco swapped its Lucky Strike logos for 555 stickers at the inaugural Chinese GP, with overalls and Davidson's third car sporting that brand's blue-and-yellow colours. Button claimed his fourth second place, 1.035sec behind the winner. Satō came from the back following an engine grid penalty to finish sixth.

After finishing third (Button) and fourth (Satō) at Suzuka, the team retained second overall despite a disappointing Brazilian GP. Button's engine was already smoking on the grid and lasted just three laps, another winning opportunity lost because he had overtaken eventual winner Montoya and was ahead of Michael Schumacher. Satō started and finished sixth.

MILD SEVEN RENAULT F1

The improved reliability dictated by new engine rules forced Renault to abandon its wide-angle philosophy and revert to a more conventional 72-degree V10 with a lineage that dated back to the Supertec customer units of 2000. The new RS24 unit's extra height raised the car's centre of gravity by 10mm, but it was reliable, produced more power and delivered a strong torque curve, even if it still fell short of Ferrari and BMW.

An unchanged driver line-up was confirmed when Jarno Trulli signed a one-year extension as Fernando Alonso's team-mate.

Fernando Alonso, Renault R24 (Monaco GP)

Jarno Trulli, Renault R24 (Belgian GP)

Franck Montagny became reserve driver after turning down a Minardi race seat, despite Renault not being able to use an additional test driver on GP Fridays. Montagny's Renault R23B was quickest during the 2–4 December test at Barcelona, where development drivers Heikki Kovalainen and José Maria López drove an F1 car for the first time. Mild Seven tobacco remained as title sponsor for an 11th season, with mobile network Telefónica added to the associate partners.

Former Cosworth chief engineer Rob White was appointed technical director of the engine facility at Viry-Châtillon, reporting to deputy managing director Bernard Dudot. Head of aerodynamics John Iley resigned at the end of 2003 and was replaced by Dino Toso. Chief designer Mark Smith left in August to become Jordan technical director.

Trulli shook down the new R24 ahead of schedule at Barcelona on 20 January, with Alonso raising hopes with fastest time on the test's last day. Officially launched in Palermo's Teatro Massimo opera house on 29 January, the R24 was another evolution, albeit with radical detailing behind the cockpit. 'The overall package is very compact,' technical director Bob Bell told *Autosport*. 'The [engine] characteristics have allowed us to sculpt the bodywork as we wanted to: the new vee angle permitted much narrower, tighter sidepods at the rear.' These were low at the back with long fins that curved around the rear wheels. The exhausts were moved back, and there were differing cooling options according to conditions, including three vents on each side and chimneys that curved outwards. Split radiators (angled top and bottom) and a smaller fuel tank aided the tight packaging. The rear wing was a development of the split-endplate design introduced during 2003 and double bargeboards were retained. Smith reduced the R24's weight while maintaining rigidity, with titanium (rather than titanium/carbon) now used in the six-speed gearbox.

With F1 president Patrick Faure stating that the team wanted to be 'one of the first three', Renault enjoyed an impressive winter thanks to pace and reliability. The R24 was difficult to drive, with its drivers complaining about its balance and twitchy handling, but its low-speed traction was better than any rival while tyre wear and fuel consumption were strengths. Despite the ban on electronic launch control, Renault maintained its lightning starts thanks to the unique 'pre-loaded' transmission.

From fifth on the grid in Melbourne, Alonso used the grass to snatch third and finished as 'best of the rest' behind the dominant Ferraris. Trulli faded to seventh after contact with Takuma Satō's BAR-Honda damaged his diffuser in the first corner. The Renaults were less competitive at the next two races although both drivers still scored points. Trulli was fifth in Malaysia and fourth in Bahrain,

Jacques Villeneuve, Renault R24 (Brazilian GP)

despite being hindered by Rubens Barrichello's unsafe release at the first pitstops. Qualifying issues scuppered Alonso's chances at both rounds and he was further delayed in Bahrain after a clash with Christian Klien's Jaguar-Cosworth at the start left him needing a new nosecone.

A new aero package for the San Marino GP featured revised wings and diffuser, with B-specification engines delivering more power. With nervous handling in qualifying trim, Alonso survived collisions with David Coulthard (lap one) and Ralf Schumacher (lap 49) to claim fourth, with Fisichella fifth. Handling was improved for the Spanish GP when Renault reverted to the 2003 front wing (with downward curvature at the centre) and revised the suspension. Trulli jumped from fourth to first at the start before leading a Renault 3–4 at the finish. He dedicated that podium to Dino Toso, who had been diagnosed with cancer.

With extra wings above the axle line and on the airbox for Monaco, the Renaults were competitive from the outset. On pole for the first time, Trulli dictated proceedings from the start and withstood Jenson Button's late pressure to score his only F1 victory. Alonso started third and initially shadowed his team-mate but was furious when he crashed in the tunnel after getting off-line while lapping Ralf Schumacher.

Trulli, who had a throat problem that caused him to lose his voice, continued to lead Renault's charge at the Nürburgring, where he qualified third but lost positions when he collided with Satō again, then recovered to finish fourth with Alonso fifth. Driveshaft failures accounted for both cars in Montréal. Relegated to the back at Indianapolis by an electronic issue on his qualifying run, Trulli salvaged fourth despite running wide as he challenged third-placed Satō. Alonso made another great start and was third until he crashed when debris caused a right-rear puncture.

Overshadowed by Trulli so far, Alonso started the French GP from pole position only to be beaten into second by the four-stopping Michael Schumacher. Trulli held third position until Barrichello forced his way past on the last corner of the race, sparking an angry exchange between Trulli and team boss Flavio Briatore. Previously in the form of his life and 13 points ahead of his much-hyped Spanish team-mate, Trulli did not score again as negotiations for 2005 eventually ended in the sack.

Renault's British GP was one to forget. Broken rear suspension was blamed for Trulli's 160mph accident at Bridge while a ten-place grid penalty for an engine change on Friday ruined Alonso's chances. In Germany, Alonso disputed second with Button before losing out when he ran over debris. Another engine upgrade at the Hungaroring, to RS24D (the C-spec only ran on the dyno), brought new cylinder heads but an engine failure sidelined Trulli in the race while Alonso trailed home third behind the Ferraris. In Belgium, Trulli used intermediate tyres to snatch pole position with Alonso third after the Ardennes rain intensified. They ran 1–2 for the opening nine laps before Trulli pitted from the lead and Alonso spun on his own oil. Trulli had his own spin when tagged by Juan Pablo Montoya at the Bus Stop chicane and finished ninth in a car that he described as 'undriveable' having 'lost grip at the rear'. Trulli's assertion that he was now being given inferior equipment was refuted by the team.

Renault failed to score at Monza, handing BAR the advantage in the contest for constructors' runner-up. Alonso spun into the gravel at the Variante della Roggi and Trulli's anonymous tenth place baffled management. But with Trulli no longer part of Briatore's driver-management empire and their relationship having deteriorated, Allan McNish and Franck Montagny – reserve drivers old and new – were mentioned as possible replacements. Jacques Villeneuve had a seat fitting two days after the Italian GP and signed a three-race deal to replace Trulli in the quest to secure second in the constructors' standings.

That gamble backfired with the lacklustre Villeneuve finishing no higher than tenth. Alonso scored on each occasion but his fourth places in China and Brazil, the latter after leading when wet-shod rivals pitted, plus fifth at Suzuka were not enough to overhaul BAR-Honda. Renault finished third overall, 14 points behind its rival.

BMW WILLIAMS F1

Ever-more restrictive rules made unconventional designs a rarity by 2004, with development by increment rather than quantum leap. It was therefore a shock when the Williams FW26-BMW was revealed at Valencia on 5 January, with the early date chosen so its engineers could hone its fundamentally different concept. Most striking was the FW26's wide, stubby 'walrus' nose, conceived to optimise the twin keel, which chief designer Gavin Fisher and head of aerodynamics Antonia Terzi adopted for the first time. The intention was to improve airflow under the car and to the spoon-shaped rear wing to regain downforce lost under the new regulations. BAR-like fences on the rear wing were introduced for the Bahrain GP before the FIA decreed that they were not legal. The short wheelbase of the FW25 was further reduced thanks to the smaller fuel tank that was now necessary. Pushrod suspension with front torsion bars and rear coil springs was retained. The front end had to be stiffened to pass the crash test, reducing the ballast available and adversely affecting weight distribution. Rather than add responsiveness, the FW26's short wheelbase made it nervous and difficult to handle.

First tested at Monza before the 2003 Italian GP, the BMW P84 engine was only slightly heavier than its best-in-class predecessor despite the need to last a whole race weekend, and BMW's Mario Theissen fully expected to reclaim the 10 percent power loss during the season. It was competitive, although Ferrari had now overtaken BMW in the outright power stakes. The FW26's narrow, aluminium seven-speed gearbox was the product of cooperation between Munich and Grove.

Williams technical director Patrick Head set out the goals for the coming season at launch: 'Since 1997 it has been the longest period in Williams's history without a championship, so our aim is to win them both.' The team was already destabilised by that time with both drivers almost certain to leave at the end of 2004. Juan Pablo Montoya had already signed for McLaren and Williams was refusing to match Toyota's offer to Ralf Schumacher.

Marc Gené re-signed as reserve driver in November with Sir Frank Williams considering his team 'fortunate to have a driver of Marc's calibre, who can test with metronomic precision and efficiency'.

Antônio Pizzonia resumed his test role after being quickest in a year-old FW25 at Valencia on 29 January. Two sons of former Williams champions, Nico Rosberg and Nelson Piquet Jr, also tested during the winter while Formula BMW Asia champion Ho-Pin Tung created 'full-colour, front-page news' in his home country when he became the first Chinese driver to test contemporary F1 machinery at Jerez on 11 December. IndyCar champion Scott Dixon impressed in the spring during four days at Paul Ricard and Barcelona, although an F1 switch never materialised.

Promising pre-season testing times led to disappointment in Australia, where the Williams-BMWs were half a second or more off Ferrari's ultimate pace and an early wheel-banging incident only increased tensions between its drivers. Montoya started third but was beaten into fourth by Ralf Schumacher after a scruffy race. Their Michelin tyres suited the Malaysian heat where Montoya took second and Schumacher survived contact with Mark Webber's Jaguar only to suffer BMW's single race-engine failure of the season. Having lost a podium in Bahrain when stuck in fourth gear for the last ten laps, Montoya finished third at Imola despite being frustrated that Michael Schumacher's vigorous opening-lap defence at Tosa went unpunished. Ralf Schumacher was seventh on both occasions following contact with Takuma Satō and Fernando Alonso respectively.

An aero upgrade was taken to the Spanish GP where the brake ducts proved too small and caused overheating. A mighty second on the grid but slow away, Montoya lost his brakes at an alarming rate and slid into a mechanic as he made a precautionary stop, without causing injury. Having nursed his car home sixth that day, Ralf Schumacher was second quickest in qualifying at Monaco but received a ten-place grid penalty for an engine change on Thursday. He progressively lost gears until he withdrew with seven laps to go,

Ralf Schumacher, Williams FW26-BMW (San Marino GP)

Juan Pablo Montoya, Williams FW26-BMW (Australian GP)

while Montoya survived another altercation with Schumacher Sr to claim fourth.

There was significant change at the top of the company after that race for Williams Grand Prix Engineering co-founder and technical director Patrick Head assumed the less hands-on role of director of engineering, with 33-year-old chief operations engineer Sam Michael promoted. The alarming slump continued during the summer, just as BMW was considering its long-term future. Eighth and ninth on the grid at the Nürburgring due to handling imbalance, they collided with each other at the first corner with Montoya blaming contact from a fast-starting Toyota for hitting the back of his team-mate's car and eliminating it, although Montoya was able to recover with eighth place. Canada seemed to be a turned point. Previously anonymous, Schumacher qualified on pole and led a strong 2–5 on the road before both Williams-BMWs were disqualified for illegal brake ducts.

Worse followed a week later at Indianapolis. Schumacher suffered a left-rear puncture in the banked Turn 13 on lap nine and thudded into the concrete retaining wall. Knocked out in that high-speed accident, he missed the next six races due to concussion and hairline fractures to two vertebrae. Montoya started from the pitlane in the spare car and was challenging the top four when the stewards black-flagged him for switching cars too late, fully 59 laps after the offence had been committed.

Such was Williams-BMW's plight that a major mechanical and aerodynamic upgrade, quoted by some to be the FW26B, was taken to the French GP without testing. So significant were the

changes that a new side-impact test was required. The twin-keel nose, engine cover and rear wing were revised with sidepods reprofiled around compact new radiators. Montoya crashed heavily in wet Friday practice, started sixth in the rebuilt car (after a couple of mistakes on his qualifying lap) and spun on his way to a disappointing eighth. The FW26s were particularly nervous at Silverstone where Montoya recovered from a slow start to finish fifth. Marc Gené completed both races in Schumacher's absence without threatening to score a point. 'It was just unfortunate for me to be driving the car at the time when it was most difficult and least competitive,' he said.

Gené was dropped for the German GP but a planned head-to-head test at Jerez between Antônio Pizzonia and Jordan's Nick Heidfeld to choose his replacement was cancelled when terms could not be agreed with Eddie Jordan, so Pizzonia returned unopposed. Williams-BMW's new aero package worked at Hockenheim where both cars scored points. Montoya qualified on the front row and finished fifth despite a poor start and blistered tyres, with Pizzonia seventh.

Further revisions tested only in the wind tunnel were taken to the Hungaroring, the most noticeable of them a standard, narrow nose and complex front-wing endplates that replaced the 'walrus' affair. Montoya made a fast start from seventh to finish fourth while Pizzonia, who had qualified a place ahead of his team-mate despite his heavier fuel load, again finished seventh. Changeable conditions compromised qualifying in Belgium, where both were denied possible podium finishes. Pizzonia was third when his gearbox

Marc Gené, Williams FW26-BMW (British GP)

failed and Montoya, who had knocked Jarno Trulli into a spin at the chicane, lost that position late on when a puncture caused terminal suspension damage.

A low-downforce set-up for Monza, including the pre-Hungary front wing and a new rear end, helped Montoya grab another front-row start, albeit 0.531sec slower than Rubens Barrichello's Ferrari. A minor gearbox problem from half distance demoted the Colombian to fifth by the finish. Pizzonia was hit by Olivier Panis's Toyota at the Variante della Roggia on lap one before recovering from the back to claim his customary seventh. That was his last appearance of 2004 for Schumacher was passed fit (and insurance formalities completed) for the last three races.

Progress made during the German driver's absence was evident to him on his return. The quicker Williams-BMW driver in China when fifth on the grid, he retired when David Coulthard's optimistic lunge at the hairpin ended in contact. That DNF gave him a beneficial qualifying slot in Japan where he translated another front-row start alongside his brother into a strong second place. Montoya finished fifth in China and was seventh in Japan after an 'off' at Suzuka's chicane.

Williams-BMW's largely frustrating campaign drew to a triumphant conclusion at Interlagos. Starting second once more, Montoya made a timely switch from intermediate to dry tyres and withstood Kimi Räikkönen's close attentions to win by 1.022sec, with Schumacher fifth. Juan Pablo and Connie Montoya chose a São Paulo McDonalds to celebrate what would be Williams's last win until the 2012 Spanish GP.

Williams-BMW beat McLaren-Mercedes into fourth as the best of the fallen giants. The repercussions of the failed 'walrus' concept were felt after the season when Terzi, who had been credited with its inspiration, resigned on 3 November, and did not work in F1 again. She was replaced as head of aerodynamics by Loïc Bigois, who had joined in March to work on the 2005 car and develop the new wind tunnel at Grove.

Antônio Pizzonia, Williams FW26-BMW (Belgian GP)

WEST McLAREN MERCEDES

West McLaren Mercedes endured a disastrous start to the 2004 campaign as it dealt with the aftermath of the MP4-18 debacle, restructured the relationship with its engine supplier and relocated to the state-of-the-art McLaren Technology Centre. However, the team did win a race for the eighth successive season and finished 2004 on the rise once more.

David Coulthard extended his contract for another year but began his ninth season with the team knowing it would be his last. Juan Pablo Montoya signed for 2005 on 17 November 2003 and McLaren exercised its option on Kimi Räikkönen in the New Year. Reserve driver Alexander Wurz, who had been free to negotiate with Jaguar, and tester Pedro de la Rosa remained for 2004. Aerodynamicist Nikolas Tombazis joined from Ferrari in April to work alongside Peter Prodromou.

Although the team was often one of the last to reveal its new car, the McLaren MP4-19 and Mercedes-Benz FO110Q engine were running at Valencia as soon as close-season testing began on 25 November. With management on both sides stressing the benefits of the unraced MP4-18 programme, Mercedes-Benz motorsport boss Norbert Haug stated: 'The MP4-18 was a completely new concept and was worth a lot for what we learned… We will feel the benefits on the 19.' The new car was a mechanical and aerodynamic refinement of that unraced machine according to technical director Adrian Newey. 'What we have tried to do,' he told *Autosport*, 'is make a reliable and raceable version of the MP4-18.' The monocoque was stiffened and its distinctive needle nose fell away to a contoured front wing that had unique endplates with a stepped leading edge.

An alternative front wing was raced from the Malaysian GP with a single central downward curve as engineers sought to eradicate understeer. The exhaust chimneys introduced on the MP4-17D at the 2003 Italian GP were retained, as were vertical brake callipers. Attention was paid to improving access to the engine and the time taken to change it. The cockpit was so tight that the 6ft 2in Wurz originally could not fit, with drivers suffering bruising before it was reconfigured with the fire extinguisher moved.

Promising pre-Christmas tests at Valencia and Jerez proved deceptive for the original MP4-19 lacked reliability and pace. The drivers struggled to generate tyre temperature in its Michelins while rear-end instability under braking and oversteer were additional traits. Engine-installation issues plagued the 2–6 February Barcelona test and Räikkönen, returning after a month's convalescence following an operation on his wrist, suffered a pit fire at Valencia.

McLaren set out on the championship trail believing it was lacking 50bhp and unsure as to whether its engine could last a race weekend. Indeed, the team suffered its worst start to a season since 1981, initially a second off the pace. Räikkönen retired from the first three races, although fifth on the Malaysian grid gave some cause for optimism. Coulthard finished eighth in Australia and sixth in Malaysia but lost another minor score when hydraulic pressure vanished in Bahrain. This poor start prompted a management restructure across team and engine partner alike, with Martin Whitmarsh becoming general manager for both McLaren Racing (rebranded from McLaren International) and Mercedes-Ilmor. Operations director Jonathan Neale replaced Whitmarsh as team MD. Hans-Ulrich Maik and Werner Laurenz left Mercedes-Ilmor and

Kimi Räikkönen, McLaren MP4-19B-Mercedes-Benz (French GP)

David Coulthard, McLaren MP4-19-Mercedes-Benz (Australian GP)

the company adopted alternate project leaders for each season, Andy Cowell leading development in 2004 with Axel Wendorff responsible for 2005. Mercedes-Benz's long-term commitment to F1 was boosted by main board director Jürgen Hubbert's decision to postpone retirement plans.

There was no immediate transformation. The MP4-19s were a handful over the kerbs at Imola, where Räikkönen salvaged eighth from the back of the grid following an engine change, while Coulthard was delayed by a first-lap clash with Fernando Alonso. Both were off the pace in Spain and had slow pitstops.

The impressive new McLaren Technology Centre was officially opened on 12 May by HM Queen Elizabeth II. This futuristic semi-circular headquarters, set in 'green-belt' land two miles north of Woking, was the largest privately funded construction project in Europe at the time. Designed by Sir Norman Foster, the 500,000sq ft scheme received government approval in 1997, with ground broken on the site the following year.

A new 'spoon' rear wing and tweaked suspension were tested before Monaco in a bid to improve handling. Räikkönen and Coulthard qualified 5–8 although Sunday only brought more disappointment. Coulthard was the innocent victim when Giancarlo Fisichella, unsighted by smoke from Takuma Satō's huge blow-up, crashed over him at the Swimming Pool while Räikkönen lost a podium finish when his engine lost pneumatic pressure. Räikkönen

started fourth and ran second at the Nürburgring before new pistons were blamed for engine failures that accounted for both cars in front of Mercedes-Benz's home support. That prompted an openly critical Hubbert to tell *Bild* that he would 'prefer finishing a race in sixth position than having the cars stopping in second'.

Work on the MP4-19B had begun in August 2003, long before the full extent of the team's woes became apparent, and Räikkönen first drove the revised car at a wet Silverstone two days after the Nürburgring debacle. The MP4-19B project team, led by chief designer Mike Coughlan, wanted to redistribute weight but was constrained by having to evolve an existing car. The new monocoque was marginally taller and waisted at the middle with cockpit size increased. Its engine was raised to enlarge the dry sump while fuel capacity was reduced in keeping with contemporary thinking. Revised aerodynamics featured a lower needle nose and new diffuser. The sidepods had marked undercuts and reshaped double winglets that drew comparison to the latest Ferrari and Renault respectively. A wider nose section was tried on either side of the summer break before being raced at Monza. All-new rear suspension aimed to alleviate oversteer.

The original MP4-19s continued to be raced in North America, where McLaren-Mercedes scored its first double points finishes of 2004. With Williams-BMW and Toyota disqualified in Canada, Räikkönen was fifth despite four stops and a drive-through penalty for crossing the pit exit line. Coulthard recovered from being spun around by Christian Klien's Jaguar at the first corner to claim ninth on the road and sixth in the revised results. Perseverance was rewarded at Indianapolis where Räikkönen and Coulthard finished 6–7 despite both being delayed.

Two MP4-19Bs were taken to Jerez for an extensive four-day test with all four drivers pressed into action. With overheating issues overcome and more than 3,000km completed, the step forward was confirmed in France and at Silverstone. Coulthard qualified third at Magny-Cours, although the cars faded to sixth and seventh in the race. Räikkönen grabbed a shock pole position for the British GP, led the early laps and challenged Michael Schumacher for victory before finishing second, splitting the Ferraris. Räikkönen continued to press Schumacher at Hockenheim until his rear wing failed on the high-speed approach to Turn 1. Coulthard was seventh and fourth in these races.

An overly cautious tyre choice for qualifying blighted Hungary before Räikkönen restored the *Silver Arrows* to the top step of the podium at Spa-Francorchamps. Tenth on the grid following a qualifying mistake in the rain, he was fifth by the end of the first lap, inherited the lead when Alonso's Renault retired and outpaced a conservative Michael Schumacher to score McLaren-Mercedes's only victory of 2004. Coulthard qualified fourth and finished seventh after a right-rear puncture and the loss of his front wing in another *contretemps* with Klien.

Räikkönen had engine issues in Italy before qualifying second and finishing third in China. Sixth at Monza after starting from the pitlane with a full fuel load, Coulthard's hopes of scoring points in China or Japan were denied by contact with Ralf Schumacher and Rubens Barrichello respectively. Sixth in Japan, Räikkönen jumped into the Brazilian GP lead from third on the grid only to lose out at the final pitstops. He shadowed Montoya home in second with Coulthard a downbeat 11th.

Fifth overall represented McLaren's worst constructors' performance in two decades.

RED BULL SAUBER PETRONAS

There was an all-new driver line-up at Hinwil with Heinz-Harald Frentzen and Nick Heidfeld released. Giancarlo Fisichella visited the factory in July and his two-year deal was announced at the 2003 Hungarian GP, with a get-out clause for 2005 if a top-three team came calling. Peter Sauber confirmed persistent rumours of Felipe Massa's return after a year testing for Ferrari when he also signed a two-year deal. Plans to run Neel Jani as Friday test driver were dropped, 'principally for budget reasons'. Red Bull-backed F3000 champion Vitantonio Liuzzi was given his first F1 test at Jerez on 16 September. Jacky Eeckelaert was promoted to head of vehicle engineering and Rémy Decorzent moved to Toyota. They were replaced as race engineers by Giampaolo Dall'Ara and Mike Krack, who worked with Fisichella and Massa respectively.

Sauber's state-of-the-art new wind tunnel was opened on 16 December 2003 and became fully operational in February. Fisichella claimed 'maybe it is the best wind tunnel in Formula 1' although Sauber lacked the budget to make full use of the facility. Existing tunnels at Emmen and Huntingdon (Lola) were used to design the Sauber C23-Petronas, with Ferrari supplying the gearbox as well as the Petronas-badged V10. The C23's resemblance to the Ferrari F2003-GA was noted at its launch in Red Bull Hangar-7 at Salzburg airport on 12 January. Whispers that it was a direct copy, and therefore illegal, were compounded by technical director Willy Rampf's abandonment of the twin-keel front suspension that Sauber had pioneered, preferring Ferrari's single-keel solution to increase rigidity and, perhaps more importantly, to integrate tyre development. The wheelbase was reduced by 5cm and the chassis was modified after it failed its initial side-impact test. British American Racing's defection to Michelin left Bridgestone with just four clients – Ferrari, Sauber and cash-strapped Jordan and Minardi – which stressed the Swiss team's importance to Maranello. The front wishbones were strengthened following a high-speed failure during Barcelona testing prompted an overnight stay in hospital for Massa. Power

Giancarlo Fisichella, Sauber C23-Petronas (Italian GP)

Felipe Massa, Sauber C23-Petronas (Chinese GP)

steering was introduced at the Bahrain GP and new wings and aero parts arrived throughout the European season.

The stopwatch soon showed that the C23 was not merely a Ferrari clone for it was initially slow if reliable. Fisichella finished the first four races (despite stalling at both pitstops in Malaysia and being spun by Ralf Schumacher in Bahrain) with ninth from the back of the grid at Imola his best result thus far. Massa outqualified his team-mate at the opening two rounds and, his engine having failed in Australia, survived an 'off' to finish eighth in Malaysia.

Seventh in Spain, Fisichella appeared well-placed in Monaco when he started tenth despite a heavy fuel load. He could not exploit that strategy when, unsighted by smoke from Takuma Satō's blow-up, he crashed over David Coulthard's McLaren in the Swimming Pool section and rolled. Understeer restricted Massa to ninth in Barcelona while he overcame tyre degradation to hold onto fifth in Monte Carlo. Fisichella missed qualifying for the European GP to conserve a set of tyres and came from the back to finish a fine sixth. A clutch issue caused a poor start for Massa before front-wing damage upset the car's handling.

There were contrasting fortunes in Canada with Fisichella inheriting fourth after both Williams-BMWs were disqualified but Massa enduring a 113G head-on impact at the hairpin when he lost a rear wheel at 165mph during the closing stages. That was caused by a rear-suspension breakage, leading to strengthening for the United States GP. Hampered by blistering tyres and lacking grip all weekend, Massa was eliminated at the first corner while late

hydraulics failure ended Fisichella's points challenge.

Only the Jordans and Minardis qualified slower in France before an upgrade for Silverstone proved a significant step forward. Vents for the innovative 'folded' radiators were repositioned on tightly packaged sidepods, which sported double rather than single winglets, and the engine cover plunged sharply to the rear. Electing not to qualify once more, Fisichella climbed through the field to sixth at Silverstone. A jammed left-rear wheel denied another score at Hockenheim, where a slow pitstop and more tyre issues thwarted Massa. Fisichella qualified and finished eighth in Hungary but Massa retired with fading brakes after starting last following an engine change on Friday.

Using extreme wet-weather tyres, both drivers qualified in the top eight in Belgium, with Fisichella starting fifth. Both cars suffered damage at the first corner but recovered to finish fourth (Massa) and fifth (Fisichella). At the Italian GP, Massa rammed Nick Heidfeld's Jordan on lap five but Fisichella finished eighth. They were light fuelled for qualifying in China so Massa lined up fourth and Fisichella seventh. Three-stopping, their tyres grained throughout the race, but they held on to score, Fisichella seventh, Massa eighth. Fisichella was eighth in Japan despite running wide at Spoon and spun away his hopes in Brazil. Massa delighted the partisan Brazilian crowd by starting fourth, leading a couple of laps in the wet and finishing eighth.

The best independent team by far, Sauber-Petronas easily beat manufacturer rivals Jaguar and Toyota as it retained sixth overall.

Mark Webber, Jaguar R5-Cosworth (German GP)

JAGUAR RACING

This was a crucial year for Jaguar Racing. Losses at the Ford Motor Company led to a budget cut and questions about Ford's long-term commitment circulated by mid-season. Jaguar Racing and Cosworth Engineering were put up for sale on 17 September 2004, on the day that Ford also announced that road-car production would cease at Jaguar's historic Browns Lane plant in Coventry.

The bleak financial outlook already had a bearing on the choice of team-mate for Mark Webber, whom Jaguar had re-signed in May 2003. The search for the number two led to Red Bull, which wanted to place F3 Euroseries runner-up Christian Klien in a race seat. He was among those assessed when testing resumed at Valencia's Circuito Ricardo Tormo on 25 November 2003. Jaguar had wanted Alexander Wurz and talks were held with Jos Verstappen, but the unheralded 20-year-old Klien was confirmed as Webber's team-mate on 2 December in a deal that bolstered Jaguar's coffers by over $10m.

Plans to retain Justin Wilson as Friday test driver were scuppered by the FIA's ruling that only drivers with six or fewer GP starts in the past two years were eligible. Townsend Bell and Alan van der Merwe were possibilities before Björn Wirdheim was the surprise choice in January. The reigning F3000 champion fulfilled that role at all 18 races and was placed on standby to race in France when Klien injured his hand in a garage incident during Jerez testing.

Tony Purnell, Head of Ford's Premier Performance Division, admitted that the Jaguar R5-Cosworth had faults even before its shakedown at Lommel airfield in Belgium. Officially launched at

the Barcelona circuit on 18 January, the evolutionary R5 was built around the monocoque from the 2003 car that had shown glimpses in Webber's hands. It was the product of a stable engineering team with Rob Taylor (vehicle design), Mark Gillan (vehicle performance) and Ben Agathangelou (aerodynamics) at the helm. Chief engineer Malcolm Oastler returned to Australia in June.

Single-keel front suspension was retained, ahead of large bargeboards and elongated sidepods. The weight of the latest 90-degree Cosworth V10 engine (CR-6) was reduced despite the need to last a full race weekend. The seven-speed gearbox was new and the pushrod suspension was revised as Jaguar sought to improve rear-tyre wear. As Taylor commented: 'We've made a significant improvement in mass, stiffness, weight, centre of gravity, all the usual things.' A controversial new rear wing used at the Spanish GP featured aerodynamic 'fences' to join the two permitted upper elements. A new diffuser was introduced for the German GP although the brake ducts that were part of that upgrade had to be removed when they overheated.

Work began on upgrading Jaguar's wind tunnels in Bedford and Bicester. Pi Research executive Tim Routsis replaced Cosworth managing director Nick Hayes in the close season as Hayes initially returned to his previous F1 technical director role before leaving in a summer reshuffle. Chairman of long-time sponsor HSBC, Sir John Bond shared his frustrations at the company's Annual General Meeting at the time. 'I share your disappointment with the team's performance,' he said. 'We are committed to the end of 2004 and

Christian Klien, Jaguar R5-Cosworth (Belgian GP)

will make an announcement at the right time.' It did not renew. There was a high-profile association with the movie *Ocean's 12* at Monaco, with a £140,000 Steinmetz diamond embedded in the nose of each car and Hollywood A-listers George Clooney, Brad Pitt and Matt Damon in attendance.

With Webber continuing in the development R4B, Klien was 3.441sec off the pace in the new car after three days (20–22 January) at Barcelona with subsequent tests beset by teething troubles. The R5 was unstable in high-speed corners before its full 2004 aero package was taken to Jerez in February with improved reliability and speed shown next time out at Valencia. Webber continued to display single-lap promise, but power deficit and continued rear tyre wear restricted Jaguar to seventh overall once more.

Webber began with top-six grid positions at the first two races only to retire. Having stopped as he lost gears in Australia, he could not make the most of his headline-grabbing front-row start in Malaysia and dropped to ninth as the anti-stall kicked in. He finally spun out after a rear puncture from a collision with Ralf Schumacher on lap five and a drive-through penalty for speeding in the pitlane. An error ruined his qualifying in Bahrain, but he rebounded by finishing eighth despite running wide on the out-lap from his second pitstop. A top-ten qualifier at the next two races, Webber faded due an electrical issue at Imola and lack of grip in Spain. Denied points in Monaco by electronics failure, he recovered from a slow start and a moment with Michael Schumacher at the Nürburgring to claim seventh. He was quickest at a Silverstone test but was lucky to walk

away from a high-speed shunt at Becketts following a puncture.

Klien finished his first four GPs without scoring a point. He was tenth after a slow pitstop in Malaysia, diced with Fernando Alonso (breaking the Spaniard's front wing) and Kimi Räikkönen in Bahrain, and retired in Spain and Monaco. On the opening lap in the Principality, he rammed Nick Heidfeld's Jordan at Mirabeau and consequently crashed his R5 at the Loews Hairpin with the promotional diamond lost. Ahead of Webber on the Canadian grid (tenth), impact with David Coulthard's McLaren at the start catapulted him into the other Jaguar, inflicting terminal suspension damage on Webber's car and leaving himself a chastened ninth following repairs and post-race disqualifications. Both retired from the United States GP, Klien after another first-lap *contretemps* and Webber when his upgraded engine caught fire.

Double finishes at the next four races showed improved reliability, Webber beating Felipe Massa and Fernando Alonso into eighth at Silverstone and overcoming oversteer to claim sixth in Germany. Tenth despite a spin in Hungary, Webber qualified seventh in the Belgian rain only to be eliminated when he hit Rubens Barrichello's Ferrari at the first corner. Klien passed Olivier Panis's Toyota and survived contact with Coulthard to claim sixth and his first F1 points. They were off the pace in Italy, where Webber finished ninth and Klien 13th following a drive-through for speeding in the pitlane. With the team now officially for sale and closure a very real possibility, talks were held with interested parties Red Bull, Arden International – whose owner Christian Horner was Jaguar's

Björn Wirdheim, Jaguar R5-Cosworth (Italian GP)

guest at the Chinese GP – and Alex Shnaider's Midland Group.

In China, Klien drove an updated R5B with new suspension and diffuser, plus a lighter chassis and lower centre of gravity. His weekend ended when contact with Michael Schumacher's Ferrari at the chicane broke his suspension. Webber finished tenth in the standard car. Shanghai proved to be a one-off for the R5B, for Jaguar reverted to standard cars for the final two races. Webber made the most of drying conditions in Japan to claim third on the grid but did not figure in the race before being forced to retire by pain from his scalding cockpit. Klien finished his difficult rookie campaign with finishes outside the top ten as Jaguar faded from the scene, with Webber eliminated from the Brazilian GP when he crashed into his team-mate after 23 laps.

The bleak final months of Jaguar Racing came to a successful conclusion when Ford agreed terms with Red Bull and Champ Car Series co-owner Kevin Kalkhoven to buy Jaguar and Cosworth respectively. Both deals were announced at 9am on Monday, 15 November, safeguarding the workforces at the respective factories in Milton Keynes and Northampton.

PANASONIC TOYOTA RACING

Toyota Motorsport continued to flex its financial muscles as it reshaped its technical team. Persistent rumours were confirmed when Renault released Mike Gascoyne on 1 December 2003, a year early, to take up a four-year contract as technical director, with

Gustav Brunner reverting to the chief designer role. Team chairman Tsutomu Tomita also assumed Ove Andersson's team principal duties when the Swede retired to take an advisory role. There were no changes in the cockpit with confirmation of Olivier Panis and Cristiano da Matta on 5 August 2003. Ricardo Zonta remained as reserve driver with Ryan Briscoe returning to the testing role.

The 2004 engine and rear end were evaluated for six weeks in a modified TF103B test chassis before the Toyota TF104 was launched at the factory in Cologne on 17 January. Gascoyne described Luca Marmorini's latest V10 (RVX-04) as 'a championship-winning engine', and it still developed over 900bhp despite having to last a whole weekend. Titanium was used to save weight and increase rigidity in the compact new seven-speed gearbox while Brunner continued to eschew the twin-keel fashion. There were curved bargeboards ahead of shorter sidepods sporting simplified single winglets, the periscope exhausts were more central, and the 'Coke bottle' rear extremely narrow. Fuel capacity was reduced in a narrower tank, but the chassis proved too heavy while lacking downforce and grip. The relatively high centre of gravity wore the rear Michelins at an unacceptable rate. Panis crashed heavily at Barcelona on 5 February and required a precautionary night in hospital.

With Australian qualifying compromised, da Matta stalled at his first pitstop and both Toyotas were lapped with only a Jordan behind at the finish. An improved tenth on the grid in Malaysia, the Brazilian finished ninth after running wide on the opening lap, while Panis was three places worse off after an error-strewn race.

Cristiano da Matta, Toyota TF104 (Bahrain GP)

The TF104s fared better at the smooth new Bahrain International Circuit where they qualified and finished in the top ten. Gascoyne had instigated a redesign of the TF104 straight after the Australian GP, but the lowered version delivered little discernible improvement at Imola. Light-fuelled, da Matta did manage to qualify tenth only to receive a drive-through penalty for speeding in the pitlane and spin out after accidently switching off the traction control. Panis started the Spanish GP from seventh but was guilty of another pitlane speeding offence before the hydraulics failed. Blighted by understeer all weekend, da Matta finished last.

Head of aerodynamics René Hilhorst moved on following a disagreement with Gascoyne, who assumed hands-on control for that area of development. The team finally scored its first points at Monaco, with da Matta sixth despite a drive-through for ignoring blue flags and Panis eighth from the pitlane. Zonta was unhurt when he crashed heavily during Monza testing following a rear blow-out on the approach to the Parabolica. The North American detour delivered fifth for Panis at Indianapolis and double disqualification in Canada due to oversized extra cooling for the brakes. The TF104s were too slow in France and Silverstone ended with another non-score, Panis going out with a spin when his fire extinguisher discharged.

Olivier Panis, Toyota TF104B (Japanese GP)

Ricardo Zonta, Toyota TF104B (Brazilian GP)

Gascoyne's updated TF104B had been scheduled for that race but was only completed in time for the German GP. Another lightened monocoque (by 9kg) was shaken down at Jerez before its all-new aero was added on Friday at Hockenheim. A five percent increase in aerodynamic efficiency was expected from a package featuring curved supports for the front wing with revised endplates. The sidepod winglets were twisted ahead of modified flick-ups and a tighter-still 'Coke bottle' rear. Exhaust chimneys on the sidepods replaced the gills seen on the original car. But the revisions did not help in Germany as Panis, having started ninth, stalled and da Matta had a race-ending puncture.

Gascoyne was adamant that the TF104B was a step forward: 'There's nothing wrong with the car,' he said after that race, 'not a single problem.' Both drivers had already been informed that

they would not be retained in 2005. Da Matta was sacked with immediate effect on 5 August with Zonta, who had been the team's third driver at every race thus far, named as his replacement. Briscoe replaced Zonta for the remaining six GP Fridays, which included a puncture-induced high-speed crash at Eau Rouge. Norbert Kreyer and Ange Pasquali left in a mid-season cull, with operations manager Richard Cregan replacing Pasquali as team manager.

Zonta's debut in Hungary proved fraught. Starting 15th, he was spun around by Mark Webber's Jaguar in the first corner. His recovery was slowed by blistered tyres and halted by electronics failure; Panis finished 11th. The Frenchman made the best of his powerful engine to claim ninth on the Belgian grid but lost his front wing at the start and recovered steadily to eighth. Zonta started last after a pre-qualifying spin, gained ten positions on the opening

Ryan Briscoe, Toyota TF104B (Belgian GP)

Jarno Trulli, Toyota TF104B (Brazilian GP)

lap, and was running fourth thanks to a race of attrition when he suffered a rare engine failure with three laps to go.

The pain continued at Monza where Panis crashed into Antônio Pizzonia at the Roggia chicane on the opening lap and Zonta finished 11th having lacked grip throughout. Panis qualified eighth in China only for the anti-stall to activate and ruin his race, while Zonta lost fifth gear and retired. New signing Jarno Trulli tested at Silverstone and Jerez, where he crashed following a puncture, before replacing Zonta in Japan and Panis in Brazil. Trulli's sixth on the grid in Japan after topping pre-qualifying was Toyota's best starting position of the year but his tyres degraded in the race, then in Brazil lost positions when it rained. Both Toyotas finished outside the top ten at those last two races as another underwhelming campaign drew to a close.

JORDAN FORD

Jordan Grand Prix's financial plight dominated its immediate future. Dublin-based investment company Merrion Capital acquired Warburg, Pincus & Co's 49.9 percent shareholding in October 2003 and Eddie Jordan was Roman Abramovich's guest at a Chelsea football match a month later. Summer rumours of Middle Eastern investment, first from Bahrain and then Dubai, did not materialise.

Eddie Jordan was angered when manufacturers did not respect the previously suggested $10m customer engine budget. Talks were held with Mercedes-Benz before terms were agreed with Cosworth to continue. The team's Ford-badged V10s were meant to be of the same specification as Jaguar's works supply, although some power was sacrificed to improve reliability. Jordan director of business affairs Ian Phillips told *Autocourse*'s Maurice Hamilton: 'We

Nick Heidfeld, Jordan EJ14-Ford (Monaco GP)

Giorgio Pantano, Jordan EJ14-Ford (Belgian GP)

Timo Glock, Jordan EJ14-Ford (Canadian GP)

Robert Doornbos, Jordan EJ14-Ford (Brazilian GP)

were probably 70bhp down on Jaguar. And it got worse… when Cosworth were up for sale.'

Giancarlo Fisichella moved to Sauber when his contract expired and Jos Verstappen, who had backing from Trust Computers, ended winter-long negotiations on 27 January 2004. Nick Heidfeld had signed an option with Jordan before Christmas and was announced as lead driver three days after the Verstappen talks ended.

The Gallaher Tobacco Group that had backed Jordan since 1996 promoted its Sobranie brand in territories where Benson & Hedges was not sold. Its preference for a British driver boosted the cause of Ralph Firman or Allan McNish for the second seat. However, both were left disappointed when late talks with Giorgio Pantano concluded with the F3000 race winner named as Heidfeld's team-mate a fortnight before the season. Jaroslav Janiš, Timo Glock and Bas Leinders all tested during the winter, although the latter crashed after just six corners of his installation lap at Barcelona. Glock also had an accident on his first day but impressed enough to sign as Friday test driver.

James Robinson replaced Gary Anderson as head of race and test engineering while Henri Durand also left after the disappointing 2003 campaign. John McQuilliam and Nicolò Petrucci continued to head the design and aero departments, without sufficient wind-tunnel time or development budget. Speaking after Heidfeld gave the Jordan EJ14-Ford its shakedown at Silverstone on 2 February, Eddie Jordan claimed: 'We have found a bigger aero increase from… last year to this than we ever found in our 14 years so far.' Financial constraints and the late go-ahead for the EJ14 dictated a simple, conventional design. Jordan reverted to a single keel and the pushrod/torsion bar suspension was completely revised. The EJ14 was shorter than its predecessor, with a stiffer, lighter monocoque. The exhausts were placed within the flick-ups at the rear of the sidepods. The smaller gearbox allowed the diffuser to be enlarged. A new deal was agreed with Bridgestone.

The EJ14 had Trust logos for that shakedown as negotiations

with Verstappen were briefly rekindled but they were removed for the official launch on 4 February. It was a surprise, not least to Verstappen and his manager Huub Rothengatter, when Trust concluded a deal with Jordan nonetheless. There was further contact between the parties and Verstappen was due to do a day's filming for Trust at Silverstone on 1 June until he pulled out claiming that he could not fit in the EJ14. Without a title sponsor once more, Jordan signed an associate deal with the Bahrain GP organisers.

For all the pre-season talk of being the fifth-best team, this was another challenging campaign with only Minardi for company. Heidfeld retired from four of the first five races, hitting two mechanics as he pitted to check his failing clutch in Australia. With no prior experience of the first three circuits, Pantano circulated steadily among the backmarkers and finished each time. There were double DNFs at Imola and Barcelona and costly accidents during Friday practice at Imola (Glock) and testing at a wet Paul Ricard (Heidfeld). The latter responded to that shunt by finishing seventh at the next race in Monaco when he switched to a three-stop strategy amid the flurry of safety-car periods, but Pantano's race ended after 12 laps when stuck in fourth gear. The Nürburgring brought Heidfeld's best starting position of 2004, 13th, and 10th place in the race.

A management dispute forced Pantano from the cockpit after Canadian Friday practice, so Glock took his place for qualifying and the race. The debutant changed his bent front wing at the first stop and survived contact with Christian Klien's Jaguar to finish 11th on the road. Heidfeld was 12th despite a botched pitstop that saw his refueller dragged along the pitlane. They were promoted to seven and eight (giving three precious championship points) when Williams-BMW and Toyota were disqualified. Pantano was the unwitting victim of the first-corner accident at Indianapolis while engine failure denied Heidfeld further points. Both Jordans had drive-through penalties at Magny-Cours and Pantano's second spin during the British GP left him beached at Abbey. Eddie Jordan refused Heidfeld permission to test for Williams-BMW with a view to replacing the injured Ralf Schumacher while unknown Israeli Chanoch Nissany was 18.501sec off the pace when he tested an EJ14 at Silverstone on 14 July.

Heidfeld parked his ill-handling car at Hockenheim before finishing the next five races outside the top ten, despite early incidents in Belgium and Italy. Pantano was 15th in Germany and retired from the next three races, twice through crashes, with Gianmaria Bruni's Minardi at Raidillon on the opening lap in Belgium and at the Parabolica in Italy. He was dropped on the Wednesday before the Chinese GP and replaced by Glock, initially as a one-off but then also for the last two races when former F1 driver David Kennedy could not broker a deal for Formula Nippon champion-elect Richard Lyons to have the seat. Glock finished 15th in all three races while Robert Doornbos took over his testing duties despite no experience of an F1 car. Heidfeld's dispiriting campaign concluded with mechanical failure after 15 laps of the Brazilian GP.

WILUX MINARDI COSWORTH/MINARDI COSWORTH

Before the end of the 2003 season, Minardi extended its Cosworth agreement for updated CR-3 engines. The back-to-back test between the Minardi PS03 and PS04 (*née* Arrows A23) to decide the design direction for 2004 was inconclusive although team owner Paul Stoddart promised 'a new PS04 in 2004 that will be the best of both worlds'. Gabriele Tredozi (technical director) and Sandro Parini based the new PS04B on the PS03 and it first turned a wheel at Imola on 17 February, with its CR-3L V10 mated to a six-speed semi-automatic gearbox. The monocoque, pushrod-activated torsion-bar suspension and engine mountings were all stiffened, the centre of gravity lowered, and weight redistributed. Loïc Bigois was responsible for the aerodynamics before he moved to Williams. Budget prevented any wind-tunnel time until February and restricted in-season test days to a rarity. Revised bodywork and diffuser were available at the opening race with subsequent aerodynamic upgrades at Imola and the Nürburgring, including a

new floor and bargeboards. Bridgestone tyres were retained.

Commercial needs remained the crucial factor in choosing drivers. Friday test driver by the end of 2003, Gianmaria Bruni was promoted to the race team, and was joined at Minardi's Vallelunga test on 10–11 December by Heikki Kovalainen, José Maria López, Norbert Siedler, Fabrizio del Monte and Narain Karthikeyan. After Jos Verstappen took his Trust Computers money elsewhere, Hungarian journeyman Zsolt Baumgartner was named as Bruni's team-mate before Christmas. Baumgartner saw out the season despite the loss of an oil sponsor in the New Year and reduced government investment. Bas Leinders was named as third driver in March but was prevented from running in Australia because he had not completed the necessary 300km in an FIA-observed F1 test. He fulfilled that requirement at a wet Fiorano before the Malaysian GP and undertook Friday testing duties at every GP thereafter. Hopes of making his race debut at Spa-Francorchamps were denied when Leinders could not raise enough backing. Sergey Zlobin tested at Vallelunga in September.

A Minardi normally finished, invariably at the back and having been lapped more than once. Australia was beset by misfires that halted Baumgartner and delayed Bruni for 17 minutes in the pits. Both finished in Malaysia, and Bruni was last in Bahrain after electronic issues forced him to start from the pitlane. Baumgartner brought up the rear at Imola, they spun out of the Spanish GP and both crashed during practice in Monaco. The power steering failed on both cars during that weekend's race but Baumgartner persevered to finish ninth.

After a double finish in the European GP, Baumgartner recovered from being pitched into a spin by Christian Klien in Canada to claim a post-disqualification tenth. Team and driver were rewarded for persistence when Baumgartner became the first Hungarian to score a point by finishing eighth in the United States, two laps behind any other car still circulating. In contrast, Bruni was involved in the first-corner mêlée and parked rather than try to get back to the pits for repairs to his suspension. In France, Baumgartner spun into the gravel and Bruni pitted on the last lap to save his gearbox.

Bas Leinders, Minardi PS04B-Cosworth (European GP)

Gianmaria Bruni, Minardi PS04B-Cosworth (Monaco GP)

The British GP was overshadowed by sporting director John Walton's death on Friday following a heart attack earlier in the week. Minardi missed Saturday practice as a mark of respect and raced with sponsor logos replaced by a 'John Boy' tribute to the popular 47-year-old. This time it was Bruni's turn to bring the car home, 16th after a slow fuel stop and drive-through penalty for ignoring blue flags.

Wilux, a Dutch bathroom equipment company, had been title sponsor since the start of the season, with the right to resell space on the car to recoup its investment. Unhappy with Stoddart's decision to replace commercial sponsorship with the Walton tribute at Silverstone, Wilux terminated the agreement after the German GP. Double tail-end finishes in Germany and Hungary were followed by an expensive weekend at Spa-Francorchamps. Having already

crashed during practice on Saturday morning, Bruni spun at Raidillon on the opening lap of the race and was collected by Giorgio Pantano's Jordan. Baumgartner was eliminated when Jenson Button crashed into him at Les Combes following a puncture. Both incidents triggered a safety car on a weekend when the Minardis had been closer than usual to the Jordans.

Bruni was treated for smoke inhalation when his car was engulfed in flames during an Italian GP pitstop while Baumgartner finished 15th after hitting a mechanic at his pitstop. A pair of 16th places followed, for Baumgartner in China and Bruni in Japan, as the PS04Bs slipped even further off the pace, with Baumgartner crashing in practice and the race at Suzuka. Both started the final race in Brazil from the pitlane and were lapped four times by the end.

Zsolt Baumgartner, Minardi PS04B-Cosworth (Japanese GP)

DRIVER PERFORMANCE

DRIVER	CAR-ENGINE	AUS	MAL	BRN	RSM	E	MC	EU	CDN	USA	F	GB	D	H	B	I	PRC	J	BR
Fernando Alonso	Renault R24	[5]3	[19]7	[16]6	[6]4	[8]4	[3]R	[6]5	[5]R	[9]R	[1]2	[16]10	[5]3	[5]3	[3]R	[4]R	[6]4	[11]5	[8]4
Rubens Barrichello	Ferrari F2004	[2]2	[3]4	[2]2	[4]6	[5]2	[6]3	[7]2	[7]2 FL	[1]2 FL	[10]3	[2]3	[7]12	[2]2	[6]3	[1]1 FL	[1]1	[15]R FL	[1]3
Zsolt Baumgartner	Minardi PS04B-Cosworth	[17]R	[17]16	[20]R	[18]15	[20]R	[19]9	[17]15	[19]10	[19]8	[20]R	[19]R	[20]16	[18]15	[18]R	[19]15	[19]16	[20]R	[19]16
Ryan Briscoe	Toyota TF104B	–	–	–	–	–	–	–	–	–	–	–	T	T	T	T	T	T	T
Gianmaria Bruni	Minardi PS04B-Cosworth	[20]NC	[16]14	[17]17	[17]R	[18]R	[20]R	[19]14	[20]R	[18]R	[19]18	[18]16	[19]17	[19]14	[17]R	[18]R	[17]R	[18]16	[20]17
Jenson Button	BAR 006-Honda	[4]6	[6]3	[6]3	[1]2	[14]8	[2]2	[5]3	[2]3	[4]R	[4]5	[3]4	[13]2	[4]5	[12]R	[6]3	[3]2	[5]3	[5]R
David Coulthard	McLaren MP4-19-Mercedes-Benz	[12]8	[9]6	[10]R	[11]12	[10]10	[8]R	[20]R	[9]6	[12]7	–	–	–	–	–	–	–	–	–
	McLaren MP4-19B-Mercedes-Benz	–	–	–	–	–	–	–	–	–	[3]6	[6]7	[4]4	[12]9	[4]7	[10]6	[9]9	[8]R	[12]11
Cristiano da Matta	Toyota TF104	[13]12	[10]9	[9]10	[10]R	[11]13	[15]6	[11]R	[12]DSQ	[11]R	[11]14	[12]13	–	–	–	–	–	–	–
	Toyota TF104B	–	–	–	–	–	–	–	–	–	–	–	[15]R	–	–	–	–	–	–
Anthony Davidson	BAR 006-Honda	T	T	T	T	T	T	T	T	T	T	T	T	T	T	T	T	T	T
Robert Doornbos	Jordan EJ14-Ford	–	–	–	–	–	–	–	–	–	–	–	–	–	–	–	T	T	T
Giancarlo Fisichella	Sauber C23-Petronas	[14]10	[12]11	[11]11	[19]9	[12]7	[10]R	[18]6	[11]4	[14]9	[15]12	[20]6	[14]9	[8]8	[5]5	[15]8	[7]7	[7]8	[10]9
Marc Gené	Williams FW26-BMW	–	–	–	–	–	–	–	–	–	[8]10	[11]12	–	–	–	–	–	–	–
Timo Glock	Jordan EJ14-Ford	T	T	T	T	T	T	T	[16]7	T	T	T	T	T	T	T	[16]15	[17]15	[17]15
Nick Heidfeld	Jordan EJ14-Ford	[15]R	[15]R	[18]15	[16]R	[15]R	[17]7	[13]10	[15]8	[16]R	[17]16	[15]15	[18]R	[16]12	[16]11	[20]14	[14]13	[16]13	[16]R
Christian Klien	Jaguar R5-Cosworth	[19]11	[13]10	[12]14	[14]14	[16]R	[14]R	[12]12	[10]9	[13]R	[13]11	[13]14	[12]10	[14]13	[13]6	[14]13	–	[14]12	[15]14
	Jaguar R5B-Cosworth	–	–	–	–	–	–	–	–	–	–	–	–	–	–	–	[15]R	–	–
Bas Leinders	Minardi PS04B-Cosworth	–	T	T	T	T	T	T	T	T	T	T	T	T	T	T	T	T	T
Felipe Massa	Sauber C23-Petronas	[11]R	[11]8	[13]12	[12]10	[17]9	[16]5	[16]9	[18]R	[15]R	[16]13	[10]9	[16]13	[20]R	[8]4	[16]12	[4]8	[19]9	[4]8
Juan Pablo Montoya	Williams FW26-BMW	[3]5	[4]2 FL	[3]13	[3]3	[2]R	[9]4	[8]8	[4]DSQ	[5]DSQ	[6]8	[7]5	[2]5	[7]4	[11]R	[2]5	[10]5	[13]7	[2]1 FL
Olivier Panis	Toyota TF104	[18]13	[14]12	[8]9	[13]11	[7]R	[13]8	[10]11	[13]DSQ	[8]5	[14]15	[17]R	–	–	–	–	–	–	–
	Toyota TF104B	–	–	–	–	–	–	–	–	–	–	–	[9]14	[13]11	[9]8	[13]R	[8]14	[10]14	–
Giorgio Pantano	Jordan EJ14-Ford	[16]14	[18]13	[15]16	[15]R	[19]R	[18]R	[15]13	[NT]DNP	[17]R	[18]17	[14]R	[17]15	[17]R	[19]R	[17]R	–	–	–
Antônio Pizzonia	Williams FW26-BMW	–	–	–	–	–	–	–	–	–	–	–	[10]7	[6]7	[14]R	[8]7	–	–	–
Kimi Räikkönen	McLaren MP4-19-Mercedes-Benz	[10]R	[5]R	[19]R	[20]8	[13]11	[5]R	[4]R	[8]5	[7]6	–	–	–	–	–	–	–	–	–
	McLaren MP4-19B-Mercedes-Benz	–	–	–	–	–	–	–	–	–	[9]7	[1]2	[3]R FL	[10]R	[10]1 FL	[7]R	[2]3	[12]6	[3]2
Takuma Satō	BAR 006-Honda	[7]9	[20]15	[5]5	[7]16	[3]5	[7]R	[2]R	[17]R	[3]3	[7]R	[8]11	[8]8	[3]6	[15]R	[5]4	[18]6	[4]4	[6]6
Michael Schumacher	Ferrari F2004	[1]1 FL	[1]1	[1]1 FL	[2]1 FL	[1]1 FL	[4]R FL	[1]1 FL	[6]1	[2]1	[2]1 FL	[4]1 FL	[1]1	[1]1 FL	[2]2	[3]2	[20]12 FL	[1]1	[18]7
Ralf Schumacher	Williams FW26-BMW	[8]4	[7]R	[4]7	[5]7	[6]6	[12]10	[9]R	[1]DSQ	[6]R	–	–	–	–	–	–	[5]R	[2]2	[7]5
Jarno Trulli	Renault R24	[9]7	[8]5	[7]4	[9]5	[4]3	[1]1	[3]4	[3]R	[20]4	[5]4	[5]R	[6]11	[9]R	[1]9	[9]10	–	–	–
	Toyota TF104B	–	–	–	–	–	–	–	–	–	–	–	–	–	–	–	[6]11	[9]12	–
Jacques Villeneuve	Renault R24	–	–	–	–	–	–	–	–	–	–	–	–	–	–	–	[12]11	[9]10	[13]10
Mark Webber	Jaguar R5-Cosworth	[6]R	[2]R	[14]8	[8]13	[9]12	[11]R	[14]7	[14]R	[10]R	[12]9	[9]8	[11]6	[11]10	[7]R	[12]9	[11]10	[3]R	[11]R
Björn Wirdheim	Jaguar R5-Cosworth	T	T	T	T	T	T	T	T	T	T	T	T	T	T	T	T	T	T
Ricardo Zonta	Toyota TF104	T	T	T	T	T	T	T	T	T	T	T	–	–	–	–	–	–	–
	Toyota TF104B	–	–	–	–	–	–	–	–	–	–	–	T	[15]R	[20]10	[11]11	[13]R	–	[14]13

FORMULA 1 RACE WINNERS

ROUND	RACE (CIRCUIT)	DATE	WINNER
1	Foster's Australian Grand Prix (Albert Park)	Mar 7	Michael Schumacher (Ferrari F2004)
2	Petronas Malaysian Grand Prix (Sepang)	Mar 21	Michael Schumacher (Ferrari F2004)
3	Gulf Air Bahrain Grand Prix (Sakhir)	Apr 4	Michael Schumacher (Ferrari F2004)
4	Gran Premio Foster's di San Marino (Imola)	Apr 25	Michael Schumacher (Ferrari F2004)
5	Gran Premio Marlboro de España (Catalunya)	May 9	Michael Schumacher (Ferrari F2004)
6	Grand Prix de Monaco (Monte Carlo)	May 23	Jarno Trulli (Renault R24)
7	Allianz Grand Prix of Europe (Nürburgring)	May 30	Michael Schumacher (Ferrari F2004)
8	Grand Prix du Canada (Montréal)	Jun 13	Michael Schumacher (Ferrari F2004)
9	United States Grand Prix (Indianapolis)	Jun 20	Michael Schumacher (Ferrari F2004)
10	Mobil 1 Grand Prix de France (Magny-Cours)	Jul 4	Michael Schumacher (Ferrari F2004)
11	Foster's British Grand Prix (Silverstone)	Jul 11	Michael Schumacher (Ferrari F2004)
12	Grosser Mobil 1 Preis von Deutschland (Hockenheim)	Jul 25	Michael Schumacher (Ferrari F2004)
13	Marlboro Magyar Nagydíj (Hungaroring)	Aug 15	Michael Schumacher (Ferrari F2004)
14	Belgian Grand Prix (Spa-Francorchamps)	Aug 29	Kimi Räikkönen (McLaren MP4-19B-Mercedes-Benz)
15	Gran Premio Vodafone d'Italia (Monza)	Sep 12	Rubens Barrichello (Ferrari F2004)
16	Sinopec Chinese Grand Prix (Shanghai)	Sep 26	Rubens Barrichello (Ferrari F2004)
17	Fuji Television Japanese Grand Prix (Suzuka)	Oct 10	Michael Schumacher (Ferrari F2004)
18	Grande Prêmio do Brasil (Interlagos)	Oct 24	Juan Pablo Montoya (Williams FW26-BMW)

A full house watches Michael Schumacher lead the German Grand Prix

DRIVERS' CHAMPIONSHIP

	DRIVERS	POINTS
1	Michael Schumacher	148
2	Rubens Barrichello	114
3	Jenson Button	85
4	Fernando Alonso	59
5	Juan Pablo Montoya	58
6	Jarno Trulli	46
7	Kimi Räikkönen	45
8	Takuma Satō	34
9	Ralf Schumacher	24
10	David Coulthard	24
11	Giancarlo Fisichella	22
12	Felipe Massa	12
13	Mark Webber	7
14	Olivier Panis	6
15	Antônio Pizzonia	6
16	Christian Klien	3
17	Cristiano da Matta	3
18	Nick Heidfeld	3
19	Timo Glock	2
20	Zsolt Baumgartner	1
21	Jacques Villeneuve	0
22	Ricardo Zonta	0
23	Marc Gené	0
24	Giorgio Pantano	0
25	Gianmaria Bruni	0

CONSTRUCTORS' CHAMPIONSHIP

	CONSTRUCTORS	POINTS
1	Ferrari	262
2	BAR-Honda	119
3	Renault	105
4	Williams-BMW	88
5	McLaren-Mercedes-Benz	69
6	Sauber-Petronas	34
7	Jaguar-Cosworth	10
8	Toyota	9
9	Jordan-Ford	5
10	Minardi-Cosworth	1

Fernando Alonso poses with his trophies after becoming the youngest World Champion to that date

2005
ALONSO FINALLY ENDS SCHUMACHER'S REIGN

Fernando Alonso withstood Michael Schumacher's pressure to win the San Marino Grand Prix

Fernando Alonso ended five years of scarlet domination in 2005 to eclipse Emerson Fittipaldi's 33-year-old record as the sport's youngest champion to date. Renault narrowly beat McLaren-Mercedes to secure its first teams' title. Kimi Räikkönen matched Alonso's seven victories but the Spaniard's greater reliability prevailed.

For Ferrari, the only leading team to use Bridgestone rubber, the fall from grace was spectacular with Michael Schumacher's win at the farcical United States GP its only one. That race was the nadir for F1 in America, for all 14 Michelin-shod drivers withdrew after the formation lap on safety grounds, leaving Bridgestone's Ferrari, Jordan and Minardi teams to entertain the furious crowd.

Another raft of regulation changes from the FIA looked to shuffle the pack, save costs and slow the cars. A relatively late change decreed that each competitor had to use the same engine for two race weekends or face ten-place grid penalties. Downforce was slashed by 25 percent by raising the front

Suspension failure caused Kimi Räikkönen's last-lap demise at the Nürburgring

Just six cars started the 2005 United States Grand Prix...

wing by 50mm, moving the rear wing forward by 150mm and reducing the height of the diffuser. For this season only, one set of tyres had to last qualifying and the race, except when damaged or for changing weather conditions, which handed Michelin a decisive advantage due to its lower wear rate than Bridgestone. Nine of the ten teams agreed to limit in-season testing to 30 days with Ferrari the exception. FIA president Max Mosley was re-elected unopposed on 28 October.

Another new qualifying procedure was introduced. Grid positions were decided by the aggregate of single-lap runs on Saturday afternoon (with running order determined by the previous race result) and Sunday morning (with race fuel). That left drivers at the mercy of the weather gods when conditions were changeable. It was universally unpopular and was dropped after six races to be replaced from the European GP by single-car qualifying on Saturday, with drivers carrying race fuel and running in the reverse order of the previous result.

The calendar expanded to 19 races with the new Hermann Tilke-designed anti-clockwise Istanbul Park, where huge traffic jams preventing many from seeing the inaugural Turkish GP. Interest for races in Egypt (within sight of the Pyramids), Dubai (with rally driver Mohammed Bin Sulayem involved), Romania and Mexico (Cancún) came to nothing. Rules governing Friday third cars were relaxed after the Bahrain GP to allow drivers who had started more than six GPs in the last

two years to participate. The FIA announced 'an immediate ban on wearing of jewelry (body piercing and heavy chains) by race and rally competitors'.

The possibility of the breakaway Grand Prix World Championship in 2008 remained, although that was weakened when Ferrari committed to the existing F1 structure until 2012. Professor Sid Watkins retired after 25 years as FIA Medical Delegate; HRH Prince Rainier of Monaco and Cosworth founder Keith Duckworth passed away.

...To the anger of local fans

MILD SEVEN RENAULT F1

Winners of the original grand prix in 1906, Renault and Michelin combined to end Ferrari's domination of the decade so far. Furthermore, 24 years and 58 days old when he clinched the drivers' title, Fernando Alonso succeeded Emerson Fittipaldi as the youngest world champion to that date.

Renowned for cost-cutting during his time at Nissan, Carlos Ghosn replaced Louis Schweitzer as chairman of Renault Group in October 2004, and instituted a review of its motor racing programmes. With his contract due to expire at the end of 2005, team principal Flavio Briatore signed a one-year extension in the spring. Alonso remained under contract while a two-year deal for Giancarlo Fisichella, who was also managed by Briatore, was announced on 28 July 2004. Franck Montagny and Heikki Kovalainen remained as reserve and test driver respectively.

Alonso gave the Renault R25 its shakedown at Valencia on 25 January, with Fisichella taking over by the end of the four-day programme. The R25 was formally launched at a packed Grimaldi Forum in Monte Carlo on 1 February. It was Tim Densham's turn to lead the design process, assisted by Martin Tolliday, while co-chief designer Mark Smith was among the recent exodus from Enstone. Dino Toso continued as head of aerodynamics despite illness, while long-serving executive director of engineering Pat Symonds remained the team's tactical and operational lynchpin.

Wind-tunnel focus was switched to the new car in the summer of 2004, before the new regulations had been finalised. Under the leadership of technical director Bob Bell and newly arrived deputy James Allison, the R24's carbon-fibre monocoque was revised and a new aerodynamic package developed while addressing mechanical weaknesses. Sidepods that swooped down and around the rear wheels had an accentuated undercut (to reduce frontal area) and cooling louvres. The front wing had a 'spoon-shaped' central section under its needle nose. Pushrod suspension was via torsion bars (all-new at the rear) with an innovative vee-keel at the front for the lower wishbones, which widened from front to back. This solution was adaptable from track to track and combined the strength of a single keel with the aero benefits of a twin. Particular attention was paid to the outer channels of the diffuser with the lower wishbones at the rear redesigned to suit.

Engine technical director Rob White, project manager Axel Plasse and the engineers at Viry-Châtillon eschewed the trend for 90-degree engines, preferring to develop the old-style narrow concept for its 72-degree V10. More compact and lighter than before, this allowed the 'Coke bottle' rear to be tighter, maintained the RS24's prodigious fuel economy and torque curve, and boosted power to the level of leading rivals. The engineers at Enstone meanwhile optimised engine installation, reduced chassis weight and lowered the centre of gravity. The relatively heavy engine and six-speed gearbox (rather than more fashionable seven-speed) concentrated weight towards the rear, helping to reduce tyre wear now that a single set had to complete qualifying and the race. Powerful new Magneti Marelli step 11 electronics controlled both engine and chassis.

Renault Sport president Patrick Faure targeted the 2005 world championships saying: 'No longer will we be satisfied to be regular podium finishers… This season, we must take regular race wins.'

Fernando Alonso, Renault R25 (Belgian GP)

Briatore was clear about what was required: 'At Renault we don't have any prima donnas. Discipline is an important value, as are rigour and the ability to hit targets. The whole team shares that approach.' Deputy managing director Bernard Dudot retired in April with White and André Lainé joint appointments in his place.

The R25 was immediately on the pace at Valencia and Jerez, with Alonso and Fisichella 1–2 at the 15–18 February Barcelona group test. That promise was confirmed from the outset in Australia, where Fisichella dominated from pole position to chequered flag. Alonso, who only started 13th after a wet track compromised Saturday qualifying, set the fastest race lap as he stormed through to finish third. The Spaniard dominated the next two races from pole, beating Jarno Trulli's Toyota by 24.327sec in Malaysia and 13.409sec in Bahrain. Fisichella retired from both races, at Sepang with a crash that also eliminated Mark Webber's Williams-BMW (the Renault driver was reprimanded for causing it) and next time out with an engine issue. He also suffered a heavy testing crash at Barcelona following a left-rear tyre failure.

With a new 'cascade' front wing on the car, Alonso made it three in a row at Imola by holding off Michael Schumacher's charging Ferrari for the last ten laps to win by 0.215sec. In contrast, Fisichella made a mistake on his first qualifying run and crashed at Tamburello five laps into the race. Kimi Räikkönen ended Renault's winning start in Spain and Monaco as momentum swung towards McLaren-Mercedes. Alonso was a distant second in his home race with Fisichella fifth after changing his front wing to cure chronic understeer. The high-downforce Monaco set-up included new bodywork, an extra flip-up on the sidepods and double-stacked

front wing. Tyre degradation slowed both drivers during the Monaco GP, where Alonso finished fourth from a front-row start and Fisichella got knocked out of the points by Trulli's strong-arm tactics at the Loews hairpin.

Alonso qualified with heavy fuel at the Nürburgring so that he could adopt a two-stop strategy. He survived contact with Ralf Schumacher at the start and inherited a lucky win when Räikkönen's suspension failed on the last lap. Having qualified badly and stalled on the grid, Fisichella came from his pitlane start to salvage sixth. They shared the second row in Canada and Fisichella was leading a 1–2 when his hydraulics failed. Now in the lead, Alonso made a mistake and tapped the wall five laps later, breaking his suspension. Those retirements compromised their qualifying running order for the United States GP but that proved immaterial due to the Michelin withdrawal at the end of the formation lap.

Alonso secured back-to-back pole positions at Magny-Cours and Silverstone. He led the French GP throughout, with F1 sceptic Ghosn in attendance, and finished second at Silverstone after Juan Pablo Montoya passed him at Becketts on the opening lap. Fisichella scored points at both races despite delays. Inheriting victory at Hockenheim after Räikkönen had a hydraulics failure, Alonso extended his points lead over the Finn to 36; Fisichella sustained damage on the opening lap when hit by Takuma Satō but snatched fourth from Michael Schumacher on the penultimate lap.

Neither scored in Hungary thanks to an overly cautious tyre choice and incident-filled races. Räikkönen scored maximum points that day to narrow Alonso's advantage and did so again in Turkey, where Alonso was second and Fisichella fourth after being delayed

Giancarlo Fisichella, Renault R25 (Australian GP)

by a faulty fuel rig. Taking care to preserve his championship lead, Alonso also took second places in Italy and Belgium as he closed in on the title. Fisichella finished third at Monza but had a challenging weekend at Spa-Francorchamps. From only 13th on the grid after changing his engine, he adopted an aggressive low-downforce set-up to aid overtaking, but the car proved a handful when it rained and he lost control exiting Eau Rouge at 160mph on lap ten, spinning into heavy impact with the barrier.

A final upgrade and D-spec engine was introduced at the Brazilian GP to reclaim some performance versus McLaren-Mercedes. This included the 'mass-damper' in the nosecone that would become a *cause célèbre* during 2006. Combined with very stiff springs to keep the front wing close to the road, this sprung weight added front-end stability by counteracting the vertical forces, giving improved aerodynamic efficiency and more consistent tyre contact with the track. After qualifying on pole and driving a controlled race to third place behind the silver cars, Alonso confirmed a first drivers' title for himself and team alike. The constructors' title was a closer affair but second and third at Suzuka gave Renault a two-point advantage with one race left. When Fisichella lost victory to Räikkönen on the very last lap in Japan, some observers questioned his future as a top-line F1 driver. Alonso, who started a rain-delayed 16th, made a great start, and counted a peerless manoeuvre on Michael Schumacher into 130R among his 14 overtakes on the way to third.

The engine was upgraded (E-spec) as a 'one-race' special for the crucial Chinese GP showdown. Alonso used the 19,200rpm now available in qualifying to head a front-row lock-out and led throughout. A drive-through penalty for blocking Räikkönen as they entered the pits relegated Fisichella to fourth, but that was enough to confirm Renault's first constructors' title.

WEST McLAREN MERCEDES/TEAM McLAREN MERCEDES

McLaren-Mercedes produced the fastest technical package of 2005 and yet lost both world titles and its star designer by the end of the year. It won more races (ten) and set more fastest laps (12) than Renault, with both teams starting from pole position on seven occasions. However, poor engine reliability, Juan Pablo Montoya's shoulder injury and a slow start to the campaign thwarted its challenge. Furthermore, technical director Adrian Newey's move to Red Bull Racing, announced on 8 November 2005, was a seismic shift for the future of F1.

McLaren's new driver line-up of Kimi Räikkönen, entering his fourth season, and Montoya had been known for over a year, with fireworks expected from two uncompromising drivers with burning personal ambition. Their very different driving styles forced McLaren to adopt a costly dual set-up programme. One advantage to dropping out of the championship top four in 2004 was the use of an additional test driver on GP Fridays, with either Pedro de la Rosa or Alexander Wurz fulfilling that role. The Austrian remained the reserve driver but was too tall to fit in the MP4-20 prior to cockpit revisions. There was a nod to the future when McLaren-Mercedes protégé Lewis Hamilton tested an MP4-19B at Silverstone on 1 December 2004.

Newey's contract was due to expire in the summer of 2005 and a short-term extension did not quell speculation about his future. Mike Coughlan remained as chief designer within a 'matrix' of engineering talent that included Paddy Lowe, Pat Fry, Tim Goss and Mark Williams. Nikolas Tombazis headed the MP4-20 aero team that included Peter Prodromou. Ola Källenius was appointed Mercedes-Ilmor managing director in the New Year, reporting to Group CEO Martin Whitmarsh. Ilmor was renamed Mercedes-Benz High Performance Engines when the German manufacturer completed

Kimi Räikkönen, McLaren MP4-20-Mercedes-Benz (Monaco GP)

Juan Pablo Montoya, McLaren MP4-20-Mercedes-Benz (Italian GP)

its 100 percent acquisition in September 2005, with founder Mario Illien retiring from F1. Title sponsor West withdrew on 31 July when a European Union tobacco advertising ban came into force, with Diageo's Johnnie Walker whisky brand added to the commercial portfolio at the next race.

The McLaren MP4-20-Mercedes first turned a wheel at the Circuit de Barcelona-Catalunya on 24 January in Räikkönen's hands. The MP4-18/19 series had been difficult to work on, so one aim was easier assembly and adjustability. Weight was moved forward to improve rear-tyre durability now that a single set had to last qualifying and the race. The monocoque and wheelbase were reduced in size and the needle nose abandoned. Newey's answer to the new front-wing regulations was a 'zero-keel' solution, with the lower wishbones at the front raised to allow them to be mounted directly to the chassis. The revised aero also included further undercut sidepods, triple-profile front wing, pronounced airbox-mounted 'horn' fins and endplate-mounted rear wing. J-dampers (inerters) were fitted to the suspension to stabilise oscillations between all four wheels. Mercedes-Ilmor alternated its lead engineer, with Axel Wendorff responsible for the two-race Mercedes V10 engine (FO100R). The new engine was reliable during pre-season running and the new seamless-shift seven-speed gearbox was said to be worth 0.3sec a lap.

The MP4-20's potential was immediately evident although the car proved difficult to balance and did not generate sufficient tyre temperature to optimise single-lap qualifying. That latter problem was compounded in Australia by both cars having to qualify when the track was wet, and driver error blighted that race and the next. Forced to take the Australian restart from the pitlane after

stalling on the grid, Räikkönen drove a wild race through the field to eighth place, while Montoya had two off-track excursions on his way to sixth. In Malaysia, the Colombian finished fourth after flat-spotting his tyres but the Finn lost a podium when his right-rear tyre deflated. Montoya's challenge then took another hit when he missed the next two races due to a shoulder injury that he blamed on an accident while playing tennis.

As Wurz had not yet driven the MP4-20 because he could not fit in the cockpit, de la Rosa replaced Montoya in Bahrain and narrowly outqualified Räikkönen. The Finn responded with third place in the race while de la Rosa completed his impressive comeback with fifth and fastest lap. Wurz raced at Imola and inherited third on his one-off return following BAR-Honda's disqualification. Starting from pole, Räikkönen lost a likely victory when a CV joint (an MP4-20 weakness) failed after nine laps. Thereafter Wurz and de la Rosa shared the third driver duties.

A major upgrade, including new wings, front suspension and revised engine, finally helped Räikkönen turn potential into points and he dominated the next two races by qualifying on pole position and leading every lap. Montoya finished seventh in Spain on his return from injury despite a spin and problems with refuelling. He was excluded from qualifying in Monaco for brake-testing Ralf Schumacher during Saturday practice but came through from the back of the grid to finish fifth. At the Nürburgring, Räikkönen was set for a third successive victory until a spectacular suspension failure on the last lap, his flat-spotted front-right tyre having placed excessive strain on a wishbone; Montoya was seventh. During testing at Paul Ricard, Wurz was fortunate to escape serious injury when a puncture caused him to crash at 200mph.

Pedro de la Rosa, McLaren MP4-20-Mercedes-Benz (Bahrain GP)

Räikkönen overcame steering issues to score a fortunate win in Montréal but was frustrated on his return to Europe after the Indianapolis/Michelin debacle. Engine failures during practice at both Magny-Cours and Silverstone resulted in ten-place grid penalties that denied likely victories, with podium places and fastest lap at both races no consolation as Fernando Alonso extended his points advantage. The Finn converted pole position into a dominant race lead at Hockenheim only to coast to a halt with hydraulics failure. As for Montoya, he was disqualified in Canada for ignoring the pit-exit red light and retired in France before easing to his first McLaren-Mercedes victory after barging his way past Alonso at Becketts on the opening lap of the British GP. Starting last in Germany after he lost control on the final corner of his qualifying lap, Montoya stormed through the field to finish second.

Victories in Hungary and Turkey sustained Räikkönen's lingering title hopes. Montoya was sidelined by CV joint failure at the Hungaroring and threw away a certain 1–2 at Istanbul Park when he tripped over Tiago Monteiro's Jordan with two laps to go, allowing Alonso to close in and steal second place. At Monza, where Montoya set the testing pace (recording 231.2mph in the speed trap), Räikkönen was quickest in qualifying but started 11th due to another engine failure and could only finish fourth when further delayed by a left-rear puncture and spin. Gifted pole position by Räikkönen's grid penalty, Montoya led from start to finish despite a tyre issue and pressure from Alonso.

The Colombian headed a front-row lock-out in Belgium, where Räikkönen shadowed him in the early laps before snatching victory by running a longer middle stint. With four laps to go, another 1–2 was lost when Antônio Pizzonia collided with Montoya while being lapped, earning the Williams-BMW driver a fine. McLaren-Mercedes's first 1–2 finish since 2000 followed in Brazil with Montoya victorious as Räikkönen's mathematical title chances ended.

Räikkönen ensured that the constructors' contest was decided at the final race. Only 17th on the grid in Japan after another engine

Alexander Wurz, McLaren MP4-20-Mercedes-Benz (San Marino GP)

failure in practice and rain when he qualified, he produced the finest drive of his F1 career to date and snatched victory from Giancarlo Fisichella on the final lap; Montoya was eliminated in an opening-lap *contretemps* with Jacques Villeneuve. Räikkönen followed up with second place in China but that was not enough to wrest the constructors' title from Renault.

So Räikkönen and McLaren-Mercedes were runners-up in the drivers' and constructors' standings. When interviewed by Bob Constanduros for *Autocourse*, Whitmarsh acknowledged that 'mistakes have been made in the team – by the mechanics, the engineers, the management and the drivers'.

SCUDERIA FERRARI MARLBORO

After five years of unbroken domination, Ferrari and Michael Schumacher slipped to third overall. Schumacher and team-mate Rubens Barrichello were under contract for the next two seasons, while Marc Gené joined Luca Badoer on the test team when he could not agree terms with Williams-BMW. Carlos Reutemann completed 17 laps of Fiorano in a Ferrari F2004 on 8 December 2004. If that was a blast from the past, there were rumours of a potential new Ferrari driver when MotoGP superstar Valentino Rossi tested in April and August.

Design of the Ferrari F2005 was suspended while the new rules were finalised, so a modified version of the all-conquering 2004 car was planned for the first four races. Technical director Ross Brawn described the resulting F2004M as a 'heavy compromise' that complied with the new aero rules. It was driven for the first time by Andrea Bertolini at Fiorano on 20 January a week before Schumacher returned from holiday to set competitive times at Barcelona. However, cautious optimism was dented when the

F2004M was slower than Michelin rivals at the Catalan venue during February. The definitive tyre compound for Australia was taken to Valencia only for that final test to be rained out, leaving Bridgestone unsure of how competitive it would be. 'They are consistent,' was Bridgestone technical director Hirohide Hamashima's assessment, 'but I would like to have found another half-second.' Rory Byrne echoed that sentiment: 'We have one tyre that is quick, but we don't know if it will last. We have another tyre that we know will last, but we don't know how quick it is.'

With Byrne planning retirement, it was Aldo Costa who coordinated the design process on the F2005. The new car was unveiled on 25 February, a week before the opening race. Engine chiefs Paolo Martinelli and Gilles Simon abandoned the intended single-race type 054 engine project following the late imposition of two-race rules. The long-life 055 V10 was developed to complete the 1,400km required during two weekends, with the focus on drivability and making the rear tyres last. The diminutive new seven-speed carbon/titanium gearbox was integral to the tightly packaged rear as Costa, John Iley (head of aerodynamics) *et al* optimised airflow to the diffuser and rear wing. Seeking to replace lost downforce, the F2005 sported extra aerofoils bow, midships and aft, comprising an ungainly central affair under the front wing (as seen on the F2004M), four on the airbox and another on the rear crash structure. Lower sidepods housed smaller radiators, with exhausts that twisted to exit from within the bodywork. Traction control, weight distribution and adaptable suspension layout were key to tyre wear. The single-keel front-suspension mounting was retained and Brembo developed the new 'total corner' braking system. The F2005's debut was originally scheduled for round five in Spain to coincide with the beginning of a two-race engine cycle.

Bridgestone's safety-first approach to the long-life tyres cost

Michael Schumacher, Ferrari F2004M (Australian GP)

qualifying time and so compromised race results. The F2005 lacked mechanical grip and its 'size-zero' gearbox proved troublesome. The close relationship with Bridgestone that had been crucial in recent seasons was now a hindrance, for the tyre company lacked another top team to help development. Shell extended its fuel partnership once more to 2010.

With Gené and Badoer conducting back-to-back development of the two cars at Mugello and Jerez, the gripless F2004Ms were blown away by Renault in Australia. Starting from the back after rain ruined qualifying and having changed his engine, Schumacher made little headway in the midfield before accepting blame for crashing into Nick Heidfeld's Williams-BMW. Barrichello made a great start from his rain-affected 11th and survived locking brakes to split the Renaults in second. Ferrari's plight was emphasised in the Malaysian heat when both started outside the top ten once more, with Schumacher's two points scant reward for an afternoon mired in the midfield. Debris stuck in Barrichello's rear wing caused oversteer, bringing on excessive rear-tyre wear that ended his race.

Schumacher and Barrichello tested the F2005 as a matter of urgency and Bridgestone introduced new rubber. Despite the complexities of introducing a new car at a long-haul 'flyaway', the debut was brought forward to Bahrain, where the F2005s had their nosecones painted black to mark the passing of Pope John Paul II. Schumacher qualified second and challenged Fernando Alonso's Renault until his hydraulics scrambled after 12 laps. Barrichello started from the back following a gearbox-ravaged qualifying and lost the final points position on the last lap with his grooved tyres worn to the core.

Imola's cooler conditions suited Ferrari and Bridgestone. A mistake at Rivazza restricted Schumacher to 13th on the grid but he used a long first stint to climb to third, then passed Jenson Button at the Variante Alta and only lost to Alonso by 0.215sec after a titanic struggle. That was a rare early highlight for the team. Tyre deficiencies in Spain meant that neither driver scored due to punctures (Schumacher) and blisters (Barrichello). In Monaco, Schumacher ran into David Coulthard's McLaren but recovered to snatch seventh from his team-mate on the last lap, a manoeuvre that angered Barrichello.

Third (Barrichello) and fifth (Schumacher) at the Nürburgring, they suffered gearbox failures in practice and qualifying respectively in Canada. Schumacher started second and made the most of a well-timed safety car to finish in that position, while Barrichello came from a pitlane start to complete a morale-boosting double podium behind Kimi Räikkönen's McLaren-Mercedes. The Michelin withdrawal after the formation lap at Indianapolis left Schumacher to score Ferrari's only victory of 2005 with Barrichello second for a hollow 1–2. Despite the lack of opposition, the Ferraris almost collided when Schumacher exited from his second pitstop, adding to internal tension.

An aero upgrade at Magny-Cours included revised front wing, bargeboards and diffuser, while a new tyre compound improved qualifying performance. Schumacher started and finished third (after a three-stop strategy) in France and sixth at Silverstone, with brake trouble restricting Barrichello to ninth and seventh respectively. Fifth at Hockenheim, Schumacher used another new Bridgestone compound in Hungary to snatch Ferrari's only

Rubens Barrichello, Ferrari F2004M (Australian GP)

Michael Schumacher, Ferrari F2005 (European GP)

pole position of the year and finish second despite his brother's late pressure. In Turkey, he spun in qualifying and hit Mark Webber's Williams-BMW during another uncomfortable afternoon languishing in the pack. With his six-year Ferrari career coming to an end, Barrichello endured a miserable run of four successive finishes in tenth place or worse. That included hitting Jacques Villeneuve's Sauber-Petronas in Germany and Jarno Trulli's Toyota at the Hungaroring, and suffering a puncture during the Italian GP, where the red cars faded to 10th (Schumacher) and 12th in front of the disappointed *Tifosi*.

With his Belgian GP already ruined by a premature switch to dry tyres, Schumacher was rammed by Takuma Satō at La Source,

but Barrichello made a late switch from wets to finish fifth. Ferrari took a step forward in Brazil when Schumacher used a good start to finish fourth while Barrichello passed Button for sixth place despite a power-steering issue. Seventh in Japan, Schumacher was reprimanded for crashing into Christijan Albers's Minardi before the start of the Chinese GP, and then spun the spare car out of the race during a safety-car period. Barrichello finished outside the top ten at the last two races of a dispiriting campaign for all concerned.

Constructors' champions since 1999, only Ferrari's 'free hit' at the United States GP preserved its distant third in the standings. 'When you are bad,' mused sporting director Jean Todt, 'it's good to have your nose in the shit, so you smell it clearly and you react.'

Rubens Barrichello, Ferrari F2005 (Monaco GP)

Ralf Schumacher, Toyota TF105B (Japanese GP)

PANASONIC TOYOTA RACING

Toyota emerged from three mediocre seasons with the third fastest car/engine package, five podium finishes, two pole positions and fourth in the constructors' standings.

Having already used its considerable resources to reshape its technical team, Toyota offered lucrative long-term contracts to a new driver pairing for 2005. Ralf Schumacher signed a three-year deal in May 2004 and Jarno Trulli's two-year agreement followed in September. Ricardo Zonta returned to his reserve role while Olivier Panis relinquished his race seat and accepted a two-year contract as test driver and ambassador. Former Michelin technician Pascal Vasselon arrived in a research and development capacity. This was Mike Gascoyne's first Toyota as technical director from start to finish. He also began the season directing on-track operations until Dieter Gass was promoted to chief race engineer from Monaco to ease pressure on the 42-year-old Englishman.

The Toyota TF105 was the first new car to be revealed when the drivers pulled the covers off in Barcelona's Estació de França railway station on 8 January. Gascoyne and Jason Somerville's aero team improved aerodynamic efficiency, with particular emphasis on the rear end. The monocoque from the unloved TF104 and its B-spec cousin was retained (albeit having shed another 10kg), as were the single-keel front-suspension mounting and titanium seven-speed

gearbox. Luca Marmorini's engine department updated the RVX-05 V10 to last two race weekends. The lower sidepods were fitted with tall cooling chimneys and pronounced flick-ups ahead of the rear wheels. The rear wing was mounted on a central support, freeing the endplates to be used solely to control airflow. Toyota renewed its Michelin contract despite speculation that it would change allegiance. An aggressive development strategy over the winter resulted in totally new aero when the cars arrived in Australia, compete with revised front wing under vertical supports that were now straight rather than curved.

Having benefitted from a dry track for first qualifying in Australia, Trulli started second but faded during the race due to rear-tyre wear. Team principal Tsutomu Tomita called it 'the best day of my life' when Trulli finished second in Malaysia from another front-row start, and he repeated that result in Bahrain. Schumacher's back-to-back top-five finishes accentuated the optimistic start to 2005. The cars were less competitive at Imola, where Schumacher's 25sec penalty for an unsafe release denied another double points score.

Armed with a revised floor and diffuser in Spain, Trulli survived a pitlane fire to beat his team-mate after a race-long duel and finish third. There were contrasting fortunes in Monaco between qualifying and the race. Trulli started fifth and ran second behind the safety car. However, he clouted a kerb at the Loews hairpin

Jarno Trulli, Toyota TF105 (Malaysian GP)

as he tried to force his way past Giancarlo Fisichella, so faded to tenth at the finish. Starting 18th after crashing at Tabac, Schumacher climbed the lap charts to claim sixth despite his brother's aggressive last-lap attention. Toyota's European GP was ruined within metres of the start. Fourth on the grid, Trulli was handed a drive-through when his mechanics were still working on the car 15sec before the formation lap, and Schumacher hit Fernando Alonso at the first corner before later spinning out of the race. Eighth at the Nürburgring, Trulli lost another podium when his brake disc shattered with eight laps to go in Canada, where Schumacher finished sixth.

Schumacher's left-rear puncture in Indianapolis's final banked corner during Friday practice caused him to crash violently for the second successive year. That ruled him out of the rest of the weekend and caused the safety fears that led all 14 Michelin runners to withdraw from the race after the formation lap. Friday

third driver Zonta took Schumacher's place for qualifying while Trulli, knowing that Toyota would not race, used minimal fuel to claim the team's first pole position.

That pole was no fluke for Trulli qualified and ran second at Magny-Cours before fading to fifth at the finish. With no French F1 driver in 2005, Panis replaced Zonta as third driver at Magny-Cours. The TF105s lacked grip at Silverstone and Trulli had a nightmare German GP thanks to a puncture and drive-through for ignoring blue flags. The cars were more competitive at the Hungaroring, where they qualified in the top five and Schumacher, a points scorer at the previous three races, finished third. Trulli's diffuser was damaged by Rubens Barrichello's Ferrari at the start but he coped with wayward handling to claim fourth.

Trulli's impressive one-lap pace continued with fifth-place grid slots for the next two races. Sixth in Turkey, he led another double score when fifth at Monza. Their switch to dry tyres while

Ricardo Zonta, Toyota TF105 (United States GP)

Olivier Panis, Toyota TF105 (French GP)

the track was still wet at Spa-Francorchamps proved too early. Schumacher lost a potential podium finish when he spun to the back, then set the fastest race lap as he recovered to seventh; Trulli started third but tumbled down the order and crashed following contact with Tiago Monteiro's Jordan. All Toyota had to show from a disappointing Brazilian GP was Schumacher's eighth place, with Trulli compromised by a ten-place grid penalty following rare engine problems in practice.

Panis tested the TF105B at Silverstone on 13–14 September with the race drivers trying the update at Jerez later that month. The car had a non-keel arrangement for the front suspension mounts, with the lower wishbones attached to the chassis and steering column raised. However, it was based around the TF105 monocoque, so the remnant of the keel remained, reducing the benefit to the airflow. Revised aerodynamics included new bargeboards and flick-up turning vanes. Toyota took the updated cars to the last two races amid its fight with Ferrari over third spot in the constructors' standings. Trulli described the heavier steering as 'very strange' and was slower than his team-mate for the first time. Having used a beneficial place in the qualifying order to snatch a surprise pole at Suzuka, Schumacher led the opening stint of the Japanese GP before trailing home eighth. Trulli spun during qualifying and was shunted out of the race by Takuma Satō's foolhardy manoeuvre at the chicane. Understeer, tyre vibrations and an ill-timed safety car ruined Trulli's Chinese GP while Schumacher took advantage of the safety cars and Giancarlo Fisichella's penalty to finish third.

BMW WILLIAMS F1

The early announcement of Juan Pablo Montoya's McLaren move meant that Williams began courting Mark Webber before the 2004 season had even started. The Australian invoked a performance clause in his Jaguar contract to sign before the summer break. Ponderous negotiations with Ralf Schumacher broke down in May. The original plan had been to rehire Jenson Button for 2005 but the Contract Recognition Board ruled in BAR-Honda's favour on 20 October 2004, by which time Mika Häkkinen had shelved comeback plans.

Giancarlo Fisichella, Jacques Villeneuve and David Coulthard were all mentioned as possibilities, and plans to test Anthony Davidson were scuppered by his contractual obligations to BAR-Honda. Patrick Head described reserve driver Antônio Pizzonia as 'probably favourite' to be Webber's team-mate, only for Nick Heidfeld to impress at Jerez in December. With reserve driver Marc Gené having joined Ferrari, Williams signed both Pizzonia and Heidfeld with testing during January used to decide who would race. It was Heidfeld, who had seemed to be on the F1 scrapheap, who was confirmed as race driver when the Williams FW27-BMW was launched at Valencia's Circuit Ricardo Tormo on 31 January. The 'inconsolable' Pizzonia was third driver once more. Among those to test during the winter were 2004 BMW champions Andy Priaulx (European Touring Cars) and Sebastian Vettel (Formula BMW). An addition to the test roster in April was 19-year-old Nico Rosberg on a long-term contract. Chief executive officer Chris Chapple was hired from Goldman Sachs with a remit to improve the management structure.

Design of the FW27 was interrupted at a crucial time by chief designer Gavin Fisher's motorcycle accident in Los Angeles in September 2004, with senior engineer Mark Loasby assuming his duties for three months. Loïc Bigois replaced Antonia Terzi as head of aerodynamics in November 2004 while John Davis, who had been responsible for bringing the new 60 percent wind tunnel online and decommissioning the old facility, left at the end of his contract. 'The new [wind tunnel]… did its first run in April 2004,' technical director Sam Michael told *Autocourse*'s Maurice Hamilton at the end of 2005, 'and, in reality, it became productive only in July and August of this year.' The new regulations allied to wind-tunnel correlation issues hindered development and meant that the FW27 lacked aerodynamic grip, leaving the team mired in the midfield.

Williams reverted to a single-keel configuration after one disappointing season with the twin-tusk 'walrus' FW26, with improved weight distribution and downforce key objectives. The FW27 was a conventional design that looked as purposeful as the original FW26 had been ungainly. The monocoque was smaller and lighter and the torsion bar suspension revised. Undercut sidepods, svelte engine cover and waisted 'Coke bottle' rear followed prevailing trends. Large sidepod-mounted chimneys were required to cool the BMW V10. The front wing's deep central 'spoon' section was replaced by a simplified version from the Turkish GP. BMW director of motorsport Mario Theissen was critical of the late switch to two-race engines and this forced an all-new V10 to be shelved and the existing unit to be developed as the P84/5. The hierarchy in Munich had been unhappy with 2004's shortcomings so another season without a title challenge was unacceptable. The FIA's threat that the team's new seamless-shift gearbox was in effect a continuously variable transmission (CVT), which had been outlawed since 1994, led Williams to continue with the old seven-speed unit,

much to Patrick Head's chagrin. Williams bucked the uncertain economic climate by signing a lucrative five-year deal with the Royal Bank of Scotland, while Hewlett-Packard remained as title partner.

Sam Michael admitted that 'aero balance and downforce levels are not where we want them to be' after the FW27's first tests, with an additional Gurney flap and untested new wings at the first race evidence of that shortfall. Sir Frank Williams described winter testing as 'really, really disappointing' as his team trailed behind Renault, McLaren-Mercedes and Ferrari. Webber took time to adapt to Williams-BMW's Carbon Industrie brakes and began the season feeling the lingering effects of a rib injury sustained in testing. The aggressive development programme was hampered by lack of physical testing of new parts and ongoing wind-tunnel correlation issues. Initial single-lap pace gave cause for optimism but the Williams-BMW partnership, which had so recently threatened Ferrari's supremacy, disintegrated with, according to *Autosport*'s Mark Hughes, 'a mediocre car powered by what had become a mediocre engine'.

Having started third in Australia, Webber was disappointed to finish fifth while Heidfeld was eliminated by Michael Schumacher while trying to pass for eighth, for which the seven-time champion later apologised. New bargeboards, front wing and sidepods were flown to Malaysia, with *Autosport* reporting £2,000 in excess baggage charges. Webber was on course to finish third when Giancarlo Fisichella crashed over his FW27, promoting Heidfeld onto the lower step of the podium. In Bahrain, they started from fourth (Heidfeld) and fifth (Webber), but Heidfeld's engine came to a smoky end and a spin-induced tyre vibration restricted Webber to sixth. The San Marino GP was ruined by poor starts and being stuck behind Jarno Trulli's slow Toyota.

Faulty valves delayed practice in Spain, where Webber bagged

Mark Webber, Williams FW27-BMW (United States GP)

Nick Heidfeld, Williams FW27-BMW (Monaco GP)

a front-row start and finished sixth with more tyre vibration, while Heidfeld was tenth after taking an engine penalty. With the strained relationship between team and engine partner at a critical juncture, Williams-BMW enjoyed its best result of 2005 in Monte Carlo. Heidfeld used an early second pitstop to pass Webber, who had been slow away from third on the grid, before both drivers passed Fernando Alonso late in the race to score a double podium, Heidfeld ahead of Webber. This improved form continued a week later at the Nürburgring when the light-fuelled Heidfeld snatched the only pole position of his F1 career and finished second. Laden with fuel, Webber made another slow getaway from third and was sidelined after hitting Montoya's McLaren-Mercedes in the first corner. The FW27s were less competitive in Canada, where Heidfeld blew an engine and Webber salvaged fifth, and withdrew before the start of the United States GP. The week after that North American furore, BMW announced its acquisition of Sauber and its divorce from Williams was confirmed before the Turkish GP.

Williams introduced a much-anticipated aerodynamic overhaul for the French GP, but wind-tunnel data did not translate into reality, so torrid weekends followed at that race and the next. Suddenly two seconds off the pace, the FW27s qualified and finished outside the top ten at Magny-Cours and Silverstone due to a lack of grip and extremely sensitive handling. Heidfeld stopped six times in France

as he tried to fix the chronic imbalance and even reverted to the old aero package for the British GP.

The car was better at Hockenheim, sixth and seventh on the grid, but neither driver scored. Webber lost 11 laps in the pits having his suspension fixed following Takuma Sato's first-lap assault and Heidfeld faded as oversteer worsened. Heidfeld led a 6–7 in Hungary despite having to feather the throttle as debris caused temperatures to soar. A spate of right-rear tyre failures in Turkey, including two each during the race, was later blamed on a new brake component. The loss of BMW and the inconsistent campaign thus far prompted Gavin Fisher's departure in September with Jörg Zander arriving from BAR-Honda a month later.

After suffering concussion in a testing crash at Monza's first Lesmo corner on 26 August, Heidfeld withdrew from the Italian GP and was also ruled out for the Belgian GP, after which a shoulder injury sustained while cycling in Switzerland curtailed the rest of his season. His replacement was Pizzonia, who finished seventh at Monza after a tenacious race but did not shine again. Pizzonia was fined $8,000 for causing an accident while being lapped by Montoya's McLaren-Meredes in Belgium, an incident that promoted Webber into fourth.

Pizzonia was hit by Coulthard as they approached the first corner of the Brazilian GP, with Webber an innocent victim requiring 25 minutes for repairs. The Australian was a strong fourth in Japan and

Antônio Pizzonia, Williams FW27-BMW (Italian GP)

Jenson Button, BAR 007-Honda (Belgian GP)

beat Button into seventh in China. Pizzonia spun during the early laps at Suzuka and suffered a last-lap puncture in China as his F1 career drew to a downbeat conclusion.

In the year that it lost its works engine partner, Williams finished fifth in the constructors' standings as its gradual decline continued.

LUCKY STRIKE BAR HONDA

Having made a quantum leap in performance during the winter of 2003/04, British American Racing's fall from grace during 2005 was extreme. The pre-season focus was on catching Ferrari with a self-proclaimed 'win-or-bust' approach, but the realities of a fundamental aerodynamic issue, race bans and no points before mid-season were bitter pills to swallow.

Honda extended its exclusive engine deal with BAR by three years in July 2004. After four years of rumours about buying a stake in the team, Honda acquired 45 percent from British American Tobacco in January (once legal obstacles presented by minority shareholder Craig Pollock had been overcome) and completed the takeover in September. Team principal David Richards, who was named a Commander of the British Empire (CBE) in the New Year's Honours List, left before the season as part of Honda's restructure, with managing director Nick Fry promoted to chief executive

officer. Yasuhiro Wada replaced Shoichi Tanaka as president of Honda Racing Development.

The tug of war over Jenson Button's services was resolved on 20 October 2004 when the Contracts Recognition Board met in Milan. It ruled in BAR-Honda's favour for 2005, with Williams having prior claim for 2006 unless Button had 75 percent of the championship leader's points tally on 21 August 2005. There had been talk of a return for Mika Häkkinen before Takuma Satō met performance clauses in his agreement and was retained. Anthony Davidson remained as reserve with Enrique Bernoldi assisting the test programme. Adam Carroll, Alan van der Merwe and James Rossiter were all part of the winter Young Driver Programme; British F3 champion Nelson Piquet Jr's first taste of the old BAR 006-Honda at Jerez on 8 February ended in the barriers. Tony Kanaan's 29 September appearance at the Spanish circuit was Honda's reward for winning the 2004 IndyCar title.

BAR launched its new challenger, the elegant 007, at the Circuit de Barcelona-Catalunya on 16 January, with a live satellite link to *Autosport* International in Birmingham's National Exhibition Centre. Technical director Geoff Willis introduced a brand-new monocoque with a distinctive shovel front wing as his answer to the new regulations. The new floor was contoured to channel air to the rear diffuser as Willis looked to reduce drag and maintain

Takuma Satō, BAR 007-Honda (Japanese GP)

Anthony Davidson, BAR 007-Honda (Malaysian GP)

downforce. Aerodynamic lower wishbones at the front were mounted to a single keel, with enlarged bargeboards. The close ties between BAR and Honda were evident in chassis development and the lightweight carbon-fibre encased seamless-shift seven-speed gearbox. Takeo Kiuchi's RA005E V10 engine was smaller and lighter than before, despite having to last two race weekends. It was the most powerful unit on the grid by the end of 2005.

The BAR 007-Honda was the first new car to run although initial testing had to be switched to Valencia because Barcelona's newly laid tarmac had not cured. Early testing pace was inconsistent and the engine initially could not complete the mileage required for two race weekends. Continued mechanical woes were compounded by both race drivers crashing, Satō at 180mph at Jerez when the rear wing broke. There were four front-row starts, and podium finishes at Hockenheim and Spa-Francorchamps, but the 007 was overly pitch-sensitive, wore through its rear tyres at a prodigious rate and was difficult to set up, with its ideal balance on a knife edge.

Reliability fears over winter were born out at the opening race in Melbourne, where the cars lacked downforce and were outside the top ten when withdrawn on the final lap. This allowed engine changes without penalty, a loophole that was closed before the next race. Worse was to come in Malaysia despite Button qualifying in the top ten for a successive race. With Davidson handed a one-off race appearance when Satō fell ill on Friday evening, both BAR-Hondas retired by the end of lap two. Button, who was sixth at the time, bemoaned the situation: 'I wouldn't have thought it was difficult to engineer an engine to last for three laps. We seem to be going backwards in every department.' A double DNF in Bahrain only darkened the mood.

Former Indianapolis 500 winner Gil de Ferran started work at Brackley as sporting director on 11 April, an appointment designed to free Willis to concentrate on technical matters. A specific

aerodynamic problem identified during the subsequent three-day Barcelona test, allied to a new floor and diffuser, allowed Button and Satō to qualify third and sixth at Imola. An apparent step forward was confirmed when they finished 3–5, Button having led for five laps, but the team was soon engulfed in crisis. The result was only confirmed after six hours of deliberation by the stewards and the FIA appealed that outcome with technical delegate Jo Bauer reporting that Button's car was 'able to run below the minimum weight limit'. The Court of Appeal judged a secondary collector tank within the main fuel cell to be illegal on 4 May, alleging that it allowed the car to run underweight until the final pitstop. BAR-Honda was disqualified from the San Marino GP and handed an additional two-race ban, which Fry described as 'wholly and grossly disproportionate', although the team reluctantly accepted the decision rather than face further sanction.

It was back to the midfield on their return at the Nürburgring, with inadequate downforce blamed, before new sidepods and set-up changes tested at Monza and Silverstone transformed the car. Button qualified on pole in Canada and third at Indianapolis, although the points dearth continued. He was on course for the podium when he crashed into Montréal's 'Wall of Champions' and Satō had to change his gearbox during the race after being rammed by Jacques Villeneuve.

After being among the Michelin runners to withdraw before the start of the United States GP, the team's dismal run ended at Magny-Cours. In finishing fourth, Button marked the start of ten successive points finishes, while Satō, who had qualified fourth, came home 11th after two off-track excursions. Button started from the front row at both Silverstone and Hockenheim and finished fifth and third respectively, with more fifths following in Hungary (despite lacking grip) and Turkey. Satō started the British GP from the pitlane after stalling on his way to the grid, then at the German GP hit Jarno

Trulli and Giancarlo Fisichella on lap one. Satō avoided trouble at the Hungaroring and withstood sweltering cockpit temperatures to finish eighth and register his only point of 2005.

They qualified and ran in the top five at Monza before refuelling issues ruined their races. In Belgium, Button recovered from poor qualifying and early oversteer to finish third after excelling in the mixed conditions; Satō was heavily criticised when he misjudged braking at La Source and turfed Michael Schumacher out of the race. 'I don't know what kind of therapy works for Taku,' the seven-time champion fumed, 'it's just another hara-kiri manoeuvre.' Button qualified fourth in Brazil only for tyre degradation to drop him to seventh by the finish. Already handed a ten-place grid penalty for the Spa-Francorchamps incident, Satō changed his engine but made no impression from the back of the grid.

Button made his fourth front-row start of the year at Suzuka but only finished fifth when his fuel flap failed to open at his first stop. Satō spent the weekend in the media glare due to recent confirmation that he was not being retained for 2006. Starting fifth at his home race, he ran wide at the first corner (glancing Rubens Barrichello's Ferrari as they skated across the gravel trap), hit Jarno Trulli's Toyota in an ill-advised overtake at the chicane and was disqualified for one accident too many. Sporting 555 branding for the Chinese GP, Button only finished eighth thanks to an ill-timed safety car while Satō served a drive-through penalty for jumping the start before he retired.

With that, BAT sold its remaining shares and one of F1's great underachievers morphed from British American Racing to Honda.

RED BULL RACING

Ford vice president Richard Parry-Jones announced the sale of Jaguar Racing to 60-year-old Dietrich Mateschitz's Red Bull energy drink company at 9am on Monday 15 November 2004, the day that championship entries were due. A one-year engine agreement existed with Cosworth Engineering, which was acquired by Champ Car co-owner Kevin Kalkhoven on the same day.

The highly rated Mark Webber activated a performance-based break clause to move to Williams-BMW. David Coulthard had agreed a two-year Jaguar contract in July and Anthony Davidson was the

choice of Tony Purnell (head of Ford's Premier Performance Division) and David Pitchforth (Jaguar Racing managing director) before Ford's withdrawal. With those arrangements voided by the takeover, two Red Bull juniors tested at Barcelona during a 24–26 November test. F3000 champion Vitantonio Liuzzi was quicker than incumbent Christian Klien in a Jaguar R5-Cosworth that featured an interim livery, plus gearbox, drivetrain and rear suspension from the 2005 car.

A week after saying that Coulthard was not part of his plans, Mateschitz told journalists at that test: 'What our team needs now is experience. There are only two drivers who have proved to be both fast and experienced, those are Nick Heidfeld and David Coulthard.' The Scot had a seat fitting at Milton Keynes on 6 December, tested at Jerez two days later and signed a one-year deal on 17 December. Identical 2005 contracts were handed to Klien and Liuzzi in the New Year, with Klien confirmed as Coulthard's team-mate on the eve of the season. Red Bull GP2 drivers Scott Speed and Neel Jani tested in March with Speed the first American in 11 years to appear during a GP weekend when he fulfilled Friday testing duties in North America.

Initially named team principal and managing director respectively, Purnell and Pitchforth left on 7 January following meetings with Red Bull adviser Dr Helmut Marko. Arden International F3000 boss Christian Horner, who had had discussions before Christmas about buying Jordan Grand Prix, was named as sporting director with immediate effect and Guenther Steiner arrived from Opel's DTM operation six days later as technical operations director. Director of engineering Ian Pocock exited the business before the season with Jordan's Mark Smith appointed deputy technical director. Another recruit from the Silverstone-based team in June was head of race and test engineering Paul Monaghan. The huge 'Energy Station' hospitality facility was visual confirmation of Red Bull's deep pockets and grand ambitions.

Rob Taylor (head of vehicle design), Mark Gillan (vehicle performance) and Ben Agathangelou (aerodynamics) led design of the Red Bull RB1-Cosworth (previously the Jaguar R6) before Gillan returned to academia in December. The RB1's maiden run in Red Bull's definitive blue, red and yellow livery came during a Jerez filming session on 7 February, two days before testing began in earnest. Particular attention was paid to the rear end to ease the tyre-wear issues that had blighted the last two Jaguars. Agathangelou

David Coulthard, Red Bull RB1-Cosworth (Brazilian GP)

Christian Klien, Red Bull RB1-Cosworth (British GP)

Vitantonio Liuzzi, Red Bull RB1-Cosworth (Monaco GP)

Scott Speed, Red Bull RB1-Cosworth (United States GP)

used the Bicester wind tunnel to finalise its new diffuser and 'Coke bottle' layout, with revised suspension geometry and a longer, narrower seven-speed gearbox. The monocoque was 15kg lighter, enabling more ballast to be used to optimise weight distribution. Michelin tyres were retained. The chassis was the best to emerge from Milton Keynes since 1999, a positive evolution despite inconsistent handling.

At Cosworth, head of development Alex Hitzinger and head of race engineering Simon Corbyn directed the latest iteration of its 90-degree V10, with exhaust chimneys integrated into the RB1's winglets. Improved but still less powerful than leading rivals, the Cosworth TJ2005 developed 860bhp at 18,300rpm and the Series 12 upgrade delivered another 30bhp from the United States GP.

Red Bull Racing's first two GPs resulted in double points scores – a feat that had eluded Jaguar Racing in five years. Liuzzi was fastest in FP1 in Australia before Coulthard and Klien annexed row three when qualifying conditions favoured them. Coulthard snatched third at the start and beat Mark Webber's Williams in their race-long battle for fourth. Klien completed a fine day by finishing seventh, and qualified in that position at the next two races when quicker than Coulthard. DC's race experience showed when he headed a Red Bull 6–8 in Malaysia and finished eighth in Bahrain. An electronic issue before the formation lap prevented Klien from starting that latter event.

Liuzzi replaced Klien for the next three races as Red Bull evaluated its juniors. Despite having started more than six GPs in the previous two seasons, Klien was allowed to take part in Friday practice at those events after Red Bull canvassed its rivals to relax that rule. The RB1s were off the pace at Imola, where Liuzzi failed to pull off a wild passing manoeuvre on Webber on his way to tenth place, which became a points-scoring eighth following BAR-Honda's disqualification. Coulthard was three places worse off after damage following contact with Felipe Massa's Sauber-Petronas caused oversteer. An upgrade including new floor was taken to Barcelona, where Liuzzi spun out on lap three and Coulthard overcame poor handling and a flat-spotted tyre to claim eighth.

Sponsored for the Monaco GP by the latest instalment of the Star Wars franchise (Episode III: Revenge of the Sith), Red Bull left the Principality empty-handed after an accident-ravaged weekend. Coulthard, the innocent victim on Saturday morning of the coming-

together between Juan Pablo Montoya and Ralf Schumacher, started seventh but was eliminated when rammed by Schumacher Sr in the aftermath of Christijan Albers's Minardi track blockage at Mirabeau. Liuzzi struggled with rear-tyre wear before he tapped a barrier and broke his rear suspension. Liuzzi was retained for a fourth and final race at the Nürburgring, where he ran sixth before fading to ninth by the finish, while Coulthard made a great start from 12th to fourth, led a lap during the first pitstops, recovered from a drive-through penalty for speeding in the pitlane, and finally reclaimed fourth. Klien returned to race action in Canada where a lack of Cosworth grunt consigned the Red Bulls to qualifying outside the top ten. Both drivers complained about poor handling but scored points, Coulthard seventh despite oversteer and Klien eighth with understeer. The team withdrew from the United States GP along with all the other Michelin runners.

Liuzzi returned to testing duties in France and retained that role for the rest of the season. Uncompetitive at that race and the next, the RB1 was improved for Germany where Klien started tenth and Coulthard finished seventh. Amid week-by-week speculation as to whether Klien or Liuzzi would drive the second car, with Marko remarking that 'so far neither has made themselves a must', both RB1s crashed on the opening lap of the Hungarian GP. Klien was launched into a roll in Turn 1 by Jacques Villeneuve's Sauber and Coulthard hit debris. Seventh (Coulthard) and eighth (Klien) in Turkey, they finished outside the top ten at Monza with DC delayed by an opening-lap altercation with Giancarlo Fisichella's Renault.

Cosworth's first engine failure during a race thwarted Coulthard in Belgium, where Klien finished ninth after prematurely changing to dry tyres. Test driver Liuzzi was uninjured in a heavy shunt at Les Combes in the Friday rain at Spa-Francorchamps. Klien was mighty in qualifying for the Brazilian and Japanese GPs where he started from sixth and fourth respectively although he faded to ninth at both events. He finished fifth in Shanghai thanks to not pitting during the second safety-car period. Eliminated in Brazil in a first-corner tangle with Antônio Pizzonia's Williams-BMW, Coulthard emphasised Red Bull-Cosworth's improved pace by qualifying and finishing sixth at Suzuka. In China, Coulthard had already pitted when Montoya's crash triggered the first safety car and therefore found his race ruined.

SAUBER PETRONAS

This was a crucial season for Peter Sauber and the 61-year-old realised that he needed manufacturer support for his team to survive. The existing Ferrari engine deal entered its ninth and final season with Felipe Massa in the second year of his contract. Giancarlo Fisichella exercised a 'top-team' clause in his contract to join Renault. Sauber admitted interest in Anthony Davidson, Gary Paffett and Vitantonio Liuzzi before opting for experience to replace Fisichella. Jacques Villeneuve, the 1997 World Champion, visited Hinwil in August and agreed a two-year deal for his full-time F1 return. Willy Rampf and Seamus Mullarkey remained as technical director and head of aero respectively.

The Sauber C24-Petronas was unveiled at Valencia's Circuit Ricardo Tormo on 14 January, with Massa completing the shakedown that day. This was an evolutionary design based around the monocoque from the C23 with its rebadged V10s now the same specification as the works units due to the two-race engine rules. Smaller exhausts were moved forward and lowered. After a single season buying Ferrari's gearboxes, Sauber built its own titanium-cased seven-speed once more to save money. The single-keel front-suspension mounting was retained and the wheelbase extended. The rear diffuser was unconventional with S-shaped outer channel and large Gurney flap. A secondary front wing tried after the launch did not generate enough downforce and upset air to the rear wing, so it was replaced by a conventional single-deck arrangement with a low, scooped centre. The aggressively undercut and curvaceous sidepods contained integrated water/oil radiators that folded horizontally to reduce height and improve packaging.

Sauber's switch to Michelin tyres was a surprise given Ferrari's close relationship with Bridgestone. The suspension had originally been designed for the Japanese rubber, so this was a compromise. Now with its own team to fund, Red Bull allowed its title partnership to expire on 31 December 2004 after a ten-year association.

The C24 lacked downforce and, without the resources or staff to maximise use of its state-of-the-art full-scale wind tunnel, Sauber failed to recover. Villeneuve spent the first half of 2005 at odds with the engineers regarding set-up. He struggled with the C24's rear-end instability under braking from the moment he spun on his very first lap in the car. With winter times poor and the final Imola test curtailed by heavy rain and snow, Sauber travelled to Melbourne in downbeat mood.

Changeable conditions for qualifying in Australia allowed Villeneuve to start from an unrepresentative fourth but he tumbled down the order to 13th at the finish. A second slower than any other Michelin runner in Malaysian qualifying, he spun out of the race as criticism mounted. Massa's pair of tenth places was all Sauber-Petronas had to show from the opening two races. The Brazilian helped the team celebrate its 200th GP by finishing seventh in Bahrain, where Villeneuve, who was 1.385sec slower in qualifying, lost eighth when David Coulthard's Red Bull hit him.

An upgrade including revised engine cover was introduced at Imola to boost downforce and improve stability. That filled Villeneuve with increased confidence and he finished sixth on the road, elevated to fourth following the disqualifications. Massa qualified eighth but an engine penalty and contact with Coulthard ruined his race. That was followed by three successive non-scores

Jacques Villeneuve, Sauber C24-Petronas (Monaco GP)

Felipe Massa, Sauber C24-Petronas (Brazilian GP)

for the team, with Monaco particularly galling when Villeneuve ran into Massa at Ste-Dévote as he attempted to take eighth place, preventing a probable double score. In Canada, Massa withstood Mark Webber's late pressure to claim fourth – the team's best result of the year – while Villeneuve qualified eighth but hit Takuma Satō's BAR-Honda on lap one and finished ninth.

On-track results may have been underwhelming but there was progress off it when BMW announced its takeover in the week following the abortive United States GP. With renewed scrutiny on Villeneuve's future now that Sauber would be a works team in 2006, he was eighth in France before messy races at Silverstone and Hockenheim. He ran over his refueller in Britain and during the German GP he was hit by Rubens Barrichello (lap 1), Robert Doornbos (lap 4) and Tiago Monteiro (lap 26), while Massa finished eighth. Both cars caught fire during the Hungarian GP. Confirmed by Ferrari for 2006, Massa tagged Nick Heidfeld's Williams-BMW at the start of the Turkish GP and was recovering from the change of nosecone when his engine failed; Villeneuve finished 11th. They both finished the next two GPs, with Villeneuve a combative sixth in Belgium as he bettered Massa for once. Starting with a heavy fuel load, the former champion briefly held second place behind the safety car, and survived a couple of off-track moments and wheel-to-wheel contact with Narain Karthikeyan to secure a much-needed result. With a car that simply was not quick enough in race trim,

both drivers finished the last three GPs with just one points score between them, achieved with Massa's sixth place in China after gambling on staying out when the safety car was deployed for a second time.

In its last season using rebadged Ferrari engines, Sauber-Petronas dropped to eighth in the constructors' standings.

JORDAN GRAND PRIX

Eddie Jordan was looking to sell his eponymous team by the end of 2004, having batted such questions away for 18 months. Canadian-domiciled Russian steel tycoon Alex Shnaider emerged as the prime candidate when talks with Arden F3000 team owner Christian Horner foundered before Christmas. Shnaider's Midland Group had planned to enter the championship in 2006 as a brand-new team, with the industrialist telling *F1 Racing*: 'We wanted to outsource much of this work. That's why we're not interested in buying an existing team.' Ex-Jordan technical chief Gary Anderson and F3 team owner Trevor Carlin were hired as consultants and Dallara was commissioned to build a purpose-built chassis. However, Bernie Ecclestone brokered the purchase of Jordan instead, which accelerated Midland's entry by 12 months, avoided the FIA's $48m new team bond and transferred Jordan's FOCA benefits. The 36-year-old Shnaider bought Eddie Jordan's 50.1 percent and

Narain Karthikeyan, Jordan EJ15B-Toyota (Brazilian GP)

Merrion group's 49.9 percent shareholdings on 21 January 2005, with the team continuing for a final year as Jordan Grand Prix.

Negotiations with Toyota for engine supply were already ongoing when Ford put Cosworth Engineering up for sale on 17 September 2004. The new two-race engine rules freed capacity at Toyota and a one-year deal was agreed in principle on the typhoon-silenced Saturday of the Japanese GP and concluded on 13 November, two days before entries for the 2005 World Championship were due. The arrangement halved Jordan's engine bill, although a race seat for Toyota reserve Ryan Briscoe was not part of the deal as had been suggested.

The Midland acquisition ended Eddie Jordan's day-to-day F1 involvement with a new management structure installed at the Silverstone factory. F3 team owner Colin Kolles was appointed

Robert Doornbos, Jordan EJ15B-Toyota (British GP)

managing director, Trevor Carlin sporting director and Adrian Burgess (from Carlin's World Series team) chief operating officer, with former rally co-driver Christian Geistdörfer in a marketing role. Renault's Mark Smith had rejoined as technical director on 1 December 2004 and was followed from Enstone by Paul Monaghan, who succeeded James Robinson as head of race and test engineering. Commercial guru Ian Phillips provided a link to the past as director of business affairs. John McQuilliam (chief designer), Simon Phillips (aerodynamics), James Key (technical co-ordinator) and Mike Wroe (electronics) remained. A Jordan employee since 1987, Andy Stevenson succeeded Tim Edwards as team manager. It was soon apparent that all was not well within the new structure for Smith quit just a week after the takeover, with the 33-year-old Key promoted in his place. Carlin grew tired of the threadbare financial realities and quit in June, and Monaghan soon joined Smith at Red Bull Racing.

With driver decisions delayed by the ownership uncertainty during the winter, the eventual choices were two rookies who had won races for Carlin in the junior categories, Narain Karthikeyan (who had tested for Jordan in 2001) and Tiago Monteiro, thanks to backing from TATA and Galp respectively. Disappointed to miss out on a race seat, Robert Doornbos continued in the third-driver role he had fulfilled at the final three GPs of 2004. Linked to the Midland/Dallara negotiations for 2006, Mexican Champ Car race winner Mario Domínguez's Silverstone test on 11 February lasted just a lap due to poor weather. Nicky Pastorelli and Roman Rusinov were named as test drivers.

Toyota delivered the first working engine on 4 February, three days before Monteiro gave the Jordan EJ15-Toyota its shakedown on a foggy Silverstone National Circuit. The late engine switch left little option but to merely adapt the EJ14 to the Toyota RVX-05 and revise

Tiago Monteiro, Jordan EJ15-Toyota (United States GP)

Nicolas Kiesa, Jordan EJ15-Toyota (German GP)

Franck Montagny, Jordan EJ15-Toyota (European GP)

its aerodynamics to comply with the new regulations, so the EJ15 was always a compromise. Carlin admitted to *Autosport*'s Andrew van de Burgt that 'we'll be doing very little to this year's car' as the team focused on 2006. Midland's corporate black livery, complete with the colours of the Russian flag, was launched in Moscow's Red Square on 25 February amid dancers and fireworks, although the cars continued to sport the yellow of Benson & Hedges throughout 2005.

Reliability was almost bulletproof, Karthikeyan's electrical failure in Bahrain the only mechanical retirement before mid-season. The first Indian to start a GP, the somewhat wild Karthikeyan was an impressive ninth in the wet first qualifying for the Australian GP and adapted more quickly than his team-mate. However, impact with a barrier at Monaco caused race-ending hydraulic issues and a crash in Canada drew public rebuke from Kolles. Monteiro improved steadily and finished every race in the first half of the season, his tenth places in Bahrain and Canada Jordan's best results thus far. Jordan was not allowed to run a third car during Friday practice in Canada due to using too many sets of tyres at the previous race, at the Nürburgring, where Franck Montagny had replaced Doornbos as a one-off.

The Michelin fiasco at Indianapolis thrust Jordan into the limelight when just the six Bridgestone runners started the race. Monteiro made the most of the opportunity to become the first Portuguese driver to stand on an F1 podium. He won the early-race tussle with Karthikeyan to lead a joyous Jordan-Toyota 3–4 behind the dominant Ferraris. That result could not hide the fact that the EJ15 was too slow, and work on a heavily updated EJ15B had already begun, although cost prohibited a new monocoque. The car featured a revised engine installation and gearbox casing, plus new suspension, radiator configuration and aero package (floor, sidepods and rear wing). The pace during initial testing at Barcelona was encouraging but overheating delayed the EJ15B's race debut.

Doornbos tried the EJ15B on Friday morning at Magny-Cours, although the race drivers relied on the standard specification to finish among the backmarkers as normal. Karthikeyan was slowed by losing gears from the second lap of the French GP and had an early electrical failure at Silverstone. The British GP was Doornbos's last Friday appearance before racing for Minardi, so Nicolas Kiesa became third driver for the rest of the European campaign. With Johnny Herbert a new public face for the team after signing a one-year contract as sporting relations director, both Jordan-Toyotas finished the next three races outside the top ten. That was despite Monteiro's clash with Jacques Villeneuve on his birthday in Germany, suffering an opening-lap puncture when hit by Christijan Albers in Hungary and dental work on an abscess in Turkey. That latter race was notable for Monteiro being the unwitting victim of second-placed Juan Pablo Montoya's clumsy attempt to lap him.

The EJ15B's cooling was improved sufficiently for the only such chassis to be taken to the Italian GP. Monteiro won the toss of a coin to be assigned the new car and was encouraged to beat the Minardis and finish 17th. Karthikeyan was last in an old-spec EJ15 despite another first-lap puncture following more contact with Albers. Both drivers had EJ15Bs in Belgium, where Monteiro claimed an excellent eighth with Karthikeyan 11th.

Kiesa's third-driver role was extended to cover the Brazilian and Chinese GPs. Sakon Yamamoto impressed when he replaced Kiesa in Japan by setting quicker lap times than the race drivers, albeit on fresh tyres and with higher revs. Monteiro's unblemished finishing record ended at Interlagos when a driveshaft broke after 56 laps. They both finished the Japanese GP before Jordan Grand Prix's 250th and final F1 appearance in China, where team members wore personalised T-shirts that featured a 'Jordan RIP 1991–2005' motif. Monteiro finished 11th but Karthikeyan was lucky to walk away from a 160mph accident.

Sakon Yamamoto, Jordan EJ15B-Toyota (Japanese GP)

Christijan Albers, Minardi PS04B-Cosworth (Australian GP)

MINARDI F1 TEAM

Team owner Paul Stoddart spent 2005 trying to sell Minardi. Eddie Irvine brokered discussions with Russian businessman Roustam Tariko and there was talk of a Dutch consortium before Red Bull's Dietrich Mateschitz met Stoddart at the Italian GP and concluded negotiations at Spa-Francorchamps, with the sale agreed for a reported $35m.

The countdown to Minardi's final F1 season included its annual 'young' driver test at Misano, on 22–26 November 2004. Patrick Friesacher, Will Power, Christijan Albers and Jeffrey van Hooydonk were quickest on successive days with Tiago Monteiro, Will Davison, Pastor Maldonado, Patrick Huisman (aged 36) and Chanoch Nissany (aged 41) also driving a Minardi PS04B-Cosworth. In addition, Euro 3000 champion Nicky Pastorelli had a couple of winter tests. Former Minardi test driver Albers was announced as the first race driver in Amsterdam on 23 December, with Friesacher preferred to Nicolas Kiesa as his team-mate.

Formula BMW Asia Champion Marchy Lee drove a PS04B

at Mugello in April in the unfulfilled hope of being Friday test driver at the San Marino GP. Nissany performed that role at the Hungarian GP, where the little-known Israeli completed eight slow laps (nearly 13 seconds off the pace) before spinning. Enrico Toccacelo replaced Nissany for three races from the Turkish GP, but World Series by Renault champion Robert Kubica was denied the necessary super licence to take part in Chinese practice because he had not completed 300km in an F1 car.

Never shy of an argument with the FIA, Stoddart entered 2004-specification Minardi PS04Bs, with old 72-degree Cosworth CR-3L engines, for the Australian GP. Without 2005-compliant aero, they were not allowed to take part on Friday despite gaining an injunction from Victoria's Supreme Court, action that led to the FIA threatening to strip the race of championship status. Minardi relented by the end of the day and its mechanics worked overnight to make the cars legal. The evil-handling PS04Bs were used at the first three races in this form, finishing at the back on each occasion when lapped three or more times. Albers was

Patrick Friesacher, Minardi PS04B-Cosworth (Malaysian GP)

Christijan Albers, Minardi PS05-Cosworth (United States GP)

set-up. Andy Tilley used the Lola wind tunnel in Huntingdon for new aerodynamics that mimicked elements of cars further up the pitlane. The deep, 'spoon'-shaped front wing had sculpted endplates ahead of large bargeboards that featured double fins. The sidepods had triangular intakes and were cut away at the bottom before cascading to the rear, with vertical strakes mounted ahead of winglets. There were large cooling chimneys with periscope exhausts adjacent to the airbox.

Minardi hoped the PS05 would be quicker than the PS04B *muletta* by a second a lap to allow it to challenge Jordan among the backmarkers. Mechanical failures sidelined both cars at Imola and, with Stoddart missing through illness, they were left on the Spanish GP grid due to an electronics malfunction, before retiring once more. Friesacher crashed out of the Spanish and Monaco GPs while Albers triggered a safety car at that latter race when he spun at Mirabeau and almost blocked the track. 'We were totally crap,' Stoddart fumed after the European GP. 'For some reason we lost all the potential we showed in qualifying and what could have been a good weekend turned into a disaster.' Albers, who received a drive-through penalty for ignoring blue flags, and Friesacher were the last drivers still circulating, 17th and 18th.

Albers was 11th (and last) after a race of attrition in Montréal before Minardi was among the three Bridgestone-shod teams to start the ill-fated United States GP. Albers and Friesacher finished fifth and sixth respectively, the last runners once more but handed precious points on a dreadful day for F1. Left-rear punctures eliminated both cars in France, with Albers fortunate to escape

forced to retire in Australia when he lost first and second gears, preventing him from restarting after his pitstop. Friesacher crashed out of the Malaysian GP on the third lap when he hit oil in Turn 1.

Technical director Gabriele Tredozi described the Minardi PS05-Cosworth as 'radical' when Albers completed 120 laps of Mugello on 15 April. Built around the first all-new monocoque in four years, the PS05 was powered by the latest-specification Cosworth TJ2005 90-degree V10. Its gearbox, with stiffer twin-part titanium casing, retained six speeds to aid reliability while the suspension was developed from PS04B's pushrod/torsion bar

Patrick Friesacher, Minardi PS05-Cosworth (British GP)

Robert Doornbos, Minardi PS05-Cosworth (Turkish GP)

Chanoch Nissany, Minardi PS05-Cosworth (Hungarian GP)

from an ensuing crash with only abrasions to one hand; the cause was traced to valve caps not being replaced at the pitstops. At Silverstone, both drivers finished in their customary positions at the back. This was Friesacher's last appearance as he made way for Robert Doornbos for the rest of the season in an all-Dutch line-up.

Albers finished ahead of some better-fancied runners at Hockenheim, where Doornbos lost time after a collision with Jacques Villeneuve. Hydraulic failures ended their Hungarian GP before a new rear wing and sidepods were introduced in Turkey. Doornbos aborted his qualifying lap when his rear brakes caught fire but he beat the Jordans in the race. Albers was withdrawn after a litany of issues ranging from refuelling malfunction to a recalcitrant gearbox. They finished the Italian GP despite Albers's opening lap 'off' at the second Lesmo and a drive-through penalty.

With the sale to Red Bull agreed that day, they outqualified both Jordans at Spa-Francorchamps only to wrongly choose full wets for the start. A new 'Renault-copy' front wing was taken to Interlagos, where Doornbos retired and Albers beat Narain Karthikeyan's Jordan into 14th. They qualified in the top 15 in the Japanese rain with Michael Schumacher, Fernando Alonso and Kimi Räikkönen for company. Both finished despite pitstop dramas when Doornbos drove into a mechanic and Albers's car caught fire. In China, Albers crashed into Schumacher's Ferrari on the way to the grid and had to switch to the spare PS05, which lacked power steering, then finished the race 16th (and last), two places

behind his team-mate, after stopping when the car shed its left-front wheel retainer.

Minardi scored seven points at Indianapolis but finished tenth and last in the constructors' standings in its final season before becoming Scuderia Toro Rosso. At Minardi's final test at Vallelunga on 23 November 2005, Juan Cáceres was fastest with Luca Filippi, Katherine Legge, Davide Rigon, Roldán Rodríguez and Chanoch Nissany also participating in that small part of F1 history.

Enrico Toccacelo, Minardi PS05-Cosworth (Italian GP)

2005 RESULTS

DRIVER PERFORMANCE

DRIVER	CAR-ENGINE	AUS	MAL	BRN	RSM	E	MC	EU	CDN	USA	F	GB	D	H	TR	I	B	BR	J	PRC
Christijan Albers	Minardi PS04B-Cosworth	17 R	19 13	18 13	–	–	–	–	–	–	–	–	–	–	–	–	–	–	–	–
	Minardi PS05-Cosworth	–	–	–	20 R	14 R	14 14	20 17	15 11	18 5	20 R	18 18	16 13	17 R	15 R	20 19	18 12	16 14	13 16	18 16
Fernando Alonso	Renault R25	13 3 FL	1 1	1 1	2 1	3 2	2 4	6 1 FL	3 R	6 DNS	1 1	1 2	3 1	6 11	3 2	2 2	4 2	1 3	16 3	1 1
Rubens Barrichello	Ferrari F2004M	11 2	12 R	–	–	–	–	–	–	–	–	–	–	–	–	–	–	–	–	–
	Ferrari F2005	–	–	20 9	9 R	16 9	10 8	7 3	20 3	7 2	5 9	5 7	15 10	7 10	11 10	7 12	12 5	9 6	9 11	8 12
Jenson Button	BAR 007-Honda	8 11	9 R	11 R	3 DSQ*	–	–	13 10	1 R	3 DNS	7 4	2 5	2 3	8 5	13 5	3 8	8 3	4 7	2 5	4 8
David Coulthard	Red Bull RB1-Cosworth	5 4	8 6	14 8	14 11	9 8	7 R	12 4	12 7	16 DNS	15 10	13 13	11 7	13 R	12 7	10 15	11 R	14 R	6 6	7 9
Anthony Davidson	BAR 007-Honda	–	15 R	–	–	–	–	–	–	–	–	–	–	–	–	–	–	–	–	–
Pedro de la Rosa	McLaren MP4-20-Mercedes-Benz	T	T	8 5 FL	T	T	–	–	T	T	T	T	–	T	T	–	T	–	T	T
Robert Doornbos	Jordan EJ15-Toyota	T	T	T	T	T	T	–	T	–	–	–	–	–	–	–	–	–	–	–
	Jordan EJ15B-Toyota	–	–	–	–	–	–	–	–	–	T	T	–	–	–	–	–	–	–	–
	Minardi PS05-Cosworth	–	–	–	–	–	–	–	–	–	–	–	17 18	19 R	17 13	18 18	17 13	18 R	15 14	20 14
Giancarlo Fisichella	Renault R25	1 1	3 R	10 R	12 R	6 5 FL	4 12	9 6	4 R	4 DNS	6 6	6 4	4 4	9 9	2 4	8 3	13 R	3 5	3 2	2 4
Patrick Friesacher	Minardi PS04B-Cosworth	16 17	20 R	19 12	–	–	–	–	–	–	–	–	–	–	–	–	–	–	–	–
	Minardi PS05-Cosworth	–	–	–	19 R	15 R	13 R	18 18	19 R	20 6	18 R	19 19	–	–	–	–	–	–	–	–
Nick Heidfeld	Williams FW27-BMW	7 R	10 3	4 R	8 6	17 10	6 2	1 2	13 R	15 DNS	14 14	14 12	7 11	12 6	6 R	NT DNP	–	–	–	–
Narain Karthikeyan	Jordan EJ15-Toyota	12 15	17 11	17 R	16 12	13 13	17 R	19 16	17 R	19 4	17 15	17 R	19 16	18 12	18 14	19 20	–	–	–	–
	Jordan EJ15B-Toyota	–	–	–	–	–	–	–	–	–	–	–	–	–	–	–	20 11	15 15	11 15	15 R
Nicolas Kiesa	Jordan EJ15-Toyota	–	–	–	–	–	–	–	–	–	–	–	T	T	T	T	T	–	–	–
	Jordan EJ15B-Toyota	–	–	–	–	–	–	–	–	–	–	–	–	–	–	–	–	–	T	T
Christian Klien	Red Bull RB1-Cosworth	6 7	7 8	7 DNS	T	T	T	T	16 8	14 DNS	16 R	15 15	10 9	11 R	10 8	13 13	16 9	6 9	4 9	14 5
Vitantonio Liuzzi	Red Bull RB1-Cosworth	T	T	T	15 8	11 R	12 R	14 9	–	–	T	T	T	T	T	T	T	T	T	T
Felipe Massa	Sauber C24-Petronas	18 10	14 10	12 7	8 10	10 11	11 9	11 14	11 4	10 DNS	9 R	16 10	13 8	14 14	8 R	15 9	7 10	8 11	10 10	11 6
Franck Montagny	Jordan EJ15-Toyota	–	–	–	–	–	–	T	–	–	–	–	–	–	–	–	–	–	–	–
Tiago Monteiro	Jordan EJ15-Toyota	14 16	18 12	16 10	17 13	18 12	15 13	17 15	18 10	17 3	19 13	20 17	18 17	20 13	14 15	–	–	–	–	–
	Jordan EJ15B-Toyota	–	–	–	–	–	–	–	–	–	–	–	–	–	–	17 17	19 8	11 R	20 13	19 11
Juan Pablo Montoya	McLaren MP4-20-Mercedes-Benz	9 6	11 4	–	–	7 7	16 5	5 7	5 DSQ	11 DNS	8 R	3 1	20 2	2 R	4 3 FL	1 1	1 14	2 1	18 R	5 R
Chanoch Nissany	Minardi PS05-Cosworth	–	–	–	–	–	–	–	–	–	–	–	–	T	–	–	–	–	–	–
Olivier Panis	Toyota TF105	–	–	–	–	–	–	–	–	–	T	–	–	–	–	–	–	–	–	–
Antônio Pizzonia	Williams FW27-BMW	–	–	–	–	–	–	–	–	–	–	–	–	–	–	16 7	15 15	13 R	12 R	13 13
Kimi Räikkönen	McLaren MP4-20-Mercedes-Benz	10 8	6 9 FL	9 3	11 R	1 1	1 1	2 11	7 1 FL	2 DNS	13 2 FL	12 3 FL	1 R FL	4 1 FL	1 1	11 4 FL	2 1	5 2 FL	17 1 FL	3 2 FL
Takuma Satō	BAR 007-Honda	20 14	NT DNP	13 R	6 DSQ	–	–	16 12	6 R	8 DNS	4 11	7 16	8 12	10 8	20 9	4 16	10 R	19 10	5 DSQ	17 R
Michael Schumacher	Ferrari F2004M	19 R	13 7	–	–	–	–	–	–	–	–	–	–	–	–	–	–	–	–	–
	Ferrari F2005	–	–	2 R	13 2 FL	8 R	8 7 FL	10 5	2 2	5 1 FL	3 3	9 6	5 5	1 2	19 R	6 10	6 R	7 4	14 7	6 R
Ralf Schumacher	Toyota TF105	15 12	5 5	6 4	10 9	4 4	18 6	8 R	10 6	NT DNP	11 7	8 8	12 6	5 3	9 12	9 6	5 7 FL	10 8	–	–
	Toyota TF105B	–	–	–	–	–	–	–	–	–	–	–	–	–	–	–	–	–	1 8	9 3
Scott Speed	Red Bull RB1-Cosworth	–	–	–	–	–	–	–	T	T	–	–	–	–	–	–	–	–	–	–
Enrico Toccacelo	Minardi PS05-Cosworth	–	–	–	–	–	–	–	–	–	–	–	–	–	T	T	T	–	–	–
Jarno Trulli	Toyota TF105	2 9	2 2	3 2	5 5	5 3	5 10	4 8	9 R	1 DNS	2 5	4 9	9 14	3 4	5 6	5 5	3 R	17 13	–	–
	Toyota TF105B	–	–	–	–	–	–	–	–	–	–	–	–	–	–	–	–	–	19 R	12 15
Jacques Villeneuve	Sauber C24-Petronas	4 13	16 R	15 11	11 4	12 R	9 11	15 13	8 9	12 DNS	10 8	10 14	14 15	15 R	16 11	12 11	14 6	20 12	8 12	16 10
Mark Webber	Williams FW27-BMW	3 5	4 R	5 6	4 7	2 6	3 3	3 R	14 5	9 DNS	12 12	11 11	6 NC	16 7	7 R	14 14	9 4	12 NC	7 4	10 7
Alexander Wurz	McLaren MP4-20-Mercedes-Benz	–	–	T	7 3	–	T	T	–	–	–	–	T	T	–	–	T	T	–	–
Sakon Yamamoto	Jordan EJ15B-Toyota	–	–	–	–	–	–	–	–	–	–	–	–	–	–	–	–	–	T	–
Ricardo Zonta	Toyota TF105	T	T	T	T	T	T	T	T	13 DNS	T	T	T	T	T	T	T	T	–	–
	Toyota TF105B	–	–	–	–	–	–	–	–	–	–	–	–	–	–	–	–	–	T	T

*Button led laps 24 and 43-46 on the road but was disqualified

FORMULA 1 RACE WINNERS

ROUND	RACE (CIRCUIT)	DATE	WINNER
1	Foster's Australian Grand Prix (Albert Park)	Mar 6	Giancarlo Fisichella (Renault R25)
2	Petronas Malaysian Grand Prix (Sepang)	Mar 20	Fernando Alonso (Renault R25)
3	Gulf Air Bahrain Grand Prix (Sakhir)	Apr 3	Fernando Alonso (Renault R25)
4	Gran Premio Foster's di San Marino (Imola)	Apr 24	Fernando Alonso (Renault R25)
5	Gran Premio Marlboro de España (Catalunya)	May 8	Kimi Räikkönen (McLaren MP4-20-Mercedes-Benz)
6	Grand Prix de Monaco (Monte Carlo)	May 22	Kimi Räikkönen (McLaren MP4-20-Mercedes-Benz)
7	Grand Prix of Europe (Nürburgring)	May 29	Fernando Alonso (Renault R25)
8	Grand Prix du Canada (Montréal)	Jun 12	Kimi Räikkönen (McLaren MP4-20-Mercedes-Benz)
9	United States Grand Prix (Indianapolis)	Jun 19	Michael Schumacher (Ferrari F2005)
10	Grand Prix de France (Magny-Cours)	Jul 3	Fernando Alonso (Renault R25)
11	Foster's British Grand Prix (Silverstone)	Jul 10	Juan Pablo Montoya (McLaren MP4-20-Mercedes-Benz)
12	Grosser Mobil 1 Preis von Deutschland (Hockenheim)	Jul 24	Fernando Alonso (Renault R25)
13	Marlboro Magyar Nagydíj (Hungaroring)	Jul 31	Kimi Räikkönen (McLaren MP4-20-Mercedes-Benz)
14	Turkish Grand Prix (Istanbul Park)	Aug 21	Kimi Räikkönen (McLaren MP4-20-Mercedes-Benz)
15	Gran Premio Vodafone d'Italia (Monza)	Sep 4	Juan Pablo Montoya (McLaren MP4-20-Mercedes-Benz)
16	Belgian Grand Prix (Spa-Francorchamps)	Sep 11	Kimi Räikkönen (McLaren MP4-20-Mercedes-Benz)
17	Grande Prêmio do Brasil (Interlagos)	Sep 25	Juan Pablo Montoya (McLaren MP4-20-Mercedes-Benz)
18	Fuji Television Japanese Grand Prix (Suzuka)	Oct 9	Kimi Räikkönen (McLaren MP4-20-Mercedes-Benz)
19	Sinopec Chinese Grand Prix (Shanghai)	Oct 16	Fernando Alonso (Renault R25)

DRIVERS' CHAMPIONSHIP

	DRIVERS	POINTS
1	Fernando Alonso	133
2	Kimi Räikkönen	112
3	Michael Schumacher	62
4	Juan Pablo Montoya	60
5	Giancarlo Fisichella	58
6	Ralf Schumacher	45
7	Jarno Trulli	43
8	Rubens Barrichello	38
9	Jenson Button	37
10	Mark Webber	36
11	Nick Heidfeld	28
12	David Coulthard	24
13	Felipe Massa	11
14	Jacques Villeneuve	9
15	Christian Klien	9
16	Tiago Monteiro	7
17	Alexander Wurz	6
18	Narain Karthikeyan	5
19	Christijan Albers	4
20	Pedro de la Rosa	4
21	Patrick Friesacher	3
22	Antônio Pizzonia	2
23	Takuma Satō	1
24	Vitantonio Liuzzi	1
25	Robert Doornbos	0

CONSTRUCTORS' CHAMPIONSHIP

	CONSTRUCTORS	POINTS
1	Renault	191
2	McLaren-Mercedes-Benz	182
3	Ferrari	100
4	Toyota	88
5	Williams-BMW	66
6	BAR-Honda	38
7	Red Bull-Cosworth	34
8	Sauber-Petronas	20
9	Jordan-Toyota	12
10	Minardi-Cosworth	7

Kimi Räikkönen leads on the opening lap of the Monaco Grand Prix

Fernando Alonso counted the Australian Grand Prix among his seven victories as he and Renault successfully defended their titles

2006

ANOTHER FOR ALONSO AS SCHUMACHER BOWS OUT

Michael Schumacher challenged Fernando Alonso in what turned out to be the last season of his Ferrari career. Renault's campaign was temporarily derailed mid-season when its 'tuned mass-damper' was banned. However, it recovered to retain both drivers' and constructors' titles 100 years after the marque won the very first grand prix in 1906.

Engines were reduced in capacity and number of cylinders to 2.4-litre V8s, with 90-degree vee angle and 95kg minimum weight stipulated. Variable-length inlet trumpets were outlawed. Old V10s were permitted as a low-cost alternative, with air intake and revs restricted to 77mm and 16,700rpm respectively. Reduced power meant that aerodynamic efficiency rather than outright downforce was crucial. Engine vibration was an anticipated by-product of the switch to V8s, and most designers moved the shorter unit forward while maintaining the wheelbase to benefit rear-end aerodynamics. A mandatory slot-gap separator was added between the rear-wing elements from the Canadian GP to prevent flexing that reduced drag and so increased top speed.

The regulation that a single set of tyres had to last for qualifying and the race was abandoned, leading to the reintroduction of tyre stops and eradicating a major advantage for Michelin. The new rules placed higher lateral loads on the tyres, which proved difficult to bring into the working temperature window with front graining a recurring complaint. Ferrari continued to defy the 30-day in-season testing limit

Michael Schumacher announced his retirement after winning the Italian GP

Felipe Massa narrowly avoids hitting Fernando Alonso in Bahrain

Jenson and John Button celebrate victory in the Hungarian GP

agreed by its rivals. Qualifying was overhauled with a single one-hour session split into three knockout stages, ending with the Q3 top-ten shoot-out for pole position. Drivers who got through to that final 20-minute segment (15 minutes from the French GP) could replace fuel for every lap completed within 110 percent of their fastest time. That was intended to get rid of the 'fuel-burn' phase when drivers circulated slowly at the start of Q3 to reduce fuel load and improve ultimate lap time.

Private equity company CVC Capital Partners acquired the 75 percent shareholding in the F1 holding group previously held by three German banks, with Bernie Ecclestone remaining at the head of the reconstituted board. The FIA formed a new Formula 1 Commission for 2008, with six teams among the various stakeholders. McLaren's omission was explained by a limit of one team per country (Williams was the British representative), although *Autosport* questioned whether it was 'a deliberate snub to a team that has not enjoyed a cosy relationship with the FIA'. Tony Scott-Andrews, a lawyer, was appointed as F1's first permanent steward to improve race-by-race consistency.

To avoid clashing with the Commonwealth Games, Melbourne was not the opening race for the first time since 1996. There were late doubts about the German and Italian GPs due to financial difficulties and noise protests respectively, although both went ahead. The Belgian GP on 17 September was cancelled when the promoter declared bankruptcy in January. Damon Hill succeeded Sir Jackie Stewart as president of the British Racing Drivers' Club, owner of Silverstone. Montréal signed a five-year contract extension to host the Canadian GP. This was the final year that cigarette branding was permitted in the European Union, which led to all tobacco companies except Philip Morris International (Marlboro) leaving F1.

Canada was Fernando Alonso's sixth win in the opening nine GPs

Fernando Alonso, Renault R26 (Bahrain GP)

MILD SEVEN RENAULT F1

The new world champions were shocked before Christmas by Fernando Alonso's announcement that he was joining McLaren-Mercedes for 2007. When the initial surprise and resentment had eased, driver and team focused on retaining those hard-won titles, with Alonso promising: 'Until the Monday after the final race, I will be driving to my maximum for Renault.' In the final season of his two-year contract, Giancarlo Fisichella's hopes that Alonso's forthcoming defection would improve his own chances of winning the World Championship proved in vain.

GP2 runner-up Heikki Kovalainen replaced Franck Montagny as reserve driver while José María López, Giorgio Mondini and Robert Kubica all received prize tests on 1 December for winning junior Renault categories. Renault Sport president for 20 years, Patrick Faure was replaced by Alain Dassas on 3 April. Renault's success in 2005 inevitably placed key staff in the shop window for rival teams with head of mechanical design Rob Marshall, who was credited with inventing the 'mass-damper', and chief mechanic Jonathan Wheatley poached by Red Bull in December.

The other teams had been testing new 2.4-litre engines for up to six months when the Renault R26 completed its shakedown at Jerez on 10 January, the first time that the all-new RS26 V8 had run on track. Alonso completed back-to-back tests of the new and old (3-litre V10) units during those four days at Jerez, with the new unit less than 0.4sec slower. Rob White continued as engine technical director and Léon Taillieu as project leader at Viry-Châtillon. The RS26 was not the most powerful engine in the field but it was the most drivable. Its excellent heat dissipation allowed use of

smaller radiators that reduced sidepod frontal area, with chimneys preferred to cooling louvres to further decrease drag.

The R26 was 'an aggressive development of a proven and successful design philosophy' according to chassis technical director Bob Bell. 'We have worked on saving weight, improving stiffness, and improving the car in every area.' Renault abandoned its policy of alternating chief designer when Mark Smith left during 2005, and Tim Densham spent a year working on the new car. The dimensions and forward positioning of the engine and slimline gearbox allowed Dino Toso's aero department to shrink-fit the 'Coke bottle' rear end. The conventional paddle-shift titanium gearbox had seven speeds for the first time. The monocoque was marginally raised around the cockpit with Renault's pioneering vee-keel retained to mount the lower-front wishbones. Another key innovation of the R25, 'mass-dampers', were fitted at the front and rear to control pitch and bounce respectively. The aggressively tapered and undercut sidepods, with very small L-shaped inlets, channelled air rearwards. The lower plane of the rear wing curved upwards at the centre and was now supported centrally, allowing elaborate drag-efficient endplates to be fitted. The car was launched in Monaco on 31 January with the definitive front wing and its simplified endplates added for Bahrain.

The R26 was fast and reliable during the winter and Alonso narrowly edged Michael Schumacher's Ferrari at the opening GP in Bahrain. Hydraulic failure during that race gave Fisichella a fresh engine for Malaysia that he used to claim pole position and dominate the race. Only seventh on the grid after carrying twice the required fuel load in error, Alonso finished second to

2006

complete Renault's second-ever 1–2 as a team, the first having been the 1982 French GP. They qualified second (Fisichella) and third (Alonso) in Australia, where Alonso warmed his tyres better in uncharacteristically cool temperatures behind the safety car to pass Jenson Button's Honda on the restart and win. Fisichella was fifth after starting from the pitlane due to stalling on the grid and a subsequent catalogue of ill-fortune.

Twelve months after their epic tussle at Imola, Alonso was narrowly beaten by Schumacher's Ferrari in the San Marino GP despite having the quicker car. Out of two-race engine sequence following his Bahrain retirement, Fisichella ran an upgraded RS26B engine at Imola but was eliminated in Q2 and so only finished eighth. Alonso took that more powerful V8 for the Nürburgring, where he beat Schumacher Sr to pole only for the positions to be reversed come race day. Fisichella again failed to make the top-ten shoot-out after being baulked by Jacques Villeneuve. There was some payback when he passed the Canadian's BMW Sauber in the final pitstops to claim sixth.

Alonso responded to Ferrari's sudden onslaught by winning the next four races, each from pole position. He delighted King Juan Carlos I and the home crowd at Barcelona and controlled the Monaco GP despite Kimi Räikkönen's early pressure. He led all but one lap at Silverstone and victory in Canada established a 25-point advantage. Fisichella scored at each of those races as the R26

displayed bullet-proof reliability. He completed an all-Renault front row in Spain only to lose second to Schumacher in the pitstops. His best three qualifying times in Monaco were deleted for impeding David Coulthard but, on a circuit where overtaking is nigh-on impossible, Fisichella forced his way past three cars to claim sixth. Fourth at Silverstone, he jumped the start in Montréal from second on the grid. The subsequent drive-through penalty dropped him to fifth and he only regained one position by the chequered flag.

Momentum swung back to Maranello at Indianapolis, where Fisichella was the quicker Renault driver from the outset. With Michelin having brought a conservative choice of compound to the scene of its 2005 debacle, Fisichella – again using an engine upgrade a race before Alonso – qualified and finished third, two places ahead of his gripless team-mate. Both drivers had the improved RS26C engine for Magny-Cours, where Ferrari/Bridgestone continued to hold sway. Alonso was able to split the Ferraris by switching to a two-stop strategy while Fisichella's understated sixth was explained by tyre graining.

There was a technical bombshell on 27 July when the FIA adjudged the 'mass-damper' to be a movable aerodynamic device. The German GP stewards declared the system as legal only for the FIA to appeal that ruling. The Renault R26 was not the only car to be fitted with the system, but its performance slumped when the 'mass-dampers' were deactivated for fear of disqualification.

Giancarlo Fisichella, Renault R26 (Chinese GP)

With Bridgestone also having an advantage, Ferrari finished 1–2 with Alonso and Fisichella a distant fifth and sixth with blistered tyres in the Hockenheim heat. Renault improved its enforced suspension revision for Hungary but left empty-handed. Alonso received a harsh two 2sec qualifying penalty for brake-testing Robert Doornbos on Friday so started the damp race from 15th. He used Michelin intermediates to lead by lap 18 only to have an issue with the right-rear wheel nut when he switched to dry tyres. The championship leader three-wheeled to a halt at Turn 2 on his out lap; Fisichella crashed.

The FIA Court of Appeal confirmed the 'mass-damper' ban on 23 August and Ferrari led Renault in qualifying for the following weekend's Turkish GP. Fisichella spun at the first corner to avoid colliding with his team-mate and was hit by Nick Heidfeld's BMW Sauber, forcing him to pit for a new nosecone; sixth place was damage limitation. The Ferraris ran 1–2 until Alonso used an early safety car to pit and jump Michael Schumacher. He held off his title rival at the second pitstops and for the rest of the race to claim a crucial second-place finish.

Renault's increasing feeling of injustice intensified at Monza when Alonso was docked his best three qualifying times for impeding Felipe Massa's final qualifying attempt. Flavio Briatore told RAI television that 'they have decided give the World Championship to Schumacher' although he later retracted his comments. Alonso's engine expired as he recovered from his tenth-place start and Fisichella came home fourth following a one-stop strategy. The cold and wet of China favoured Renault and Michelin but the decision not to change Alonso's rear tyres at a pitstop and slow second stop restricted him to second as Schumacher drew level in the standings.

With Bridgestone outperforming Michelin in Japanese qualifying, Alonso passed both Toyotas and beat Massa out of the pits to claim second. That became first (and a decisive ten-point advantage) when Schumacher's engine failed. Fisichella was third in both China and Japan. Alonso retained the drivers' title by finishing second in Brazil with Renault constructors' champions once more.

SCUDERIA FERRARI MARLBORO

Ferrari and Bridgestone rebounded from a disastrous 2005 campaign to challenge Renault/Michelin throughout 2006. Already helped by the reintroduction of tyre pitstops bringing Bridgestone back into play, the mid-season 'mass-damper' ban appeared to hand Ferrari a decisive advantage. However, in a year dominated by speculation about whether Michael Schumacher would extend his contract or retire, both driver and team ultimately fell short.

Part of the Ferrari set-up since 2001 and managed by Jean Todt's son Nicolas, Felipe Massa signed a one-year contract as Rubens Barrichello's replacement on 2 August 2005. Luca Badoer and Marc Gené extended their test deals. Valentino Rossi continued to assess a potential switch from two wheels to four before committing in May to remain in MotoGP.

Gené had been entrusted with the new V8's track debut at Fiorano on 2 August 2005 in a modified Ferrari F2004 but it was Schumacher who first drove the new-for-2006 Ferrari 248F1 (2.4-litres, 8-cylinders) at the damp test track on 16 January. This was the latest offering from the Ross Brawn-led engineering powerhouse that included Aldo Costa (head of design and development), Rory Byrne (design consultant) and John Iley (head

Michael Schumacher, Ferrari 248F1 (French GP)

Felipe Massa, Ferrari 248F1 (Hungarian GP)

of aerodynamics). Perceived aero deficiencies from the overly cautious F2005 were addressed. Having used a single keel since 1996, Ferrari opted to increase front-suspension options with a vee-shaped alternative that was deeper than Renault's pioneering iteration. Mirrors were moved to the outer edges of the sidepods, which were more compact and aggressively undercut thanks to the smaller engine's reduced cooling requirements. The rear wing was centrally supported to allow greater flexibility in endplate design. In keeping with leading rivals, Ferrari maintained the wheelbase of the F2005 (305cm) with the shorter engine moved forward to enhance rear-end aero, which included a completely new split diffuser with tall central section that extended to the beam wing, and curvaceous outer channels. Reworked suspension retained Sachs rotary shock absorbers at the rear. A triple-tier front wing first seen during Ferrari's extended pre-season Bahrain test featured a pronounced central 'spoon' section rather than the flat 'snowplough' of 2005.

Nikolas Tombazis returned from McLaren on 1 March as chief designer following his brief sojourn in Woking, reporting to Costa. Byrne's retirement plans at the end of 2006 were delayed when he agreed a two-year extension in the autumn. Tyre development engineer Gérard Brussoz arrived from Michelin in a research and development role. Ferrari did not follow the 30-day testing limitations agreed by its rivals.

The legality of a new rear wing at the Bahrain GP was challenged due to high-speed flexing that was thought to reduce drag. The update duly passed scrutineering and Schumacher led Massa in a qualifying 1–2 to equal Ayrton Senna's record 65 pole positions. Massa was ninth after a debut that included a spectacular spin and slow pitstop while second-placed Schumacher was narrowly beaten out of his final pitstop by Fernando Alonso's winning Renault. That was partly due to having to refuel a lap early because one of his Q3 laps had been over 110 percent of his pole time, such were the fine margins in 2006.

A manufacturing issue caused both drivers, plus Red Bull Racing's

David Coulthard, to take fresh engines and a ten-place grid penalty in Malaysia. Massa and Schumacher finished fifth and sixth on a day for damage limitation. Tyre warm-up issues eliminated both Ferraris in second qualifying for the Australian GP. Massa also crashed during that session and collided with Christian Klien and Scott Speed at the start of the race. Ferrari's day of woe was completed when Schumacher crashed at the final corner on lap 33.

Having solved the piston issues that had ruined the Malaysian GP and forced limited revs to be used so far, Ferrari harnessed full power and an aero upgrade (with twin-plane front wing) to good effect at Imola. Schumacher, starting from a record 66th pole position, covered Alonso's strategy to score his 85th GP victory. Fourth that day, Massa had a new race engineer for the European GP with Rob Smedley replacing Gabriele delli Colli. Modified suspension and aero tweaks helped Ferrari's continued resurgence at the Nürburgring. Having lined up behind Alonso on the grid, Schumacher's four consecutive record laps before his second pitstop resulted in another win with third-placed Massa on the podium for the first time. The title battle swung back in Renault's favour in Spain with the Ferraris well-beaten into second (Schumacher) and fourth (Massa).

The duel continued in Monaco, where Schumacher's 1m 13.898s was good enough for provisional pole position. However, his final qualifying attempt was slower, so he slid wide at La Rascasse and stalled the car, preventing anyone from beating his time. Schumacher and the team denied that it had been deliberate but condemnation was universal. Demoted to the back of the grid by the stewards as a consequence, Schumacher came from the pitlane to finish fifth. Massa finished ninth after a Q1 mistake in Casino Square also relegated him to the back.

The Ferraris qualified on the second row at Silverstone, where Schumacher passed Kimi Raïkkönen's McLaren for second at the final pitstops and Massa finished fifth. Both drivers struggled for tyre temperature in Canadian qualifying. Schumacher made a poor start from fifth and spent the first stint looking at Jarno Trulli's Toyota gearbox. A late safety car saved his race, and he took advantage of Räikkönen's mistake on the penultimate lap to snatch second; Massa was fifth again.

Tyre performance swung back to Bridgestone at the next two races as Ferrari locked out the front row. Having ended Alonso's run of five successive pole positions, Schumacher led a dominant 1–2 in the United States after passing his team-mate at the first pitstops. An even more extreme 'Coke bottle' rear end was introduced at Magny-Cours and Schumacher used it to secure pole and an eighth French GP victory with Massa third. That momentum gathered pace in Germany following the FIA's 'mass-damper' ruling, for Ferrari had not perfected its version of the system and suffered far less than Renault, allowing Schumacher to head yet another emphatic 1–2.

Ferrari's run ended at a damp Hungaroring. Handed a 2sec qualifying penalty for overtaking under red flags during practice, Schumacher was overly robust as he battled Pedro de la Rosa's McLaren, including cutting the chicane, and he broke a track rod as he tried to keep Nick Heidfeld's BMW Sauber at bay in the closing stages. He was classified ninth, one place behind Massa, before both gained a position following Robert Kubica's disqualification. In Turkey, Massa upstaged his team-mate by leading another qualifying 1–2 to claim his first pole position. The Brazilian then raced to an untroubled breakthrough victory after both drivers pitted when the safety car was deployed. Schumacher finished third after losing track position to Alonso by being stacked in the pits and running wide at the triple-apex Turn 8.

At the United States GP, Schumacher had informed senior management of his decision to retire at the end of the season, hoping to keep the matter private as he challenged for his eighth title. However, speculation intensified when it became clear that Räikkönen would join in 2007, and an emotional Schumacher finally confirmed his intention after winning the Italian GP, where Massa finished outside the points. Schumacher only qualified sixth at a cold and wet Shanghai, but passed both Renaults late on to score his 91st victory and join Alonso on 116 points with two races remaining. Compromised by an engine penalty, Massa's one-stop race ended when he ran into David Coulthard's Red Bull.

Schumacher was left needing a mathematical improbability

when he suffered his first race-engine failure since 2000 while leading the Japanese GP. Starting from pole, Massa finished second behind champion-elect Alonso. A technical issue denied Schumacher the chance of pole for his final race at Interlagos. He responded to a puncture early in the race by charging back to fourth. Wearing special overalls in the colours of the Brazilian flag, Massa took advantage of his team-mate's misfortune to take pole and win 'the easiest race I've ever done'.

This was the end of an era. In addition to Schumacher's retirement, technical director Ross Brawn took a sabbatical in 2007 and engine director Paolo Martinelli accepted an executive role within the parent Fiat corporation.

TEAM McLAREN MERCEDES

The announcement on 8 November 2005 that McLaren technical director Adrian Newey was moving to Red Bull Racing on a three-year deal shocked the team and F1 in general. The strength in depth at Woking was further tested when aerodynamics chief Nikolas Tombazis returned to Ferrari in March, with Peter Prodromou promoted. Rob Taylor arrived from Red Bull at the start of the season as senior designer to work under Mike Coughlan.

A plan for a satellite 'B-team' was evaluated during 2004. That included the sale of intellectual property of the year-old chassis by McLaren Applied Technologies, supply of Mercedes-Benz engines, and lease of McLaren's old factory in Albert Road, Woking. On 16 October 2004, Grand Prix Investments announced that 'Team Dubai F1 will enter the FIA Formula One World Championship with effect from the 2006 season', confirming it would pay the $48m FIA new-team bond and that 'Team Dubai F1 has also entered into exclusive negotiations with both Mercedes-Benz and McLaren for supply of engines and technical assistance'. The formal launch in November did not happen and the project foundered when sufficient investment was not forthcoming.

Juan Pablo Montoya and Kimi Räikkönen, who had a minor knee operation during the close season, entered the final year of their contracts. There were doubts about their extended futures, with Montoya unhappy that McLaren had not already exercised its option for 2007 and Räikkönen considering an offer from Ferrari.

Kimi Räikkönen, McLaren MP4-21-Mercedes-Benz (Bahrain GP)

Juan Pablo Montoya, McLaren MP4-21-Mercedes-Benz (European GP)

Alexander Wurz moved to Williams-Cosworth after five years as reserve, to be replaced by Pedro de la Rosa. DTM champion Gary Paffett was added to the testing roster before Christmas following promising outings at Jerez, Barcelona and Valencia.

Markus Duesmann, technical director of Mercedes-Benz High Performance Engines, oversaw development of the 2.4-litre Mercedes-Benz FO108S V8 with project leader Andy Cowell. It was track-tested in a modified MP4-20B in May, with development intensified from September. Although engine failures in practice at four GPs had scuppered Räikkönen's 2005 challenge, initial reliability issues with the new V8 and a power deficit (by 30bhp) led to the old V10 also being used into the New Year. Duesmann, who had only joined in April 2005, was placed on 'gardening leave' in June when he agreed to move to BMW, with Cowell and Alex Wendorff sharing his responsibilities.

With traditional Papaya orange adopted as its testing livery, the McLaren MP4-21-Mercedes made its debut at Barcelona on 23 January but this was curtailed by another V8 engine failure. The final car of McLaren's Newey era was an evolution of the concepts that had made its predecessor so aerodynamically efficient. Improved reliability and tyre warm-up in cool or qualifying conditions were key objectives. Prodromou reported that 'thousands of hours of wind-tunnel testing' had been spent optimising the slim rear packaging around the narrower V8 and its ancillaries, all of which meant that the old rev-restricted V10 was too large to be an emergency alternative. The front end was completely reworked around a 'zero-keel' configuration and saw the return of the needle nose, plus swooping tri-plane front wing with accentuated central 'spoon' section. There was a smaller engine cover complete with 'horn' wings and undercut sidepods that featured small triangular intakes. The MP4-21 had a relatively long wheelbase that helped move weight rearwards and manage airflow to the rear wing, which, unusually for 2006, was supported by the endplates. The carbon-cased seven-speed seamless-shift gearbox was elongated. Räikkönen was blunt in his assessment of the team's weakness: 'The biggest part of the problem is the engine.' Mercedes-Benz motorsport chief Norbert Haug admitted: 'We are not where we want to be with the V8 programme.' Furthermore, the MP4-21 lacked aero efficiency and front downforce, with understeer a consequence.

In its definitive chrome, black and red livery, the MP4-21 looked, said Autosport's Mark Hughes, 'gorgeous in all its shrink-wrapped, reflective silver glory. It's visibly aerodynamically adventurous… with not a straight line to be seen and hardly a curve that isn't multi-planed.' Engine issues initially masked the MP4-21's potential and Mercedes was out-developed by rivals from Maranello and Viry-Châtillon during 2006. However, Räikkönen raised hopes by setting the winter's fastest time at Valencia so far on 17 February, with long-run pace increasingly impressive.

Räikkönen was the first driver to suffer from the new knock-out qualifying when a wishbone broke in Q1 to leave him last on the grid in Bahrain, but he stormed through the field to third thanks to his alternate one-stop strategy, with Montoya qualifying and finishing an unhappy fifth. Extra cooling holes required in the Malaysian heat increased drag and lap times. Having locked out the third row, Räikkönen was hit by Christian Klien at the start and Montoya finished fourth, with Ron Dennis 'looking forward to the upgrades which should allow us to show our true potential'.

The FIA demanded wing changes to the MP4-21 before the Australian GP, where Montoya endured a torrid afternoon. He spun while warming his tyres on the way to the grid but reclaimed his fifth-place grid slot when the start was aborted. He was delayed by queuing behind the sister car in the pits, spun during a safety-car period and rode the kerbs so hard that the engine kill switch activated. Räikkönen changed his nosecone during a pitstop to cure understeer and finished second when closing on Fernando Alonso's winning car. The deficit to Renault and Ferrari continued at Imola, where Montoya led a McLaren-Mercedes 3–5 after spending most of the race in traffic.

Räikkönen used the new Mercedes Phase 4 engine upgrade at the Nürburgring to finish fourth, just 1.128sec behind second-placed Alonso. McLaren-Mercedes lacked pace in Spain, where Kimi made a great start from ninth to fifth, and finished in that position. Montoya made poor getaways at both races before retiring, due to engine failure at the Nürburgring and blaming his traction control when he spun in Spain. Quickest in Q1 and Q2 at Monaco, Räikkönen was denied the chance of pole position when Michael Schumacher parked his Ferrari at La Rascasse at the end of the top-ten shoot-out. That restricted the McLaren-Mercedes to the second row but Räikkönen challenged for victory until his heat shield caught fire for the second time that weekend, elevating Montoya to second. Increasingly frustrated by his season so far, Räikkönen disappeared to his boat rather than return to the pits.

The Finn qualified on the front row at Silverstone and challenged Alonso for the lead during the early stages, but Schumacher Sr beat him at the second round of pitstops so he had to settle for third. Montoya finished a distant sixth at Silverstone after nursing first-lap damage caused by Jacques Villeneuve's BMW Sauber. Räikkönen

pressured the Renaults during the opening stint in Canada before clutch issues at both pitstops denied a possible win. He slipped to third when he ran wide at Turn 10 on the penultimate lap and Schumacher took advantage.

Montoya's prospects for 2007 were harmed by incidents at both North American races. Having crashed out of the Canadian GP, he ran into the back of his team-mate in the second corner of the United States GP and both were eliminated in the resulting four-car pile-up. Aware that he would not be retained for another season, Montoya phoned his former Champ Car employer Chip Ganassi on the day after that Indianapolis debacle and signed to race in the 2007 NASCAR Cup. McLaren immediately replaced him with Pedro de la Rosa on a race-by-race basis from the French GP.

With the engine revving to 20,000rpm for the first time, the cars qualified in the top ten at Magny-Cours and scored points after adopting a three-stop strategy, Räikkönen disappointed with fifth and de la Rosa seventh after losing time at the start. Räikkönen grabbed a shock pole at Hockenheim although a faulty fuel sensor meant he had to refuel ten laps before Michael Schumacher planned to stop, compromising strategy options. Although tyre blisters, a slow stop and a hydraulic issue added more delay, he passed Jenson Button to claim third. He repeated that pole at the Hungaroring (with a more representative fuel load) and built a 20sec lead during the first stint only to crash into Vitantonio Liuzzi's Toro Rosso-Cosworth. An early retirement in Germany, de la Rosa started the Hungarian GP from fourth and survived contact with Schumacher Sr to finish a career-best second. Räikkönen crashed on the second lap of the Turkish GP having sustained damage at the start, while de la Rosa was fifth.

The Finn snatched his third pole in four races when just 0.002sec quicker than Schumacher's Ferrari at Monza and finished second. De la Rosa's engine failed as speculation mounted that he would be replaced by GP2 points leader Lewis Hamilton or test driver Gary Paffett. The Spaniard was confirmed for the next two races and, having survived a spin in Shanghai, inherited fifth when two cars tangled on the final lap. Räikkönen stormed into second during his first stint only for a throttle issue to deny another possible victory.

Pedro de la Rosa, McLaren MP4-21-Mercedes-Benz (Brazilian GP)

Jenson Button, Honda RA106 (Hungarian GP)

Neither McLaren-Mercedes made Q3 in Japan, where Kimi salvaged fifth. Hamilton was quicker than de la Rosa during a Jerez test but was not drafted in for the Brazilian GP 'This is a hero-to-zero sport, so why risk it?' was Ron Dennis's reasoning. Räikkönen started his final race for McLaren-Mercedes from the front row but faded to fifth with de la Rosa eighth.

Having failed to win a GP for the first time since 1996, McLaren-Mercedes was a distant third in the constructors' standings.

LUCKY STRIKE HONDA RACING F1 TEAM

Jenson Button's on-off 2005 move to Williams-BMW led to contingency talks with Rubens Barrichello as a possible replacement and the Brazilian finally agreed a three-year deal in the summer. With Honda acquiring British American Tobacco's remaining shares in the Brackley-based team and the Williams-BMW partnership broken, Button negotiated his way out of his commitment to Williams to sign a new three-year deal (with options for another two) with the rebranded Honda F1 Team. That left Honda favourite Takuma Satō out in the cold and Anthony Davidson, who craved a race seat, reluctantly accepting the third-driver role once more. One positive for Davidson's profile was that he tested on the Friday at every GP because Honda was no longer one of F1's four top teams.

Honda was the first manufacturer to run its V8 engine, the RA806E, when Davidson and Enrique Bernoldi drove a BAR 006-based test chassis at Mugello on 27–28 April 2005. A two-year-old chassis was chosen due to the recurring front aerodynamic

issues that blighted the 007. The Honda RA106 was launched at Barcelona on 25 January with two cars immediately available for testing as the team aimed to rebound. Gestation for the latest offering from technical director Geoff Willis had included the resignation of chief designer Jörg Zander in October 2005 and William Toet's acrimonious departure two months later. Mariano Alperin, who had been with British American Racing since it acquired Tyrrell in 1998, was appointed chief aerodynamicist in May 2006. Gary Savage (deputy technical director), Kevin Taylor (chief designer) and Mark Ellis (chief engineer) all remained.

The RA106 followed the emerging trend for removing the keel under its nose with the front wishbones attached directly to the monocoque, clearing airflow to the floor and sculpted sidepods, which were less undercut than those of rivals and featured pronounced shoulders. Focus was placed on the front-end aerodynamics and eradicating the pitch sensitivity of the 2005 car, with a shallow twin-plane front wing introduced at the start of February. The rear wing was centrally mounted on two supporting pylons. A longer-wheelbase version was built during the summer. Engine project leader Takeo Kiuchi returned to the road-car division and Yosuke Sekino replaced him. The engine again drove through a carbon-cased seven-speed seamless-shift gearbox.

BAT's Lucky Strike cigarette brand remained as title sponsor for this final season of tobacco sponsorship. Integrating the Brackley-based race team with Honda's research facility in Tochigi was challenging, although there was progress and the renamed team finally achieved its maiden F1 victory.

Rubens Barrichello, Honda RA106 (Bahrain GP)

The Honda RA106 and new engine were reliable during the winter. Button was quickest at the final Barcelona test to illustrate its single-lap pace, although the long runs were less positive. That qualifying potential was confirmed at the start of the campaign but race problems – both performance and procedural – angered management in Tokyo and limited results for half a season. That said, Button led the opening three races and scored points on each occasion. Fourth in Bahrain despite a poor start, he qualified on the front row in Malaysia and finished third. He took pole and led the opening laps in Australia but could not generate sufficient tyre temperature to defend his position at the four safety-car restarts and faded to fifth by the time his engine failed on the last lap. Barrichello struggled to adapt during these three GPs, especially to the traction control, but did challenge his team-mate during the opening laps in Bahrain until a gearbox issue stymied progress. A ten-place grid drop for changing his engine followed by a stop-go for speeding in the pitlane ruined his Malaysian GP. The Brazilian's qualifying in Australia was foiled by an inopportune red flag and he spent 23 laps stuck behind Takuma Satō before finishing seventh.

Suspension and aerodynamics were modified for Imola to improve tyre warm-up but qualifying success – Button second and Barrichello third – did not translate to race results. The right-rear wheel jammed at Button's first stop, then he was signalled to leave while the refuelling hose was still attached at the second and lost more time while a mechanic removed the broken fuel nozzle, all of which left him seventh at the end. Barrichello's fuel rig failed at his first stop before braking issues restricted him to tenth. He outqualified Button for the first time at the Nürburgring (fourth) and finished fifth, with the Englishman retiring.

Button's set-up change during qualifying for the Spanish GP caused understeer so fifth-placed Barrichello was the leading Honda on the grid once more. They circulated in tandem during the first stint before Button, running a lap longer, took the advantage as they finished sixth and seventh. Barrichello qualified fifth in Monaco with enough fuel to complete a mammoth 45-lap first stint but lost a podium finish when he sped in the pitlane and dropped to fourth thanks to a drive-through penalty. Button missed Q3 and struggled with traffic and an unbalanced car throughout. At Silverstone,

Barrichello qualified sixth before fading and Button, who only started 19th due to a procedural error in qualifying, spun on his own oil after just eight laps.

That latest disappointment prompted Honda Japan to appoint Honda Racing Developments engineering director Shuhei Nakamoto, whose reputation had been forged in World Superbikes, as senior technical director. That effectively demoted Willis, who had already relinquished the trackside element of his all-consuming job to concentrate on finessing the team's £25m full-scale Brackley wind tunnel that had been finished three months ahead of schedule in May. A team spokesman confirmed 'discussions are taking place with Geoff Willis regarding his future role with the team' during the Canadian GP weekend and his departure was announced in August. Jacky Eeckelaert, who had arrived from Sauber in the winter to co-ordinate operations between the F1 team's Brackley base and R&D facilities in Tochigi, took on Willis's circuit-based duties when promoted to engineering director.

Both cars made the top-ten shoot-out in Montréal but neither Honda scored, with Button losing eighth to David Coulthard with three laps to go. In America, Button was eliminated on the first lap and Barrichello qualified fourth and finished sixth. A modified front wing with extra element introduced at Magny-Cours diverted air from the radiators and caused overheating, necessitating drag-inducing extra holes in the bodywork and loss of pace, with engine issues causing retirement. The engine was upgraded and electronics revised for the German GP, where rear-end stability was also improved. Both cars qualified in the top six and Button finished fourth to score his first points since Spain.

That upturn continued in Hungary, where Barrichello qualified third with Button fourth. The decision to start Barrichello on full wets proved a mistake and an early change to intermediates restricted him to fourth. Starting 14th due to an engine change on Saturday, Button revelled in changing conditions to score his breakthrough GP victory at the 113th attempt once Fernando Alonso had relinquished the lead.

Fourth in Turkey, Button crashed heavily at the Parabolica during testing at Monza with suspension failure blamed. A new Stage 4 engine that formed the basis for the 2007 unit had an improved

Anthony Davidson, Honda RA106 (Chinese GP)

torque curve when it was introduced at the Italian GP, although the team reverted to old units when Davidson suffered two failures on Friday. With top-ten grid positions now the norm, they split strategies to claim another double score, Button fifth after two-stopping and Barrichello sixth having pitted once.

The RA106s ran in 555 livery at Shanghai, where they locked out row two after setting identical times. Barrichello suffered excessive tyre wear during the damp early laps while Button again starred in changeable conditions, passing his team-mate and Nick Heidfeld's BMW Sauber on the last lap to grab fourth; Barrichello dropped to sixth after hitting Heidfeld on that chaotic final lap. The Stage 4 engine was used at Suzuka after the Monza failures had been traced to a manufacturing fault. Another opening-lap tangle with Heidfeld

forced Barrichello to change his nosecone and relegated him to an afternoon at the back. Button made a good start and passed both Toyotas to score another fourth. Only 14th on the grid for the Brazilian finale due to a traction-control issue, Button adopted an attacking strategy to claim third while local hero Barrichello was disappointed with seventh.

BMW SAUBER F1 TEAM

BMW's main board had rejected motorsport director Mario Theissen's suggestion that it should have its own team in 2003 but he made a renewed proposal in early 2005. Purchase of Sauber began with talks regarding an engine-supply deal but, on 22 June

Nick Heidfeld, BMW Sauber F1.06 (French GP)

Jacques Villeneuve, BMW Sauber F1.06 (Monaco GP)

2005, BMW announced it would buy Crédit Suisse's 63.25 percent shareholding in the Swiss team over the next three years. Board director Burkhard Göschel declared that 'this decision is a strong, long-term affirmation of BMW's commitment to Formula 1', with team and chassis officially renamed BMW Sauber. Peter Sauber retained his minority stake and Crédit Suisse received free space on the car during that transitional period. Walter Riedl, who had been with the BMW F1 programme since its inception in 1999, was named managing director of BMW Sauber. Petronas remained as major partner with Intel added to the corporate portfolio.

BMW Sauber immediately began a vigorous recruitment drive to raise headcount from 280 to more than 400 by the end of 2007. Expanding the aero department and making 24-hour use of Sauber's impressive wind tunnel were key priorities for Theissen and long-time technical director Willy Rampf. Honda refugee Willem Toet joined on 13 January as senior aerodynamicist with Seamus Mullarkey redeployed. Former British American Racing/ Williams chief designer Jörg Zander began work in that role on 1 July. Felipe Massa's erstwhile race engineer Mike Krack replaced Honda-bound Jacky Eeckelaert as head of vehicle engineering. Sauber engine chief Osamu Goto left in the winter to form powertrain consultancy Geo Technology.

Robert Kubica, BMW Sauber F1.06 (Italian GP)

Massa moved to Ferrari while speculation about talks with Mika Häkkinen was quashed. Former Sauber favourite Nick Heidfeld signed a three-year contract in September after impressing Theissen at Williams. The press statement that 'this fills the first cockpit in the new BMW team' placed Jacques Villeneuve's future in doubt, despite his firm contract for 2006. Talks with Flavio Briatore to put Heikki Kovalainen in the second seat were not fruitful and Villeneuve was finally confirmed on the World Championship entry in November. World Series by Renault champion Robert Kubica impressed as third driver.

Launched in central Valencia on 16 January, the BMW Sauber F1.06 was an evolution of the Sauber C24. Heinz Paschen's engine department in Munich began work on the new BMW V8 (P86) in November 2004. It was track-tested in mid-2005 and developed 720bhp at 18,900rpm by the start of the season. Paschen left BMW in July and was replaced as head of F1 powertrains by Mercedes-Benz recruit Markus Duesmann, although he was only free to start work on 1 January 2007. The front of the F1.06's monocoque and nose were lowered to remove the C24's single keel with lower wishbones now mounted directly to the chassis. The shorter V8 and slimmer Sauber-built gearbox allowed Rampf greater scope for reduced rear-end drag and increased aerodynamic efficiency. The radiators were smaller due to reduced cooling requirements with large chimneys emanating from the reworked sidepods. The rear wing was mounted via its endplates. Theissen was quick to dampen ambitions: 'This is a several years' programme, but we have the confidence, we have the resources and the patience and the dedication to get there.'

With expectations raised by Kubica's fastest FP1 time in Bahrain, Villeneuve narrowly missed Q3 while a mistake restricted Heidfeld to tenth on the grid. The German's race was ruined by a first-corner *contretemps* with Nico Rosberg while Villeneuve was running ninth when his engine blew up without warning. Roles were reversed in Malaysia where Villeneuve started tenth (following engine penalties for quicker cars) and Heidfeld's engine failed when on course to finish fifth, elevating Villeneuve to seventh. Both drivers made it into Q3 and scored points in Australia, with Heidfeld fourth despite tyre warm-up issues and

Villeneuve sixth after starting from the penultimate row following another engine change.

The F1.06 lacked grip at Imola and the Nürburgring. Heidfeld, suffering a stomach bug, crashed at the second Rivazza during qualifying for the San Marino GP, where both BMW Saubers languished outside the top ten. Docked his three fastest qualifying times at the Nürburgring for baulking Giancarlo Fisichella in Q2, Villeneuve finished eighth and Heidfeld repeated that result in Spain. The German was seventh at the next three races with the newly married Villeneuve eighth at Silverstone despite hitting Juan Pablo Montoya on lap one. An aero and engine upgrade transformed the F1.06s for the British GP, with both drivers qualifying and finishing in the top ten during their most competitive weekend to date.

Villeneuve crashed in Canada and Heidfeld was launched into a triple roll in the first-corner mêlée at Indianapolis. Villeneuve had qualified sixth at that latter race and was in that position when his engine let go. Sauber traditionally faded during the second half of the season due to lack of development, but new parts now came thick and fast with shifts in the wind tunnel operating six days a week. Central to the Silverstone improvement had been a new rear wing that BMW Sauber had to abandon by the French GP amid accusations that it was flexing to widen the slot gap and reduce straight-line drag. The F1.06s also had McLaren-like airbox-mounted 'horns' and two unsightly vertical nose fins at Magny-Cours. The FIA banned the 'twin-tower' fins before the next race, citing impaired 'forward and/or lateral vision of the driver', although aesthetics may have played a part. Traffic ruined Villeneuve's qualifying and thus compromised his French GP; Heidfeld finished eighth after waving Pedro de la Rosa through when wrongly shown a blue flag.

There was contact between the team-mates on the opening lap of the German GP, damaging both cars. Villeneuve eventually crashed heavily after an underwhelming afternoon and did not attend the post-race debrief. He told Theissen that he was still suffering from headaches on the following Tuesday and was promptly replaced by Kubica for the rest of the season, effectively ending his F1 career. The impressive Kubica outqualified Heidfeld

Sebastian Vettel, BMW Sauber F1.06 (Chinese GP)

at the Hungaroring and finished seventh only to be disqualified for having an underweight car, a shortfall blamed on excessive tyre wear. Heidfeld revelled in changing weather to finish third despite contact with a defensive Michael Schumacher. Having tested at Jerez on 5 July and received his super licence on the Wednesday before the Turkish GP, 19-year-old Sebastian Vettel replaced Kubica as third driver. His first lap brought a pitlane speeding fine but fastest times at Istanbul and Monza indicated his talent.

Heidfeld qualified in the top five at the next two races only for both to be compromised, by first-lap contact with Giancarlo Fisichella in Turkey and Michael Schumacher easing him onto grass at the first corner at Monza. Kubica qualified in the top eight at both races and claimed third place in Italy, a podium finisher at only the third attempt. Heidfeld had been a genuine threat for victory in Italy so eighth after serving a drive-through penalty for speeding in the pitlane was a severe disappointment. He entered the final lap in China in fourth place only to be blocked by backmarkers and spin while avoiding Takuma Satō's Super Aguri, which relegated the angry German to seventh. Kubica hit Robert Doornbos on the first lap before a premature change to dry tyres thwarted his fightback with the track still wet.

They were eighth and ninth in Japan, where Heidfeld refused to let the faster Kubica pass. In Brazil, both BMW Saubers progressed to Q3 for the seventh time, but they collided on lap four and Heidfeld sustained further damage when he hit Vitantonio Liuzzi. Two more 'offs' at Turn 1 were followed by an accident in the closing stages. With Kubica ninth, only Toyota's double DNF ensured that BMW Sauber held onto fifth in the standings.

PANASONIC TOYOTA RACING

Toyota was well prepared for the new engine rules and aimed to win races and challenge for the title. Luca Marmorini's 2.4-litre V8 (designated RVX-06) began bench-testing in March 2005 and test driver Olivier Panis was three seconds slower than with the old 3-litre unit when it made its track debut at Jerez in July. Toyota had had one of the best engines by the end of the V10 era but its V8 fell short during 2006.

It was a shock when the new Toyota TF106 emerged in the Barcelona pitlane on 29 November 2005 – the first day of winter testing – although in truth this was little more than the TF105B converted to V8 power, with unchanged bodywork. Toyota's switch to Bridgestone from Michelin, winners of all but one race in 2005, was part of a wider road-car deal rather than a racing decision. Panasonic extended its title partnership for another three years. A second wind tunnel at the Cologne factory was commissioned before the end of 2005.

Jarno Trulli and Ralf Schumacher remained under contract for a second season together while Ricardo Zonta and Olivier Panis were retained as reserve and test driver respectively. Chief designer Gustav Brunner left on 19 December 2005 following 'operational changes to its [Toyota's] chassis department', which prompted legal action. Tyre expert Pascal Vasselon was promoted to head of vehicle design and development.

The Toyota TF106 was officially launched to the press on 14 January, with the Toyota Yaris production line in Valenciennes the chosen venue. The TF105B's zero-keel front suspension arrangement was retained although remnants of the keel

Ralf Schumacher, Toyota TF106B (German GP)

Jarno Trulli, Toyota TF106B (Brazilian GP)

remained. In an extensively reworked rear end to improve tyre wear, Penske shock absorbers – mounted longitudinally on the conventional paddle-shift gearbox – replaced the previous rotary arrangement. The Bridgestone switch compromised suspension geometry after four years with Michelin rubber. The rear wing was mounted centrally, and power steering revised. The 2006 aero package was added at Vallelunga on 14–16 February but cold temperatures rendered tyre data inconclusive. 'We have a new front and rear wing,' technical director Mike Gascoyne told *Autosport*, 'more sculpted sidepods, a modified diffuser, restyled engine cover and floor.' The TF106 did not have the aggressively undercut sidepods of the Renault R26, and the shorter V8 engine was not moved as far forward as possible, negating the aero gains enjoyed by others. Team president John Howett was unequivocal about the aims for the coming season: 'We'll be looking for our first win among many.'

For all the fine words and ambitions, the Bahrain GP was a stark reality check when both drivers qualified and finished outside the top ten. In unexpectedly cool conditions, the TF106s did not generate enough tyre temperature so lacked grip and performance. The sweltering heat of Malaysia helped in that regard, and Schumacher came from the back of the grid (following an engine failure in qualifying) to finish eighth. The fastest Bridgestone qualifier when sixth in Australia, Schumacher

benefitted from four safety cars to claim a morale-boosting third, despite a drive-through penalty for pitlane speeding. Having suffered first-lap damage at both races, Trulli was ninth in Malaysia and eliminated in Australia.

That all was not well was evident when Gascoyne left three days after the Australian GP following a disagreement with senior management. 'Toyota Motorsport and Mike Gascoyne have developed different opinions about the future direction of the technical operations in the team's chassis and engineering areas,' read a statement, 'which have resulted in the need for change on both sides.' The technical department was reorganised under Vasselon's stewardship with the technical director and chief designer roles made redundant.

They started the next three races from inside the top ten although further points scores proved elusive. Schumacher's engine failed during the European GP, and he lost his front wing in a half-hearted attempt to pass Trulli on lap 16 of the Spanish GP. The definitive 2006 car – the TF106B that had been promised since the start of the season – was introduced at Monaco. This had a brand-new monocoque that eradicated the last trace of the keel, plus a longer gearbox and repositioned engine. Trulli qualified sixth despite a heavy fuel load and would have finished third but for a hydraulics glitch within sight of the flag that promoted Schumacher into eighth. An engine penalty at Silverstone consigned Trulli to an afternoon in the midfield traffic while Schumacher made a poor start and was hit by Scott Speed and Mark Webber on the opening lap.

Trulli ended a run of 13 non-scoring races by qualifying fourth and nursing his misfiring TF106B home sixth in Montréal. A suspension problem during qualifying for the United States GP forced him to start from the pitlane but he charged through the field to claim fourth. Schumacher retired from both races, his gripless car withdrawn in Canada after a drive-through penalty, numerous off-track adventures and four unscheduled pitstops.

There was a major upgrade at the French GP with revised aero, new suspension and a new-spec engine in Schumacher's car. Trulli headed a promising qualifying 4–5 and led during the pitstops only for a leaking brake calliper to deny a podium. Schumacher also lost that opportunity with a sticking wheel nut at his first stop, although he did salvage fourth. In Germany, Trulli came from the back following another grid penalty to finish seventh, with Schumacher ninth following a first-lap collision with David Coulthard and subsequent drive-through. Schumacher scored points at the next two races despite being hamstrung by Bridgestone's intermediate tyres in Hungary and by an engine penalty and change of nose broken in the first corner in Turkey.

Their low-downforce Monza set-up lacked outright pace although Trulli capitalised on a good start to finish seventh, with Schumacher beaten by the Toro Rossos. Both were eliminated in Q1 for the Chinese GP and retired. In contrast, they filled the second row in Japan where they scored points – Trulli sixth and Schumacher seventh – despite Trulli not letting his faster team-mate pass when ordered to do so on the radio. Critical team members believed that cost Schumacher the chance of finishing fourth. The Italian matched Toyota's best starting position with third at Interlagos, where both had rear-suspension failures in the opening ten laps. That denied Toyota the chance of stealing fifth from BMW Sauber in the World Championship.

RED BULL RACING

The extent of Red Bull Racing's ambition was laid bare when Adrian Newey signed a three-year deal as chief technical officer on 8 November 2005. F1's most respected designer started work in Milton Keynes at the end of February with his focus primarily on 2007. A concerted recruitment campaign included Jonathan Wheatley and Rob Marshall from Renault as team manager and chief designer respectively. Race engineer Humphrey Corbett and logistics manager Gianfranco Fantuzzi joined from Toyota. Mark Smith was promoted to technical director with Ben Agathangelou remaining as head of aerodynamics. Guenther Steiner moved to America to set up Red Bull's NASCAR operation and head of vehicle design Rob Taylor left for McLaren.

Talks were held with BMW and Honda to replace Cosworth before a two-year deal with Ferrari was announced on 23 April 2005. David Coulthard extended his contract by a year and

Christian Klien, Red Bull RB2-Ferrari (Canadian GP)

David Coulthard, Red Bull RB2-Ferrari (Australian GP)

Christian Klien was preferred to Vitantonio Liuzzi for Red Bull's senior team. Scott Speed was announced as third driver at the 2005 Italian GP but was transferred to Scuderia Toro Rosso following the acquisition of Minardi, with Robert Doornbos confirmed as Red Bull reserve before Christmas.

Coulthard completed the Red Bull RB2-Ferrari's shakedown at Silverstone on 15 December while the definitive aero package was being finalised in the recently recommissioned wind tunnel in Bedford. The RB2 featured Renault-inspired vee-shaped front keel for the suspension mounts, 'mass-damper' and undercut sidepods. There was a double-deck front wing and narrow 'Coke bottle' rear beneath the endplate-mounted wing. Red Bull continued with

Michelin tyres despite speculation to the contrary. Smith described the design philosophy to *Autosport*: 'Minimised aero volume, maximised aero performance, minimised mechanical packaging, minimised compliances, minimum centre of gravity height and optimised weight distribution.' A seamless-shift gearbox was introduced during the season.

A misunderstanding with Ferrari regarding heat-dissipation data was blamed for inadequate cooling. Large holes were cut in the sidepods as an emergency fix during testing and factory-based meetings of senior technical staff were held over the Christmas holidays to find a solution. Revised bargeboards and sidepods were introduced at the 14–17 February Valencia test

Robert Doornbos, Red Bull RB2-Ferrari (Chinese GP)

with the radiators angled into the airflow, giving increased drag. The RB2 did not complete any long runs pre-season and the error compromised the final specification. Lacking straight-line speed and aerodynamic efficiency, Red Bull stopped developing the RB2 after the French GP to concentrate on Newey's all-new 2007 car. Newey's summer was interrupted by high-speed accidents during historic events: he crashed his Ford GT40 at the second Mulsanne chicane during the Le Mans Classic and was hospitalised overnight when he lost control of his Jaguar Lightweight E-type on the Lavant Straight while practising for the Goodwood Revival.

Warned by Dietrich Mateschitz that he must beat Coulthard if he wanted to prolong his Red Bull career, Klien outperformed the Scottish veteran in Bahrain by starting and finishing eighth. He repeated those qualifying efforts in Malaysia where both cars retired with hydraulic failures. Coulthard was handed eighth in Australia when Speed was penalised for ignoring yellow flags; Klien crashed heavily following a sudden loss of downforce. A major off-track development at Imola was the double-deck Energy Station that provided hospitality for both Red Bull-owned teams. The RB2s retired at Imola and the Nürburgring – Coulthard having collided with Liuzzi's Toro Rosso-Cosworth at the start – and finished outside the top ten in Spain.

With one-off backing from the *Superman Returns* movie at Monaco, Coulthard started from an improved seventh and avoided trouble to finish third. He celebrated Red Bull's first podium in a Superman cape, which was all that sporting director Christian Horner wore for his dip in the Energy Station's swimming pool. A revised RB2 (described by Horner as 'a subtle upgrade') at the British GP featured new suspension, electronics and aero package, but Red Bull did not build on that Monaco result.

That Klien had beaten his team-mate at the opening two races was long forgotten. Pressure to retain his drive mounted with no-scores in North America. He lost eighth in Canada when he ran wide in the closing stages and was eliminated in the first-corner pile-up

at Indianapolis. Coulthard scored points on both occasions with eighth place from the back of the Canadian GP grid after an engine change and seventh in the United States. Coulthard and Klien qualified ninth and 12th respectively in France and finished in those positions. Coulthard was hit by Ralf Schumacher on lap one of the German GP after making it through to the top-ten shoot-out for the second successive race. Klien avoided the accidents to finish eighth and score his first point since the opening race. A fuel leak forced him to start the Hungarian GP from the pitlane in the spare car and he made little headway before spinning into the Turn 3 gravel. Coulthard was an excellent fifth in the changeable conditions despite separate incidents with Robert Kubica, Michael Schumacher and Rubens Barrichello.

A two-stop strategy proved to be a disadvantage in Turkey, where Klien ran as high as sixth before fading to 11th. He repeated that result at Monza, one place ahead of Coulthard as the draggy RB2 suffered on the long straights. With the Toro Rossos next to finish, Horner observed: 'Unfortunately, Christian headed a not particularly fast Red Bull train today.' Informed that he was not being retained by either F1 team, Klien was dropped with immediate effect when he turned down a Red Bull-sponsored Champ Car or DTM drive for 2007. Robert Doornbos, whose major claim to fame during 15 Friday practice appearances had been incidents with Fernando Alonso in Hungary and Turkey, replaced Klien for the last three races, with Michael Ammermüller testing on the Friday of the Chinese, Japanese and Brazilian GPs.

Starting from an excellent tenth in China, where both drivers crashed into rival cars, Doornbos finished each of his races, albeit without troubling the top ten. Both drivers were well off the pace at Suzuka and Interlagos, where the frustrated Coulthard was sidelined by gearbox failures.

After the optimism engendered by the switch to Ferrari power and euphoria surrounding Newey's signature, seventh overall was a disappointing return as Red Bull regressed.

Michael Ammermüller, Red Bull RB2-Ferrari (Japanese GP)

Mark Webber, Williams FW28-Cosworth (Chinese GP)

WILLIAMS F1 TEAM

The Williams FW28-Cosworth showed initial promise but poor reliability and inconsistent performance marred the team's season, with aerodynamic inefficiency and rear handling issues on corner entry to blame. That resulted in the nine-time constructors' champions slumping to an 'unacceptable' eighth in the standings after its worst season since 1978.

The team's BMW engine contract did not expire until 2009 but Munich's purchase of Sauber further soured an already strained relationship. Wanting a clean break, Williams held talks with Honda and Toyota before agreeing an exclusive one-year deal with Cosworth. The prototype of the 2.4-litre V8, developed by Alex Hitzinger and Simon Corbyn, ran on the dyno in October 2004 with development continued throughout 2005. The Cosworth CA2006 was the first new unit to rev beyond 20,000rpm and had a slight power advantage over its rivals at the start of the campaign. Williams chief executive officer Chris Chapple said: 'If we don't win the World Championship this year it won't be because of Cosworth', although better-funded manufacturers developed at a quicker rate. The sidepods sported triple winglets to improve downforce but they proved drag-heavy. The loss of BMW had financial as well as technical consequences, which was exasperated by Hewlett Packard's withdrawal. Williams switched from Michelin to Bridgestone tyres.

The Jenson Button saga continued, with the BAR-Honda driver contracted to Williams for 2006 unless he scored 75 percent of the championship leader's points by 21 August 2005. However, Button wanted to stay with Honda and, with another trip to the Contract Recognition Board looming, he agreed compensation to cut his ties with Williams on 16 September. Mark Webber was in the second year of his contract and test driver Nico Rosberg, who had recently won the inaugural GP2 Series, was named as Webber's team-mate on 3 November. McLaren tester Alexander Wurz joined Narain Karthikeyan on the testing strength and was the Friday third driver at every race. Team manager Dickie Stanford took a sabbatical and was replaced by Tim Newton. Ed Wood joined the design department from Prodrive in March 2006.

Teething issues with the new seven-speed seamless-shift gearbox hampered initial tests of the Williams FW27C-Cosworth *muletta*. However, Rosberg topped the Jerez timing screens on 20 January, and fears that Williams may have to start the year with a conventional gearbox proved unfounded. The FW28 was launched at the factory in Grove a week later with chief aerodynamicist Loïc Bigois seeking improved efficiency that the FW27 had lacked. The front wishbone mounts followed McLaren's zero-keel solution, below a lower nose. The twin-plane front wing spouted extra winglets in high-downforce trim. Sidepods were raised to shoulder height and fitted with vertical extensions to the fore. Heavy undercuts directed air to the 'Coke bottle' rear and endplate-

Nico Rosberg, Williams FW28-Cosworth (French GP)

supported wing. Williams was the first team to follow McLaren's lead and use inerters in the suspension to optimise tyre contact at all four corners. Transmission guru Jörg Zander had joined from BAR-Honda in October 2005 but resigned after just six months as chief designer, citing family reasons.

Initial signs in Bahrain were good as both cars scored points with Rosberg sensational. He lost 45 seconds in a first-corner *contretemps* with Nick Heidfeld before setting fastest lap as he stormed back to seventh, one place behind Webber. 'We were the fastest car out there today,' technical director Sam Michael told *Autosport*, 'and we would have been on for a much stronger result if we'd been less conservative. We won't do that again.' They qualified third (Rosberg) and fourth (Webber) in Malaysia but retired early as the mechanical

gremlins began. In Australia, Rosberg made a mistake on his Q2 qualifying run and was eliminated at the first corner. Webber started seventh with a heavy fuel load and was leading during the first pitstops when his gearbox failed.

Webber was sixth at Imola and Rosberg seventh at the Nürburgring, where both cars started at the back following a precautionary engine change and a ten-place grid penalty. 'We just weren't quick enough,' was Webber's assessment when they failed to score points in Spain. Wurz was quickest in second practice for the Monaco GP with the FW28 more competitive in high-downforce trim. Both race drivers made it to the top-ten qualifying shoot-out, with Webber an excellent second on the grid. A mistake on the second lap at Ste-Dévote dropped him to third but he challenged

Alexander Wurz, Williams FW28-Cosworth (Bahrain GP)

for victory only for leaking exhaust gases to ignite the electrics. Rosberg's stuck throttle completed a frustrating double DNF.

The FW28's inconsistency was highlighted at Silverstone, where its suspect aero efficiency was exposed. Eliminated in Q1 for that race and the next, Webber was a victim of the opening-lap collision between Scott Speed and Ralf Schumacher at Silverstone. Rosberg missed scoring a point by 0.709sec. Starting sixth in Canada, the confident rookie was barged into the wall by Juan Pablo Montoya's aggressive move after a lap. The Williams-Cosworths were slow at Indianapolis, where Rosberg's ill-handling car finished last, and Webber was launched skyward by Christian Klien at the first corner – the first of four successive retirements.

Searching for its early form, Williams took an upgrade at Magny-Cours to increase downforce without the associated drag that had hindered performance thus far. A grid penalty at the French GP consigned Rosberg to a frustrating afternoon in the midfield before his own run of four successive DNFs. Webber's water leak in Germany denied a fifth-place finish. He qualified in that position in Hungary only to crash on the opening lap. They avoided the first-corner mêlée in Turkey and completed the opening lap inside the top six, but lost the strategic advantage of being fuelled heavy when the safety car was deployed. Webber finished tenth, which was, according to Sam Michael, 'about where the car is currently at'.

Without a top-eight finish in ten races, the FW28s qualified at the back of the midfield in China when rain favoured its Michelin rivals.

Webber recovered from spinning after he had changed to dry tyres to finish eighth and score a single point. Rosberg made Q3 on his first visit to Suzuka and finished in tenth position; Webber crashed at the chicane. Williams had announced a new long-term contract with Toyota in the summer, so Brazil represented Cosworth's final GP for the rest of the decade, after 39 years as a fixture in the F1 paddock. The team planned to use 20,000rpm for the whole race distance for the first time but a sad finale saw Rosberg run into the back of Webber's car on the opening lap. With Webber out on the spot, Rosberg crashed heavily without completing the lap following a subsequent failure.

SCUDERIA TORO ROSSO COSWORTH

The Toro Rosso STR01-Cosworth V10 was the most contentious technical package of 2006. Red Bull doubled its F1 stake in September 2005 by paying a reported $35m for Minardi, which it rebranded Scuderia Toro Rosso (Italian for 'Team Red Bull'). Franz Tost joined as team principal once his BMW contract as track operations manager expired on 31 December 2005 and Red Bull owner Dietrich Mateschitz persuaded Gerhard Berger, whom he had sponsored as long ago as 1986, to acquire a 50 percent stake in February. Christijan Albers and Robert Doornbos left once negotiations with Red Bull were concluded, with the latter named reserve driver for the senior team. Red Bull juniors Vitantonio Liuzzi

Vitantonio Liuzzi, Toro Rosso STR01-Cosworth (Australian GP)

Scott Speed, Toro Rosso STR01-Cosworth (Malaysian GP)

Neel Jani, Toro Rosso STR01-Cosworth (United States GP)

and Scott Speed were placed in Toro Rosso race seats, with Speed the first American F1 race driver since Michael Andretti in 1993. A1GP star Neel Jani was Friday test driver at every race.

The controversy was two-fold when the STR01 broke cover in February. Its visual similarity to the 2005 Red Bull prompted accusations of it being an illegal copy. Tost told *Autocourse* that 'this year's car is a development of the RB1, last year's Red Bull car. It was changed a little bit on the aerodynamic side and on the mechanical side, but many components were carried over from the RB1.' The FIA ruled that Toro Rosso had not 'borrowed' Red Bull's intellectual property in contravention of the Concorde Agreement because it was Ford that owned the IP for the RB1 as it began life as the Jaguar R6. The second contention as aired by Midland's Colin Kolles was that the restricted V10 engine, which had been allowed as an affordable alternative for the low-budget Minardi concern, 'doesn't belong in Formula 1 anymore, it is not in the regulations. Red Bull is spending hundreds of millions… and bullshitting the whole world. If they are in front of us on the grid in Bahrain, then they will have a problem.'

Before the takeover, Minardi had agreed a two-year deal for 3-litre Cosworth TJ2005 V10 engines, restricted to 16,700rpm and 77mm air intake. With in-season development prohibited and hitting the rev limiter on longer straights, Kolles's fears of an unfair advantage proved unfounded, with Toro Rosso even allowed an additional

300rpm for qualifying from the Hungarian GP. The car used Red Bull's seven-speed gearbox. Toro Rosso switched to Michelin tyres and gradually changed elements of the brakes from AP to Hitco/Brembo during the season. Erstwhile Minardi technical director Gabriele Tredozi was released before the 2006 Italian GP and replaced a month later by Cosworth head of F1 development Alex Hitzinger. One Minardi stalwart who was promoted was new chief race engineer Laurent Mekies.

Midland and Super Aguri questioned the FIA about Toro Rosso's eligibility to score points when they were outqualified in Bahrain and Malaysia, although there was no formal protest. Those concerns were emphasised by Speed's performance in Australia when he beat David Coulthard's Red Bull into eighth. However, a 25sec penalty for overtaking under yellow flags dropped him to 11th in the final results and during the subsequent hearing he was fined $5,000 for 'using abusive language to another competitor'. Eleventh at the opening two races, Liuzzi split the Red Bulls in qualifying for the Australian GP and passed Michael Schumacher for eighth on lap 12 only to be denied points when he ran into Jacques Villeneuve.

Poor qualifying and locking brakes ruined the San Marino GP before Speed finished 11th at the Nürburgring, where Liuzzi and Coulthard crashed at the start. Liuzzi was tenth in Monaco but lacked straight-line speed in Spain and at Silverstone. They both escaped

Q1 at that latter race, where Speed made a great start only to invite suspension damage with an unwise move on Ralf Schumacher at Becketts. Speed finished tenth in Montréal while Liuzzi lost his front wing by clipping Mark Webber's Williams as he overtook.

Having shown glimpses thus far, Toro Rosso scored its first championship point at Indianapolis when Liuzzi came from the back of the grid to finish eighth. Speed outqualified the senior Red Bulls on home soil only to be eliminated in the Turn 1 pile-up. In France, Speed was tenth despite severe back pain due to a heavy practice shunt on Friday, and Liuzzi repeated that result in Germany by forcing his way past Coulthard at the hairpin.

Handed a 300rpm boost from the Hungarian GP, they failed to escape Q1 at that race or the next. With the V10's torque expected to give Toro Rosso an advantage on the twisty Hungaroring, Liuzzi's birthday celebrations turn sour when he was hit by Kimi Räikkönen as he slowed to let the McLaren lap him. Speed spun after prematurely switching to dry rubber before the track was ready. An opening-lap incident in Turkey delayed Speed and allowed Liuzzi to jump into seventh, but the Italian lost places to quicker cars before an electronics malfunction caused him to spin and stall.

Reliable but slow in a straight line at Monza, they qualified for the Chinese GP in 11th (Speed's best grid position of the year) and 13th thanks to Michelin's superior intermediate tyres. On a one-stop strategy, Liuzzi finished tenth despite another spin while Speed could not generate sufficient tyre temperature and tumbled down the order. Both spun during the Japanese GP, where Liuzzi had already collided with Mark Webber at the start and Speed withdrew with late power-steering failure. Toro Rosso's maiden F1 season ended in Brazil with both cars finishing outside the top ten,

as had become the norm, with 11th-placed Speed the leading Red Bull-backed finisher. Liuzzi's eighth place in America translated into ninth in the constructors' standings. There had been progress but Mateschitz was entitled to demand more in the future.

MF1 TOYOTA/SPYKER MF1 RACING

As soon as Alex Shnaider had rebranded Jordan Grand Prix as Midland Formula 1 (MF1), the steel magnate was looking to offload the team, having inherited 'financial disarray'. Shnaider originally planned to enter F1 in 2006 and had commissioned Dallara to build the chassis, with initial design work started in 2004. The purchase of Jordan led to technical director James Key having to co-ordinate the existing structure at Silverstone, including chief designer John McQuilliam and head of aero Simon Phillips, with Dallara's technical team at Varano, which augmented the wind-tunnel work. Sporting director Adrian Burgess described the resulting Midland M16-Toyota (continuing the Jordan numbering sequence but replacing 'EJ' with 'M') as 'very much a joint effort'.

A one-year extension was agreed with Toyota so the M16 was specifically designed around the new 2.4-litre RVX-06 V8 engine. Expected engine parity with the works Toyota team did not materialise. The M16 was built around a new monocoque and revised aerodynamics, with a double-deck front wing resembling the championship-winning Renault R25's version. Midland persisted with a twin keel to mount new front suspension, although this structure was shallower than before, while the sidepods were taller and wider than the norm, and two central pylons supported the rear aerofoil. Reduced fuel capacity, engine size and ancillaries

Tiago Monteiro, Midland M16-Toyota (Malaysian GP)

Christijan Albers, Midland M16-Toyota (San Marino GP)

Giorgio Mondini, Midland M16-Toyota (Spanish GP)

Adrian Sutil, Midland M16-Toyota (French GP)

Markus Winkelhock, Midland M16-Toyota (Australian GP)

aided rear-end packaging. The new (non-seamless-shift) seven-speed gearbox was longer, and the engine was moved forward.

The first F1 team to be entered under a Russian licence, Midland made its official debut at the 7–11 December Jerez test with an old Jordan EJ15B-Toyota repainted in the definitive red, silver and black livery. Already confirmed as race drivers by that time were Christijan Albers, who transferred his backing from Minardi on a one-year deal, and Tiago Monteiro in his second season. Nicky Pastorelli was originally announced as reserve driver but was not among the personnel when the M16 was unveiled at Silverstone on 3 February. Managing director Colin Kolles used that occasion to announce that Friday duties would be shared between Giorgio Mondini at nine races with Markus Winkelhock (the son of the late Manfred) and Adrian Sutil promised four apiece. Sutil eventually only appeared three times but impressed. Roman Rusinov tested away from race weekends and Fabrizio del Monte was added to that bloated line-up in April.

There was optimistic pre-season talk of challenging Williams and Red Bull in the midfield but only the Super Aguri-Hondas proved slower. Teething troubles hindered progress in Bahrain although Monteiro finished, and both drivers saw the chequered flag in Malaysia. Hydraulics accounted for Monteiro in Australia (only his second retirement in 22 GPs thus far) while Albers passed Takuma Satō to claim tenth. The disappointing form at those opening flyaways had consequences, for Adrian Burgess and chief mechanic Ricky Taylor left with immediate effect on 6 April.

A new aero package at Imola included a revised front wing and diffuser, but the disappointments continued. Albers was pitched into an opening-lap barrel roll by Yūji Ide's Super Aguri and Monteiro came home last. They finished the European GP at the back as well. In

Spain, Monteiro beat Satō in the race not to be last while Albers ran over his own broken front wing and caused terminal damage to the undertray. They pressed the self-destruct button at two of the next three races by colliding on the opening lap in Monte Carlo and at Montréal's Circuit Gilles Villeneuve.

Upgrades for the intervening British GP helped an M16 escape Q1 for the first time, in Monteiro's hands. He did that again in Hungary, then both drivers managed it at Indianapolis, and Albers in France. However, the closest they came to scoring a point during that period was in America, where Monteiro was ninth until 'Satō made an unrealistic move' at a safety-car restart and crashed into the unhappy Portuguese driver. Outside the top ten as normal in Germany, they were disqualified for running flexible lower rear-wing elements, which the team blamed on glue melting in the hot conditions. They survived the changeable conditions in Hungary to register Midland's best F1 finishes, Monteiro ninth and Albers tenth, albeit three laps off the pace.

Despite denials, negotiations to sell the team were now ongoing. Michiel Mol, owner of the Lost Boys internet and fashion brand that sponsored Albers, opened discussions with Shnaider at the Malaysian GP and talks lingered throughout the summer. Luxury car brand Spyker confirmed it had joined Mol's M-Consortium bid on the day after the Turkish GP, where a triple-plane front wing and new bargeboards had been introduced. Both Monteiro and Albers, who made it to Q2 once more only to have a third successive engine penalty, crashed out of the race.

The sale was finalised on the Saturday of the Italian GP for a reported £57m, with the cars renamed Spyker MF1 M16-Toyotas and the team rebranded Spyker MF1 Racing. Mol immediately

Ernesto Viso, Spyker MF1 M16-Toyota (Brazilian GP)

hired Mike Gascoyne as chief technology officer, the ex-Jordan man returning to the team he had left in 2001. With the cars running in Midland livery for the last time before adopting Dutch orange, Albers mixed it with the midfield independents until delayed by a puncture. Monteiro had brake issues all weekend and finally parked the unstable car.

Sporting relations director Johnny Herbert left when his contract expired before the Chinese GP. Spyker continued the policy of rotating Friday third drivers with Alexandre Prémat and Ernesto

'E.J.' Viso given their opportunity in China and Brazil respectively. Albers had his qualifying time deleted in China for missing the weighbridge and was penalised 25sec for blocking Nick Heidfeld on the last lap of the race. He outqualified both Red Bulls and a Toro Rosso in Japan, where his driveshaft failure littered the chicane with debris, including a rear wheel and wing. Monteiro spun and stalled having just changed to dry tyres in China and was lapped twice in Japan. An eventful but ultimately points-free season ended with another lowly double finish in Brazil.

Alexandre Prémat, Spyker MF1 M16-Toyota (Chinese GP)

SUPER AGURI F1

When Honda dropped Takuma Satō for 2006, former GP driver Ukyo Katayama said that 'the whole of Japan did not take this well'. Faced with a backlash in its homeland, Honda looked to place Satō in a satellite team and ex-F1 star Aguri Suzuki announced his entry for the 2006 World Championship at a Tokyo press conference on 1 November. With just 128 days before the start of the season, Super Aguri F1 acquired the old Arrows factory at Leafield, Oxfordshire and set about recruiting a workforce of 100 plus, including managing director Daniele Audetto (ex-Ferrari, Lamborghini and Ligier) and chief technical officer Mark Preston (ex-Arrows and McLaren). Honda transferred 14 engineers from its research operation in Tochigi. Preston was promoted to technical director and chief race engineer Graham Taylor named as sporting director after the European season.

Suzuki needed to acquire the intellectual property rights to a chassis design that had to be manufactured in-house to comply with the Concorde Agreement. Initial plans for the year-old BAR 007 were shelved so 2002-vintage Arrows A23 chassis were bought from Paul Stoddart, with parts augmented from around the globe. 'We found out there was an Arrows used as a show car in a Melbourne airport duty-free display area,' Satō later told *Motor Sport*. 'The team bought it and shipped it to the UK, and that was my race car!' These chassis were modified to take 2.4-litre Honda V8 power and updated to 2006 aerodynamic regulations. Honda's RA806E engine had to be raised to fit the old Arrows gearbox and this adversely affected the centre of gravity. Super Aguri raced under a Japanese licence with that national identity extended to its Bridgestone tyres; 2005-specification rubber was

used at the first four races because the latest compounds caused vibrations that upset the power steering.

The team's entry was initially refused when the $48m bond did not reach the FIA before the 15 November deadline. Now needing the unanimous approval from the existing teams, the resubmitted paperwork was approved on 26 January, once legal niceties with the FIA and rival teams had been concluded.

Terms on a long-term deal with Satō were finalised in February, with Honda test driver Anthony Davidson's chances of a full-time race seat receding due to the preference for an all-Japanese line-up. 'It is the intention to start the team with a very strong Japanese identity and having two Japanese drivers is an important part of that,' Audetto told *Autosport*. Kosuke Matsuura and Sakon Yamamoto were mentioned before Formula Nippon runner-up Yūji Ide was announced.

The Super Aguri SA05-Honda passed its crash test on 3 February, 11 days before its systems check at Gloucestershire's Kemble airfield. Three days of pre-season Barcelona testing on 21–23 February concluded with Satō and Ide slowest. The 2006 aero kit was first run at Silverstone on the eve of the cars being freighted to Bahrain for the opening race. Additional structures required to pass the crash test added weight and prevented ballast being used to redistribute weight. The cars usually qualified at the back, but Satō was an extremely fast starter, especially once the upgraded SA06 was introduced at the German GP.

Managing to have three cars ready for the Bahrain GP was an achievement in itself. They were predictably slow (Ide was 8.839sec off the pole time) but Satō described it as 'a fantastic result' when he finished 18th after being lapped four times. He

Takuma Satō, Super Aguri SA05-Honda (Monaco GP)

Takuma Satō, Super Aguri SA06-Honda (Brazilian GP)

Yūji Ide, Super Aguri SA05-Honda (Australian GP)

Franck Montagny, Super Aguri SA05-Honda (Spanish GP)

Franck Montagny, Super Aguri SA06-Honda (Italian GP)

was last again in Malaysia while mechanical failures sidelined Ide at both races. A new front wing was introduced in Australia, where they qualified and finished in the last two positions. Satō made a good start and kept Rubens Barrichello's works Honda at bay until he pitted on lap 23. Out of his depth so far, Ide was reprimanded for crashing into Christijan Albers at Imola's Villeneuve chicane on the opening lap of the San Marino GP, launching the Midland-Toyota into a barrel roll. Satō spent 44 laps at the back before spinning out of the race at Rivazza.

When Ide was dropped before the European GP 'following advice received from the FIA', one of the more underwhelming F1 careers ended. Hired on a race-by-race basis from the Nürburgring, former Renault reserve Franck Montagny ventured that 'the car was not as slow as I expected, so I was pleasantly surprised'. Satō gained 12 places at the start before both cars retired with hydraulic issues. Satō was 17th at two of the next three races and Montagny 16th in Monaco, with a Super Aguri invariably the last car circulating.

Delayed by a front-wing change in Canada, Satō was battling Tiago Monteiro for last place when he crashed on the final lap. He outqualified a Williams at Indianapolis but both drivers were eliminated in incidents with rival cars during the early laps. Lack of spare parts precluded a Friday test driver until Yamamoto took that role for the British, Canadian, United States and French GPs. Satō's gearbox failed on lap one in France while Montagny, the only local driver on the grid, finished 16th.

There was wholesale change before the German GP as Yamamoto replaced Montagny and Satō gave the '90 percent new' Super Aguri SA06-Honda its shakedown on Silverstone's Stowe circuit. This car was based around a lighter version of the SA05 monocoque with new carbon floor helping save 20kg. It was fitted with Honda's seven-speed seamless-shift aluminium-cased gearbox, which meant the engine could be lowered to improve the centre of gravity. The aerodynamics were totally reworked with taller, contoured sidepods that improved airflow to the rear end. The SA06's planned introduction at Magny-Cours was delayed due to a gearbox-installation issue. Half a second quicker than in the old car, Satō qualified among the Midlands and Toro

Sakon Yamamoto, Super Aguri SA05-Honda (British GP)

Rossos at Hockenheim and the Hungaroring. He led both Albers and Monteiro at that latter race until delayed by a clutch issue in the pits. A crash in the morning forced Yamamoto to use the old SA05 spare car to qualify in Germany. He started the German GP from the pitlane in his repaired SA06 but retired and spun at the first corner of the Hungarian GP.

A third SA06 was completed before the Turkish GP and Montagny used it for Friday testing duties for the rest of the campaign. His surprise seventh place in FP2 at Shanghai was Super Aguri's highest session ranking all season. Satō had new suspension for qualifying at Istanbul Park but lost 23 minutes in the pits after a first-corner altercation with Monteiro. His floor delaminated during the Italian GP, costing a couple of seconds a lap. Yamamoto spun out of the Turkish GP and lost hydraulics when running last at Monza.

Penalised for an engine change in China, Satō revelled in the damp conditions to finish 14th, only to be disqualified for blocking Nick Heidfeld on the last lap. With fervent home backing at Suzuka, Satō outqualified and finished ahead of Monteiro. Super Aguri's best showing of the year came at Interlagos where Satō finished tenth – ahead of a Red Bull-Ferrari and both Toro Rosso-Cosworths and Spyker-Toyotas – with Yamamoto completing his third race in succession. That prompted Preston to declare: 'For the first time this year we were racing, rather than just driving around.'

Sakon Yamamoto, Super Aguri SA06-Honda (Japanese GP)

2006 RESULTS

DRIVER PERFORMANCE

DRIVER	CAR-ENGINE	BRN	MAL	AUS	RSM	EU	E	MC	GB	CDN	USA	F	D	H	TR	I	PRC	J	BR
Christijan Albers	Midland M16-Toyota	18 R	15 12	17 11	20 R	16 13	18 R	16 12	18 15	19 R	14 R	15 15	21 DSQ	22 10	22 R	–	–	–	–
	Spyker MF1 M16-Toyota	–	–	–	–	–	–	–	–	–	–	–	–	–	–	18 17	22 15	16 R	17 14
Fernando Alonso	Renault R26	4 1	7 2 FL	3 1	5 2 FL	1 2	1 1	1 1	1 1 FL	1 1	5 5	3 2	7 5	15 R	3 2	10 R	1 2 FL	5 1 FL	4 2
Michael Ammermüller	Red Bull RB2-Ferrari	–	–	–	–	–	–	–	–	–	–	–	–	–	–	–	T	T	T
Rubens Barrichello	Honda RA106	6 15	20 10	16 7	3 10	4 5	5 7	5 4	6 10	9 R	4 6	13 R	6 R	3 4	13 8	8 6	3 6	8 12	5 7
Jenson Button	Honda RA106	3 4	2 3	1 10	2 7	6 R	8 6	13 11	19 R	8 9	7 R	17 R	4 4	14 1	6 4	5 5	4 4	7 4	14 3
David Coulthard	Red Bull RB2-Ferrari	13 10	19 R	11 8	14 R	12 R	21 14	7 3	11 12	22 8	17 7	9 9	10 11	12 5	16 15	14 12	12 9	17 R	18 R
Anthony Davidson	Honda RA106	T	T	T	T	T	T	T	T	T	T	T	T	T	T	T	T	T	T
Pedro de la Rosa	McLaren MP4-21-Mercedes-Benz	–	–	–	–	–	–	–	–	–	–	8 7	9 R	4 2	11 5	7 R	7 5	13 11	12 8
Robert Doornbos	Red Bull RB2-Ferrari	T	T	T	T	T	T	T	T	T	T	T	T	T	T	T	10 12	18 13	22 12
Giancarlo Fisichella	Renault R26	9 R	1 1	2 5	11 8	11 6	2 3	9 6	5 4	2 4	3 3	7 6	5 6	7 R	4 6	9 4	2 3	6 3	6 6
Nick Heidfeld	BMW Sauber F1.06	10 12	11 R	8 4	15 13	13 10	10 8	15 7	9 7	13 7	10 R	11 8	15 R	10 3	5 14	3 8	8 7	9 8	8 17
Yūji Ide	Super Aguri SA05-Honda	21 R	18 R	22 13	22 R	–	–	–	–	–	–	–	–	–	–	–	–	–	–
Neel Jani	Toro Rosso STR01-Cosworth	T	T	T	T	T	T	T	T	T	T	T	T	T	T	T	T	T	T
Christian Klien	Red Bull RB2-Ferrari	8 8	8 R	13 R	17 R	15 R	14 13	11 R	14 14	12 11	16 R	12 12	12 8	13 R	10 11	16 11	–	–	–
Robert Kubica	BMW Sauber F1.06	T	T	T	T	T	T	T	T	T	T	T	T	9 DSQ	8 12	6 3	9 13	12 9	9 9
Vitantonio Liuzzi	Toro Rosso STR01-Cosworth	15 11	13 11	12 R	16 14	14 R	15 15	12 10	13 13	15 13	20 8	22 13	16 10	17 R	18 R	17 14	13 10	15 14	15 13
Felipe Massa	Ferrari 248F1	2 9	21 5	15 R	4 4	3 3	4 4 FL	21 9	4 5	10 5	2 2	2 3	3 2	2 7 FL	1 1	4 9	20 R	1 2	1 1
Giorgio Mondini	Midland M16-Toyota	–	T	–	T	–	T	T	T	T	T	–	–	–	T	–	–	–	–
	Spyker MF1 M16-Toyota	–	–	–	–	–	–	–	–	–	–	–	–	–	–	T	–	–	–
Franck Montagny	Super Aguri SA05-Honda	–	–	–	–	21 R	20 R	20 16	20 18	21 R	19 R	20 16	–	–	–	–	–	–	–
	Super Aguri SA06-Honda	–	–	–	–	–	–	–	–	–	–	–	–	–	T	T	T	T	T
Tiago Monteiro	Midland M16-Toyota	19 17	16 13	20 R	19 16	18 12	17 16	17 15	16 16	18 14	15 R	18 R	18 DSQ	16 9	19 R	–	–	–	–
	Spyker MF1 M16-Toyota	–	–	–	–	–	–	–	–	–	–	–	–	–	–	20 R	18 R	21 16	21 15
Juan Pablo Montoya	McLaren MP4-21-Mercedes-Benz	5 5	5 4	5 R	7 3	8 R	12 R	4 2	8 6	7 R	11 R	–	–	–	–	–	–	–	–
Alexandre Prémat	Spyker MF1 M16-Toyota	–	–	–	–	–	–	–	–	–	–	–	–	–	–	T	–	–	–
Kimi Räikkönen	McLaren MP4-21-Mercedes-Benz	22 3	6 R	4 2 FL	8 5	5 4	9 5	3 R	2 3	3 3 FL	9 R	6 5	1 3	1 R	7 R	1 2 FL	5 R	11 5	2 5
Nico Rosberg	Williams FW28-Cosworth	12 7 FL	3 R	14 R	13 11	22 7	13 11	8 R	12 9	6 R	21 9	19 14	14 R	18 R	14 R	12 R	15 11	10 10	13 R
Takuma Satō	Super Aguri SA05-Honda	20 18	17 14	21 12	21 R	20 R	19 17	19 R	21 17	20 15	18 R	21 R	–	–	–	–	–	–	–
	Super Aguri SA06-Honda	–	–	–	–	–	–	–	–	–	–	–	17 R	19 13	21 R	21 16	21 DSQ	20 15	19 10
Michael Schumacher	Ferrari 248F1	1 2	14 6	10 R	1 1	2 1 FL	3 2	22 5 FL	3 2	3 2	1 1 FL	1 1 FL	2 1 FL	11 8	2 3 FL	2 1	6 1	2 R	10 4 FL
Ralf Schumacher	Toyota TF106	17 14	22 8	6 3	6 9	10 R	6 R	–	–	–	–	–	–	–	–	–	–	–	–
	Toyota TF106B	–	–	–	–	–	–	10 8	7 R	14 R	8 R	5 4	8 9	9 6	15 7	13 15	16 R	3 7	7 R
Scott Speed	Toro Rosso STR01-Cosworth	16 13	12 R	18 9	18 15	17 11	16 R	18 13	15 R	17 10	13 R	14 10	19 12	20 11	17 13	15 13	11 14	19 18	16 11
Adrian Sutil	Midland M16-Toyota	–	–	–	–	T	–	–	–	–	–	T	–	–	–	–	–	–	–
	Spyker MF1 M16-Toyota	–	–	–	–	–	–	–	–	–	–	–	–	–	–	–	–	T	–
Jarno Trulli	Toyota TF106	14 16	9 9	9 R	9 R	7 9	7 10	–	–	–	–	–	–	–	–	–	–	–	–
	Toyota TF106B	–	–	–	–	–	–	6 17	22 11	4 6	22 4	4 R	20 7	8 12	12 9	11 7	17 R	4 6	3 R
Sebastian Vettel	BMW Sauber F1.06	–	–	–	–	–	–	–	–	–	–	–	–	–	T	T	T	T	T
Jacques Villeneuve	BMW Sauber F1.06	11 R	10 7	19 6	12 12	9 8	22 12	14 14	10 8	11 R	6 R	16 11	13 R	–	–	–	–	–	–
Ernesto Viso	Spyker MF1 M16-Toyota	–	–	–	–	–	–	–	–	–	–	–	–	–	–	–	–	–	T
Mark Webber	Williams FW28-Cosworth	7 6	4 R	7 R	10 6	19 R	11 9	2 R	17 R	16 12	12 R	10 R	11 R	5 R	9 10	19 10	14 8	14 R	11 R
Markus Winkelhock	Midland M16-Toyota	T	–	T	–	–	–	–	–	–	–	–	T	T	–	–	–	–	–
Alexander Wurz	Williams FW28-Cosworth	T	T	T	T	T	T	T	T	T	T	T	T	T	T	T	T	T	T
Sakon Yamamoto	Super Aguri SA05-Honda	–	–	–	–	–	–	T	T	T	–	T	–	–	–	–	–	–	–
	Super Aguri SA06-Honda	–	–	–	–	–	–	–	–	–	–	–	22 R	21 R	20 R	22 R	19 16	22 17	20 16

2006

FORMULA 1 RACE WINNERS

ROUND	RACE (CIRCUIT)	DATE	WINNER
1	Gulf Air Bahrain Grand Prix (Sakhir)	Mar 12	Fernando Alonso (Renault R26)
2	Petronas Malaysian Grand Prix (Sepang)	Mar 19	Giancarlo Fisichella (Renault R26)
3	Foster's Australian Grand Prix (Albert Park)	Apr 2	Fernando Alonso (Renault R26)
4	Gran Premio Foster's di San Marino (Imola)	Apr 23	Michael Schumacher (Ferrari 248F1)
5	Grand Prix of Europe (Nürburgring)	May 7	Michael Schumacher (Ferrari 248F1)
6	Gran Premio Telefónica de España (Catalunya)	May 14	Fernando Alonso (Renault R26)
7	Grand Prix de Monaco (Monte Carlo)	May 28	Fernando Alonso (Renault R26)
8	Foster's British Grand Prix (Silverstone)	Jun 11	Fernando Alonso (Renault R26)
9	Grand Prix du Canada (Montréal)	Jun 25	Fernando Alonso (Renault R26)
10	United States Grand Prix (Indianapolis)	Jul 2	Michael Schumacher (Ferrari 248F1)
11	Grand Prix de France (Magny-Cours)	Jul 16	Michael Schumacher (Ferrari 248F1)
12	Grosser Mobil 1 Preis von Deutschland (Hockenheim)	Jul 30	Michael Schumacher (Ferrari 248F1)
13	Magyar Nagydíj (Hungaroring)	Aug 6	Jenson Button (Honda RA106)
14	Petrol Ofisi Turkish Grand Prix (Istanbul Park)	Aug 27	Felipe Massa (Ferrari 248F1)
15	Gran Premio Vodafone d'Italia (Monza)	Sep 10	Michael Schumacher (Ferrari 248F1)
16	Sinopec Chinese Grand Prix (Shanghai)	Oct 1	Michael Schumacher (Ferrari 248F1)
17	Fuji Television Japanese Grand Prix (Suzuka)	Oct 8	Fernando Alonso (Renault R26)
18	Grande Prêmio do Brasil (Interlagos)	Oct 22	Felipe Massa (Ferrari 248F1)

DRIVERS' CHAMPIONSHIP

	DRIVERS	POINTS
1	Fernando Alonso	134
2	Michael Schumacher	121
3	Felipe Massa	80
4	Giancarlo Fisichella	72
5	Kimi Räikkönen	65
6	Jenson Button	56
7	Rubens Barrichello	30
8	Juan Pablo Montoya	26
9	Nick Heidfeld	23
10	Ralf Schumacher	20
11	Pedro de la Rosa	19
12	Jarno Trulli	15
13	David Coulthard	14
14	Mark Webber	7
15	Jacques Villeneuve	7
16	Robert Kubica	6
17	Nico Rosberg	4
18	Christian Klien	2
19	Vitantonio Liuzzi	1
20	Scott Speed	0
21	Tiago Monteiro	0
22	Christijan Albers	0
23	Takuma Satō	0
24	Robert Doornbos	0
25	Yūji Ide	0
26	Sakon Yamamoto	0
27	Franck Montagny	0

CONSTRUCTORS' CHAMPIONSHIP

	CONSTRUCTORS	POINTS
1	Renault	206
2	Ferrari	201
3	McLaren-Mercedes-Benz	110
4	Honda	86
5	BMW Sauber	36
6	Toyota	35
7	Red Bull-Ferrari	16
8	Williams-Cosworth	11
9	Toro Rosso-Cosworth	1
10	Midland-Toyota	0
11	Super Aguri-Honda	0

Fernando Alonso and Kimi Räikkönen head the field before the British Grand Prix

ANOTHER FOR ALONSO AS SCHUMACHER BOWS OUT 217

Ferrari's Kimi Räikkönen, seen celebrating in Australia, beat McLaren-Mercedes duo Fernando Alonso and Lewis Hamilton by a single point

2007

FERRARI VERSUS McLAREN
ON AND OFF THE TRACK

Lewis Hamilton and Fernando Alonso face the press after qualifying in Hungary

The 2007 season was overshadowed by the 'Spygate' affair that engulfed Ferrari and McLaren. Disaffected Ferrari technical manager Nigel Stepney was accused of passing a confidential 780-page dossier on the Ferrari F2007 to McLaren chief designer and former colleague Mike Coughlan. With legal proceedings launched in Modena and London, Stepney was sacked, and Coughlan suspended on 3 July. Honda was briefly drawn into the saga three days later when it issued a statement to confirm speculation that chief executive officer Nick Fry had met both men in the spring 'with a view to investigating job opportunities'. The World Motor Sport Council initially ruled

Max Mosley and Ron Dennis held an awkward photo call at the Belgian GP

on 26 July that there was insufficient evidence that Ferrari data had been used within McLaren. However, McLaren was excluded from the 2007 constructors' championship and fined a record $100m when the WMSC reconvened on 13 September following new email evidence. Although professing its innocence, McLaren did not appeal the penalty as it sought closure from the unhappy affair that had divided paddock opinion.

In an unconnected case, Renault appeared before the WMSC on 6 December 2007 when an ex-McLaren engineer who had joined in 2006 was found to have technical information from his former employers. Renault was judged to have breached article 151c of the international sporting code but escaped punishment, mirroring the original 'Spygate' outcome in July.

On track, the 2007 drivers' championship ended in a three-way showdown between Ferrari's Kimi Räikkönen and warring McLaren-Mercedes drivers Fernando Alonso and rookie Lewis Hamilton. Hamilton appeared on course for the title with two races to go but Räikkönen overturned a 17-point deficit to snatch his only World Championship title.

At odds with the FIA since the 2005 United States GP fiasco, Michelin withdrew at the end of 2006, leaving Bridgestone as exclusive tyre partner and effectively bringing forward by 12 months the FIA's intention to have a single tyre supplier. Bridgestone brought two compounds of dry tyres to each event with both the prime and white-striped option having to be used during the race. That the Michelin teams had to adjust was expected, but it was not straightforward for previous

Robert Kubica suffered a violent 185mph accident during the Canadian Grand Prix

Bridgestone clients either for these control tyres generated oversteer that suited some drivers more than others.

McLaren questioned the flexibility of Ferrari's floor in Australia with stringent load tests introduced as a result. Engine revs were limited to 19,000rpm as part of a three-year engine freeze (to 2006 Japanese GP specification) following extensive negotiations with the manufacturers. Safety-car rules were revised with backmarkers now permitted to unlap themselves before a restart, with the pitlane closed while they did so. Only two cars could be used in practice so most teams did not field an additional third driver on Friday. The two-race engine rule introduced in 2005 only applied to Saturday and Sunday of each race weekend, with teams free to change on Friday.

A customer-car row rumbled on throughout 2007. Teams had had to build their own cars since 1981 and the contemporary Concorde Agreement stated: 'A constructor is a person… who owns the intellectual property rights to the rolling chassis it currently races, and does not incorporate in such chassis any part designed or manufactured by any other constructor.' Spyker claimed that the Toro Rosso and Super Aguri were copies of the Red Bull and Honda respectively. It was eventually agreed in December that both teams could continue to run customer cars until the end of 2009, after which they had to become fully fledged constructors.

Imola was dropped while Spa-Francorchamps, complete with revised chicane and redeveloped facilities, returned following a one-year absence. Bahrain and Interlagos extended contracts

until 2013 and 2015 respectively. The Nürburgring and Hockenheim agreed to alternate a single German race, with the former holding its final European GP in 2007. The Japanese GP switched to a very wet Fuji Speedway on a long-term contract. The Indianapolis Motor Speedway only signed a one-year extension for 2007 as it reconsidered its F1 future. Switzerland repealed the law that had banned circuit racing since the 1955 Le Mans disaster. Testing was restricted to 30,000km excluding young-driver tests.

The year saw the growth of computational fluid dynamics (CFD) to complement existing wind-tunnel testing.

Sebastian Vettel hit the back of Mark Webber in Japan

SCUDERIA FERRARI MARLBORO

Kimi Räikkönen was announced as Michael Schumacher's replacement at the 2006 Italian GP although the taciturn Finn's lucrative three-year deal had been agreed in secret for over a year. Schumacher's retirement allowed Felipe Massa to extend his race deal for another two years. Luca Badoer and Marc Gené remained as test drivers despite reduced permissible mileage.

The chassis and engine departments were reorganised when Ross Brawn took a year off and Paolo Martinelli transferred to Fiat. Brawn's job was split with head of human resources Mario Almondo named technical director and chief race engineer Luca Baldisseri assuming his trackside role. Both men reported to new group chief executive officer Jean Todt. Martinelli's deputy, Gilles Simon, was promoted while head of design and development Aldo Costa, consultant Rory Byrne, aero chief John Iley and sporting director Stefano Domenicali continued in unchanged roles. Technical manager Nigel Stepney took a factory-based role and felt overlooked in the reshuffle.

Philip Morris International extended its title partnership until 2011 despite the European Union ban on tobacco advertising and rival teams agreeing to seek non-tobacco sponsors. The Ferraris carried full Marlboro branding in Bahrain, Monaco and China with a barcode displayed elsewhere. Vodafone switched to McLaren-Mercedes as title partner.

There was surprise when the Ferrari F2007 was revealed at Maranello on 14 January because the wheelbase had been extended contrary to conventional wisdom at the time. The longest car in that year's field, it had weight shifted rearward, with the extra 85mm ahead of the driver to increase space for the bargeboards and aero to work. New chief designer Nikolas Tombazis adopted a zero keel for the first time, while the radiators were as flat as possible to increase the undercut to the sidepods, accelerating airflow to the rear 'Coke bottle' and wing. Cooling slats were preferred to chimneys and the split rear beam was retained to maximise the height of the central diffuser. The carbon-cased 'quick-shift' gearbox was Ferrari's answer to rival seamless units.

The bulletproof reliability that had characterised the Schumacher/Brawn era deserted Ferrari at vital moments, and the F2007's ride over bumps and kerbs was not optimal. Development was compromised for two weeks in the middle of the season when the wind tunnel broke down.

That said, the F2007 was increasingly competitive during the winter and that pace was confirmed in Australia when Räikkönen dominated with pole position, fastest lap and victory. Thoughts that the pre-season favourite may cruise to the title proved premature for he struggled with the control tyres until the summer. Massa started the Australian GP at the back following a gearbox issue in first qualifying, so he used a one-stop strategy to salvage sixth. The floor was stiffened for Malaysia to pass the more stringent FIA tests introduced following McLaren-Mercedes's observations. The extreme heat in Malaysia forced cooling holes to be cut into the bodywork, adding drag. However, Ferrari's single-lap pace remained, for Massa qualified on pole for the next three races. Outrun by the McLaren-Mercedes drivers in race trim, Massa faded to fifth in Malaysia due to a poor start and a couple of mistakes during the race. Criticised in the media, he responded by dominating the Bahrain and Spanish GPs. Räikkönen, eclipsed by his inexperienced team-mate, started each of those three races from third. Having also finished third in Malaysia and Bahrain, he was holding that position when his electrics failed on lap nine in Barcelona. Extensive revisions to the F2007 in Spain with longer sidepods, new front wing, bargeboards, rear suspension, and underbody were designed to improve cooling and reclaim downforce lost in the rigid floor.

The long wheelbase proved a hinderance in Monaco's tight confines with third-placed Massa finishing over a minute behind the McLaren-Mercedes duo. After clipping the barrier at the exit of the Swimming Pool in Q2, the heavy-fuelled Räikkönen was consigned to a long afternoon in traffic and an eighth-place finish. Outpaced by McLaren-Mercedes in North America, Räikkönen salvaged fifth from the Canadian GP despite damaging his front wing when he hit Massa at the start and after collecting debris from Robert Kubica's

Kimi Räikkönen, Ferrari F2007 (Brazilian GP)

Felipe Massa, Ferrari F2007 (European GP)

accident. Massa was disqualified for ignoring a red pit-exit light in Canada and finished third on the Indianapolis road course, where Räikkönen recovered from a slow start to claim fourth. The first hints of what was to come began to surface when a team spokesman said, amid rumours of sabotage to the oil systems at the Monaco GP, 'Ferrari has taken action against Nigel Stepney and there is now an investigation.'

Of more immediate concern, Räikkönen was only fourth in the drivers' standings with a 26-point deficit to Lewis Hamilton. Facing criticism in the press and with title hopes fading, the Finn had the F2007 and its control tyres to his liking when the circus arrived in France. With a new front wing that accentuated the central 'spoon' section, he scored back-to-back victories at Magny-Cours and Silverstone as the 'Spygate' affair engulfed F1's top two teams. Pole-winner Massa completed a Ferrari 1–2 in France, where he was unhappy when strategic calls favoured Räikkönen, and finished fifth in England after starting from the pitlane. Räikkönen took advantage of problems encountered by McLaren-Mercedes in qualifying for the European GP to annex pole position only for his hydraulics to fail in the race. Having started third, Massa appeared on course for victory until a late shower gave Alonso the advantage.

Räikkönen was narrowly beaten by Hamilton in Hungary, where Q2 errors by team and driver meant Massa had a frustrating race outside the top ten. They qualified first (Massa) and third (Räikkönen) in Turkey and ran 1–2 for every lap bar the pitstops. McLaren-Mercedes dominated in Italy as the F2007s struggled over Monza's kerbs. Massa retired from third while the one-stopping Räikkönen, who had crashed heavily at the Ascari chicane during Saturday practice, lost second position to Hamilton's audacious

overtaking manoeuvre with ten laps to go. McLaren's exclusion from the constructors' championship was announced before the following week's Belgian GP, thereby handing Ferrari that title. With his neck still sore from his Monza shunt, Räikkönen led a Ferrari front-row lock-out before controlling proceedings to win at Spa-Francorchamps for the third successive year, 4.695sec ahead of second-placed Massa. Ferrari blamed delayed receipt of a pre-race email for starting the Japanese GP on intermediate tyres rather than extreme wets as the FIA had mandated. The resulting early pitstop dropped their cars to the back of the field. Räikkönen and Massa recovered to third and sixth respectively, the Brazilian having also received a drive-through penalty for overtaking behind the safety car.

Seventeen points behind Hamilton with two races to go, Räikkönen scored Ferrari's 200th GP victory in China to prolong his slim title hopes. Third that day, Massa qualified on pole for his home race at Interlagos and led the opening two stints as Ferrari dominated. Needing victory and the McLaren-Mercedes drivers to stumble, Räikkönen passed the compliant Massa at the final pitstops to lead another 1–2 finish. With Hamilton's 36sec gearbox glitch and Alonso off the pace, Räikkönen clinched a shock drivers' title by a single point and even allowed himself a rare smile on the podium.

BMW SAUBER F1 TEAM

BMW Sauber's upwardly mobile trajectory continued in its sophomore season as a works entity with its F1.07 the third fastest car on the grid. The team scored points at every race and both drivers qualified for the top-ten shoot-out without fail.

Nick Heidfeld, BMW Sauber F1.07 (Chinese GP)

The consistent Swiss/German team was elevated to constructors' runner-up following the exclusion of McLaren-Mercedes.

BMW Sauber revealed its 2007 driver line-up at the final race of 2006. Impressive newcomer Robert Kubica was retained alongside the already contracted Nick Heidfeld, with Sebastian Vettel confirmed as reserve driver. Timo Glock joined the testing strength in November, dovetailing the role with his successful GP2 campaign. Vettel took part in FP1 in Australia and Malaysia before BMW Sauber decided to concentrate on its race drivers throughout the weekend.

Heidfeld gave the BMW Sauber F1.07 its shakedown at Valencia on 16 January. With chief designer Jörg Zander having joined Willy Rampf's technical department on 1 July 2006, the F1.07 was an evolution of the 2006 car that had shown glimpses of race-winning pace. The design process benefitted from the wind tunnel operating 24 hours a day from October and correlation from the recently commissioned 'Albert2' computational fluid dynamics supercomputer, at the time the largest industrial computer in Europe. The F1.07 had completely new front aerodynamics with a higher nose and sculpted wing. The aggressively undercut sidepods featured elaborate winglets and larger intakes while the cooling system was overhauled. There was a narrow rear end, with air channelled to the endplate-mounted rear wing and diffuser. The BMW V8 engine (P86/87 to reflect its lineage following the engine freeze) drove through a new titanium-cased seven-speed seamless-shift gearbox developed in Munich and internally termed QSG (quick-shift gearbox). The RCC (race car controller) engine

management system was also new. Weight was saved to increase the ballast available to optimise distribution and tyre performance.

The F1.07 showed promising pace during the winter although gearbox hydraulic issues restricted mileage and left the drivers guarded about their chances in Australia. Qualifying for the opening three long-haul races confirmed the F1.07 as the closest challenger to Ferrari and McLaren-Mercedes. Heidfeld's three successive fourth-place finishes included passing Fernando Alonso's McLaren-Mercedes around the outside of Bahrain's Turn 4. Kubica had all manner of issues at the first two races. His Australian GP ended when unable to shift from fifth gear and he was last in Malaysia after a catalogue of problems that began with hitting the back of Heidfeld's car in the first corner. 'It is better to forget this race quickly,' was Kubica's verdict. He was sixth in Bahrain despite losing downforce when the fuel flap stuck open.

A new front wing with accentuated central section was introduced at the Spanish GP, where Kubica started fifth and finished fourth. Already delayed when he was released from his first pitstop before the front-right wheel had been reattached, Heidfeld retired when his gearbox failed. Revised power steering arrived for the Monaco GP, which yielded fifth (Kubica) and sixth (Heidfeld). Kubica's frightening barrel roll after clipping Jarno Trulli's Toyota was the abiding image of the Canadian GP, the Pole emerging with just a sprained ankle. Second in Canada, Heidfeld had hydraulics failure after 55 laps of the United States GP. Kubica was ruled out of that race on medical grounds with Vettel his impressive replacement.

Robert Kubica, BMW Sauber F1.07 (Spanish GP)

Starting his debut from seventh, Vettel ran across the grass amid the Turn 1 chaos before recovering to eighth by the finish, making him the first teenager to score an F1 point.

Kubica was back on the pace when he returned in France and was fourth at that race and the next. Suffering from back cramp on Friday at Magny-Cours, Heidfeld finished fifth in France and sixth at Silverstone. There were departures in the summer for Zander and aerodynamicist John Owen, both destined for Honda.

Heidfeld was the quicker BMW Sauber driver at the Nürburgring, where he qualified fourth before flying home overnight to see his new-born son. A collision in the second corner of the race involved both drivers, denying them the chance of a podium or even better.

Kubica spun and was hit by Lewis Hamilton's McLaren-Mercedes while Heidfeld suffered a bent track rod, but both finished the race, Heidfeld passing Kubica for sixth place on the penultimate lap.

When Vettel joined Scuderia Toro Rosso from the Hungarian GP, Glock was promoted to reserve driver. Heidfeld started from the front row and withstood Fernando Alonso's pressure to finish third, following that with fourth in both Turkey and Italy. Kubica faded during the Turkish GP and was fifth in both Hungary and at Monza. A ten-place grid penalty ruined Kubica's Belgian GP while Heidfeld ran wide at La Source following a poor getaway before gaining two positions in the pitstops to claim fifth. Both cars misfired during the Japanese GP deluge with Kubica also handed a harsh drive-through

Sebastian Vettel, BMW Sauber F1.07 (United States GP)

penalty following an incident with Hamilton. The Pole recovered to take seventh after being passed by Felipe Massa on the last lap. Third behind the safety car, Heidfeld turned into Jenson Button's Honda at the original restart and sustained substantial damage that eventually led to his withdrawal with a couple of laps to go.

In China, hydraulic failures in practice and wrong tyre choice during the wet/dry race restricted Heidfeld to seventh. Planning one pitstop, Kubica made an early switch to dry tyres that brought him into contention for the team's breakthrough victory. He took the lead on lap 33 only for the hydraulics to fail moments later. A successful campaign concluded with another double score in Brazil. Running fourth in the closing stages, Heidfeld ran wide when Nico Rosberg made an aggressive move into Turn 1 that allowed Kubica, who had reduced his revs due to an overheating engine, to take fifth, 0.766sec ahead of his team-mate.

ING RENAULT F1 TEAM

Renault's close working relationship with Michelin had been a cornerstone of its recent success, so the enforced switch to single-make Bridgestone tyres hit the team harder than any other. With Fernando Alonso bound for McLaren-Mercedes, Renault exercised its option on Giancarlo Fisichella's services and Heikki Kovalainen was promoted from reserve to the second race seat. Ricardo Zonta and Nelson Piquet Jr signed as test drivers. Team principal Flavio Briatore extended his contract to the end of 2008. Pat Symonds became executive director of engineering, handing some of his trackside duties to chief race engineer Alan Permane. Japan Tobacco (Mild Seven) withdrew after 13 years with the Enstone-based team and Telefónica did not renew following Alonso's departure. Dutch bank ING agreed a three-year title-sponsorship deal in October 2006. Renault also supplied engines to Red Bull Racing, marking the first time since 1997 that it had serviced more than one team.

Amsterdam was chosen as venue for the launch of the Renault R27 on 24 January in deference to the new title partner. This was further evolution of a winning concept, albeit with ING's garish white, orange and blue colours added to the yellow of Renault. The bodywork was described as 'refined and clean' with aerodynamic mirrors moved from the monocoque to the leading outer edge of the trademark undercut sidepods. The mirrors needed additional supporting brackets at the first race to reduce vibration. The vee-keel was retained for the lower-front wishbones and channelled air towards an elegantly waisted 'Coke bottle' rear end. Weight was redistributed further forward to better suit the Bridgestone rubber, although rear wear was an issue. The new seamless-shift seven-speed gearbox was evaluated in a modified R26 when testing resumed on 28 November.

There were questions about the strength of the driver line-up and whether Fisichella had the consistency to fill the void left by Alonso. The R27 lacked balance, especially in high-speed corners, with inherent front instability eventually traced to a wind-tunnel correlation issue connected to the tyre modelling. Double champions for the previous two seasons, Renault achieved just one podium finish during 2007.

That Renault had slipped into the midfield was evident at the first three long-haul races. In Australia, Fisichella withstood Felipe Massa's pressure to finish fifth while Briatore reported that 'Kovalainen had a horrible race'. He told Italian television that the tenth-placed Finn 'did almost everything wrong' after a couple of grassy moments and a spin. New front-wing endplates were introduced in Malaysia although the lack of front-end downforce persisted. 'We are lacking grip,' Fisichella complained on Friday, 'and that makes the car nervous and inconsistent to drive', so both Renaults were eliminated in Q2 for the first time since the introduction of knock-out qualifying. Running fuel-heavy for a long first stint, they finished sixth (Fisichella) and eighth (Kovalainen) in Malaysia, then repeated the strategy in Bahrain to claim eighth and ninth respectively.

Kovalainen made it through to Q3 for the first time in Barcelona where fuel-rig problems forced both drivers to make an extra pitstop, costing seventh-placed Kovalainen a couple of positions; Fisichella's chances had already been ruined by a first-lap mistake. With Monaco's stop-start nature helping mask the high-speed handling deficiencies, Fisichella recovered from a practice crash at Ste-Dévote to qualify and finish fourth – his best result of the

Heikki Kovalainen, Renault R27 (Canadian GP)

Giancarlo Fisichella, Renault R27 (Monaco GP)

season – but Kovalainen did not threaten the top ten. Starting last in Canada after crashes on Friday (practice) and Saturday (first qualifying) and an engine change, Kovalainen used a low-downforce set-up to climb through the field to finish fourth as others faltered. 'Fisi' was disqualified for leaving the pitlane when the red light was showing. They both made Q3 at Indianapolis, where Kovalainen qualified sixth, led during the first pitstops and finished fifth; Fisichella's one-stop race was ruined when he spun on lap two.

Chassis technical director Bob Bell reorganised the aero department with Dino Toso, who had been fighting cancer since 2004, taking a conceptual view as director of aerodynamic technology. His ongoing day-to-day responsibilities were handled by deputy technical director James Allison until new head of aero Dirk de Beer arrived at the end of the season from BMW Sauber. There was also change at group level when Renault Sport president Alain Dassas moved to Nissan in the autumn and was succeeded by Bernard Rey.

Mid-season progress continued at Magny-Cours, where the R27s occupied the third row. Kovalainen lost a lap changing a right-rear puncture caused by first-lap contact with Jarno Trulli's Toyota at the Adelaide hairpin. Fisichella finished sixth despite understeer. At Silverstone, Kovalainen led a Renault 7–8 in qualifying and the race as excessive rear tyre wear persisted. A new 'bri-plane' (a cross between bi- and tri-plane) front wing introduced at the European GP had a squarer central section and additional slot gap in the main element. Kovalainen finished eighth at the Nürburgring and Hungaroring with Fisichella compromised on both occasions. He lost time when stacked in the pits as they changed to dry tyres at the former race and had a five-place grid penalty for impeding Sakon Yamamoto in Hungary.

Kovalainen continued to outperform his more experienced colleague by scoring points in Turkey, Italy and Belgium. Fisichella rammed Trulli at the first corner of the Turkish GP and, having been eliminated in Q2 at Monza, understeered from lap two at Monza because of rear-wing damage from an altercation with David Coulthard. He started the Belgian GP from the pitlane only to crash on the opening lap due to his cold brakes.

Having chosen a dry set-up for Japanese GP qualifying, they did not make it into Q3 when rain fell. That allowed the team to fill its cars with fuel and record its best result of the year. They ran longer than anyone else once the safety car was finally withdrawn after 19 very wet laps and were briefly 1–2 before making their own pitstops. Kovalainen benefitted from the Mark Webber/Sebastian Vettel *contretemps* to claim a fine second place with Fisichella fifth. That was in stark contrast to the following week's Chinese GP that saw Renault have its worst qualifying of 2007 and finish outside the points. An underwhelming title defence concluded with both cars crashing out of the Brazilian GP, Fisichella having driven into the path of Sakon Yamamoto's Spyker as he rejoined the track after running wide in Turn 1.

Reliability and the exclusion of McLaren-Mercedes helped Renault into a distant third place in the constructors' standings.

AT&T WILLIAMS

Williams announced a three-year customer-engine deal with Toyota on 27 July 2006, preferring the commercial opportunities of a manufacturer alliance to its existing Cosworth partnership. Nico Rosberg had completed the first year of a long-term deal and reserve driver Alexander Wurz was promoted when Mark Webber signed for Red Bull in August. Toyota protégé Kazuki Nakajima,

Nico Rosberg, Williams FW29-Toyota (Belgian GP)

whose father Satoru had raced for Lotus and Tyrrell from 1987 to 1991, joined Narain Karthikeyan as test drivers. Nakajima tested on four GP Fridays when his GP2 programme allowed.

Chief executive officer Chris Chapple left Williams by mutual consent on 10 November 2006 and was replaced by Rio Tinto executive Adam Parr. The design department was restructured as soon as the FW28's shortcomings became apparent with Ed Wood taking the vacant chief designer role. Senior systems engineer John Russell returned after three years in the Australian V8 Supercar Championship with a brief to seek better reliability. Renault's Jon Tomlinson started work as head of aerodynamics in March 2007 and soon prompted Loïc Bigois's move to Honda. Technical director Sam Michael focused on car performance with chief operations engineer Rod Nelson hired from Renault to assume his on-track duties.

Former chief mechanic Dickie Stanford ran the test team while Frank Dernie's special projects engineer contract ended.

An extensive winter test programme with the interim Williams FW28B-Toyota began at Silverstone on 19 September with Karthikeyan behind the wheel. The new FW29 was unveiled at Grove on 2 February with body shape and undercut sidepods simplified to reduce drag. Those sidepods each featured a combined T-wing and exhaust chimney assembly. The nose was lowered with tri-plane front wing and zero-keel redesigned. Split upper elements were attached on either side of the nose at most races, with a McLaren-style full-width 'bridge' used at the Italian and Belgian GPs. The rear wing was now centrally supported with a split beam that increased space for the central diffuser. The Toyota RVX-07 engine drove through the latest seamless-shift

Kazuki Nakajima, Williams FW29-Toyota (Brazilian GP)

Alexander Wurz, Williams FW29-Toyota (Canadian GP)

aluminium gearbox that had been track-tested since the autumn. Communications giant AT&T was the new title partner although Chinese computer company Lenovo and Royal Bank of Scotland had larger branding.

Improved speed and reliability were displayed during a promising winter programme, with the initial 2007 aero package tried at Barcelona after most rivals had decamped to Bahrain for the final test. Disappointed to qualify outside the top ten in Australia, Rosberg sealed a strong seventh by passing Ralf Schumacher's Toyota, while Wurz was the victim of a collision with David Coulthard's Red Bull. In Malaysia, Rosberg qualified an excellent sixth and was on course to finish in that position when his hydraulics failed. Wurz recovered from 20th on the grid to ninth place following Q1 gear-selection issues. They finished the Bahrain GP where they had started, Rosberg 10th and Wurz 11th.

Pre-Spanish GP testing was curtailed when Rosberg and Nakajima crashed; come the race, Rosberg finished sixth while Wurz went out on the opening lap after hitting Schumacher's Toyota. Rosberg qualified in the top seven in Monaco and Canada only to be delayed, the respective causes being traffic and a stop-go penalty (for refuelling when the pitlane was closed). Using a one-stop strategy at those races, Wurz finished seventh in Monaco and came from the penultimate row of the grid in Canada to finish third, marking Williams's first podium since 2005. Rosberg lost sixth in the United States when leaking oil caught fire with four laps to go.

A new front wing was taken to Magny-Cours, where Rosberg started and finished ninth. Wurz was eliminated in Q1 for the third successive race amid rumours that he would be replaced by Nelson Piquet Jr. Wurz outqualified Rosberg for the first time at Silverstone

but that coincided with Williams-Toyota's least competitive weekend of 2007. Rosberg crashed out of the European GP during the early downpour, but Wurz survived the chaos to finish fourth, just 0.263sec behind third-placed Webber. Rosberg qualified for Q3 at the next four races and started the Hungarian GP from fourth position. He scored successive seventh places at that race and the next (Turkey) and was sixth in the Italian and Belgian GPs. Wurz was classified outside the top ten at the first three of those races and retired at Spa-Francorchamps.

Another fine Saturday performance from Rosberg in Japan was to no avail when he needed a new engine for the race. Both cars retired, with Wurz eliminated by Takuma Satō's Super Aguri-Honda on the safety-car restart. Having announced that this would be his last GP appearance, Wurz finished 12th in China, where both drivers complained of poor balance. Replacing Wurz, Nakajima made his F1 debut in Brazil, Sam Michael stating: 'Kazuki's qualifying was poor, but his racing was outstanding. He overtook people who had been racing a lot longer.' Unfortunately, he knocked over three mechanics at his first pitstop, thankfully without injury. Rosberg completed an excellent maiden season by finishing fourth in Brazil to consolidate Williams-Toyota's fourth in the constructors' standings.

RED BULL RACING

There was much anticipation surrounding the first Red Bull to be designed by chief technical officer Adrian Newey. Development of the 2006 Red Bull RB2-Ferrari stopped after that year's French GP to concentrate time and resources on the new creation. Newey was adamant that works-specification Renault V8s were preferable to the older units supplied by Ferrari, so an alternative deal was negotiated. As there was another year left on the Ferrari contract, this supply was eventually transferred to Scuderia Toro Rosso. Ferrari had argued that its agreement was with Red Bull Racing, rather than with the Red Bull corporation, but Jean Todt eventually relented.

McLaren colleagues Peter Prodromou and Giles Wood followed Newey to Milton Keynes in the winter of 2006/07. Prodromou joined when his McLaren contract expired on 1 November 2006 and became head of aerodynamics after Ben Agathangelou's departure in May 2007. Described as 'one of the cleverest people I know' by Newey in his autobiography *How To Build A Car*, Wood was responsible for installation of a driver-in-the-loop simulator in Milton Keynes. David Coulthard signed another contract extension and Mark Webber returned to the team he had raced for when it was Jaguar Racing. Michael Ammermüller was reserve driver, a role that Sébastien Buemi fulfilled at the Hungarian GP.

The 'uncompromising' Red Bull RB3-Renault completed its private shakedown on 24 January, two days before a low-key launch at the Circuit de Barcelona-Catalunya. Newey had ignored the RB2 as its basis and continued his evolutionary design philosophy that had served McLaren so well, albeit having to start the process from memory and with a clean sheet of paper due to his switch. Integral to the RB3 were the zero-keel front-suspension layout Newey had introduced in 2005 and a shape that resembled the McLaren MP4-21 with tightly packaged 'Coke bottle' rear and tri-plane front wing. The nose was lower and wider than on the RB2, with aggressively undercut sidepods that had relatively small inlets. The mirrors were originally attached to the outside of the sidepods but moved to the cockpit after one race. The sculpted rear wing featured louvred endplates and two central supports. Late confirmation of Renault

RS27 V8 engines meant that a conventional paddle-shift gearbox was retained for the start of the season. The new version of the seamless-shift gearbox proved fragile when it was finally ready to race in Spain.

Hydraulic failures during successive tests at Barcelona, Valencia and Jerez prompted sporting director Christian Horner to admit 'we're about four weeks behind where we'd ideally like to be'. The RB3 lacked downforce in its original guise with Newey concerned that there were correlation issues with the Bedford wind tunnel, which was temporarily closed while these were resolved.

Webber's seventh on the Australian GP grid showed potential but a fuel-flap problem delayed his pitstop and caused extra drag. Coulthard was eliminated in first qualifying and then crashed over Alexander Wurz's Williams after 48 laps of the race. Coulthard retired from the next two races while Webber failed to translate top-ten starts into points. Starting the Bahrain GP from 21st following a gearbox issue in qualifying, Coulthard stormed through the field until a driveshaft failed. Webber had a recurrence of the fuel-flap issue before his own gearbox problems meant that promising race pace went unrewarded.

Webber had a reliability-ravaged weekend in Spain and, having qualified ninth, Coulthard finished fifth despite losing third gear in the new seamless-shift gearbox during the closing stages. Hopes were high for Monaco where both drivers progressed to Q3 only for Coulthard to be demoted for blocking Heikki Kovalainen. Sunday was a disappointment, however, for Webber retired and Coulthard struggled with understeer following opening-lap contact with Vitantonio Liuzzi. The rear wings had flexed during the Spanish GP so had to be strengthened to comply with the revised load tests introduced in Canada. Coulthard did not finish either North

David Coulthard, Red Bull RB3-Renault (Brazilian GP)

Mark Webber, Red Bull RB3-Renault (Malaysian GP)

American race thanks to gearbox failure (Montréal) and a first-corner accident (Indianapolis). Webber qualified and finished both races in the top ten, including seventh place in Indiana.

Off the pace in France and England (where the cars had a one-off livery featuring the faces of 30,000 contributors to the Wings for Life charity), Red Bull bounced back at the chaotic European GP at the Nürburgring. Webber produced another stellar qualifying performance (sixth) and was quick all day to finish third. Fifth-placed Coulthard completed a double score from the back of the grid, the Scot even leading a lap when others pitted for dry tyres. There was also a new technical director at this juncture as Geoff Willis, a colleague of Newey's at both Leyton House and Williams, replaced Mark Smith, who moved to Spyker in August rather than accept another role.

The Hungarian and Turkish GPs were spent at the tail end of the top ten with a McLaren-style 'bridge' front wing fitted at that latter event. In Italy, Coulthard spun in Q1 when his gearbox lost oil, then crashed in Curva Grande on lap two of the race due to front-wing damage. Ninth after a race-long battle with Jenson Button's Honda at Monza, Webber converted another Q3 appearance into seventh place at Spa-Francorchamps.

Torrential rain at Fuji offered the midfield pack an opportunity. Suffering from food poisoning, Webber started seventh with a heavy fuel load and was second when the safety car was deployed on lap 42. Hopes of a podium finish were dashed when Sebastian Vettel's Toro Rosso hit him before the restart, gifting Coulthard a fourth-place finish. Red Bull-Renault's improvement continued at the final two races where it had two cars in Q3 for the first time. Coulthard started the Chinese GP from fifth only for both drivers to switch to dry tyres just as rain returned, leaving the Scot eighth at the end. Despite contact with Kazuki Nakajima's Williams, Coulthard finished ninth in Brazil, while Webber started from a season-best fifth only to be halted by a transmission failure after 14 laps. There had been glimpses of promise, but poor reliability – especially with the tightly packaged transmission – limited Red Bull-Renault to fifth overall.

PANASONIC TOYOTA RACING

Year six of Toyota's expensive F1 programme brought more of the same, with the Cologne-based under-achievers no closer to scoring that elusive victory. The team's management-by-committee culture resulted in another underwhelming campaign in the midfield and sixth in the constructors' standings.

Ralf Schumacher was in the final year of his original deal and Jarno Trulli committed until the end of the decade by signing a three-year extension. Test drivers Ricardo Zonta and Olivier Panis left with Super Aguri's Franck Montagny hired and F3 driver Kamui Kobayashi among those to test during the winter. John Howett remained as president of Toyota Motorsport while team principal Tsutomu Tomita left to run the Toyota-owned Fuji Speedway in June and was replaced by Tadashi Yamashina.

Mark Gillan (ex-McLaren and Jaguar) returned from academia to begin work as head of aerodynamics on 1 January 2007. Pascal Vasselon co-ordinated development of the Toyota TF107 with ex-Williams engineers Mark Tatham and Jason Somerville leading design and aerodynamics respectively. The TF107 was the first new car to be launched at an exhibition hall in Cologne on 12 January, three days after its shakedown at Paul Ricard. Former technical director Mike Gascoyne began this evolution of his TF106B before his departure. Its curved nose was raised with the sharply angled lower wishbones mounted directly to the chassis as before. Their proximity to the upper front wishbones reduced set-up options with a sensitive front end and fallibility over kerbs. The trend for aggressively undercut sidepods was investigated and ignored. Engine and elongated gearbox were brought forward to improve weight distribution and rear aerodynamics. The TF107 had a conventional paddle-shift gearbox at launch before the seamless unit developed with Williams was ready. The car lacked aero efficiency and was overly pitch-sensitive, while weak launch control frequently led to poor starts. An internal process review to improve reliability was only partially successful.

Expectations were tempered during the winter with both drivers vocal in their frustration. 'We have this problem with the car,' Trulli told reporters. 'General handling, grip and consistency. On top of that, reliability has been an issue for the past two weeks.' That initial gloom was alleviated by Q3 appearances in Australia and Malaysia, Trulli and Schumacher starting eighth and ninth on both occasions. Trulli made a slow getaway in Australia and trailed his eighth-placed team-mate home after a troubled race. The Italian finished seventh in Malaysia and Bahrain, with Schumacher outside the top ten.

An aero upgrade (wings, floor and rear bodywork) for Barcelona helped Trulli maintain his single-lap pace with sixth on the grid, but low fuel pressure forced him to take the restart from the pitlane and eventually curtailed his race. With his F1 future in doubt, Schumacher blamed traffic for the first of three successive Q1 eliminations and opening-lap damage contributed to his eventual exit from the Spanish GP. Neither driver made third qualifying in Monaco, where they started poorly and only beat the Super Aguris and a Spyker after anonymous races. Having both suffered front-suspension failures on the Canadian kerbs during practice, Trulli was involved in Robert Kubica's race accident before later crashing on his own in Turn 1. Eighth in Montréal, Schumacher slid into David Coulthard at the first corner of the United States GP while Trulli beat the other Red Bull of Mark Webber into sixth after a race-long duel.

Starting the French GP from eighth, Trulli collided with Heikki Kovalainen at the hairpin on lap one and Schumacher was tenth after an afternoon spent in traffic. With his contract due for renewal, Schumacher's form then seemed to improve, for he joined Trulli in Q3 at the next three races. The quicker Toyota man for once at Silverstone, he started sixth although neither driver finished due to differing handling issues. Trulli had a new chassis for the next race at the Nürburgring where strategy errors as the weather changed resulted in last place. Schumacher fared better until he ran into Nick Heidfeld's BMW Sauber. Hungary was the German's strongest performance of his last F1 season, starting fifth and finishing sixth to equal Toyota's best result of 2007.

With new floor and front wing for Turkey, Schumacher reverted to Q1 elimination and Trulli was spun around at the first corner by Giancarlo Fisichella. Both finished outside the top ten and that pattern continued in Monza's low-downforce trim. Trulli's two-stop strategy at Spa-Francorchamps was ruined by one-stopping rivals (including Schumacher) when he ran wide at the start.

There was no happy homecoming at the wet Fuji Speedway, where they failed to qualify for the top-ten shoot-out, Schumacher having damaged his car in a Q1 altercation with Sakon Yamamoto. In the race, Trulli did not figure after spinning behind the safety car

Ralf Schumacher, Toyota TF107 (Italian GP)

Jarno Trulli, Toyota TF107 (Turkish GP)

and Schumacher, already delayed by drowned electronics, parked his car with a late puncture. A new floor and diffuser introduced at Fuji were discarded for the Chinese GP, where Schumacher qualified sixth but spun three times in the race, stalling the engine on his final pirouette. A gripless Trulli did not make his customary Q3 appearance and was equally out of sorts during the race. In Brazil, Trulli started and finished eighth following a three-stop strategy while Schumacher made a low-key exit from F1.

SCUDERIA TORO ROSSO

The customer-car row continued to simmer with rivals keen to assess similarities between the latest Toro Rosso and Adrian Newey's Red Bull RB3. Presentation of the Toro Rosso STR02 was delayed until 13 February, with design attributed to Red Bull Technology (RBT), Newey's employer and a sister company to the senior team. Six Toro Rosso engineers spent the winter at RBT's premises in Milton Keynes modifying installation, ancillaries and cooling to accommodate a new engine. Red Bull had been dissatisfied with Ferrari during 2006 so sought alternative arrangements and passed the second year of the contract to its junior team, a change that was only accepted by the *Scuderia* in December. The Ferrari F1-056H engine drove through a conventional gearbox before Red Bull's seamless-shift unit became available to Toro Rosso at Magny-Cours. Fabrication of the STR02 was farmed out to third-party companies 'in Germany and Austria' and there was some in-house development such as a 'bridge' front wing at the Italian GP.

Confirmed as Toro Rosso's first race driver, Vitantonio Liuzzi gave the STR02 its shakedown as dusk approached on 13 February. The fate of Scott Speed remained uncertain due to 'contractual

issues' and better-funded Narain Karthikeyan and Tiago Monteiro were possible alternatives. Speed tested the STR02 at Bahrain's Sakhir circuit on 24 February and his status as second driver was announced later that day.

The prolonged negotiations with Ferrari about the engine switch and teething troubles at Red Bull Racing had inevitable consequences for Toro Rosso. Limited track time during the winter meant the opening flyaway races were tantamount to extended test sessions with the unsorted STR02s a handful in Australia. A technical reshuffle followed before the next race in Malaysia when Toro Rosso technical director Alex Hitzinger, who had only arrived from Cosworth on 1 November, transferred to RBT as head of advanced technologies, with Giorgio Ascanelli replacing him. Both Toro Rossos finished the Malaysian GP despite an early collision but they retired in Bahrain, Speed due to an opening-lap skirmish and Liuzzi with hydraulics failure.

An aero upgrade at the Spanish GP included revised sidepods and rear wing aimed at improving aero efficiency. Both cars had transmission issues during qualifying and retired, Speed following a high-speed left-rear puncture. Liuzzi qualified a respectable 12th in Monaco and Canada but crashed out of both races. Ninth in the Principality after his most assured race so far, Speed also progressed to Q2 in Montréal only to crash over Alexander Wurz's Williams while trying to pass it. They were classified in the United States despite Liuzzi's late water leak. A shock third (Speed) and fifth (Liuzzi) on Friday afternoon at Magny-Cours proved a mirage for both cars retired from the race, and from the British GP too. Liuzzi crashed into Anthony Davidson at the first corner at Magny-Cours and Speed had another altercation with Wurz at Silverstone. They were victims of the downpour at the Nürburgring's Turn 1 on lap

Vitantonio Liuzzi, Toro Rosso STR02-Ferrari (Brazilian GP)

three of the European GP with Liuzzi perilously close to hitting a rescue tractor in the chaos.

Speed's future had been in doubt all year and he was sacked on the Tuesday before the Hungarian GP following an angry confrontation with team principal Franz Tost after the European GP. Sebastian Vettel was hired until the end of 2008 and the 20-year-old accumulated mileage in unfamiliar machinery by finishing his first three races for Toro Rosso. Informed that he was also surplus to requirements in 2008, Liuzzi beat the German youngster in Turkey and at Monza, albeit in 15th and 17th positions respectively,

and was 12th after a slow pitstop in Belgium.

Heavy rain swept Fuji during the Japanese GP weekend with Vettel both star and villain of the story. He coaxed a STR02 into the top-ten shoot-out for the first time, qualifying eighth, and briefly led the race when Lewis Hamilton pitted. He was third during the final safety-car period when he crashed into the back of Mark Webber's second-placed Red Bull as the pack closed up, losing podium finishes for both senior and junior teams. 'A little bit of day-dreaming cost both teams a lot of points,' was Webber's post-race judgement on the distraught Vettel. Liuzzi lost an eighth-place

Scott Speed, Toro Rosso STR02-Ferrari (European GP)

finish when he was handed a 25sec penalty for overtaking Adrian Sutil under yellow flags. There was redemption for both drivers at the rain-affected Chinese GP. With new parts having improved the STR02s, they narrowly missed out on Q3 after their best combined qualifying so far, although Vettel was penalised five grid positions for impeding Heikki Kovalainen. They split strategies to finish fourth (Vettel one-stopping) and sixth (Liuzzi two-stopping) to score Toro Rosso's only points of 2007. Q2 qualifiers once more in Brazil, Vettel's hydraulics failed and Liuzzi had his nosecone dislodged by Giancarlo Fisichella's Renault. Toro Rosso's Chinese results rescued a difficult campaign, and vaulted the team above Honda, Super Aguri and Spyker in the standings.

HONDA RACING F1 TEAM

Honda endured a nightmare season with an uncompetitive car and a controversial marketing campaign rather than sponsorship. Correlation issues with the new wind tunnel were blamed for inconsistent handling, which was pitch-sensitive and unstable at the rear under braking. With compromised aerodynamic efficiency, including poor downforce, the Honda RA107's potential was already a concern for the drivers when its ecological My Earth Dreams livery was revealed at London's Natural History Museum on 26 February with a high-resolution satellite image of the world replacing conventional logos. Simon Fuller's 19 Management, whose high-profile clients included David Beckham and the Spice Girls, was involved in this unexpected marketing direction, which drew

Sebastian Vettel, Toro Rosso STR02-Ferrari (Chinese GP)

criticism in some quarters as a case of F1 'greenwashing'.

Jenson Button and Rubens Barrichello remained under contract. Anthony Davidson left after five years as test and reserve driver to be replaced by Red Bull refugee Christian Klien, with James Rossiter and Mike Conway joining as test drivers. Mariano Alperin was appointed head of aerodynamics while Simon Lacey moved to McLaren. Button missed pre-Christmas tests at Barcelona and Jerez due to a rib injury from karting, so Klien and Rossiter had additional track time. Third-generation IndyCar race winner Marco Andretti also completed three test days at Jerez during the winter in a year-old Honda RA106.

Jenson Button, Honda RA107 (Australian GP)

Rubens Barrichello, Honda RA107 (Monaco GP)

Rossiter conducted the unpainted RA107's shakedown at Silverstone on 22 January before testing began in earnest at Barcelona three days later. Senior technical director Shuhei Nakamoto spoke of a new 'Honda philosophy of being adventurous and experimental' in the creation of the RA107, which was a complete reworking of the under-performing 2006 car. Honda eschewed the trend for undercut sidepods with an unusually large squared frontal area that sported substantial external side fins. The exhausts exited from the centre of the radically tapered sidepods with radiators mounted horizontally. The engine cover and 'Coke bottle' rear end were extremely narrow to optimise airflow to the diffuser and centrally mounted rear wing. Four suspension layouts were tried during the winter as the team adapted to Bridgestone tyres. The narrow nose drooped down at the front, with an angular lower section at the centre of the wing and zero-keel suspension mount. The wheelbase was extended and the engine moved forward to redistribute weight, which was aided by lighter internals to the titanium-cased seven-speed gearbox.

Indifferent testing times were blamed on an interim aerodynamic package although those issues remained when 2007-specification aero arrived for the Bahrain test. Two seconds off the pace in Australia (and slower than Honda's Super Aguri client team), both cars finished outside the top ten at that race and the next, while Button spun and stalled after a couple of laps of round three in Bahrain.

Nakamoto's lack of F1 experience was questioned in the press and Honda launched a major aero recruitment drive in the spring. Formerly with British American Racing, Loïc Bigois was headhunted from Williams to lead the department with John Owen (BMW Sauber), François Martinet (Williams) and Peter Coysh (McLaren) also hired. That spelt the end of Mariano Alperin's brief tenure as head of aerodynamics and by the end of the summer he had moved to BMW Sauber. Jörg Zander had already been poached from the Swiss/German team as deputy technical director by that time although he was not free to start work until December. The team issued a statement confirming that chief executive officer Nick Fry had met with both Mike Coughlan and Nigel Stepney, the central characters in the espionage story that was engulfing McLaren and Ferrari, to assess potential future opportunities. Chief race engineer Craig Wilson was promoted to oversee all aspects of vehicle performance as Honda looked to turn around its fortunes.

Such was Honda's plight that a major aero upgrade was already underway before the season started. A succession of new front wings began with a higher central section in Malaysia and continued throughout the campaign with limited discernible effect. Nose-mounted 'Dumbo ears' were not raced but another revised front wing, bargeboards, sidepods and floor were introduced for the Spanish GP. Both cars made second qualifying at that race only for them to collide when Button attempted to pass

Barrichello after his first pitstop. The Brazilian finished 10th with Button 12th after pitting for a new nosecone.

New sidepods with increased undercut plus revised side fins and chimneys proved a step forward during a four-day session at Paul Ricard. Both drivers qualified for Q3 for the first time in Monaco, where they filled the fifth row of the grid and ran in tandem all race but again without scoring, Barrichello 10th and Button 11th. Button could not select a gear on the grid in Canada, where Barrichello used long first and second stints to climb into third by the time of a late safety car. He timed his change to super-soft tyres too late, after the race had gone green once more, which denied the chance of a top-five finish. The Hondas collided at the start of the United States GP: trying to avoid a spinning car, Barrichello launched Button into the air and could not continue, but the Englishman was able to nurse his damaged car to a much-delayed finish.

With wind-tunnel correlation issues apparently solved, a heavily revised RA107 was tested at Jerez two days after the United States GP, with completely new front suspension, different brake ducts and another aero upgrade. With both cars starting in the midfield as normal, Button made a strong start to the French GP and passed a couple of cars to claim eighth for Honda's first point of 2007. Back pain – a legacy of his Indianapolis shunt – forced Button to sit out FP2 at Silverstone with Klien substituting for that one session. The Englishman returned on Saturday only to be eliminated in Q1 at that race and the next. Ninth (Barrichello) and tenth (Button) at Silverstone, they were ultimately disappointed at the Nürburgring. Barrichello's diffuser was damaged on the opening lap but, with wet weather the great leveller, Button stormed from 20th to fifth in two

laps before aquaplaning into the Turn 1 gravel.

With another new front-wing design in Hungary featuring two slots rather than one, the RA107s were even slower than normal. They started the Turkish GP from the back after an installation issue forced both to change engines for the race. Button was delayed at the first corner before he overtook ten cars, but 13th at the end, four places ahead of his dispirited team-mate, was scant reward. The cars were better in low-downforce Monza set-up, qualifying in the top 12 and finishing eighth (Button) and tenth (Barrichello).

They were back among the also-rans at Spa-Francorchamps, where Button observed: 'I'd rather we just concentrate on next year. This car is horrible to drive, and I don't enjoy coming to the races.' A 'bridge' front wing with upper element curving over the nose was not raced. Button excelled when it rained in Japan and China. He qualified sixth at Fuji and was fourth behind the safety car when the race belatedly went green for the first time. However, Nick Heidfeld chopped across his bow on the restart and dislodged the Honda's front wing; that Button continued without realising the wing was missing highlighted Honda's aerodynamic woes. After Takuma Satō's Super Aguri hit him on the last lap, the Englishman was classified 11th. Button started the Chinese GP from tenth and finished fifth when among the first to risk dry tyres. Barrichello finished tenth in Japan and was delayed in China by a collision with Anthony Davidson and ill-timed tyre changes. Double engine failure in Brazil concluded a dispiriting campaign.

Barrichello failed to score a point for the only time in his F1 career while Button's Chinese score saved Honda from the embarrassment of being beaten by Super Aguri in the constructors' championship.

Christian Klien, Honda RA107 (British GP)

Takuma Satō, Super Aguri SA07-Honda (Canadian GP)

SUPER AGURI F1

Super Aguri was better prepared than for its hastily assembled debut in 2006. The Super Aguri SA07-Honda was described as an interim test car when it made its track debut in Barcelona on 28 November. The SA07 was officially designed and built at Honda's Tochigi research and development facility in collaboration with Super Aguri engineers, using the Honda RA807E engine and seamless-shift carbon gearbox. Spyker managing director Colin Kolles judged it to be a direct copy of the 2006 Honda RA106 rather than Super Aguri's intellectual property as demanded by the Concorde Agreement. Quicker than the works Hondas at the start of the year, Super Aguri scored points before mid-season but then slipped down the order as its limited budget dwindled.

Aguri Suzuki's management structure of managing director Daniele Audetto, technical director Mark Preston, sporting director Graham Taylor and team manager Mick Ainsley-Cowlishaw remained stable. Peter McCool was chief designer and Ben Wood

head of aerodynamics. Honda test driver Anthony Davidson was finally rewarded with a full-time race drive alongside Takuma Satō. Sakon Yamamoto and James Rossiter were employed as test drivers. The team used the 50 percent wind tunnel at the National Physical Laboratory at Teddington.

Promise and reliability during the winter was confirmed when Satō qualified for Q3 in Australia with Davidson 11th on the grid, ahead of both works Hondas. After Davidson's anti-stall kicked in at the start, Adrian Sutil's Spyker launched him into the air at the first corner but the English driver persevered to finish 16th despite car damage and a jarred back. Davidson was also 16th in Malaysia after another anti-stall episode at his first pitstop. Satō was the quickest Honda-powered qualifier for both races but finished them outside the top ten.

Engine failure accounted for both drivers in Bahrain, Davidson having completed enough laps to be classified 16th yet again. Satō then benefitted from Giancarlo Fisichella's late pitstop in Spain to claim eighth and score Super Aguri's first point. Both cars

Anthony Davidson, Super Aguri SA07-Honda (British GP)

were lapped twice in Monaco but became more competitive in Montréal, where Satō narrowly missed out on Q3 before passing Ralf Schumacher and Fernando Alonso in the last five laps to snatch sixth. Davidson opted for a one-stop strategy and was up to third, and on course for an even better finish than his team-mate, when he hit a beaver, forcing two unscheduled pitstops (to remove the unlucky animal and then to change the damaged wing and for soft tyres). Davidson finished 11th at that race and the next; Satō spun out of the United States GP.

They were eliminated in Q1 at Magny-Cours and Silverstone, where Satō finished and Davidson retired. With both cars through to second qualifying at the Nürburgring, wet-weather specialist Satō passed six cars on the opening lap and ran in the top ten before his hydraulics failed. Davidson was the highest Honda driver on the Hungarian and Turkish grids but in the first of those races his suspension was broken by Fisichella's side-on assault. He finished 14th in Turkey and Italy despite damage at both races following first-lap contact with others. Satō finished 16th at Monza having had his brakes catch fire on the way to the grid.

The cars lacked balance in Belgium and were a handful in the Japanese rain. Satō was last in his home race after separate incidents with Alexander Wurz and Jenson Button, while Davidson's throttle sensor failed. The Englishman escaped first qualifying in China only to be spun around by Rubens Barrichello on the second lap, resultant damage to a brake duct eventually leading to retirement; Satō finished 14th. At the last race in Brazil, Super Aguri received a $10,000 fine it could scarcely afford due to a tyre-allocation misdemeanour on Friday. They filled two of the last three finishing positions in the race.

Thanks to Satō's scores, Super Aguri was ninth in the constructors' championship, just two points behind the works Honda team. All was not well off the track by this stage. Oil trading company SS United had been named as Super Aguri's prime sponsor on the eve of the season, but its logos were removed for the last three races due to non-payment. Talks with Spanish entrepreneur Alejandro Agag began at the Hungarian GP but led nowhere, so Super Aguri faced a bleak winter.

ETIHAD ALDAR SPYKER F1 TEAM

Spyker needed a new engine partner when Toyota signed a long-term deal with Williams on 27 July 2006. Previous owners Midland had already agreed a deal with Cosworth before the sale to Spyker Cars was finalised at the Italian GP. Spyker immediately reversed that decision and switched to Ferrari, leaving Cosworth without a client team. Christijan Albers was also reconfirmed at that Italian GP. Impressive on three Friday appearances that year, Japanese F3 champion Adrian Sutil signed a two-year deal to partner Albers. Renovation of Spyker's Brackley wind tunnel as a 50 percent scale facility was not due to be completed until mid-season so chief technology officer Mike Gascoyne, who had started work when his Toyota contract expired on 1 November 2006, arranged a supplementary deal with Jean-Claude Migeot's Aerolab (formerly Fondmetal Technologies) tunnel in northern Italy.

Technical director James Key's Spyker F8-VII-Ferrari was launched at Silverstone on 5 February, with the new owners adopting numbering conventions that dated back to Spyker's origins as an automobile and aeroplane manufacturer. The 'F' referred to the line (racing cars), '8' to the number of engine cylinders and 'VII' to the year expressed as a Roman numeral.

Gascoyne's late arrival and delayed confirmation of engine partner meant that the F8-VII was a 'conservative update' of the unsuccessful Midland M16, with old monocoque retained to save time and money. The aero package was revised with conventional bargeboards and sidepods that were undercut for the first time. These had to be raised to accommodate the larger radiators (by ten percent) required by the Ferrari F1-056H engine. The conventional (non-seamless-shift) seven-speed gearbox had an aluminium casing as before. Radiators and exhausts were moved forward to transfer weight towards the front. The marginally elongated nose was lowered with a zero-keel adopted for the first time, with lower-front wishbones mounted to the chassis. Spyker intended to run test drivers on GP Fridays and announced Fairuz Fauzy, Adrián Vallés, Markus Winkelhock and Guido van der Garde (despite a contractual tug-of-war with Super Aguri). All four drove during the winter but Spyker concentrated its efforts on the race drivers during race

Christijan Albers, Spyker F8-VII-Ferrari (Malaysian GP)

Adrian Sutil, Spyker F8-VIIB-Ferrari (Brazilian GP)

weekends to develop the recalcitrant F8-VII. Sutil brought backing from Medion computers and deals with title partner Etihad Airlines and Aldar property group were announced before the season.

With Gascoyne keen to downplay chances before his B-specification car was completed, the well-balanced Spyker-Ferraris lacked both grip and aero efficiency so failed to escape Q1 all season. In Australia, Albers crashed and Sutil served two drive-

through penalties during a chastening debut. The team missed the Sepang test to finish a completely new aerodynamic package with revised bargeboards, floor and diffuser for the Malaysian GP. Both Spyker-Ferraris were out by the end of lap seven in Malaysia, Sutil having hit Jenson Button's Honda in Turn 4 and Albers with his car on fire, and they were the last two cars still circulating in Bahrain and Barcelona. Off track, chief executive officer Victor Müller departed

Markus Winkelhock, Spyker F8-VII-Ferrari (European GP)

and owner Michiel Mol expanded his role amid Spyker's road-car financial struggles.

Sutil was a shock fastest when it rained for FP3 in Monaco. Unfortunately, it was dry for qualifying, although he did beat a Toyota and Super Aguri to line up 19th. Fading brakes were blamed when he crashed out of the race in Casino Square, while Albers had a driveshaft failure in the closing laps. Accidents accounted for both cars in Canada before they finished the United States GP at the back. France was a disaster: Albers damaged his monocoque on the kerbs on Friday and left his race pitstop with refuelling hose still attached and mechanics scattered in the pitlane; Sutil was last after serving a stop-go penalty for speeding at his stop.

'Commercial difficulties' were blamed when Albers was sacked after finishing 15th at Silverstone, where Sutil's engine failed. Markus Winkelhock replaced Albers for the European GP, where he enjoyed a remarkable start to the only F1 race of his career. He qualified last but decided to start from the pitlane on intermediate tyres as heavy rain fell during the formation lap. He led lap two by 19sec when quicker cars crashed (including Sutil) or changed to wet-weather tyres and continued to head the field when the safety car was deployed, but tumbled down the order when the racing resumed and retired with hydraulic failure. Roldán Rodríguez, Christian Klein and Narain Karthekeyan were all mentioned as possible permanent replacements before Sakon Yamamoto signed for the last seven races.

Sutil beat Rubens Barrichello's Honda in Hungary but Yamamoto crashed after four laps. The planned debut of Gascoyne's F8-VIIB at the Turkish GP was delayed when it failed its rear-impact test. Sutil battled Sebastian Vettel's Toro Rosso during that race before fuel pressure caused both drivers to stall in the pits. The F8-VIIB was taken to the Monza group test with the McLaren Electronic Control Unit and four-race gearbox required by the 2008 rules. The radiators were revised, rotary Sachs rear dampers replaced, and aero updated. That coincided with news of yet another new owner at a press conference in Mumbai on 3 September. Mol negotiated the sale of the troubled Spyker Automobielen's controlling interest to Indian entrepreneur Vijay Mallya.

Gascoyne had promised 'a big improvement in the stability of the rear of the car' but the F8-VIIBs remained rooted to the back of the field in low-downforce Monza configuration. They edged closer to the midfield at Spa-Francorchamps, where Sutil used soft tyres for a storming opening lap and first stint, beating both Super Aguris for 14th by the finish. With rain the great leveller at Fuji, Sutil passed Barrichello and Jarno Trulli to finish ninth on the road, with Yamamoto 12th. That got even better after the race for Sutil was promoted into eighth when Vitantonio Liuzzi received a 25sec penalty for passing him under yellow flags.

The Spyker-Ferraris were less competitive in China despite more rain, with Yamamoto last and Sutil crashing after prematurely changing to dry tyres. Spyker's only complete F1 season concluded in Brazil with both drivers starting from the back row and eliminated in incidents with rivals. The point scored in Japan gave Spyker-Ferrari tenth in the constructors' standings.

Sakon Yamamoto, Spyker F8-VIIB-Ferrari (Belgian GP)

VODAFONE McLAREN MERCEDES

McLaren entered 2007 with a new title sponsor, a fully competitive technical package and one of the most talented driver line-ups in Formula 1 history. And yet this was among the most traumatic seasons to engulf any team due to toxic in-fighting and the infamous 'Spygate' affair. The team was stripped of its constructors' points and handed a record fine, while both Lewis Hamilton and Fernando Alonso missed winning the drivers' title by a single point.

There were two seismic announcements from Woking in December 2005. Telecommunications giant Vodafone, which had sponsored Ferrari since 2002, was confirmed as title partner from 2007 'at least into the next decade' on 14 December. Five days later, news of Alonso's three-year deal to leave Renault and join McLaren from 2007 was a complete shock. GP2 champion Hamilton was preferred to Pedro de la Rosa and Gary Paffett when he was confirmed as Alonso's team-mate on 24 November 2006. De la Rosa remained in a test and reserve capacity, but Paffett returned to DTM touring cars. Mika Häkkinen's run in a McLaren MP4-21-Mercedes at Barcelona on 30 November was his first serious F1 test in five years.

The engineering exodus to Milton Keynes continued when head of aerodynamics Peter Prodromou joined Red Bull Racing after his contract expired on 1 November 2006. Honda's Simon Lacey switched to McLaren-Mercedes later that month. McLaren shareholders Ron Dennis and Mansour Ojjeh both sold 15 percent stakes to the Bahraini Mumtalakat Holding Company in January. Mercedes-Benz retained a 40 percent shareholding, with Dennis and Ojjeh now having 15 percent each.

The McLaren MP4-22-Mercedes was launched on the evening of 15 January at an hour-long parade and fireworks in Valencia, with an estimated 200,000 lining the streets to catch a glimpse of local hero Alonso and rookie Hamilton in reliveried MP4-21s. Testing of the new car began two days later at the Circuit Ricardo Tormo outside the city. The MP4-22 was an evolution of the concept originally introduced in 2005 with 'size-zero' aerodynamics and bodywork (in chrome and 'rocket' red) so tight that 'bumps and blisters' were required to cover some elements. The torque curve of the Mercedes-Benz FO108T engine was improved while its excellent heat rejection allowed smaller, more aerodynamic chimneys that

Lewis Hamilton, McLaren MP4-22-Mercedes-Benz (Hungarian GP)

emanated from accentuated undercut sidepods. The engine cover, which still featured 'horn' wings, was so low that a central fin was required to meet regulations. The triple-element front wing was mounted via its middle tier, with deep central 'spoon' section that protruded ahead of the drooping needle nose and outer fins on its large endplates. Its rear wing was centrally supported by twin pylons that were forward-mounted at an angle from mid-season to improve airflow. The seven-speed seamless-shift gearbox was a lighter development. The inboard torsion bar/pushrod suspension was revised to suit the standard Bridgestone rubber, with zero-keel retained at the front. With adaptable suspension and a shorter wheelbase than its principal rival, the MP4-22 had better tyre warm-up than the Ferrari F2007 – useful for qualifying and at low-speed circuits. The car was superb at riding kerbs although its front tyres tended to overheat in high-speed corners, causing increased wear. Initial braking issues were solved with improved cooling.

Weather, teething issues and Hamilton's first substantial crash as an F1 driver interrupted pre-season testing. That said, the MP4-22's outright pace was such that being 0.8sec shy of Kimi Räikkönen's pace in Australia was disappointing. Having spoken of learning from Alonso during his rookie campaign, Hamilton matched the reigning champion during the winter and displayed fearsome self-confidence and speed in Melbourne. He drove around the outside of Alonso and Robert Kubica's BMW Sauber in the first corner and

only lost second place to his team-mate when he was baulked by Takuma Satō. Hamilton finished third after a mighty debut that Sir Stirling Moss called 'the greatest breath of fresh air we've had ever since I started following F1'.

Malaysia's extreme heat suited McLaren-Mercedes and Alonso and Hamilton, who started second and fourth for a successive race and beat the Ferraris off the line to run 1–2 throughout, barring pitstops, with Alonso winning and Hamilton holding off Räikkönen for second. Hamilton repeated that result in Bahrain, where Alonso struggled home fifth.

A new front wing with curved 'bridge' element that stretched between the endplates and over the nose passed scrutineering for the Spanish GP despite suggestions that it contravened the flexible bodywork rule. Alonso started second but ran wide at the first corner so, on another Ferrari day, the unruffled Hamilton led a McLaren-Mercedes 2–3 to lead the championship. Alonso's relationship with team and team-mate was already strained and only grew worse in Monaco despite a dominant weekend. Alonso led a front-row lock-out and Hamilton was frustrated when he was ordered to pit before he could exploit the five extra laps of fuel he was carrying. That denied him the opportunity to challenge Alonso's first place and prompted an FIA enquiry that cleared McLaren of issuing illegal team orders.

Hamilton only had to wait two weeks for his breakthrough

success, for he won both North American races from pole position to establish a ten-point championship lead. Starting second on both occasions, Alonso finished seventh in Montréal due to a stop-go penalty for stopping when the pitlane was closed and was narrowly beaten by Hamilton at Indianapolis. The Ferrari F2007 was the quicker car at Magny-Cours, where gearbox failure during qualifying restricted Alonso to seventh at the finish, while Hamilton started from the front row and finished third.

With the 'Spygate' story unravelling and impressive new McLaren Brand Centre hospitality structure in use for the first time, Hamilton snatched pole position in the closing minutes of qualifying for the British GP. Räikkönen's Ferrari was the class of the field on Sunday with Alonso leading a McLaren-Mercedes 2–3 after starting with a heavier fuel load than his team-mate. Hamilton's title challenge faltered at the Nürburgring: uninjured in a 160mph qualifying crash, he slid into the Turn 1 gravel as the heavens opened early in the race but a tractor lifted the car out of the gravel and he finished ninth; Alonso passed Massa for victory with five laps to go, narrowing Hamilton's advantage to two points.

The simmering feud between the McLaren drivers exploded during qualifying for the Hungarian GP. Hamilton did not allow Alonso to lead the Q3 fuel-burn phase as ordered, and the Spaniard delayed leaving the pits long enough to stop his young team-mate from starting his final qualifying attempt. Alonso lost pole position when the stewards handed him a five-place grid penalty later that evening, and stripped McLaren-Mercedes of any constructors' points earned in the race. Promoted to pole following Alonso's penalty, Hamilton withstood Räikkönen's pressure to win with Alonso fourth. McLaren's appeal against those lost constructors' points was due on 19 September but would be rendered immaterial by developments in the 'Spygate' affair.

With Dennis trying to calm tensions between his drivers before the Turkish GP, Hamilton's front-right puncture handed third place behind the Ferraris to Alonso. With a new 'Spygate' hearing looming, Alonso led a McLaren-Mercedes 1–2 in qualifying and the race at Monza. Fifth in Turkey, Hamilton snatched second from the one-

stopping Räikkönen with a great manoeuvre into the first chicane.

As well as the driver feud, the World Motor Sport Council verdict (exclusion from the constructors' championship and a $100m fine) overshadowed an emotionally charged Belgian GP weekend. No match for the Ferraris at Spa-Francorchamps, Alonso beat Hamilton in qualifying as they filled row two and aggressively forced his rival wide on the exit of La Source. He won the subsequent drag race after entering Eau Rouge side by side to effectively settle their fractious dice over third position.

Imperious in the wet at Fuji, Hamilton beat Alonso to pole position by 0.070sec and survived contact with Robert Kubica's BMW Sauber to win, while Alonso crashed after 42 laps when he aquaplaned on the flooded track surface. Looking to have a decisive points advantage with two races to go, Hamilton claimed pole for the following week's Chinese GP but was left out too long on old intermediate tyres as the track dried. With his right-rear worn to the core, he lost control on the wet pit entry and became beached in the gravel trap. Räikkönen beat Alonso to victory as they both eroded Hamilton's points lead.

Needing fifth in Brazil to secure the title, Hamilton started second but lost out to both Ferraris off the line before Alonso passed him in the Senna 'S'. He immediately tried to regain third at Subida do Logo and dropped to eighth when he ran wide. His title hopes all but ended when 'a malfunction in the hydraulics system which cleared itself within 36 seconds' left him in neutral. He fought back from last to seventh, which was not enough. Without the pace to challenge the Ferraris, Alonso finished third, which handed Räikkönen an unlikely World Championship by a single point from both McLaren-Mercedes drivers. Hamilton was runner-up due to having scored more second-place finishes than Alonso.

McLaren appealed the Brazilian result when FIA technical delegate Jo Bauer reported that fuel from the Williams-Toyotas and BMW Saubers had been chilled more than was permitted. However, the International Court of Appeal ruled the appeal inadmissible due to procedural issues and the race result (and therefore Räikkönen's title) were confirmed on 15 November.

Fernando Alonso, McLaren MP4-22-Mercedes-Benz (Monaco GP)

2007 RESULTS

DRIVER PERFORMANCE

DRIVER	CAR-ENGINE	AUS	MAL	BRN	E	MC	CDN	USA	F	GB	EU	H	TR	I	B	J	PRC	BR
Christijan Albers	Spyker F8-VII-Ferrari	21 R	20 R	22 14	21 14	22 19	21 R	22 15	20 R	22 15	–	–	–	–	–	–	–	–
Fernando Alonso	McLaren MP4-22-Mercedes-Benz	2 2	2 1	4 5	2 3	1 1 FL	2 7 FL	2 2	10 7	3 2	2 1	6 4	4 3	1 1 FL	3 3	2 R	4 2	4 3
Rubens Barrichello	Honda RA107	16 11	22 11	15 13	12 10	9 10	13 12	15 R	13 11	14 9	14 11	18 18	22 17	12 10	17 13	17 10	16 15	11 R
Jenson Button	Honda RA107	14 15	15 12	16 R	14 12	10 11	15 R	13 12	12 8	18 10	17 R	17 R	21 13	10 8	12 R	6 11	10 5	16 R
David Coulthard	Red Bull RB3-Renault	18 R	13 R	21 R	9 5	13 14	14 R	11 R	16 13	12 11	20 5	10 11	13 10	20 R	11 R	12 4	5 8	9 9
Anthony Davidson	Super Aguri SA07-Honda	11 16	18 16	13 16	15 11	17 18	17 11	16 11	19 R	19 R	15 12	15 R	11 14	14 14	20 16	19 R	14 R	20 14
Giancarlo Fisichella	Renault R27	6 5	12 6	7 8	10 9	4 4	9 DSQ	10 9	5 6	8 8	13 10	13 12	10 9	15 12	22 R	10 5	18 11	12 R
Lewis Hamilton	McLaren MP4-22-Mercedes-Benz	4 3	4 2 FL	2 2	4 2	2 2	1 1	1 1	2 3	1 3	10 9	1 1	2 5	2 2	4 4	1 1 FL	1 R	2 7
Nick Heidfeld	BMW Sauber F1.07	3 4	5 4	5 4	7 R	7 6	3 2	5 R	7 5	9 6	4 6	2 3	6 4	4 4	6 5	5 14	8 7	6 6
Christian Klien	Honda RA107	–	–	–	–	–	–	–	NT DNP	–	–	–	–	–	–	–	–	–
Heikki Kovalainen	Renault R27	13 10	11 8	12 9	8 7	15 13	22 4	6 5	6 15	7 7	7 8	11 8	7 6	7 7	9 8	11 2	12 9	17 R
Robert Kubica	BMW Sauber F1.07	5 R	7 18	6 6	5 4	8 5	8 R	–	4 4	5 4	5 7	7 5	5 8	6 5	14 9	9 7	9 R	7 5
Vitantonio Liuzzi	Toro Rosso STR02-Ferrari	19 14	16 17	18 R	16 R	12 R	12 R	19 17	17 R	16 16	19 R	16 R	15 15	19 17	13 12	14 9	11 6	14 13
Felipe Massa	Ferrari F2007	22 6	1 5	1 1 FL	1 1 FL	3 3	5 DSQ	3 3	1 2 FL	4 5	3 2 FL	14 13	1 1	3 R	2 2 FL	4 6	3 3 FL	1 2
Kazuki Nakajima	Williams FW29-Toyota	T	T	–	–	–	–	T	–	–	–	–	–	–	–	–	T	19 10
Kimi Räikkönen	Ferrari F2007	1 1 FL	3 3	3 3	3 R	16 8	4 5	4 4 FL	3 1	2 1 FL	1 R	3 2 FL	3 2 FL	5 3	1 1	3 3	2 1	3 1 FL
Nico Rosberg	Williams FW29-Toyota	12 7	6 R	10 10	11 6	5 12	7 10	14 16	9 9	17 12	11 R	4 7	8 7	8 6	5 6	16 R	15 16	10 4
Takuma Satō	Super Aguri SA07-Honda	10 12	14 13	17 R	13 8	21 17	11 6	18 R	22 16	21 14	16 R	19 15	17 18	17 16	18 15	21 15	20 14	18 12
Ralf Schumacher	Toyota TF107	9 8	9 15	14 12	17 R	20 16	18 8	12 R	11 10	6 R	9 R	5 6	16 12	18 15	10 10	15 R	6 R	15 11
Scott Speed	Toro Rosso STR02-Ferrari	17 R	17 14	19 R	22 R	18 9	16 R	20 13	15 R	15 R	18 R	–	–	–	–	–	–	–
Adrian Sutil	Spyker F8-VII-Ferrari	20 17	21 R	20 15	20 13	19 R	20 R	21 14	21 17	20 R	21 R	21 17	19 21	–	–	–	–	–
	Spyker F8-VIIB-Ferrari	–	–	–	–	–	–	–	–	–	–	–	–	21 19	19 14	20 8	21 R	21 R
Jarno Trulli	Toyota TF107	8 9	8 7	9 7	6 R	14 15	10 R	8 6	8 R	10 R	8 13	8 10	9 16	9 11	8 11	13 13	12 13	8 8
Sebastian Vettel	BMW Sauber F1.07	T	T	–	–	–	–	7 8	–	–	–	–	–	–	–	–	–	–
	Toro Rosso STR02-Ferrari	–	–	–	–	–	–	–	–	–	–	20 16	18 19	16 18	16 R	8 R	17 4	13 R
Mark Webber	Red Bull RB3-Renault	7 13	10 10	8 R	19 R	6 R	6 9	9 7	14 12	11 R	6 3	9 9	12 R	11 9	7 7	7 R	7 10	5 R
Markus Winkelhock	Spyker F8-VII-Ferrari	–	–	–	–	–	–	–	–	–	22 R	–	–	–	–	–	–	–
Alexander Wurz	Williams FW29-Toyota	15 R	19 9	11 11	18 R	11 7	19 3	17 10	18 14	13 13	12 4	12 14	14 11	13 13	15 R	18 R	19 12	–
Sakon Yamamoto	Spyker F8-VII-Ferrari	–	–	–	–	–	–	–	–	–	–	22 R	20 20	–	–	–	–	–
	Spyker F8-VIIB-Ferrari	–	–	–	–	–	–	–	–	–	–	–	–	22 20	21 17	22 12	22 17	22 R

FORMULA 1 RACE WINNERS

ROUND	RACE (CIRCUIT)	DATE	WINNER
1	ING Australian Grand Prix (Albert Park)	Mar 18	Kimi Räikkönen (Ferrari F2007)
2	Petronas Malaysian Grand Prix (Sepang)	Apr 8	Fernando Alonso (McLaren MP4-22-Mercedes-Benz)
3	Gulf Air Bahrain Grand Prix (Sakhir)	Apr 15	Felipe Massa (Ferrari F2007)
4	Gran Premio de España Telefónica (Catalunya)	May 13	Felipe Massa (Ferrari F2007)
5	Grand Prix de Monaco (Monte Carlo)	May 27	Fernando Alonso (McLaren MP4-22-Mercedes-Benz)
6	Grand Prix du Canada (Montréal)	Jun 10	Lewis Hamilton (McLaren MP4-22-Mercedes-Benz)
7	United States Grand Prix (Indianapolis)	Jun 17	Lewis Hamilton (McLaren MP4-22-Mercedes-Benz)
8	Grand Prix de France (Magny-Cours)	Jul 1	Kimi Räikkönen (Ferrari F2007)
9	Santander British Grand Prix (Silverstone)	Jul 8	Kimi Räikkönen (Ferrari F2007)
10	Grand Prix of Europe (Nürburgring)	Jul 22	Fernando Alonso (McLaren MP4-22-Mercedes-Benz)
11	Magyar Nagydíj (Hungaroring)	Aug 5	Lewis Hamilton (McLaren MP4-22-Mercedes-Benz)
12	Petrol Ofisi Turkish Grand Prix (Istanbul Park)	Aug 26	Felipe Massa (Ferrari F2007)
13	Gran Premio d'Italia (Monza)	Sep 9	Fernando Alonso (McLaren MP4-22-Mercedes-Benz)
14	ING Belgian Grand Prix (Spa-Francorchamps)	Sep 16	Kimi Räikkönen (Ferrari F2007)
15	Fuji Television Japanese Grand Prix (Fuji)	Sep 30	Lewis Hamilton (McLaren MP4-22-Mercedes-Benz)
16	Sinopec Chinese Grand Prix (Shanghai)	Oct 7	Kimi Räikkönen (Ferrari F2007)
17	Grande Prêmio do Brasil (Interlagos)	Oct 21	Kimi Räikkönen (Ferrari F2007)

The Ferraris lead at Spa-Francorchamps as the rival McLaren-Mercedes go wheel to wheel

DRIVERS' CHAMPIONSHIP

	DRIVERS	POINTS
1	Kimi Räikkönen	110
2	Lewis Hamilton	109
3	Fernando Alonso	109
4	Felipe Massa	94
5	Nick Heidfeld	61
6	Robert Kubica	39
7	Heikki Kovalainen	30
8	Giancarlo Fisichella	21
9	Nico Rosberg	20
10	David Coulthard	14
11	Alexander Wurz	13
12	Mark Webber	10
13	Jarno Trulli	8
14	Sebastian Vettel	6
15	Jenson Button	6
16	Ralf Schumacher	5
17	Takuma Satō	4
18	Vitantonio Liuzzi	3
19	Adrian Sutil	1
20	Rubens Barrichello	0
21	Scott Speed	0
22	Kazuki Nakajima	0
23	Anthony Davidson	0
24	Sakon Yamamoto	0
25	Christijan Albers	0

CONSTRUCTORS' CHAMPIONSHIP

	CONSTRUCTORS	POINTS
1	Ferrari	204
2	BMW Sauber	101
3	Renault	51
4	Williams-Toyota	33
5	Red Bull-Renault	24
6	Toyota	13
7	Toro Rosso-Ferrari	8
8	Honda	6
9	Super Aguri-Honda	4
10	Spyker-Ferrari	1
–	McLaren-Mercedes-Benz	*0

*Excluded from the Constructors' Championship

Lewis Hamilton beats Robert Kubica into the first corner in Australia as Felipe Massa loses control

2008

LAST-GASP TITLE FOR TRIUMPHANT HAMILTON

Lewis Hamilton celebrates his dramatic title success in Brazil

The Concorde Agreement for 2008–12 remained unsigned. Agreement between the teams, FIA and Formula One Management regarding F1's financial structure had not been reached during six years of negotiations so the threat of a breakaway by the Grand Prix Manufacturers' Association (BMW, Honda, DaimlerChrysler, Renault and Toyota) remained. The Formula One Teams' Association was formed at a meeting in Maranello on 29 July 2008 to represent a unified voice in shaping the future, with Ferrari's Luca di Montezemolo its founding chairman.

The FIA opened a tender process for the vacant 12th team franchise, with David Richards's Prodrive preferred to Carlin Motorsport and the Jean Alesi-led Direxiv concern in April 2006. Prodrive wanted to take advantage of proposals in the Concorde Agreement to allow customer cars rather than build its own chassis. Planning permission for a factory and test track at Honiton was granted in August 2006, a deal for customer McLaren MP4-23-Mercedes was sealed and backing found from the Icelandic Baugur Group. However, those plans were scuppered during the winter of 2007/08 amid uncertainty regarding the eligibility of customer cars. Tony Scott-Andrews left his position as permanent race steward with the FIA's Alan Donnelly overseeing a new three-person panel appointed from race to race.

The minimum cockpit height was raised to improve driver head protection. McLaren Electronic Systems won the tender to supply a standard Electronic Control Unit (ECU), which allowed the FIA once again to ban electronic driver aids such as traction control. Gearboxes had to last four race weekends with a five-place grid penalty for any transgression. Spare cars were banned, and 5.75 percent biofuel was mandatory.

Lewis Hamilton won the drivers' championship at the second attempt in the most dramatic of circumstances. Needing to finish fifth at Interlagos to become the sport's youngest champion, he passed Timo Glock's Toyota at the last corner of the Brazilian GP to snatch the title from Ferrari's Felipe Massa. Ferrari sealed its eighth constructors' championship in ten years.

Team principals gathered for a Formula One Teams' Association meeting before the Italian Grand Prix

Time allowed for wind-tunnel work and computational fluid dynamics was restricted. Q3 was reduced to ten minutes with no fuel top-up to eliminate the unsatisfactory fuel-burn phase. With a major regulation change in 2009, designers took a largely evolutionary and conservative approach.

FIA president Max Mosley survived a vote of no confidence in the governing body's General Assembly following allegations published in the *News of the World* on 30 March. Mosley successfully sued the British tabloid for breach of privacy. His predecessor, Jean-Marie Balestre, died on 27 March aged 86.

A pre-season test at Barcelona was overshadowed by racist taunts from a minority aimed at Lewis Hamilton and his McLaren team. 'The federation wants to show its absolute repulsion at these incomprehensible events,' read a statement from the Real Federación Española de Automovilismo, 'as well as showing its support to the McLaren team and especially its driver, Lewis Hamilton. These kind of madmen who confuse sporting rivalry with violence must know the federation will have no tolerance with them.'

Bernie Ecclestone continued to expand the championship outside its European roots with Singapore holding F1's first night event. That street race immediately became a popular fixture on the calendar, although its inaugural edition is best remembered for Nelson Piquet Jr's deliberate crash that contributed to Renault team-mate Fernando Alonso's surprise victory. Hermann Tilke modified the area around Valencia's port to hold the European GP. Magny-Cours won a late reprieve to stage one last French GP and Indianapolis was dropped. Spa-Francorchamps and the Hungaroring extended their contracts to 2012 and 2016 respectively, while Canadian GP only went ahead once overnight resurfacing of parts of the

Pitstop disaster for Felipe Massa in Singapore

Île Notre-Dame circuit, which had broken up during practice and qualifying, was completed an hour before the start. Representatives of both Hyderabad and Cape Town had held talks with Ecclestone for a GP in 2007 or 2008, although it was 2023 when international racing (the Formula E World Championship) first visited those cities. Perennial rumours of races in New York and Las Vegas came to naught once more.

Nelson Piquet Jr crashed his Renault on lap 14 of the Singapore Grand Prix

VODAFONE McLAREN MERCEDES

McLaren-Mercedes rewarded Lewis Hamilton's exceptional rookie campaign with a contract extension to the end of 2012 while Fernando Alonso's inevitable departure was confirmed on 10 December. Interest in Sebastian Vettel and Nico Rosberg was rebuffed, so displaced Renault star Heikki Kovalainen was named as Hamilton's team-mate four days later. Overlooked for a race seat once more, Pedro de la Rosa remained as reserve driver and Gary Paffett returned to testing duties.

The Mercedes-Benz Museum in Stuttgart-Untertürkheim hosted the understated unveiling of the McLaren MP4-23-Mercedes on 8 January when team principal Ron Dennis declared that 'this is a year of forward thinking' following 12 turbulent months. Mike Coughlan's contract as chief designer was formally terminated before the season and team manager Dave Ryan was promoted to sporting director. The MP4-23 was an evolution of the car that had scored more points than any other in 2007, with Tim Goss as chief engineer and Simon Lacey head of aerodynamics. Ferrari's Marcin Budkowski joined the aero team in October 2007. The wheelbase was marginally longer to improve rear-tyre wear at fast circuits by elongating the latest seven-speed carbon-fibre gearbox and shifting the engine slightly forward. The MP4-23's responsive front end complemented Hamilton's aggressive driving style and preference for oversteer.

The elegant narrow nose remained, with 'spoon' front wing suspended beneath curved twin supports. The upper element of the 'bridge' wing pioneered in 2007 featured split outer sections.

Winglets behind the front wing were added later and 'horn' wings on the airbox were no more. The tightly packaged bodywork and aerodynamics were refined, with small apertures by the roll hoop to channel air to the airbox and centrally mounted rear wing. Ancillaries for the Mercedes-Benz FO108V were revised to improve reliability and efficiency within the freeze regulations, while new exhausts and Mobil's fuel development also boosted power. McLaren Electronic Systems now supplied the ECU to the whole grid so there were no issues adapting, unlike some rivals.

Competition at the front was as fierce as it had ever been. Both Ferrari and McLaren had two new chassis to test from launch and upgrades at almost every race. 'The rate of development has ramped to new levels,' engineering director Paddy Lowe told *Autocourse*, 'it's like a war.' Ferrari was the narrow pre-season favourite but Hamilton enjoyed the perfect start to his year by dominating the Australian GP from pole position. Third on the grid, Kovalainen was set to finish second before a third safety car ruined his strategy. A momentary loss of power when he inadvertently activated his pitlane speed limiter dropped him to fifth.

Malaysia was a stark contrast for they qualified behind the Ferraris and were both demoted five grid positions for driving slowly on the racing line in Q3. Kovalainen finished third with Hamilton fifth following a slow first pitstop when the front-right wheel nut seized. Bahrain brought no improvement. Having crashed on Friday, Hamilton dropped from third to tenth at the start when his anti-stall kicked in, then two ragged laps – twice hitting the back of Alonso's Renault, the second time dislodging

Lewis Hamilton, McLaren MP4-23-Mercedes-Benz (Australian GP)

Heikki Kovalainen, McLaren MP4-23-Mercedes-Benz (European GP)

his front wing and briefly launching him skyward – ruined his race. Kovalainen set the fastest race lap as he recovered from a flat-spotted front-right tyre during his first stint to finish fifth.

Ferrari maintained its advantage on the return to Europe, although Hamilton kept his title hopes alive with podium finishes in Spain and Turkey. Kovalainen was lucky to emerge largely unscathed from a 145mph shunt at Barcelona's Turn 9, while at Istanbul Park, where he qualified on the front row, a rear puncture at the start when clipped by Kimi Räikkönen's front wing spoiled his race. Lady luck smiled on Hamilton during the damp early laps at Monaco. He hit the Tabac barrier on lap six when running second, so the team topped up his already heavy fuel load as they changed his punctured right-rear intermediate tyre. That proved crucial for Hamilton's extended stint handed him the lead when Felipe Massa pitted at half distance and he stayed there. Kovalainen started from the pitlane due to an electronic issue and finished eighth after a frustrating afternoon in traffic.

Hamilton's title hopes took a battering at the next two races. He dominated the Canadian GP from pole before pitting behind the safety car at the end of lap 19. Slower away than Räikkönen or Robert Kubica, Hamilton failed to stop for the red pit-exit light and crashed into the Finn's stationary Ferrari, eliminating both cars. New aero at Magny-Cours included revised front wing and sidepod edges, winglets and chassis-mounted turning vanes. Grid penalties dropped Hamilton ten places (for causing the Montréal pitlane pile-up) and Kovalainen five (impeding Mark Webber in qualifying). Hamilton was then handed a drive-through for leaving the track and gaining an advantage on the opening lap – game over. Ninth due to tyre graining in Canada, Kovalainen finished fourth in France.

The pre-British GP test at Silverstone saw yet another new front wing, now featuring four elements. A dorsal fin on the engine cover tried at Hockenheim was not raced. Facing criticism in the media, Hamilton responded to his recent travails by winning the British GP by 68.577sec after one of the finest wet-weather drives in history.

Kovalainen started that race from his only F1 pole position but spun twice on the way to a disappointing fifth. German GP victory was hard-fought due to McLaren not pitting Hamilton during the mid-race safety-car period. Fourth after stopping under green-flag conditions on lap 50, Hamilton passed Nick Heidfeld, Felipe Massa and Nelson Piquet Jr to regain the advantage his pace merited. Kovalainen was fifth despite oversteer.

Hamilton led a McLaren-Mercedes front-row lock-out at the Hungaroring, where the MP4-23s sported yet another aero makeover. He lost out to Massa at the start and during his second stint flat-spotted his left-front tyre, which suddenly deflated on lap 41 to leave Massa in a clear lead. When the Ferrari's engine expired with three laps to go, Kovalainen was handed a popular maiden victory. Fifth in Hungary, Hamilton overcame a painful neck and illness to start and finish second in Valencia when no match for title rival Massa; Kovalainen finished fourth.

Starting from his third pole position in four races, Hamilton lost the Belgian GP lead when he spun at the start of lap two, allowing Räikkönen to take advantage into Les Combes. However, late rain handed Hamilton significantly more traction than his rival. He passed the gripless Ferrari into the chicane with two laps to go but did not make the corner so immediately gave the lead back. Rather than wait to make the inevitable overtake at the top of the hill, Hamilton repassed the Ferrari at La Source and won by 14.461sec, such was his dominance in those treacherous conditions. However, two hours after celebrating on the podium, Hamilton was handed a controversial 25sec penalty for leaving the track and gaining an advantage, which demoted him to third and sparked outrage in the national media, with McLaren-Mercedes unsuccessful when it appealed. Kovalainen made a poor start from third on the grid and received a costly drive-through penalty when he tapped Mark Webber's Red Bull into a spin.

Hamilton was slowest in Q2 for the Italian GP after his team misread the worsening weather conditions. He finished seventh despite the wet weather that normally favoured him. Kovalainen qualified on the front row and finished second on a day when he had been expected to take advantage of Hamilton's misfortunes with victory. Hamilton was third in Singapore when unable to pass David Coulthard's slower Red Bull for 23 laps. Kovalainen's race was compromised by a damaged floor and becoming stacked behind Hamilton at the pitstops.

They qualified 1–3 in Japan before pole-winner Hamilton threw away his chances of extending his points' lead inside two laps. He locked up and overran at the first corner, forcing Kimi Räikkönen wide and eventually earning a drive-through penalty. He also collided with Massa on lap two even though he was about to change his flat-spotted front tyres. Kovalainen was third when his engine failed after 16 laps. Pole position, fastest lap and an assured victory in China meant that Hamilton only had to finish fifth at Interlagos to claim the World Championship. Kovalainen's handling issues were caused by front tyres that had been fitted the wrong way round, although a hydraulic problem later rendered that error immaterial.

The 2008 Brazilian GP remains among the most dramatic F1 showdowns in history. With Massa cruising to victory, a conservative Hamilton controlled his own title destiny until it rained with eight laps to go. He switched to wet tyres but lost fifth to Sebastian Vettel with two laps remaining. Starting his final lap 13.144sec behind Timo Glock, he passed the dry-shod Toyota for fifth at Junção on the dash to the line to clinch McLaren-Mercedes's first drivers' title since 1999 by a single point. Kovalainen finished seventh in the race and in the final standings, while McLaren-Mercedes was runner-up in the constructors' title.

SCUDERIA FERRARI MARLBORO

Ross Brawn held talks about returning from his year-long sabbatical before accepting the challenge of rebuilding the faltering Honda team. Stefano Domenicali was named team principal on 1 January in addition to responsibility for the *Gestione Sportiva* division, with Jean Todt stepping aside. Technical director for a year, Mario Almondo moved into an operational role and was replaced by Aldo Costa. Gilles Simon's engine department was now also responsible for electronics. Ferrari had a long relationship with Magneti Marelli and was unhappy that McLaren Electronic Systems won the FIA tender to supply the standard ECU. Nikolas Tombazis and John Iley headed design and aerodynamics respectively while chief race engineer Luca Baldisseri became sporting director. Philip Morris's barcode livery replaced Marlboro branding at all 18 races.

That Kimi Räikkönen and Felipe Massa were already contracted for 2008 did not stop paddock gossip regarding their futures. Ferrari extended Massa's deal until the end of 2010 when it confirmed an unchanged line-up on 16 October. Michael Schumacher was fastest at Barcelona on the opening two days of winter testing (13 and 14 November) but did not want to return. Chris Dyer and Rob Smedley continued as race engineers for Räikkönen and Massa respectively.

Ferrari was the first team to reveal its new challenger when the evolutionary F2008 was launched in Maranello on 6 January. The wheelbase of its elongated predecessor was marginally reduced, a change that Costa described as 'just a small refinement' while remaining coy about exact dimensions. The sculpted twin-plane front wing flowed either side of a higher nose, which was an interim solution for the opening three races while the definitive nose was

Kimi Räikkönen, Ferrari F2008 (European GP)

Felipe Massa, Ferrari F2008 (European GP)

delayed until it passed its crash test. This featured a channel from bottom to top of the chassis ahead of the splitter that generated front downforce without compromising rear-end performance. Cooling was redesigned with the top of the sidepods having optional louvres, which were larger on the left-hand sidepod because it housed the oil radiator as well as a water radiator. The airbox was very narrow ahead of the tightly packaged rear end. The zero-keel was retained, while new rear suspension was intended to solve the F2007's poor ride over bumps and unsatisfactory performance in slow corners. The rear Sachs rotary shock absorber was replaced by a conventional set-up. Cockpit dimensions were reduced by aerodynamic revisions to the monocoque. Tyre warm-up issues in cool conditions hindered qualifying. Inherent understeer helped Massa outperform Räikkönen.

Räikkönen gave the F2008 its shakedown at a cold Fiorano on the day after its launch. A promising six-day test followed in Bahrain before the 2008 aero package was added at Barcelona. Pre-season favourites after narrowly outpacing McLaren-Mercedes during the winter, Ferrari's Australian GP was an incident-filled nightmare. Massa spun at the first corner before hitting David Coulthard's Red Bull as they disputed tenth place. Räikkönen started 15th following a Q1 fuel-pump issue and had a couple of 'offs' at Turn 3. Both had engine failures although Räikkönen was classified eighth.

Ferrari won the next three races to confirm the F2008's underlying pace and championship credentials. Massa led a qualifying 1–2 in Malaysia but spun out of the race soon after losing the lead to Räikkönen in the pits with the reigning champion untroubled thereafter. Under pressure due to errors at the opening two races, Massa controlled the Bahrain GP throughout with Räikkönen second. The new nose was central to a major upgrade in Spain, where Räikkönen was quickest on Friday, qualified on pole position and led all but four laps. Massa completed Ferrari's second successive 1–2 finish.

Reverting to the original nose (without holes) for the Turkish GP did not compromise performance and Massa converted pole into his third successive Istanbul victory with Räikkönen third. Ferrari's winning streak ended in Monaco despite Massa heading another qualifying 1–2 and leading from the start. However, he took to the Ste-Dévote escape road on lap 16, lost radio contact and finished third. Räikkönen received a drive-through penalty for a grid infringement and ran into the back of the luckless Adrian Sutil's Force India as they approached the chicane in the closing stages. Ferrari had an off weekend in Canada thanks to a disastrous lap behind the safety car. Räikkönen was at standstill waiting for the red pit-exit light to turn green when he was rear-ended by Lewis Hamilton. Having been stacked behind his team-mate, Massa received no fuel when it was his turn so had to stop again a lap later. That dropped him to the back of the field although he salvaged fifth by the finish.

Ferrari was back on top at Magny-Cours, where Räikkönen claimed the *Scuderia*'s 200th pole position. He was set for victory until a broken exhaust handed victory, and the championship lead, to his team-mate. Kimi held on to finish second such was Ferrari's advantage. Massa's big accident at Stowe on Friday set the tone for his torrid British GP weekend. Only ninth on the grid after missing his final qualifying run, he spun five times in the wet and trailed home in last position; Räikkönen finished fourth. McLaren-Mercedes held sway at Hockenheim, where Massa qualified on the front row but dropped to third in the race following an inopportune safety-car intervention. Räikkönen was a lacklustre sixth on the grid and at the finish.

A dorsal fin on the engine cover was introduced in Hungary, where additional cooling louvres were necessary to combat the heat. Massa jumped from third to first at the start and was leading by 5.876sec with three laps to go when his engine failed, promoting Räikkönen to third. Massa dominated the European GP at Valencia although Ferrari was fined €10,000 for an unsafe release at his second pitstop. Having already run over mechanic Pietro Timpini as he left the pits prematurely, Räikkönen lost third place to another engine failure. A faulty batch of conrods was subsequently blamed for those costly issues.

Aiming for his fourth successive Belgian GP victory, a particularly feisty Räikkönen passed Massa and both McLarens during the opening two laps and led until rain arrived with three laps to go. With far superior grip in the conditions and using his fine wet-weather skills, Hamilton closed rapidly and passed Räikkönen before cutting the chicane and having to yield the position as they started the penultimate lap. The Englishman retook the lead metres later at La Source and Räikkönen spun and then crashed as the rain intensified on that lap. A cautious second on the road, Massa was handed victory two hours later when Hamilton received a controversial 25sec penalty for leaving the track and gaining an advantage during his dice with Räikkönen.

The F2008s could not generate sufficient tyre temperature during rain at Monza although Massa did finish ahead of his title rivals in sixth with Räikkönen ninth. Now trailing Hamilton by a single point, Massa led the Singapore GP from pole before Nelson Piquet Jr's crash triggered a safety car on lap 14. Massa was one of those to stop but left with the fuel hose still attached because Ferrari's recently introduced traffic-light system prematurely changed to green. A subsequent drive-through penalty doubled Massa's agony, while Räikkönen's late accident as he challenged for fourth compounded a terrible evening for Maranello. Revised bargeboards were taken to Japanese GP, where Räikkönen finished third after being run wide by Hamilton's locked-up McLaren-Mercedes at the first corner. Massa, who made a mistake on his final qualifying attempt and received a drive-through penalty for crashing into Hamilton on lap two, finished seventh.

They were second (Massa) and third (Räikkönen) in Shanghai after swapping positions to help the Brazilian's title chances at the final race in his home city of São Paulo. Massa annexed the sixth pole of his impressive season, set the fastest race lap, and scored

the victory he required to spark short-lived jubilation in the Ferrari pit. Hamilton was 13.144sec shy of the fifth place he needed when he started the final lap but, having already changed to wet-weather tyres, passed Timo Glock's dry-shod Toyota at the last corner to deny Massa the title. Räikkönen was third with confirmation of Ferrari's 16th constructors' title almost lost in the drama.

BMW SAUBER F1 TEAM

BMW motorsport director Mario Theissen outlined the company's timeline to *Autocourse*'s Bob Constanduros in 2006. 'We are in a two-year transition phase. We will have all the people on board by the end of 2007. The factory expansion will also be ready by the end of next year, so we should have everything in place to be competitive and challenge the top teams in 2008.' He was true to his word for the BMW Sauber F1.08 was immediately fast enough to take advantage of any slip from Ferrari and McLaren-Mercedes. Great reliability and Robert Kubica's maturing talent meant both team and driver briefly led their respective championship standings, with the 1–2 finish in Canada the undoubted highlight. However, BMW Sauber switched its focus to 2009 so did not maintain the development pace of its rivals and fell away in the second half of the season.

Robert Kubica and Nick Heidfeld were confirmed as race drivers on 27 August 2007 with Theissen noting: 'Robert is a rough diamond we want to polish up into a winning driver.' The chief designer role vacated by Jörg Zander was filled by head of composite design Christoph Zimmermann in October 2007. Willem Toet led an aerodynamics department that included Seamus Mullarkey and recent recruit Mariano Alperin. Factory developments were completed and the last of the 430 staff positions at Hinwil filled by November 2007. British F3 Champion Marko Asmer drove a BMW Sauber F1.07 at Jerez in December and was eventually named as test driver, with Christian Klien reserve.

Technical director Willy Rampf described the F1.08 as a 'radical evolution' when it was launched at Munich's BMW Welt on 14 January. Increased front-end stability and improved aerodynamic efficiency were promised as the triplane front wing (with squared lower centre), intricate detailing, reduced sidepods and conventional rear end were fashioned in the wind tunnel at Hinwil. Nose-mounted 'antler' wings channelled air to the sidepods and rear wing and were widely copied. There were airbox-mounted 'horns' while the adjacent T-wings now extended the full width of each sidepod and enclosed the exhaust chimneys. Wheelbase was slightly extended to accentuate the floor and aero ahead of the bargeboards. The pushrod suspension was revised at the front and completely new at the back to improve drivability and counteract the traction-control ban. Theissen blamed winter bench-test gearbox failures on the interface with the standard ECU. The BMW P86/8 was the first engine project overseen by ex-Mercedes-Benz head of powertrain Markus Duesmann. The aggressive and consistent Kubica revelled in the F1.08's improved front-end stability but Heidfeld initially struggled with tyre warm-up.

Robert Kubica, BMW Sauber F1.08 (Canadian GP)

The first test at Valencia was disappointing as correlation between track, wind tunnel and Albert2 computational fluid dynamics supercomputer had to be verified. However, instability – especially in windy conditions – and set-up issues were solved by the third test and fears that BMW Sauber had slipped into the midfield were assuaged in Australia. Kubica qualified and ran second before being hit by Kazuki Nakajima's Williams during a safety-car period. Having qualified fifth with a heavy fuel load, Heidfeld benefitted from rapid pitstops and the high rate of attrition to finish second. Kubica was second in Malaysia while Heidfeld recovered from tenth following Jarno Trulli's first-lap nudge to set the fastest race lap and finish sixth.

Kubica was light-fuelled to claim his, and BMW Sauber's, first pole position in Bahrain. Wheelspin off the line and a mistake on lap two lost that advantage but his strategy played out sufficiently to secure third behind the Ferraris. Heidfeld's fourth place gave the consistent BMW Sauber outfit a single-point lead in the constructors' standings. That glory was short-lived for Ferrari finished 1–2 in Spain, where Kubica qualified and finished fourth. A penalty for refuelling during the second safety-car period dropped Heidfeld out of the points to ninth.

BMW Sauber was less competitive during qualifying for the Turkish and Monaco GPs as they struggled to generate front-tyre temperature. Fourth after a good start at Istanbul Park, Kubica maintained his title challenge by finishing second in Monaco, outperforming the car's potential in the wet. Heidfeld was fifth in Turkey but failed to progress to Q3 in Monaco, ending a sequence

of 28 consecutive appearances. Heavy damage caused by Fernando Alonso's Renault ruined Heidfeld's race after 13 laps.

A year on from barrel-rolling out of the 2007 Canadian GP, Kubica was quick from opening practice in Montréal. He qualified on the front row and ran second until the leaders pitted behind the safety car after 19 laps. Kubica and Kimi Räikkönen stopped for the red pit-exit light, but Lewis Hamilton crashed into the Ferrari as he accelerated away from his box. That handed the heavy-fuelled Heidfeld the lead before his only pitstop, after which Kubica passed his team-mate and led a BMW Sauber 1–2 to score a first victory for team and driver alike. Leading the drivers' championship, Kubica urged the team to 'give me 100 percent to try to maybe defend it until the last race'. However, Theissen insisted on equal focus for both drivers and Kubica grew increasingly frustrated when BMW Sauber's development resource was diverted to 2009.

They were back behind F1's top two teams at Magny-Cours, where Kubica started and finished fifth with Heidfeld outside the top ten. Having alleviated his front-tyre warm-up issues, Heidfeld was quicker for once when rain fell at Silverstone, finishing second behind the imperious Hamilton. Kubica, who did not set a Q3 time due to a rear-suspension issue, made his first race error of 2008 when he aquaplaned off the track. In Germany, Heidfeld did not make it into Q3 but led for three laps by not pitting behind the safety car and set fastest lap on the way to fourth place; Kubica was only seventh after his tyres degraded.

BMW Sauber had a weekend to forget in Hungary with incorrect tyre pressures contributing to the lack of pace. Heidfeld

Nick Heidfeld, BMW Sauber F1.08 (Italian GP)

was eliminated in Q1 and never recovered; Kubica surpassed the car's limits once more to qualify fourth but faded to eighth as he oversteered to the finish. Podium finishes for Kubica (third in Valencia) and Heidfeld (second at Spa-Francorchamps despite hitting Heikki Kovalainen at the start) signalled a resurgence although the previous consistency had deserted the team. The decision to load Heidfeld's car with fuel before qualifying in Valencia was 'a disaster' and Kubica was restricted to sixth in Belgium by poor car balance and a problem with the fuel rig.

Starting in the midfield at rain-drenched Monza, they used one-stop strategies and timely switching to intermediate tyres to climb the lap charts, Kubica closing to within 14 points of the championship leader by finishing third, with Heidfeld fifth. Kubica then badly harmed his title chances in Singapore because of a stop-go penalty for pitting when the pitlane was closed, while Heidfeld finished sixth after a three-place grid penalty for impeding another car.

The BMW Saubers lacked grip at the final three races as lingering title hopes ended. Starting sixth at Fuji, Kubica seized the lead when Hamilton forced the leaders wide at the first corner but Alonso displaced him at the pitstops, leaving the Pole to finish second after withstanding Räikkönen's challenge; one-stopping Heidfeld was ninth. Their fading competitiveness was illustrated by Kubica failing to make Q3 in China and Brazil. His mathematical title hopes ended when he finished sixth in Shanghai. Brazil marked the first time in 34 races that BMW Sauber did not score a point. Kubica's decision to start on dry tyres proved overly brave and he dropped behind Räikkönen to fourth in the championship on countback. Heidfeld was fifth in Shanghai (despite another grid penalty for impeding) and tenth at Interlagos.

BMW Sauber finished a clear third behind Ferrari and McLaren-Mercedes in the constructors' championship.

ING RENAULT F1 TEAM

Fernando Alonso returned to the team for which he had won back-to-back championships in 2005 and 2006. Renault's stuttering campaign eventually included two wins although success in the inaugural Singapore GP would soon be called into question. The Renault R28 was initially a second off the pace but its impressive development rate was such that it was the third quickest car by the end of the season.

Alonso's relationship with McLaren-Mercedes unravelled during 2007 and he met with Renault team principal Flavio Briatore and executive director of engineering Pat Symonds at the Japanese GP. A 'mutual parting of the ways' with McLaren-Mercedes was announced on 2 November. Rumours of talks with Honda, Toyota and Red Bull followed before his much-anticipated return to Enstone was confirmed on 10 December, with Nelson Piquet Jr's promotion from reserve driver also announced. Lucas di Grassi replaced Piquet with Romain Grosjean and Sakon Yamamoto named as development drivers at the car launch. Dirk de Beer began work as head of aerodynamics in February while a new $50m computational fluid dynamics system came onstream in the autumn.

Alonso was quickest in the old car on his return to a Renault cockpit at Jerez on 15 January, six days before his shakedown of the new R28 at Valencia. The car was presented to the press at Renault's communications headquarters in Boulogne-Billancourt on 29 January. Bob Bell (technical director, chassis), James Allison (deputy technical director), Tim Densham (chief designer) *et al* switched focus to the new car in the summer of 2007, believing the problems of the R27 had been identified. The front end was extensively reworked, with arched low nose integrated with the sculpted front wing that replaced the previous cascade arrangement. This featured an upper 'bridge' element and additional low-slung angular centre. The bottom-front wishbones were mounted directly to the monocoque instead of Renault's trademark vee-keel. The undercut sidepods had unusually curved inlets while weight and aero balance were shifted forwards to optimise rear-tyre wear following a year's experience of the control Bridgestones. Former chief aerodynamicist Dino Toso lost his long battle against cancer on 13 August 2008.

Early races confirmed that the R28 lacked downforce and traction, and Renault had also fallen further behind in the power stakes. While rivals had made performance gains from permitted changes to improve reliability under the engine freeze, Renault had disbanded much of the engine team in Viry-Châtillon so could not respond. Direct comparison between the Adrian Newey-designed Red Bull and Toro Rosso suggested that the Renault RS27-2008 V8 was up to 35bhp shy of Ferrari. That was countered by impressive chassis development in the second half of the campaign.

Alonso only failed to progress to the top-ten shoot-out on three occasions and took opportunities when they arose. He scored points at the opening two races when fourth in Australia and eighth in Malaysia. Piquet's difficult maiden season started at the back when he qualified between the two Super Aguris in Melbourne. Damage from opening-lap skirmishes caused his retirement that day and Piquet was 11th a week later at Sepang. Alonso was only tenth in Bahrain after being hit twice by old nemesis Lewis Hamilton in the opening two laps; Piquet withdrew with gearbox issues.

Lacking aero efficiency and balance thus far, the R28 had its first major upgrade at the Spanish GP and sported a Red Bull-inspired dorsal fin on the engine cover, aerodynamic brake ducts and a new diffuser. Inerters (J-dampers) in revised front suspension optimised tyre contact and were added to the rear suspension for Monaco. Alonso used the new set-up to qualify second in Barcelona while Piquet made Q3 for the first time, but pace did not translate

into points for Alonso's engine failed and Piquet crashed into Sébastien Bourdais's Toro Rosso during the early laps. After sixth place in Turkey, Alonso's overly optimistic move on Nick Heidfeld at Monaco's hairpin failed. Piquet was eliminated in first qualifying at both races and Monaco saw him crash at Ste-Dévote after switching to dry tyres on a wet track.

Alonso qualified fourth in Montréal but crashed again when challenging the eventual second-placed BMW Sauber of Heidfeld, while Piquet retired after terminal brake wear. The Brazilian relieved mounting internal pressure by passing Alonso in France to claim seventh and score his first championship points. Alonso was fuelled for a short opening stint and three-stop strategy that was compromised by a poor start from third on the grid.

They qualified in the top seven at Silverstone and Alonso lay fourth until he lost a couple of late positions when powerless to defend on well-worn wet tyres. Piquet crashed at Abbey after his final pitstop when on course to score more points. Alonso's torrid German GP included incidents aplenty, but Piquet enjoyed his day of days. Opting for a one-stop strategy after another Q1 elimination, the Brazilian benefitted from the safety car shortly after half distance and led for six laps when the two-stoppers refuelled. Track position was key as only Hamilton could pass so Piquet held onto a career-best second place. Fourth (Alonso) and sixth (Piquet) in Hungary after Renault's most competitive weekend so far, both were eliminated in Q2 for the European GP on Valencia's street circuit. Lap one was disastrous as Alonso lost his rear wing when hit by Kazuki Nakajima and Piquet required a new nose after running into David Coulthard. Alonso retired with Piquet consigned to an afternoon outside the top ten.

Alonso returned to form at Spa-Francorchamps by qualifying

Fernando Alonso, Renault R28 (Singapore GP)

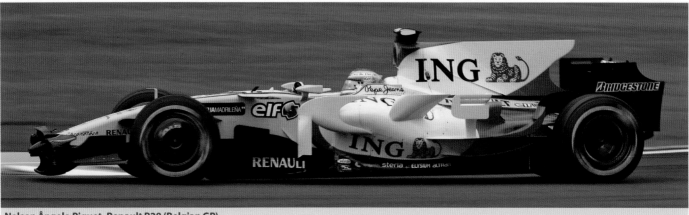
Nelson Ângelo Piquet, Renault R28 (Belgian GP)

sixth and challenging whether wet or dry. He switched to intermediate tyres with just a lap to go and snatched fourth from Sebastian Vettel's Toro Rosso on the line by a scant 0.098sec. Renault expected to be uncompetitive at Monza but an early change to intermediates vaulted one-stopping Alonso into fourth at the finish. Piquet spun out of the Belgian GP at Fagnes after 15 laps and was a lacklustre tenth in Italy.

Renault arrived in Singapore with the future of both drivers in doubt for differing reasons, and the withdrawal of its parent car company a possibility. With a revised front wing and a power boost from new Elf fuel, Alonso showed that the R28 was well-suited to the bumpy streets with quickest times in FP2 and FP3. However, he started only 15th when unable to complete a lap in second qualifying due to a fuel-system issue. Using super-soft tyres for a short 12-lap opening stint, Alonso was well-placed when Piquet triggered the safety car by crashing a lap after the Spaniard's pitstop. Alonso then used the inherent speed shown in free practice and some misfortune for others to take the lead on lap 34 and score an unlikely victory. Outrageous fortune or man-made circumstance? It emerged during 2009 that Piquet had crashed deliberately to hand Alonso his tactical advantage. The result stood but Renault received a suspended ban and both Flavio Briatore and Pat Symonds left F1, albeit to eventually return.

Fourth on the grid for the Japanese GP, Alonso used the McLaren/Ferrari first-corner confusion to emerge in second place. By going a lap further in his first stint than Robert Kubica's leading BMW Sauber, he pounced for his second successive victory with Piquet a strong fourth. That Renault now had the third-quickest car was confirmed in China where Alonso qualified and finished fourth, with eighth-placed Piquet completing another double score that clinched fourth in the constructors' standings. Alonso's second place in the Brazilian rain put him fifth in the drivers' rankings but Piquet spoiled partisan hopes by crashing on the opening lap.

PANASONIC TOYOTA RACING

Rumours of Toyota's imminent withdrawal were dismissed by motorsport president John Howett as 'malicious scaremongering' although pressure from the main board to deliver victory within two years was palpable. Jarno Trulli had a contract for two more seasons and speculation that Toyota would drop him as well as Ralf Schumacher proved false. A two-year deal with GP2 champion Timo Glock was announced in November when the Contract Recognition Board ruled that BMW Sauber did not have prior claim. Kamui Kobayashi replaced Franck Montagny as reserve driver.

Revealed in Cologne on 10 January, the Toyota TF108 was a departure from the Mike Gascoyne-led concept of the previous two seasons. General manager (chassis) Pascal Vasselon and a project team led by John Litjens followed Ferrari's lead by extending the wheelbase to increase stability. With Mark Gillan now leading the aero department for the complete design cycle, the nose was lower with twin-plane front wing underneath a raised 'bridge' element. The sidepods were undercut for the first time with flatter radiators amidst a reconfigured cooling system. Larger bargeboards were moved backwards. The latest V8 engine (RVX-08) was smaller, which allowed the airbox and 'Coke bottle' rear to be more tightly packaged. The four-race seamless-shift gearbox was designed and built in-house following a year collaborating with Williams. The rear wing was centrally supported and the suspension layout from the TF107 was retained, albeit with inerters all round and shallower lower-front wishbone angle. Veteran engineer Frank Dernie joined on a consultancy basis on 29 August 2007, attending selected races and on hand to advise on the 2009 car. The TF108 was a well-balanced improvement on its predecessor, with wider set-up window, more usable downforce, and predictable handling throughout a corner. The car was easy on its tyres although this meant Toyota struggled on conservative tyre compounds.

Quickest on the final day of Barcelona testing (27 February) thanks to a low-fuel glory run, Trulli was a regular in the qualifying top ten during 2008. Sidelined by battery failure in Australia, he was third on the grid in Malaysia when both McLarens were penalised and recovered from a poor start to claim fourth despite Lewis Hamilton's late pressure. Sixth in Bahrain, he finished eighth in Spain after being told to change his undamaged front wing.

Glock did not score a point for the first six races. Grid penalties (for a gearbox change and impeding Fernando Alonso) dropped him to the last row in Australia, where he crashed. Opening-lap contact with Nico Rosberg at Sepang caused terminal rear-

Timo Glock, Toyota TF108 (German GP)

suspension damage. Gearbox issues restricted him to ninth in Bahrain and he rammed David Coulthard's Red Bull during the Spanish GP. Both drivers finished outside the points after disappointing races in Turkey and Monaco.

Neither Toyota made Q3 in Canada, a first for 2008, but both used one-stop strategies to score points, Glock fourth and Trulli sixth. That mini resurgence continued in France where the team mourned the death of original team president Ove Andersson during a historic rally in South Africa. Boosted by new front and rear wings and revised suspension, Trulli qualified fourth and finished third, and dedicated Toyota's first podium for two years to Andersson. Glock faded from sixth at the start with tyre graining.

Toyota reverted to an old rear-wing support when failure caused Trulli's high-speed crash at Stowe corner during practice for the

British GP. Eliminated in Q2 at Silverstone, Trulli gained seven places on the opening lap and snatched seventh from Kazuki Nakajima on the last lap. Twelfth after a couple of grassy moments in England, Glock was hospitalised when he crashed heavily during the German GP. Trulli started that race from fourth but a late mistake on worn tyres cost him points.

They qualified in the top ten in Hungary with fifth-placed Glock ahead. He drove a strong race despite a slow first pitstop and used track position to claim a career-best second place. Seventh in Hungary, Trulli led a Toyota 5–7 at the European GP in Valencia. They were eliminated in Q2 for the Belgian GP and left the Ardennes without adding points to their tally. Trulli's lightning-fast start was to no avail for Sébastien Bourdais crashed into him in the first corner, causing damaged to the Toyota's gearbox and diffuser. Glock

Jarno Trulli, Toyota TF108 (Canadian GP)

finished eighth on the road only to be demoted by a 25sec penalty for ignoring yellow flags. The rain that fell throughout the Italian GP weekend masked Toyota's low-downforce weaknesses. Both started from inside the top ten but fitting full wets at their scheduled stop was a mistake and any chance of points was lost with subsequent changes to intermediate tyres.

The Toyota TF108 did not ride Singapore's bumps well but Glock nevertheless starred, starting seventh and finishing fourth. Having just missed out on Q3, Trulli fuelled for one stop and gained track position when Nelson Piquet Jr triggered the original safety-car period. The Italian led for five laps only to be denied fifth place when his hydraulics failed. They filled row four at Fuji, where Glock's suspension broke over a kerb and Trulli finished fifth. Trulli's Chinese GP effectively ended in the first turn when hit by Bourdais's Toro Rosso once more; Glock stopped once on the way to seventh.

Trulli qualified second at Interlagos but it was Glock who assumed centre stage during the dramatic closing stages of that title decider. He remained on dry tyres despite late rain and entered the final lap 13.144sec ahead of Lewis Hamilton, who needed to overtake to clinch the title. Unable to defend against the wet-shod McLaren as the rain intensified, Glock lost 18.605sec in that final lap with Hamilton snatching the crucial fifth place at the last corner. Trulli was eighth after a mid-race spin.

After its dismal 2007, Toyota finished a much-improved fifth overall with a podium apiece for its drivers. Surely, 2009 would deliver the victories that team and corporation craved?

SCUDERIA TORO ROSSO

Scuderia Toro Rosso and Sebastian Vettel were among the headline stories of 2008. The team that had been Minardi just three seasons earlier won a GP and outscored its better-funded parent outfit, while the youngster emerged as a star of the very near future. However, the tightening of customer-car rules, due in 2010, prompted Dietrich Mateschitz to reconsider why he owned a second team, with sale a real possibility.

Sebastian Vettel, Toro Rosso STR02B-Ferrari (Turkish GP)

Nicolas Todt had arranged for Sébastien Bourdais to test a Toro Rosso STR01-Cosworth at Jerez in December 2006 and the Champ Car star was confirmed as Vettel's 2008 team-mate on 15 August 2007. His Toro Rosso career began at the Barcelona test on 13 November, just two days after clinching his fourth successive Champ Car title for Newman-Haas Racing.

Toro Rosso started 2008 with an updated version of its old car and the fully sorted STR02B's winter promise was confirmed in Melbourne. Vettel qualified ninth in Australia but retired from the first four rounds. He was the victim of first-lap accidents in Australia, Bahrain and Spain, and his hydraulics caught fire in Malaysia. With attrition especially high during the Australian GP, Bourdais lay fourth when his engine let go with three laps remaining, but he was nevertheless classified seventh. He spun on the opening lap in Malaysia, finished 15th in Bahrain and collided with Nelson Piquet Jr on lap seven of the Spanish GP.

With the regular men on the long-hauls, F3 driver Brendon Hartley conducted the straight-line shakedown of the Toro Rosso STR03-Ferrari at Vairano on 2 April. This was essentially Adrian Newey's Red Bull RB4 with Melbourne-spec aerodynamics, a monocoque moulded at Carbo Tech in Salzburg and a Ferrari 056 V8 engine, which required increased cooling ancillaries but provided a handy extra 35bhp. In addition, technical director Giorgio Ascanelli led a development path that redistributed weight rearwards and introduced Toro Rosso's own braking system. Furthermore, the STR03 was transformed by an aero update in France.

The STR02B's final appearance in Turkey saw Bourdais's brakes fail and Vettel finish last after a puncture and four pitstops. The STR03 had been due at that race but a lack of spare parts and Bourdais's Barcelona testing crash on 16 April delayed its appearance to Monaco – never a good place to debut new machinery. Serving a five-place grid drop because the STR03 had a different gearbox from the STR02B's unit he had used to finish the Turkish GP, Vettel climbed from the last row to claim an impressive fifth. Bourdais followed David Coulthard's Red Bull into the barriers at Massenet during the wet opening laps.

Crashes for both drivers curtailed Saturday running in Canada. Vettel started from the pitlane having not run in qualifying and finished eighth thanks to a patient one-stop race while Bourdais finished last. An aero upgrade at Magny-Cours helped both STR03s escape Q1 for the first time although they spent the race in the midfield and finished outside the top ten. Having qualified for Q3 at Silverstone and Hockenheim, Vettel had another first-lap incident (with Coulthard) in Britain but claimed eighth in Germany, beating Fernando Alonso and Jarno Trulli. Bourdais finished both events without threatening the scorers.

Vettel retired in Hungary, where Bourdais was last following a five-place grid penalty (for impeding Nick Heidfeld in first qualifying), a flash fire during his pitstop, and an extra stop to clear extinguishant residue from his visor. That race proved an anomaly, for both drivers progressed to Q3 at the next three races. They started and finished in the same positions at the European GP, Vettel (quickest in second qualifying) sixth and Bourdais tenth. The

Sébastien Bourdais, Toro Rosso STR02B-Ferrari (Malaysian GP)

Frenchman topped the timesheets in Q1 for the Belgian GP and outqualified his team-mate as they filled row five. Bourdais was fifth when it began to rain late in the race but that all changed on the last lap. Vettel took fifth and the gripless Frenchman lost another two positions before the chequered flag.

That double score was the prelude to Toro Rosso's dream weekend at a very wet Monza. Vettel revelled in the conditions to become the youngest driver thus far to start from pole position and to win a GP. Predicting that using intermediate tyres at the start would cause rapid wear and an early stop, Ascanelli light-fuelled Vettel's car for qualifying and committed to a two-stop strategy.

Vettel duly delivered a shock pole and 'a perfect drive from start to finish' according to team principal Franz Tost. Bourdais qualified fourth but lost a lap by stalling on the grid.

Now a regular in the top-ten shoot-out, Vettel continued his fine form with fifth in Singapore and sixth at Fuji. Bourdais starred during that latter race and would have finished ahead of his team-mate in sixth but for a harsh 25sec penalty for impeding Felipe Massa as he left the pits after his second stop. Both qualified in the top ten in China and Brazil. They slipped out of the points in Shanghai, Vettel ninth following a slow pitstop, Bourdais 13th due to a front-wing change after being clipped by Trulli in the first corner.

Sebastian Vettel, Toro Rosso STR03-Ferrari (Italian GP)

Sébastien Bourdais, Toro Rosso STR03-Ferrari (Japanese GP)

At Interlagos, Vettel ran as high as second by changing early to dry tyres and was a factor all day. He passed Lewis Hamilton with three laps to go (which threw the title destiny into doubt) and finished fourth. Bourdais, who hated the STR03's tendency to oversteer, had another altercation with Trulli's Toyota.

Toro Rosso beat the senior Red Bull Racing by ten points to secure sixth overall and Vettel completed a fine first full F1 season with eighth in the drivers' standings.

RED BULL RACING

The Red Bull RB4 and Toro Rosso STR03 were both designed by Red Bull Technology in Milton Keynes and were ostensibly the same car apart from different engines – Renault and Ferrari respectively. Given the budget disparity, that the junior team won a race and beat its parent company in the championship prompted questions about the respective powerplants and added pressure on Red Bull Racing to deliver.

David Coulthard was confirmed as Mark Webber's team-mate for another year on the Friday of the 2007 British GP, with GP2 hopeful Sébastien Buemi named reserve driver in the New Year. Sebastian Vettel made his Red Bull testing debut at Barcelona on 26 February while deputising for Coulthard, who had injured his neck.

The Red Bull RB4-Renault made its track debut at Jerez on 16 January with its 2008 aerodynamic package withheld until later that winter. This was the evolutionary product of the design team that chief technical officer Adrian Newey had assembled since arriving, including Geoff Willis (technical director), Rob Marshall (chief designer) and Peter Prodromou (head of aerodynamics). There was an understandable family resemblance to the RB3, albeit with a stubby nose to optimise the 'bridge' front wing. Suspension was finessed and wheelbase unchanged despite a new monocoque, with packaging under the bodywork much revised to shift weight further forward and protect the rear tyres. The new floor and diffuser rebalanced downforce to the fore while recovering rear-end stability now that traction control was banned. A vertical extension was added to the outer edges of the sidepods at the Spanish GP

and nose-mounted deflectors were introduced in Singapore. The RB3's gearbox had been unreliable so the pinion and final drive in an all-new four-race seven-speed unit were strengthened and cooling improved. Red Bull retained the same engine supplier from year to year for the first time although both power and torque were of concern with the Renault RS27-2008. A pronounced 'shark' or dorsal fin on the airbox at the 1–3 February Barcelona test improved cornering stability and was widely copied by rival teams.

An aerodynamically efficient step forward, the RB4's impressive high-speed balance was offset by disappointing low-speed traction. The Renault engine's power deficit was evidenced by direct comparison with the Toro Rosso-Ferrari, prompting tension between Red Bull Racing and its engine supplier. Over the season, Webber enhanced his reputation and won the internal qualifying battle 16–2. Coulthard scored the team's only podium – third in Canada – but his final year in F1 brought uncharacteristic incidents with other cars.

Willis was tasked with improving reliability and this bore fruit during testing, so it was disappointing when both drivers had issues at the Australian GP. Denied the opportunity of joining Coulthard in Q3 by a brake-disc failure, Webber was eliminated in a first-lap incident, while Coulthard was taken out of tenth place by an overly optimistic Felipe Massa. Red Bull's woes continued during practice in Malaysia where suspension failure caused Coulthard to crash and Webber's engine failed, although the Australian started sixth and claimed successive seventh-place finishes at that race and the next.

Ninth in Malaysia, Coulthard's difficult start continued with Q1 eliminations and race incidents in Bahrain and Spain. In Bahrain, a first-lap clash with Adrian Sutil's Force India punctured a tyre, and a new nose was required 19 laps later following a tangle with Jenson Button. Contact with Sutil and Timo Glock at successive corners on the opening lap at Barcelona forced another unscheduled tyre change. Webber's points-scoring run continued with fifth in Spain and seventh in Turkey. Both drivers had started within the top ten at that latter race, where Coulthard finished ninth and noted: 'I've looked around my car and there's no damage, so at least we finished a race without colliding with anyone.'

Webber inherited fourth in Monaco when Kimi Räikkönen ran into Sutil in the closing stages. Coulthard was fast enough to progress to Q3 but crashed at the chicane later in the second session, then hit the barrier at Massenet after seven laps of the race. It was Webber's turn to shunt at the end of Q2 in Canada, where Coulthard used a heavy fuel load and one-stop strategy to score an unexpected third place thanks to a timely safety car. Webber led a qualifying 6–7 in France and finished sixth despite brake issues. Ninth in France but outpaced by his team-mate thus far, Coulthard announced on the Thursday before the British GP that he would retire from F1 at the end of the season.

Webber qualified second at Silverstone, only for Red Bull hopes to be extinguished within a lap of the race. Coulthard collided with Sebastian Vettel as they avoided a spinning Ferrari. Webber lost control at Chapel and was last by the time he rejoined, then spun again on the way to tenth. That was the first of four successive

Mark Webber, Red Bull RB4-Renault (Hungarian GP)

non-scores as the team lost ground. Webber went out with a punctured oil cooler in Germany and finished ninth in Hungary, having started both races eighth. The European GP at Valencia was the nadir with neither quick enough for the top ten. Coulthard was delayed by incidents with Rubens Barrichello and Nelson Piquet Jr at Hockenheim and Valencia respectively.

Webber ended that slump with eighth at Spa-Francorchamps despite losing three places when Heikki Kovalainen spun him around at the chicane. The potential of Newey's chassis was confirmed at rain-affected Monza when Red Bull and Toro Rosso filled three of the top four grid positions. Unfortunately for the senior team, it was Vettel who dominated throughout. Webber, who qualified third when the rain was at its heaviest, found his race compromised by traffic and a spin, so eighth was scant reward for

outright pace. Coulthard also spun and more positions were lost when he collided with Kazuki Nakajima.

Both cars were called into the pits as soon as Piquet triggered the safety car in Singapore and that tactic should have been rewarded with a double score. Webber was on course to finish second (or better) when his gearbox selected two gears at once, a glitch that was blamed on an electro-magnetic surge from an underground train passing below. Coulthard found himself stacked behind his team-mate at that original stop and dropped from fourth to seventh after trying to leave his second stop with the fuel hose still attached.

In Japan, Coulthard outqualified Webber for the first time since Australia but was tagged by Sébastien Bourdais and Nelson Piquet Jr in the first corner, causing suspension damage that led to a crash in Turn 2; Webber used a one-stop strategy to finish eighth. Webber

David Coulthard, Red Bull RB4-Renault (French GP)

was handed a ten-place grid penalty for the Chinese GP after using one engine too many for the season. The cars carried white Wings For Life charity livery for the final round in Brazil. Tenth in China, Coulthard was knocked out of his last GP by Nico Rosberg in the second corner, while Webber could only finish ninth.

At the end of an increasingly frustrating campaign, Red Bull was seventh in the constructors' standings.

AT&T WILLIAMS

Williams endured its fourth successive season without a victory as it slumped to eighth in the constructors' standings. Nico Rosberg's contract was extended to the end of 2009 amid interest from McLaren-Mercedes and Toyota, with Kazuki Nakajima confirmed for the second seat shortly after his debut at the 2007 Brazilian GP. Narain Karthikeyan was replaced by A1GP star Nico Hülkenberg as test and reserve driver.

'The 2008 car is an evolution of the FW29,' technical director Sam Michael told *Autosport*, 'but almost everything on the car is new. Last year's car was a good base, but we've found further returns both aerodynamically and mechanically.' The FW30 was the first Williams with recently promoted chief designer Ed Wood and head of aerodynamics Jon Tomlinson at the helm. There was continuity of engine supply (Toyota) for the first time in four years. Much of the aerodynamic development was at the back with the diffuser redesigned to interact with the revised suspension to improve stability. The three-piece front wing had a full-width 'bridge' over its lower nose. Its angular central 'spoon' section was replaced by a shallower curve in the low-downforce Spa-Francorchamps and Monza set-ups. The sidepods were lowered with more aero-efficient cooling louvres on the upper surfaces instead of chimneys. These had the T-wing package from the FW29 integrated with the vertical forward extensions from the FW28. Weight was saved despite an extended wheelbase, although more rearward distribution

than most impaired performance at high-speed tracks during an inconsistent campaign. That was accentuated when Williams stopped development in April to concentrate on 2009.

Hülkenberg's shakedown of the FW30 at Valencia's Circuit Ricardo Tormo on 21 January included an 'off' but was deemed successful. Long-run pace was promising although the front wing had to be modified when Nakajima crashed at Barcelona's first corner on 1 February when the mounting failed. When Nakajima topped the time sheets for a day that winter, it raised hopes of being 'best of the rest' behind Ferrari and McLaren-Mercedes. Confirmation of that potential at the first race proved a false dawn although Rosberg did star on a couple of notable occasions.

Gearbox issues hindered progress during practice for the Australian GP, but Rosberg qualified seventh, initially ran fourth and finished third to score his first F1 podium. Nakajima recovered from a front-wing change at the end of lap one and contact with Robert Kubica's BMW Sauber behind the safety car to claim sixth. Malaysia was a disaster for they qualified poorly (Nakajima last when penalised for his Kubica incident) and finished outside the top ten following unscheduled pitstops, Rosberg for a new front wing when he rammed Timo Glock's Toyota on the opening lap and Nakajima to change a punctured tyre. Rosberg made Q3 in Bahrain, starting and finishing eighth, with Nakajima 14th after stalling at the start and spinning on lap two.

Upgrades in Spain included new wings front and rear, and modified suspension. Facing criticism within the team, Nakajima outqualified his team-mate for the first time, albeit having both been eliminated in Q2, and finished seventh. Rosberg made a great start and was ahead of Nakajima when his engine failed. The single upper element of the front wing was separated into three individual sections in Turkey, where Giancarlo Fisichella's Force India eliminated Nakajima at the first corner and Rosberg finished eighth. Rosberg started the next two races from inside the top six only to lose potential podium finishes by hitting rival cars. He lost

Nico Rosberg, Williams FW30-Toyota (Belgian GP)

Kazuki Nakajima, Williams FW30-Toyota (Canadian GP)

his front wing against the back of Fernando Alonso's Renault on the opening lap of the Monaco GP and then crashed in the Swimming Pool section 59 laps later. He was running fourth in Montréal when involved in the pitlane pile-up, for which he also received a ten-place grid penalty in France. Seventh in Monaco despite a slow pitstop, Nakajima crashed in Canada.

Magny-Cours and Silverstone exposed the FW30's high-speed fallibility with the drivers among the backmarkers. Rosberg was even eliminated in first qualifying for the British GP, such was his car's erratic handling. Both spun in the British rain but Nakajima's timely switch to full wets resulted in eighth place despite being passed by Jarno Trulli on the last lap; Rosberg was ninth. They finished the next two races outside the points but Valencia brought improvement. Rosberg made Q3 for the first time in five races and scored his first point since May when eighth. Nakajima lost his front wing in the Turn 1 mêlée after a poor start. The cars were off the pace at Spa-Francorchamps.

Monza marked the 500th race since the formation of Williams Grand Prix Engineering. Rosberg helped the celebrations with fifth on the grid thanks to an excellent low-downforce configuration. However, he switched to full wets rather than intermediate tyres during the race and called in five laps later to redress the situation, dropping out of the points and behind one-stopping Nakajima. The FW30 suited the stop-start nature of Singapore's streets, where both drivers qualified for the top-ten shoot-out for the first time and also scored points. Running on empty, Rosberg had to refuel during the first safety-car period and led for 11 laps before serving his 10sec stop-go penalty for stopping when the pitlane was closed. That denied a shock victory, but Rosberg recovered to finish second with Nakajima eighth.

Williams was not immune from the worsening economic outlook. Royal Bank of Scotland needed a government bailout in October and the Baugur Group, whose Hamley's and mydiamonds. com brands were team partners, entered administration.

The FW30s were back outside the top ten due to the high-speed corners at Fuji and Shanghai. An increasingly frustrating campaign came to a suitably underwhelming conclusion in the Brazilian rain. Both were eliminated in Q1 and hit David Coulthard's Red Bull at the first corner. They continued although 12th (Rosberg) and 17th (Nakajima) was all that could be achieved.

Rather than challenge BMW Sauber for third as had been suggested pre-season, Williams-Toyota slumped to eighth overall.

HONDA RACING F1 TEAM

Honda restructured its senior management after the disastrous 2007 campaign with Ross Brawn announced as team principal on 12 November. 'Brawn now faces a challenge equal to the one he faced when he joined the *Scuderia* [Ferrari] in 1997,' wrote Steve Cooper in *Autosport*, 'to turn a perennial under-achiever into a world champion.' Nick Fry remained as chief executive officer with both reporting to Hiroshi Oshima (managing officer, Honda corporate communications). Keita Muramatsu replaced Yasuhiro Wada as Honda Racing Developments president before the season. Jenson Button had a long-term contract and Rubens Barrichello signed a one-year extension in July. Alexander Wurz replaced Christian Klien as reserve before Christmas, with GP2 hopefuls Luca Filippi and Mike Conway retained as test drivers. Anthony Davidson stood in while Wurz competed at Le Mans.

Brawn and deputy technical director Jörg Zander, who reported to senior technical director Shuhei Nakamoto, arrived after design for the Honda RA108 had been completed. Having first run in plain white at Valencia on 23–24 January, the RA108 and its modified 'Earthdreams' livery were presented at Brackley on 29 January, when Brawn stated: 'We have to get back into a respectable point-scoring position.' Initial plans for the RA108 were in place when head of aerodynamics Loïc Bigois arrived from Williams in the summer of 2006. He reworked what he could, adopting a new concept instead of the flawed aero that had blighted the unloved RA107. Seeking aerodynamic improvement, the chassis was narrowed and the wheelbase extended. The twin-plane front wing was conventional, under a nose that was raised to improve airflow to the floor and bargeboards, which had been moved back. The sidepods had conservative undercuts and T-wings that enclosed the exhaust chimneys. Installation for the RA808E engine was improved with revised airbox and exhausts key to unlocking much-needed extra power. Work on computational fluid dynamics that had been sub-contracted to Adrian Reynard's Advantage CFD consultancy was brought in-house. Chief designer Kevin Taylor left in August 2008, with Zander effectively taking hands-on control for the 2009 car.

The new car was more predictable than its predecessor, but testing suggested it was even less competitive with pronounced oversteer, poor ride over kerbs and inadequate aerodynamic efficiency, plus it had the least powerful engine in the field; only Super Aguri was slower over the winter. However, the definitive Melbourne aerodynamic package introduced at the final Jerez test, including a new floor and engine cover, was suddenly worth a couple of seconds a lap.

The cars qualified in the midfield for the opening three long-haul races, albeit without scoring a point. Button was eliminated on the opening lap of the Australian GP and finished tenth in Malaysia. Barrichello received penalties in Australia (for refuelling during a safety-car period) and at Sepang (speeding in the pitlane), and was disqualified from sixth in Melbourne for exiting the pitlane when the red light was showing. Button made the top-ten qualifying shoot-out for the first time in Bahrain but was delayed on lap one by a puncture and crashed into David Coulthard's Red Bull as he recovered; Barrichello was 11th.

Honda's first major upgrade at the Spanish GP included the latest iteration of the 'Dumbo wings' that had been tried in 2007. Use of new front-wheel fairings was delayed by a race when the brakes overheated. Barrichello was denied points when Giancarlo Fisichella's Force India hit his RA108 in the pitlane so it was Button who claimed sixth.

Barrichello celebrated breaking Riccardo Patrese's record 256 GP starts in Turkey, where the Hondas languished outside the top ten all weekend. The Brazilian's run of 22 races without scoring a point ended with sixth place in Monaco. Eager to exploit the wet conditions on the opening lap, Button passed Barrichello (at the hairpin) and Mark Webber (chicane) before colliding with Nick Heidfeld in the Swimming Pool section. Another incident with Heikki Kovalainen confirmed that this was not to be Button's day. With another season already a write-off, Brawn switched the technical team's focus to the new 2009 regulations.

There were contrasting fortunes in Canada. Loss of power spoiled Button's Q1 while Barrichello made his only Q3 appearance of 2008 and finished seventh. With a heavy fuel load but feeling ill, Barrichello even led for seven laps before his only pitstop; 11th was all Button could salvage from a dismal weekend. Both cars were eliminated in Q1 at Magny-Cours and Silverstone as their lack of development showed. However, correct tyre choices as the weather changed during the British GP delivered the year's highlight. With Button stranded in the Bridge gravel trap after pushing harder than the conditions allowed, Barrichello overcame his own spin and a refuelling issue to take a surprise third.

Respite was brief for they were back among the tailenders at Hockenheim and finished outside the top ten in Hungary (where Barrichello had a refuelling fire) and at Valencia. New rear

Jenson Button, Honda RA108 (Singapore GP)

Rubens Barrichello, Honda RA108 (British GP)

suspension at the Hungarian GP was the last upgrade of the season. The malaise continued at Spa-Francorchamps where the RA108s lacked grip and Barrichello lost gears. Their low-downforce cars were undrivable in the wet at Monza, conditions in which both drivers normally excelled. In Singapore, Barrichello took advantage of the safety car only for his engine to fail; Button finished ninth. Only the Force Indias were slower in qualifying for the Japanese GP, where the Honda men just beat Kazuki Nakajima's delayed Williams. Barrichello, who coped better than Button as the team tumbled down the grid, made it into second qualifying for the final two races but they finished outside the top ten as normal.

This dismal campaign came amidst a worsening economic recession and falling road-car sales. Even so, it was a total shock when the Honda Motor Company announced its immediate F1 withdrawal on 5 December, leaving Ross Brawn and Nick Fry with the winter to secure the team's future under a new identity.

FORCE INDIA FORMULA ONE TEAM

Due diligence into Vijay Mallya's takeover of Spyker was completed on 28 September 2007 with the Silverstone-based team assuming yet another new identity for the new season. 'The Force India name will clearly bring hundreds of millions of Indian fans closer to Formula 1,' said the industrialist. Colin Kolles remained as team principal and Adrian Sutil signed for a second season despite reported interest from Williams and McLaren. Wanting experience to complement Sutil's raw potential, Force India evaluated Vitantonio Liuzzi, Christian Klien, Ralf Schumacher, Franck Montagny and Giancarlo Fisichella. Confirmation came on 10 January of Fisichella's return to the team formerly known as Jordan. Liuzzi was named reserve driver a month later during an ostentatious team launch in Mumbai.

Chief technology officer Mike Gascoyne revised the engineering structure before Christmas with technical director James Key and design director Mark Smith reporting to him, now that Smith had

Giancarlo Fisichella, Force India VJM01-Ferrari (Brazilian GP)

Adrian Sutil, Force India VJM01-Ferrari (Belgian GP)

served his notice with Red Bull Racing. With chief designer John McQuilliam moving to Wirth Research after the 2007 season, Akio Haga and Ian Hall, who returned after three years with Toyota, were named as design project managers for the 2008 and 2009 cars respectively. The refurbishment of the 50 percent wind tunnel in Brackley was completed in the summer of 2007, with additional time booked at the Lola and Aerolab facilities.

Liuzzi gave the Force India VJM01-Ferrari its shakedown at Barcelona on 25 February. This was a development of the recently introduced Spyker F8-VIIB with chassis, conventional seven-speed gearbox and running gear retained. There was a new cooling system, updated aero package (albeit with too much drag) and revised rear suspension (to increase stability). The VJM01 lacked grip and expectations were modest as the focus was already on 2009. Mallya's first season was a difficult experience with Monaco the notable if ultimately disappointing exception.

Australia set the tone with both cars eliminated in first qualifying and retirements from the race. Sutil crashed on Saturday and Fisichella was an innocent victim of the first-corner mêlée. Revised aerodynamics in Malaysia, including shrouded mirrors, failed to arrest the qualifying malaise. Sutil made a great start only for his hydraulics to fail after five laps while 12th-placed Fisichella was lapped at that race and the next. Sutil also finished in Bahrain despite needing a new front wing following his first-lap collision with David Coulthard. Sutil spun on lap one in Spain, where Fisichella finished tenth – Force India's best result of 2008 – despite a pitlane incident with Rubens Barrichello's Honda. Both drivers were involved in first-lap incidents in Turkey with Fisichella out and Sutil delayed.

Rain was the great leveller in Monaco, where Sutil ended an outstanding race in tears. He had climbed into fourth position when the safety car was deployed following a late crash. Unfortunately, with the safety car withdrawn once more, Kimi Räikkönen lost control on the approach to the chicane with ten laps to go and crashed into the unsuspecting German, causing terminal suspension damage and turning 'a dream to a nightmare' for the Force India driver. Fisichella retired from his 200th GP with a 'box full of neutrals'.

The Force Indias retired in Canada – Fisichella having spun – and finished last in France. An aerodynamic and mechanical upgrade at the pre-British GP test included revised sidepods with cooling louvres instead of exhaust chimneys, new diffuser, and a dorsal fin on the airbox. Track time was curtailed when Fisichella hit the wall at Becketts and both drivers crashed during the rain-affected race. They finished on the lead lap in Germany, although Fisichella received a 25sec penalty for unlapping himself behind the safety car.

Force India became the final team to introduce a seamless-shift gearbox when it was used during Friday practice for the Hungarian GP. It was not raced until Valencia because the old units had to complete their four-race cycle. With the quick-shift 'box reliable and worth a couple of tenths a lap, Fisichella finished the European GP in 14th place and Sutil crashed. In Belgium, Sutil was 13th despite a spin and Fisichella's race was compromised when he hit Kazuki Nakajima's gyrating Williams.

Force India escaped Q1 for the first time when Fisichella lined up 12th in Italy, before they filled the back row at the last four races. Fisichella's home race ended in the Parabolica gravel after another incident with Coulthard's Red Bull. Sutil came last after switching to dry tyres for the final ten laps. In Singapore, Fisichella did not pit when Nelson Piquet Jr's crash triggered the safety car, so ran third until stopping in green-flag conditions and completing the race as the last car still circulating; Sutil crashed when avoiding Felipe Massa's spun Ferrari. They retired from the Japanese GP and Sutil's gearbox failed in China. Fisichella finished last in Shanghai and Interlagos, having stalled at his second stop at that latter race. Sutil was 16th in Brazil.

Takuma Satō, Super Aguri SA08-Honda (Bahrain GP)

SUPER AGURI F1

Unpaid sponsorship during 2007 and the forthcoming customer-car ban placed Super Aguri's future at serious risk. The winter of 2007/08 was spent minimising expenditure as Aguri Suzuki tried to find new investment and sought more Honda backing. The uncertain financial outlook delayed confirmation of drivers Takuma Satō and Anthony Davidson as well as the 19 February launch of the Super Aguri SA08-Honda. This was a modified 2007 Honda with roll hoop and gearbox updated to comply with new regulations and more stringent FIA crash testing.

Super Aguri ran a young-driver test on behalf of Honda in November 2007. In an exercise that rekindled the previous year's tensions with Colin Kolles of the renamed Force India team, Andreas Zuber, Mike Conway and Luca Filippi all drove a white Honda RA107 at Barcelona without affecting the works team's permitted 30,000km test allocation. Satō and Davidson completed a combined total of just eight days of winter testing in a Super Aguri SA07B-Honda and their participation in Australia was only announced on the Monday before the race, amid investment talks with Dubai International Capital (DIC) and automotive consultant Martin Leach's Magma Group.

Struggling with little preparation, a shortage of spare parts and inadequate budget, the Super Aguri-Hondas were eliminated in Q1 at the opening four races. In Australia, Davidson was involved in a first-lap skirmish while the fast-starting Satō's transmission failed at half distance. Davidson led lowly double finishes at the next two races when 15th in Malaysia and 16th in Bahrain. Satō ran wide on lap 28 at Sepang and was beaten out of the pits at his second stop by his team-mate at Sakhir.

DIC, which was also in negotiations to buy Liverpool Football Club, withdrew its interest on 16 April and Super Aguri only confirmed it would compete in Spain on the Friday before the race. Satō ran as high as ninth before damaging his nose and finishing last; Davidson's radiator was holed by a stone thrown up by Nelson Piquet Jr's accident. There was to be no reprieve: Suzuki withdrew from the championship and closed his F1 team on 6 May.

Anthony Davidson, Super Aguri SA08-Honda (Malaysian GP)

DRIVER PERFORMANCE

DRIVER	CAR-ENGINE	AUS	MAL	BRN	E	TR	MC	CDN	F	GB	D	H	EU	B	I	SGP	J	PRC	BR
Fernando Alonso	Renault R28	[11] 4	[7] 8	[10] 10	[2] R	[7] 6	[7] 10	[4] R	[3] 8	[6] 6	[5] 11	[7] 4	[12] R	[6] 4	[8] 4	[15] 1	[4] 1	[4] 4	[6] 2
Rubens Barrichello	Honda RA108	[10] DSQ	[14] 13	[12] 11	[11] R	[12] 14	[14] 6	[9] 7	[20] 14	[16] 3	[18] R	[17] 16	[19] 16	[16] R	[16] 17	[18] R	[17] 13	[13] 11	[15] 15
Sébastien Bourdais	Toro Rosso STR02B-Ferrari	[17] 7	[18] R	[15] 15	[16] R	[18] R	—	—	—	—	—	—	—	—	—	—	—	—	—
	Toro Rosso STR03-Ferrari	—	—	—	—	—	[16] R	[18] 13	[14] 17	[13] 11	[15] 12	[19] 18	[10] 10	[9] 7	[4] 18	[17] 12	[10] 10	[8] 13	[9] 14
Jenson Button	Honda RA108	[12] R	[11] 10	[9] R	[13] 6	[13] 11	[11] 11	[20] 11	[16] R	[17] R	[14] 17	[12] 12	[16] 13	[17] 15	[19] 15	[12] 9	[18] 14	[18] 16	[17] 13
David Coulthard	Red Bull RB4-Renault	[8] R	[12] 9	[17] 18	[17] 12	[10] 9	[15] R	[13] 3	[7] 9	[11] R	[10] 13	[13] 11	[17] 17	[14] 11	[13] 16	[14] 7	[11] R	[15] 10	[14] R
Anthony Davidson	Super Aguri SA08-Honda	[22] R	[21] 15	[21] 16	[21] R	—	—	—	—	—	—	—	—	—	—	—	—	—	—
Giancarlo Fisichella	Force India VJM01-Ferrari	[16] R	[17] 12	[18] 12	[19] 10	[19] R	[20] R	[17] R	[17] 18	[19] R	[20] 16	[18] 15	[18] 14	[20] 17	[12] R	[20] 14	[20] R	[20] 17	[19] 18
Timo Glock	Toyota TF108	[19] R	[10] R	[13] 9	[14] 11	[15] 13	[10] 12	[11] 4	[8] 11	[17] 12	[11] R	[3] 2	[13] 7	[13] 9	[9] 11	[7] 4	[8] R	[12] 7	[10] 6
Lewis Hamilton	McLaren MP4-23-Mercedes-Benz	[1] 1	[9] 5	[3] 13	[5] 3	[3] 2	[3] 1	[1] R	[13] 10	[4] 1	[1] 1	[1] 5	[2] 2	[1] 3	[15] 7	[2] 3	[1] 12	[1] 1 FL	[4] 5
Nick Heidfeld	BMW Sauber F1.08	[5] 2	[5] 6 FL	[6] 4	[9] 9	[9] 5	[12] 14	[8] 2	[11] 13	[5] 2	[12] 4 FL	[15] 10	[8] 9	[5] 2	[10] 5	[9] 6	[16] 9	[9] 5	[8] 10
Heikki Kovalainen	McLaren MP4-23-Mercedes-Benz	[3] 5 FL	[8] 3	[5] 5 FL	[6] R	[2] 12	[4] 8	[7] 9	[10] 4	[1] 5	[3] 5	[2] 1	[5] 4	[3] 10	[2] 2	[5] 10	[3] R	[5] R	[5] 7
Robert Kubica	BMW Sauber F1.08	[2] R	[4] 2	[1] 3	[4] 4	[5] 4	[5] 2	[2] 1	[5] 5	[10] R	[7] 7	[4] 8	[3] 3	[8] 6	[11] 3	[4] 11	[6] 2	[11] 6	[13] 11
Felipe Massa	Ferrari F2008	[4] R	[1] R	[2] 1	[3] 2	[1] 1	[1] 3	[6] 5	[2] 1	[9] 13	[2] 3	[3] 17	[1] 1 FL	[2] 1	[6] 6	[1] 13	[5] 7 FL	[3] 2	[1] 1 FL
Kazuki Nakajima	Williams FW30-Toyota	[13] 6	[22] 17	[16] 14	[12] 7	[16] R	[13] 7	[12] R	[15] 15	[15] 8	[16] 14	[16] 13	[11] 15	[19] 14	[18] 12	[10] 8	[14] 15	[17] 12	[16] 17
Nelson Ângelo Piquet	Renault R28	[21] R	[13] 11	[14] R	[10] R	[17] 15	[17] R	[15] R	[9] 7	[7] R	[17] 2	[10] 6	[15] 11	[12] R	[17] 10	[16] R	[12] 4	[10] 8	[11] R
Kimi Räikkönen	Ferrari F2008	[15] 8	[2] 1	[4] 2	[1] 1 FL	[4] 3 FL	[2] 9 FL	[3] R FL	[1] 2 FL	[3] 4 FL	[6] 6	[6] 3 FL	[4] R	[4] 18 FL	[14] 9 FL	[3] 15 FL	[2] 3	[2] 3	[3] 3
Nico Rosberg	Williams FW30-Toyota	[7] 3	[16] 14	[8] 8	[15] R	[11] 8	[6] R	[5] 10	[19] 16	[20] 9	[13] 10	[14] 14	[9] 8	[15] 12	[5] 14	[8] 2	[15] 11	[14] 15	[18] 12
Takuma Satō	Super Aguri SA08-Honda	[20] R	[19] 16	[22] 17	[22] 13	—	—	—	—	—	—	—	—	—	—	—	—	—	—
Adrian Sutil	Force India VJM01-Ferrari	[18] R	[20] R	[20] 19	[20] R	[20] 16	[18] R	[16] R	[18] 19	[18] R	[19] 15	[20] R	[20] R	[18] 13	[20] 19	[19] R	[19] R	[19] R	[20] 16
Jarno Trulli	Toyota TF108	[6] R	[3] 4	[7] 6	[8] 8	[8] 10	[8] 13	[14] 6	[4] 3	[14] 7	[4] 9	[9] 7	[7] 5	[11] 16	[7] 13	[11] R	[7] 5	[7] R	[2] 8
Sebastian Vettel	Toro Rosso STR02B-Ferrari	[9] R	[15] R	[19] R	[18] R	[14] 17	—	—	—	—	—	—	—	—	—	—	—	—	—
	Toro Rosso STR03-Ferrari	—	—	—	—	—	[19] 5	[19] 8	[12] 12	[8] R	[9] 8	[11] R	[6] 6	[10] 5	[1] 1	[6] 5	[9] 6	[6] 9	[7] 4
Mark Webber	Red Bull RB4-Renault	[14] R	[6] 7	[11] 7	[7] 5	[6] 7	[9] 4	[10] 12	[6] 6	[2] 10	[8] R	[8] 9	[14] 12	[7] 8	[3] 8	[13] R	[13] 8	[16] 14	[12] 9

FORMULA 1 RACE WINNERS

ROUND	RACE (CIRCUIT)	DATE	WINNER
1	ING Australian Grand Prix (Albert Park)	Mar 16	Lewis Hamilton (McLaren MP4-23-Mercedes-Benz)
2	Petronas Malaysian Grand Prix (Sepang)	Mar 23	Kimi Räikkönen (Ferrari F2008)
3	Gulf Air Bahrain Grand Prix (Sakhir)	Apr 6	Felipe Massa (Ferrari F2008)
4	Gran Premio de España Telefónica (Catalunya)	Apr 27	Kimi Räikkönen (Ferrari F2008)
5	Petrol Ofisi Turkish Grand Prix (Istanbul Park)	May 11	Felipe Massa (Ferrari F2008)
6	Grand Prix de Monaco (Monte Carlo)	May 25	Lewis Hamilton (McLaren MP4-23-Mercedes-Benz)
7	Grand Prix du Canada (Montréal)	Jun 8	Robert Kubica (BMW Sauber F1.08)
8	Grand Prix de France (Magny-Cours)	Jun 22	Felipe Massa (Ferrari F2008)
9	Santander British Grand Prix (Silverstone)	Jul 6	Lewis Hamilton (McLaren MP4-23-Mercedes-Benz)
10	Grosser Preis Santander von Deutschland (Hockenheim)	Jul 20	Lewis Hamilton (McLaren MP4-23-Mercedes-Benz)
11	ING Magyar Nagydíj (Hungaroring)	Aug 3	Heikki Kovalainen (McLaren MP4-23-Mercedes-Benz)
12	Telefónica Grand Prix of Europe (Valencia)	Aug 24	Felipe Massa (Ferrari F2008)
13	ING Belgian Grand Prix (Spa-Francorchamps)	Sep 7	Felipe Massa (Ferrari F2008)
14	Gran Premio Santander d'Italia (Monza)	Sep 14	Sebastian Vettel (Toro Rosso STR03-Ferrari)
15	Singtel Singapore Grand Prix (Marina Bay)	Sep 28	Fernando Alonso (Renault R28)
16	Fuji Television Japanese Grand Prix (Fuji)	Oct 12	Fernando Alonso (Renault R28)
17	Sinopec Chinese Grand Prix (Shanghai)	Oct 19	Lewis Hamilton (McLaren MP4-23-Mercedes-Benz)
18	Grande Prêmio do Brasil (Interlagos)	Nov 2	Felipe Massa (Ferrari F2008)

Lewis Hamilton locks up as he attempts to convert pole into the lead at Fuji Speedway

DRIVERS' CHAMPIONSHIP

	DRIVERS	POINTS
1	Lewis Hamilton	98
2	Felipe Massa	97
3	Kimi Räikkönen	75
4	Robert Kubica	75
5	Fernando Alonso	61
6	Nick Heidfeld	60
7	Heikki Kovalainen	53
8	Sebastian Vettel	35
9	Jarno Trulli	31
10	Timo Glock	25
11	Mark Webber	21
12	Nelson Ângelo Piquet	19
13	Nico Rosberg	17
14	Rubens Barrichello	11
15	Kazuki Nakajima	9
16	David Coulthard	8
17	Sébastien Bourdais	4
18	Jenson Button	3
19	Giancarlo Fisichella	0
20	Adrian Sutil	0
21	Takuma Satō	0
22	Anthony Davidson	0

CONSTRUCTORS' CHAMPIONSHIP

	CONSTRUCTORS	POINTS
1	Ferrari	172
2	McLaren-Mercedes-Benz	151
3	BMW Sauber	135
4	Renault	80
5	Toyota	56
6	Toro Rosso-Ferrari	39
7	Red Bull-Renault	29
8	Williams-Toyota	26
9	Honda	14
10	Force India-Ferrari	0
11	Super Aguri-Honda	0

Jenson Button celebrates becoming World Champion by finishing fifth in Brazil

2009
A FAIRYTALE YEAR FOR BUTTON AND BRAWN

Jenson Button's Brawn-Mercedes leads at the start of the Monaco Grand Prix

The most fundamental rule changes in a quarter of a century reshuffled the F1 pack, with wing dimensions changed to improve overtaking. The front wing increased in width to 1,800mm with six-degree driver-adjustable upper flaps that could be activated twice a lap. The rear wing decreased in width to 750mm and was now level with the top of the airbox. Aerodynamic appendages such as bargeboards, winglets and airbox 'horns' were banned in specific areas of the car. With the front wing the full width of the car, controlling airflow outside the tyres was key.

The so-called double diffuser was crucial to the outcome of the 2009 World Championship. The maximum height of the rear diffuser was reduced to 175mm but Brawn, Williams and

The Brawn diffuser photographed at the Belgian Grand Prix

Toyota exploited wording in the regulations to add a second central diffuser into the crash structure with air channeled through gaps between the two. A protest by Ferrari, Red Bull and Renault at the Australian GP was turned down with the decision confirmed by the FIA Court of Appeal on 15 April, by which time the other seven teams were already working on their own interpretations.

Each driver had eight engines for the season, with a ten-place grid penalty for exceeding that limit. Renault and Honda agitated for the engine freeze to be relaxed so performance could be equalised. Maximum revs were reduced from 19,000 to 18,000rpm. The drive towards a more ecological future included the optional Kinetic Energy Recovery System (KERS), which stored energy lost under braking in batteries or a flywheel, and delivered an extra 80bhp for 6.7 seconds per lap. With KERS adding at least 25kg and prompting some safety concerns, only McLaren-Mercedes, Ferrari, BMW Sauber and Renault raced the system.

Slick tyres were reintroduced for the first time since 1998 but a proposed ban on tyre warmers was cancelled following opposition from the Grand Prix Drivers' Association. Testing was limited to 15,000km with none from the start of the season to the New Year. Wind tunnels were restricted to 60 percent models and a speed of 50 metres per second. F1 factories had to be closed for a total of six weeks during the season, including a summer break after the Hungarian GP. The controversial pitlane closure at the start of a safety-car period was abandoned, with drivers now having to abide

Sebastian Vettel's Red Bull-Renault dominated the inaugural Abu Dhabi Grand Prix as he clinched second in the championship

by a minimum delta time to reach the pits to prevent them speeding past an incident.

The worldwide economic recession and recent withdrawal of three manufacturers hastened the need for cost control. FIA president Max Mosley campaigned for contentious new regulations in 2010, including provision for a £40m budget cap with technical freedoms for teams that chose to adhere. The Formula One Teams' Association objected with only Williams and Force India entering the 2010 championship by the deadline in May. FOTA's remaining members announced the breakaway Grand Prix World Championship on 18 June. Compromise was reached six days later with Mosley not standing for re-election, the budget cap dropped, and cost control managed by FOTA. A new Concorde Agreement (to the end of 2012) was finally signed on 1 August. Jean Todt succeeded Mosley as FIA president on 23 October after defeating 1981 World Rally Champion Ari Vatanen.

Bernie Ecclestone proposed that gold, silver and bronze medals should replace championship points with the title going to the driver with the most race wins. That was met with scepticism by most, but the FIA World Motor Sport Council initially ratified the concept on 17 March, albeit without awarding medals, although that was rescinded.

The Australian GP started at 5pm as part of an extended deal that safeguarded the race until 2015. Half points were awarded in Malaysia after heavy rain forced the race to be abandoned. The Japanese GP was held at a redeveloped Suzuka as part of an agreement to alternate the venue,

although Fuji Speedway gave up its right to host in 2010. Abu Dhabi began its long-term contract as the final round of the year with a race that started in daylight and finished in darkness. The Hermann Tilke-designed circuit featured a spectacular hotel over the track, a pit exit via a tunnel and precious few overtaking opportunities. The French GP lost its place on the calendar eight years after Bernie Ecclestone had said: 'I can't imagine the championship without its oldest and most prestigious race.' Plans for a circuit outside Paris at Disneyland or Flins-sur-Seine went unfulfilled, and it was 2018 before the event returned at Paul Ricard. With the cancellation of the Canadian GP, there was no North American round despite the obvious economic benefits.

FIA presidents future and present, Mohammed Bin Sulayem and Jean Todt

Jenson Button, Brawn BGP001-Mercedes-Benz (Monaco GP)

BRAWN GP FORMULA ONE TEAM

Brawn Grand Prix secured both world championships in its only F1 season – a unique achievement. Jenson Button won six of the opening seven races before better-funded rivals caught up. His struggle with tyre-temperature issues during the summer put his prospects in jeopardy, with Rubens Barrichello challenging his friend and team-mate by winning twice, but then Button rallied at the penultimate race to complete one of the feel-good stories of recent F1 history.

When Honda announced its withdrawal on 5 December 2008, team principal Ross Brawn, chief executive officer Nick Fry and contracted lead driver Button were defiant. Brawn sought to rescue the team and secure engines but the 700-strong workforce had to be placed on three months' notice and testing cancelled while he set about the task. Interest was reported from the likes of Prodrive, Magna Group and Force India before Brawn and Fry acquired the team for £1 in a rescue package that included a substantial dowry from Honda to avoid punitive closure costs. The goodwill up and down the pitlane extended to McLaren helping arrange Mercedes-Benz engines in February. The Honda payment and television money due to the team provided just enough budget to compete in 2009 although there were 270 redundancies and Button agreed to take a pay cut.

Barrichello had been expected to leave after 2008 with Honda chasing Fernando Alonso until he signed for Renault. Bruno Senna and Lucas di Grassi tested at Barcelona in an apparent shoot-out for the second seat, with the former impressing by lapping within three tenths of Button. However, with in-season testing banned

and the late appearance of the new car, Brawn opted for experience when Barrichello was named as Button's team-mate in March. That was initially for the first four races although he stayed for the whole campaign. Jörg Zander began the year as deputy technical director but left on 19 June to form an engineering consultancy. John Owen was project leader for design while head of aerodynamics Loïc Bigois oversaw three separate concept teams in wind tunnels at Brackley, Teddington (Ben Wood leading a group from the defunct Super Aguri Honda 'B' team) and Tochigi.

Development of the recalcitrant Honda RA108 stopped in mid-2008 to maximise opportunities presented by the regulation changes. 'We've got KERS, slick tyres, a different aero package,' mused Ross Brawn about the new challenges in the autumn. 'For sure somebody is going to get it right on the money and a few teams are going to miss the boat.' It was Brawn who was right on the money with the Brawn BGP001-Mercedes (*née* Honda RA109).

Button shook down the BGP001 at Silverstone on 6 March as the takeover was announced. It was immediately obvious that Brawn had stolen a march on its rivals, with Barrichello and Button a second quicker than anyone else at the following week's Barcelona test. Key to this performance was the double diffuser, which radically increased downforce. In the memoir he co-wrote with Ed Gorman, Fry credited junior Honda aerodynamicist Saneyuki Minagawa with the idea.

The full-width front wing featured complex endplates that channelled air around the wheels. The distinctive drooping nose had small turning vanes on either side and a splitter ahead of the floor. Sidepods were set back to create space for small

Rubens Barrichello, Brawn BGP001-Mercedes-Benz (Singapore GP)

bargeboards behind the area where aerodynamic appendages were now banned. The sidepod intakes were relatively small with a pronounced undercut to the fore.

Honda was first to test its KERS, in May 2008, but discarded it. That turned out to be a good decision because KERS proved an expensive and heavy distraction in 2009. Also contributing to the BGP001's success was the switch from Honda's engine to the more powerful Mercedes-Benz FO108W, although the positioning of its crankshaft meant the gearbox and rear suspension had to be raised by 6mm. Only three BGP001s were built.

Such was its testing pace that Brawn Grand Prix went from the edge of extinction to overwhelming pre-season favourites in a fortnight. Plain white bodywork with black and fluorescent yellow trim was evidence of its lack of sponsorship, although a late deal was struck with Richard Branson's Virgin Group. With the cars on the front row in Australia, Button led all the way from pole position. Barrichello, who made a poor start and changed his front wing at the first pitstops following contact with Kimi Räikkönen, moved up from fourth to second after Sebastian Vettel and Robert Kubica collided, finishing 0.807sec behind his team-mate.

Button made a slow getaway from pole in Malaysia so ran third during the opening dry stint. Some searing laps before his pitstop were rewarded with the lead as rain arrived and he was ahead by 22.722sec when the event was red-flagged. Barrichello received a grid penalty for changing his gearbox and was fifth when rain stopped play. Nine days later, on 14 April, the FIA International Court of Appeal upheld the ruling by the Australian GP stewards that the diffusers on the Brawn, Toyota and Williams were legal.

Red Bull dominated in the Shanghai rain, where the Brawn-Mercedes finished third (Button) and fourth (Barrichello) having struggled to generate tyre temperature. Concerns about engine overheating in Bahrain qualifying meant they started fourth (Button) and sixth (Barrichello) but Button took third from Lewis Hamilton on the second lap and passed the Toyotas during the first pitstops to ease to another victory. Barrichello was fifth after three stops and an afternoon spent in traffic. Button snatched pole for the Spanish GP in the dying moments but lost the lead to his team-mate at the start. However, he switched from a three- to a two-stop strategy and headed another 1–2 after Barrichello struggled in his final stint. That result was repeated in Monaco, where Button's only mistake was to park his winning car in the wrong place, which meant he had to run around the track to the royal box.

Red Bull had its own double diffuser in Monaco and the light-fuelled Sebastian Vettel qualified on pole in Turkey. However, Button took advantage of Vettel's opening-lap mistake at Turn 9 and dominated thereafter in what Ross Brawn called 'the most impressive drive I have seen from him'. Button's sixth victory in seven races gave him a 26-point lead over Barrichello, who made another poor start and retired when his gearbox overheated.

It was unfathomable at the time that Button would not win again all year as the struggle to generate tyre temperature in cooler European conditions threatened to derail his title charge. This coincided with a heavy revamp for the Red Bull RB5 at Silverstone that transformed it into the pacesetting machine. The quicker Brawn driver throughout the British GP weekend, Barrichello started second and finished third with Button only sixth.

Barrichello repeated that qualifying performance at the Nürburgring and survived contact with Mark Webber to lead until the first pitstops. However, Brawn switched to three-stop strategies to alleviate the tyre issues that dropped both cars out of contention for victory. Button was fifth with an angry Barrichello sixth having lost more time at his second stop due to an issue with his fuel rig. They struggled in the Hungarian heat with seventh-placed Button complaining that 'the car was very difficult to drive with a lot of rear-tyre graining… our pace is nowhere'.

Brawn-Mercedes returned to form at the European and Italian GPs with Barrichello to the fore. He qualified third at Valencia and used his heavier initial fuel load to jump both McLaren drivers in the pitstops and win by 2.358sec. They qualified on the third row in Italy with enough fuel for the optimum one-stop strategy. The in-form Barrichello dominated once he, and then Button, passed the similarly fuelled Heikki Kovalainen on the opening lap. Barrichello qualified fourth for the intervening Belgian GP, where he recovered from another poor start to finish seventh, after which an oil leak caused a fire. Seventh in Valencia, Button was punted out of the Belgian GP by Romain Grosjean on lap one at Les Combes and completed a Brawn-Mercedes 1–2 at Monza.

Now 16 points ahead, Button was eliminated in second qualifying for the Singapore GP but Barrichello failed to take advantage. Handed a five-place grid penalty for changing his gearbox when he crashed in Q3, Barrichello stalled at his second pitstop so lost fifth position to Button. Both had grid penalties in Japan for failing to slow for yellow flags and finished in the minor points positions, Barrichello seventh just 0.833sec ahead of Button.

Barrichello qualified on pole for the penultimate round at Interlagos and led the opening 20 laps before being jumped by Mark Webber and Robert Kubica in the pits. He dropped to eighth after a late puncture caused by contact when Hamilton passed him. That left Button, who had qualified in a 'disastrous' 14th position, needing fifth place to clinch the drivers' crown with a race to spare. He made incisive early overtaking manoeuvres, including finally passing an obdurate Kamui Kobayashi, to claim that position and the title. Cue his joyous rendition of 'We Are The Champions' as he returned to the pits. Brawn Grand Prix also clinched an unlikely constructors' title that day. More relaxed than for months, the new champion overtook Barrichello on the opening lap of the Abu Dhabi GP as they finished third and fourth behind the Red Bulls.

RED BULL RACING

Red Bull Racing enjoyed its breakthrough campaign in 2009 with six victories and second in both the drivers' and constructors' championships. Adrian Newey took the opportunity of new rules to make a significant step forward and only the FIA ruling in favour of the Brawn-Mercedes double diffuser prevented title success. The beautifully crafted Red Bull RB5-Renault was modified once that decision was confirmed in the FIA International Court of Appeal and ended the year as the class of the field.

Having signed a one-year contract extension before the 2008 British GP, Mark Webber had his winter preparations interrupted for nearly three months by a broken right leg sustained in a charity cycling event in Tasmania on 22 November when an oncoming car hit him. Sebastian Vettel was promoted from Scuderia Toro Rosso to replace David Coulthard, who retired from F1. Five-time

Sebastian Vettel, Red Bull RB5-Renault (Chinese GP)

Mark Webber, Red Bull RB5-Renault (Belgian GP)

World Rally Champion Sébastien Loeb impressed when he tested at Barcelona on 17 November 2008 but did not take it further. Head of race engineering Paul Monaghan assumed a wide-ranging role that included liaising with the FIA on regulatory matters, with Ian Morgan appointed head of race and test engineering. During Webber's enforced absence, Red Bull juniors Brendon Hartley and Sébastien Buemi joined Vettel in testing.

Red Bull shared its reserve driver with Toro Rosso during 2009 with Hartley named before the season. However, Coulthard replaced him at the first four races while his super licence was approved. The New Zealander's tenure only lasted four races before another junior, Jaime Alguersuari, replaced him at the Nürburgring. Coulthard was placed on standby once more when the Spanish youngster was promoted to the Toro Rosso race seat in Hungary.

Introduction of the RB5-Renault was delayed until 9 February – two days before Webber returned to the cockpit – to give Adrian Newey as much time as possible to interpret the regulations. His solution was unique with a return to pullrod rear suspension after a 22-year absence. The scalloped nose had raised outer edges to meet the required height dimensions, under which the intricate front wing had a cambered and adjustable upper element with endplates that channelled air around the wheels. Bargeboards and turning veins guided air to undercut sidepods that fell away to a very low rear. The dorsal fin on the engine cover was retained. The rear-suspension configuration allowed the gearbox to be lowered by 15mm and space created by the revised diffuser dimensions to be exploited. That lowered the centre of gravity and improved airflow to the narrow 'Coke bottle' rear, aerodynamic upper wishbones, beam wing and into the single diffuser. Red Bull benefitted from the FIA's decision to allow Renault to unfreeze its engine specification to equalise performance. The team abandoned development of its KERS system during the winter.

Vettel set the testing pace at Jerez, until everyone was blown away by the Brawn-Mercedes. That the RB5 was the second quickest car was confirmed by Vettel starting third at the opening two races. Webber lost his front wing at the first corner in Australia and was

the last runner still circulating at the finish. Vettel held second until three laps from the end when, slowed by overly worn tyres, he did not yield to Robert Kubica in Turn 3 and slid into the BMW Sauber, damaging both cars. They continued for another two corners before both crashed simultaneously. Vettel continued once more despite the front-left wheel hanging off his car, for which the team was fined $50,000 and the driver penalised ten grid positions in Malaysia. Webber was sixth in the Malaysian monsoon but Vettel spun out.

Newey was not present to witness the team's breakthrough victory in China for he was hard at work developing Red Bull's double diffuser. Vettel led a qualifying 1–3 and dominated when it rained on Sunday despite being rear-ended by Sébastien Buemi's Toro Rosso behind the safety car. Webber recovered from a spin to pass Jenson Button and claim second. Webber's Bahrain GP was ruined when he was impeded by Adrian Sutil and therefore eliminated in Q1. Vettel spent the first stint trapped behind Lewis Hamilton's KERS-equipped McLaren-Mercedes after dropping from third to fifth at the start. He jumped Jarno Trulli's Toyota at the second stops and was 7.187sec behind Button's winning Brawn-Mercedes by the finish. Vettel qualified second in Spain but again fell behind a KERS-equipped car (Felipe Massa's Ferrari) at the start and so could not challenge the Brawn-Mercedes duo. Webber passed Fernando Alonso on the opening lap and beat Vettel into third place thanks to a long middle stint.

Red Bull's double diffuser was ready for Monaco although this upgrade was compromised by the RB5's unique rear-suspension layout. Vettel started fourth but crashed at Ste-Dévote after 15 laps while Webber enjoyed a strong run to fifth. That Red Bull had taken a step forward was confirmed in Turkey when Vettel snatched pole position, albeit with a light fuel load. His Turn 9 mistake on the opening lap ceded track position to Button and he dropped behind second-placed Webber when he switched to a three-stop strategy.

There was a major overhaul for the British GP with the axle line moved rearward in relation to the engine, gearbox and chassis. That eased load on the rear tyres (wear had been an issue thus far) and created space to optimise the double diffuser. The nose was raised and a new engine cover worked in concert with the rear aerodynamics in what was a B-spec redesign in all but name. The result was a crushing display at Silverstone, where Vettel dominated from pole with Webber second, and the leading Brawn-Mercedes 41.175sec behind. There was a surprise departure amid that success for technical director Geoff Willis left with immediate effect before the German GP.

Red Bull-Renault's newfound status as pacesetters was reinforced at the Nürburgring where Webber claimed a dominant first pole position. He was slow away from the line and jinked right into Rubens Barrichello's Brawn-Mercedes on the run to Turn 1 before clipping Hamilton's rear tyre. Handed a drive-through penalty for hitting Barrichello, Webber had the pace to recover and cruise to a maiden GP victory at the 130th attempt. Vettel completed Red Bull-Renault's second successive 1–2. Beaten to pole for the Hungarian GP by Alonso's light-fuelled Renault, Vettel damaged his suspension in the first-corner fracas and eventually retired. Webber finished third on a track that exposed the RB5's slow-corner weakness.

The team's title hopes took a hit in Valencia. Vettel had already lost time due to a refuelling issue when his engine failed, while Webber dropped out of the points when engineers had to check that he had received a full tank. The Renault engine's lack of top-end power compared with Mercedes-Benz showed at Spa-Francorchamps and Monza, although Vettel was the quickest driver during the Belgian GP as he recovered from eighth on the grid to finish third, while Webber finished ninth for the second successive weekend following a drive-through penalty for an unsafe release at his first pitstop. They started the Italian GP from the fifth row with the RB5s in ultra-low-downforce trim to boost straight-line speed. Webber tangled with Kubica on the opening lap while Vettel held on to eighth at the finish.

Metal plates were fitted under the gearbox in Singapore to avoid a repeat of Webber's freak 2008 retirement and a new front wing improved slow-corner performance. Denied pole by an untimely red flag, Vettel started second but dropped to fourth when penalised for speeding in the pitlane at his final pitstop. Webber crashed in Turn 1 when his right-front brake disc failed. Vettel maintained his lingering title hopes by dominating the Japanese GP from pole position. Webber crashed at the first Degner curve during Saturday practice and missed qualifying while his car was rebuilt. He started from the pitlane but three pitstops in the opening four laps (to fix a loose headrest and then for a puncture) turned his afternoon into an extended test session.

Vettel's title aspirations effectively ended during first qualifying at Interlagos. Heavy rain before he could set a competitive time meant that he did not progress, after which he climbed from 15th on the grid to fourth at the finish. Webber qualified on the front row and showed that the RB5 was still the class of the field by taking the lead at the first pitstops and controlling proceedings thereafter. Red Bull and Vettel clinched second in their respective championships in Abu Dhabi with his fourth win of the year, while Webber withstood Button's late pressure to complete another Red Bull 1–2.

VODAFONE McLAREN MERCEDES

Lewis Hamilton's title defence was compromised by the engineering resources and development required to achieve that last-gasp success in 2008. McLaren-Mercedes began the year 2.9sec off the pace after drastically miscalculating the downforce that could be generated under the new rules. It was remarkable that the team turned around the fortunes of its recalcitrant MP4-24, at least with Hamilton at the wheel and on circuits where aerodynamic efficiency was not critical.

The McLaren MP4-24-Mercedes was launched at the McLaren Technology Centre on 16 January. Ron Dennis used the occasion to announce that Martin Whitmarsh would replace him as team principal from 1 March. He remained as chairman and chief executive officer of the McLaren Group before officially severing his ties with the F1 team a month later to concentrate on McLaren Automotive. Head of race operations Steve Hallam joined Michael Waltrip's NASCAR team in the close season. Members of Bruce McLaren Motor Racing when it was created for the 1963 Tasman Cup, Teddy Mayer died on 30 January while Tyler Alexander retired two months later.

Reserve driver Pedro de la Rosa gave the MP4-24 its track debut at the new Autódromo Internacional do Algarve near Portimão on the day after its launch. Pat Fry was chief engineer for the MP4-24 within the engineering matrix led by directors Neil Oatley and Paddy Lowe. The front wing's main element was suspended under the nose by twin supports, with two upper planes that cascaded to either side. Sidepods were unusual with less pronounced undercut sides than before to accommodate the KERS, which was the best in the field and was raced at every event except Silverstone. The rear wing had slots above extended and lower endplates. The front-wing endplates initially guided some airflow inside the front wheels, leading to high-speed stalling of the conventional single diffuser.

With a dire lack of rear downforce and aero stability, respectable times at the first Jerez test were only achieved by using a wide 2008-specification rear wing. Pre-season was spent testing new parts – floor, wings and bodywork – as the team tried to make the aerodynamics work in unison and claw back its deficit to the pacesetters. The pessimism was confirmed during qualifying for the Australian GP when the MP4-24s brought up the rear in second qualifying, with Hamilton beginning his title defence from 18th on the grid due to a five-place penalty after gearbox failure prevented him from setting a Q2 time. His fastest race lap was 1.314sec off the pace but he drove a steady race and inherited third when Jarno Trulli was penalised for overtaking him behind the safety car.

The Hamilton/Trulli safety-car incident dominated the build-up to the following week's Malaysian GP. Hamilton and sporting director Dave Ryan originally denied that the McLaren driver had been instructed to let Trulli past and this was reiterated when the stewards reinvestigated at Sepang on the Thursday. After the submission of further evidence, however, an apologetic and emotional Hamilton was excluded from the Australian results a day later for misleading the stewards. Ryan left the team he had joined in 1974 two days after the Malaysian GP and McLaren received a

Lewis Hamilton, McLaren MP4-24-Mercedes-Benz (Hungarian GP)

suspended three-race ban when it appeared before the World Motor Sport Council on 29 April.

Heikki Kovalainen retired from the opening two races without completing a lap, in Australia because he was involved in the first-corner altercation between Mark Webber and Rubens Barrichello and in Malaysia through spinning out. Hamilton ended his troubled Malaysian weekend with seventh place. An interim new floor was fitted for the Chinese GP with raised central diffuser. Hamilton qualified for the top-ten shoot-out at that race and the next as slow progress was made. During the Shanghai downpour he had several off-track excursions, the last of which handed Kovalainen fifth place. Bahrain masked the MP4-24's issues and Hamilton finished fourth.

The Spanish GP upgrade included new front wing, floor and double diffuser. However, the diffuser continued to stall in fast corners. McLaren-Mercedes did not score a point for four races although Kovalainen did qualify seventh in Monaco, where the slow corners reduced the aero deficiencies. He had gearbox issues in Spain, crashed in the Swimming Pool section in Monaco and broke his rear suspension at Silverstone in a clash with Sébastien Bourdais. Ninth in Spain, Hamilton was eliminated in first qualifying at Monaco, Istanbul and Silverstone, such was McLaren's plight.

Matters improved with an aerodynamic overhaul on Hamilton's car at the Nürburgring. New front-wing endplates guided air outside the wheels while the sidepods were wider at the rear, reducing the 'Coke bottle' but allowing for better radiator exits. The rear bodywork was redesigned and the bottom diffuser lowered to increase the area for the upper deck. That transformed

the previously under-performing machines, with both MP4-24s qualifying on the third row. Hamilton leapt from fifth to challenge Barrichello and Webber for the lead into Turn 1, but the Australian's front wing clipped his right-rear tyre and caused a puncture that ruined his afternoon. Kovalainen finished eighth on a much-improved showing for the team.

The competitive turnaround was completed at the slow-speed Hungaroring. Hamilton started fourth and used KERS to pass Webber for second on the fifth lap before taking the lead when Fernando Alonso pitted seven laps later. The reigning champion was untroubled thereafter and Kovalainen completed a notable day by finishing fifth. As a one-off at the European GP, Hamilton used a chassis with shorter wheelbase (by 7.5cm) and redistributed weight to claim pole, with Kovalainen second in the standard MP4-24. Hamilton led until a slow final pitstop, when the mechanics, expecting Kovalainen, did not have his tyres ready, leaving him second with his team-mate fourth.

The long-radius corners at Spa-Francorchamps showed that the MP4-24's high-speed issues remained. Both cars were eliminated in second qualifying and Hamilton was knocked out of the race on the opening lap at Les Combes by Jaime Alguersuari's Toro Rosso. Hamilton led a qualifying 1–4 at Monza and was lying third when he crashed at the first Lesmo corner on the last lap. Fourth in Valencia and sixth at Spa-Francorchamps, Kovalainen was the best-placed driver on the preferable one-stop strategy at Monza, so it was a disappointment when he faded to sixth during a lacklustre race.

McLaren-Mercedes's final upgrade in Singapore included a

Heikki Kovalainen, McLaren MP4-24-Mercedes-Benz (Brazilian GP)

new front wing and undertray. A KERS issue on Friday forced the mechanics to work overnight to rectify Hamilton's car and he repaid their effort with a dominant pole-to-flag victory, with Kovalainen seventh. Hamilton qualified and finished third at Suzuka despite his KERS not working for half the race and a gearbox malfunction at his second pitstop. Kovalainen needed a new gearbox when he crashed in final qualifying at Suzuka's second Degner corner and he lost any hope of points by clashing with Adrian Sutil at the chicane on lap 14.

Neither driver made it through Q1 at Interlagos, where Hamilton stormed through the field to third having pitted once. Kovalainen had an incident-filled race from a first-lap spin (caused by Sebastian Vettel) to leaving his pitstop with the fuel hose still attached, the incident splashing Kimi Räikkönen's Ferrari with fuel that briefly caught fire. Hamilton dominated qualifying in Abu Dhabi before a problem with the right-rear brake slowed and then stopped him. A gearbox issue in Q2 and loss of KERS during the race handicapped Kovalainen's last outing for the team.

Given the team's poor performance before Germany, it was some recovery to reach third in the constructors' standings, with Hamilton twice a winner and fifth overall.

SCUDERIA FERRARI MARLBORO

Ferrari won just once in its worst campaign since 1993. Company president Luca di Montezemolo highlighted three reasons for that predicament. Firstly, 'grey rules with different interpretations… Second is KERS, introduced to have a link between F1 and advanced research for road cars. We have done it immediately even if it meant a lot of money and problems with safety and reliability… The last reason is that we started the new car late and I feel that inside the team there has been a little bit too much of a presumptuous approach.' The overly conservative Ferrari F60 lacked the grip of its double-diffuser rivals, and its KERS was not as good as the Mercedes-Benz version. Furthermore, Felipe Massa sustained serious injury and the occasional strategic errors remained.

Kimi Räikkönen eschewed talk of retirement by extending his contract to the end of 2010, although that would prove to be a costly

decision for the Scuderia, while Massa was committed for 2009. Test drivers Marc Gené and Luca Badoer re-signed in September and started testing a Ferrari F2008 with wings set to replicate expected downforce levels once track activity resumed in November.

The Ferrari F60 was the first new car to be revealed when it ran at Mugello on 12 January, with its designation marking 60 years since the first Ferrari F1 car. The KERS, which was developed in conjunction with Magneti Marelli, had its storage battery under the fuel tank, giving a raised centre of gravity when the tank was full. The wheelbase remained long with shorter sidepods to create space for small bargeboards, while the mirrors doubled as turning vanes. The exhausts were exposed at launch, but these were covered in revised sidepods by the end of testing. The front wing and rear diffuser were conventional although development of the twin-deck version began as soon as it became clear that these would be declared legal. The gearbox casing was wider and lower than before, limiting the area available for the double diffuser once it was developed. Ferrari sacrificed development of the F60 and turned its attention to 2010 when it decided not to alter the gearbox. The F60 was extremely kind on its tyres but not good at generating front-tyre temperature, which hindered single-lap performance and did not suit Räikkönen's driving style.

There had been stability at the top of Aldo Costa's technical team during design and build of the F60, with Nikolas Tombazis, John Iley and Gilles Simon leading the design, aerodynamics and engine/electronics groups. However, Iley left in the summer and Simon was replaced by Luca Marmorini in October. Chris Dyer was promoted to chief race engineer with Andrea Stella now engineering Räikkönen's car and Rob Smedley continuing to work with Massa.

Four days' testing at a damp Mugello followed the launch with favourable initial impressions before two of the days in Bahrain were lost to sandstorms. There were reliability concerns about the new systems and the F60 was a second slower than the Brawn-Mercedes when they ran together at Barcelona in March. Ferrari was one of those to protest the double diffusers in Australia, although that was rejected by the FIA International Court of Appeal on 15 April.

Massa and Räikkönen started the Australian GP from sixth and

Felipe Massa, Ferrari F60 (German GP)

seventh on the grid respectively, with Massa initially third before experiencing excessive tyre wear and an upright/suspension issue. Räikkönen was set to finish in that position until he damaged his front wing against the Turn 7 wall. Delayed by the subsequent pitstop, his differential failed with three laps to go. Massa was sitting in the garage as others went quicker and eliminated him from first qualifying in Malaysia. Still on course to score points, he pitted for full wets a lap before the red flag. Räikkönen inexplicably switched to wet tyres while the track was still dry and they were worn out by the time rain did arrive to prompt the red flag.

Ferrari restructured its trackside operations in response to the Malaysian errors and its worst start to a campaign since 1992. Sporting director Luca Baldisserri was redeployed in a factory role with Dyer also covering that brief. KERS was disabled for the Chinese

GP as they failed to score once more: Massa, who made a mistake in Q2, lost a podium finish when his electrics failed behind the safety car, while Räikkönen finished in an anonymous tenth position. The Finn finally ended the non-scoring run with sixth in Bahrain, where Massa had front-wing damage at the start, temperamental KERS and a loss of telemetry.

Major changes for Spain included a lighter chassis (to offset the weight of KERS) and new wings, albeit with compromised double diffuser. This was a step forward with the scarlet cars 1–2 on Saturday morning. Unfortunately, the operational issues remained for Räikkönen repeated Massa's Malaysian Q1 elimination as he sat in the garage. Massa started fourth but faded to sixth when forced to 'lift and coast' due to being short-fuelled at his final stop; Räikkönen's hydraulics failed.

Kimi Räikkönen, Ferrari F60 (Belgian GP)

Giancarlo Fisichella, Ferrari F60 (Abu Dhabi GP)

Ferrari enjoyed its most competitive weekend so far at Monaco, where the rear bodywork and floor were refined with new exhaust exits and improved airflow to the double diffuser. Räikkönen only missed pole position by 0.025sec and finished third despite a slow second pitstop, while Massa set the fastest race lap on his way to fourth. Winner of the past three Turkish races, Massa finished sixth at Istanbul Park while Räikkönen made a poor start and came home ninth. Massa showed the F60's improved pace with fourth place at Silverstone, where the wheelbase was shortened to reduce rear-tyre wear and shift weight forward, and third in Germany; in those races

Räikkönen respectively finished eighth and retired with radiator damage having survived earlier contact with Adrian Sutil.

Ferrari's travails thus far were put into perspective by Massa's serious head injuries at the Hungaroring. He was following Rubens Barrichello during second qualifying when the Brawn-Mercedes lost a spring that pierced Massa's helmet and fractured his skull. He was released from hospital in Budapest nine days later but missed the rest of the season. The race saw Räikkönen make an aggressive start and raise morale by finishing second after his best performance of the season so far.

Ferrari asked Michael Schumacher to replace Massa for the rest of the season and the 40-year-old tested a Ferrari F2007 at Mugello on 31 July, but neck injuries from a motorcycle racing accident in February precluded any comeback and Badoer stepped in. Having not started an F1 race since 1999 or even tested during the current season, Badoer was hopelessly off the pace at the European and Belgian GPs, qualifying and finishing last. He was 2.570sec slower than Räikkönen in Q1 in Valencia, where his race included a spin and drive-through penalty. He crashed during first qualifying at Spa-Francorchamps, where his deficit to his team-mate fell to 1.378sec. Third in Valencia, Räikkönen took full advantage of KERS on the long straights and fast corners in Belgium, jumping from sixth to second at the start, passing surprise pole-sitter Giancarlo Fisichella's Force India on the Kemmel straight after an early restart, and maintaining his narrow lead to the finish. By scoring his fourth Belgian GP victory by 0.939sec, Räikkönen broke Ferrari's winless 2009 streak.

Thrust into the limelight by his Belgian performance, Fisichella

Luca Badoer, Ferrari F60 (Belgian GP)

Jarno Trulli, Toyota TF109 (Spanish GP)

replaced Badoer for the rest of the season, although those five races proved to be a disappointing footnote to his F1 career. Ninth on debut at Monza was his best result as he finished on each occasion without threatening to score points. He did not qualify in the top ten during that time and was eliminated in first qualifying in Singapore, Japan, Brazil (having spun) and Abu Dhabi.

In contrast, Räikkönen's rich vein of form continued at Monza just as the *Scuderia* was negotiating to pay off his 2010 contract to accommodate Fernando Alonso. He qualified third, lost that position when he stalled in the pits but regained it when Lewis Hamilton crashed on the last lap. Räikkönen was uncompetitive in Singapore, where the F60 displayed its slow-speed shortcomings, but finished fourth at Suzuka and sixth in Brazil, despite changing his front wing when clipped by Mark Webber on the opening lap. An uncompetitive 11th on the grid in Abu Dhabi and 12th in the race rounded off Räikkönen's first Ferrari career.

PANASONIC TOYOTA RACING

Faced with posting its first-ever annual loss in March 2009, Toyota considered following Honda out of F1 before the corporation's chief executive officer, Katsuake Watanabe, confirmed its continued participation on 23 December amid the need to cut costs. That included the 15 January launch of the Toyota TF109 being via the internet rather than by invitation, followed by redundancies in the spring. Toyota also terminated Fuji's contract to host the Japanese GP in 2010.

Team manager Richard Cregan accepted a senior role at the new Abu Dhabi circuit before the end of 2008 and respected engine boss Luca Marmorini quit in January 2009 with Kazuo Takeuchi his replacement. Jarno Trulli and Timo Glock entered the final year of their current deals and reserve driver Kamui Kobayashi re-signed. Pascal Vasselon continued to run the chassis department with Mark Gillan as head of aerodynamics. There were subtle management changes before the British GP as withdrawal remained a very real possibility. Team principal Tadashi Yamashina relocated from Cologne to the Japanese headquarters.

The Toyota TF109 first ran at the Autódromo Internacional do Algarve on 18 January with Kobayashi entrusted with its shakedown. Toyota's KERS was not raced despite the company's commitment to hybrid technology in its road cars. Toyota was one of three teams to base its design around the controversial double diffuser, with the tallest central section of all. The car had a high nose with well-aligned front wing suspended by angled supports with endplates configured to guide air around the front wheels. The sidepods were even more undercut than had first been seen on the TF108. The lower-front wishbones had high mounting points that compromised low-speed traction.

The combination of no KERS and a double diffuser meant that Toyota showed early-season promise, however, initial race-winning pace was followed by a mid-season malaise as too many upgrades failed to work as predicted. Podium finishes in Singapore and Japan did not save the season or the team.

Toyota was busy with the Australian scrutineers at the opening race of the season. Not only were the double diffusers protested, but both cars were excluded from qualifying due to flexing rear wings. Trulli finished third to confirm winter testing pace only to be handed a 25sec penalty for overtaking Lewis Hamilton behind the late safety car. That decision was overturned before the next race and Hamilton was disqualified when he and his sporting director were found to have misled the stewards. Glock was fourth in Australia (fifth on the road) after narrowly avoiding Fernando Alonso's Renault when he momentarily lost control. Trulli led a qualifying 2–3 in Malaysia although Glock lost places off the line and was trapped behind the KERS-boosted Alonso. Toyota's decision to switch the German onto intermediates when most chose full wets proved inspired and at times he lapped 15 seconds quicker than anyone else. Having then switched to full wets himself, he passed Nick Heidfeld for second place moments before the race was red-flagged. The result was declared at the end of lap 31 with Glock classified third and Trulli fourth.

Briefly second in the constructors' standings, Toyota scored two more points when it rained in China. Following a mistake in second qualifying and a gearbox change, Glock started from the pitlane and finished seventh despite an incident with Heidfeld. Disappointed to only qualify sixth, Trulli's race ended when Robert Kubica's BMW Sauber crashed over him in the murk. Qualifying for the Bahrain GP confirmed the TF109's early pace for Trulli led a front-row lock-out, albeit on low fuel. Glock made the better start to lead a Toyota 1–2 until pitting, when switching to the slower medium rubber proved an error. Trulli managed to hold onto third position by the finish with Glock only seventh.

New wings front and rear for the Spanish GP made the car less stable and were ditched, so Toyota struggled at that race and the next. Trulli crashed into Nico Rosberg and Adrian Sutil at the start of the Spanish GP, and both cars were eliminated in first qualifying at Monaco when unable to generate tyre temperature. An upgrade for Turkey included an expanded central section to the diffuser as the team tried to regain performance. Trulli qualified fifth and finished a strong fourth despite locking brakes. Glock salvaged eighth from a weekend in the midfield.

After taking seventh (Trulli) and ninth (Glock) at Silverstone, an upgrade for the German GP did not solve the tyre warm-up issues that ruined qualifying at that race and the next. Penalised for impeding Alonso in Q1 at the Nürburgring, Glock used a one-stop strategy to come from the pitlane to finish ninth. Trulli spent his afternoon at the back after an early pitstop for a new front wing. They were eliminated in second qualifying for the Hungarian GP before adopting long opening stints to score points, Glock sixth and Trulli eighth. Glock set the fastest race lap in Valencia thanks to a short final stint on super-soft tyres. He had already been delayed by a first-lap incident with Sébastien Buemi, and neither Toyota troubled the top ten.

Trulli qualified on the front row at Spa-Francorchamps and was well-placed due to his heavy fuel load. However, a slow start effectively ruined his podium chances for he damaged his front

Timo Glock, Toyota TF109 (British GP)

Kamui Kobayashi, Toyota TF109 (Abu Dhabi GP)

wing in the first-corner concertina and was running last when his brakeless car was retired; a refuelling issue denied Glock points. Lacking power and off the pace at Monza, the cars received new front and rear wings in Singapore as part of a final upgrade and Glock finished a merited second.

Kamui Kobayashi replaced Glock on Friday at Suzuka due to illness. The German returned for qualifying but crashed at the final corner during Q2 and was ruled out of the race due to leg and back injuries. Trulli bounced back from his sub-standard Singapore GP by qualifying and finishing second in Japan. Trulli's opening-lap attempt to drive around the outside of Adrian Sutil in Brazil went wrong when he lost control and crashed into the Force India. The Italian berated his rival by the side of the track and was fined for his actions. Kobayashi replaced Glock at the final two races and finished both. Ninth on debut following a robust battle with Kazuki Nakajima, he made his one-stop strategy at Abu Dhabi work to lead a Toyota 6–7 at the finish.

Toyota's F1 future had been in doubt all year and planning for 2010 was placed on hold until a board meeting in November to sign off its budget. Team president John Howett had been critical of the drivers and there was interest in signing Kimi Räikkönen with Kobayashi expected to remain as his team-mate. However, Yamashina announced the immediate closure of Toyota's F1 operation at an emotional press conference in Tokyo on 4 November. The Japanese giant left the sport after eight seasons without the victory it desired.

BMW SAUBER F1 TEAM

The global economic downturn had far-reaching effects up and down the pitlane with the independents in danger and major manufacturers under pressure. BMW motorsport director Mario Theissen told *Autosport* in May 2008: 'There is definitely more pressure from the board. We have reduced our powertrain budget and the budget cap will limit chassis development.' Crédit Suisse ended its association with the team it had once co-owned due to difficulties in the banking sector.

Technical director Willy Rampf scaled back by becoming technical co-ordinator on 1 November 2008. Managing

director Walter Riedl assumed his managerial and production responsibilities while Rampf retained his on-track role and leadership of vehicle concept. BMW Sauber exercised its option on Robert Kubica for 2009 and confirmed Nick Heidfeld's continued stay in October. Christian Klien's first test of KERS at Jerez on 22 July 2008 was marred when a mechanic was knocked over by an electric shock when he touched the car.

BMW Sauber's preparations for the regulation changes had been extensive, as Riedl explained at launch: 'We started last February, took in a lot of tests, built two interim cars… I think we are prepared.' Having stopped developing the 2008 car mid-season, BMW Sauber concentrated exclusively on its 2009 aerodynamics once testing resumed on 17 November. Use of the KERS, which was air-cooled and fitted with a superconductor, depended on circuit and driver, for the taller Kubica was particularly penalised by the extra weight. As BMW had been vehemently opposed to KERS being postponed until 2010, the team's abandonment of it – due to aerodynamic compromise and its extra 25–30kg outweighing any performance advantage – after just four races was a surprise.

The new F1.09 first turned a wheel at Valencia's Circuit Ricardo Tormo on 20 January. With the ancillary horn and antler wings of the F1.08 banned, there were turning vanes under the flat nose, rudimentary box-like front-wing endplates and distinctive sidepods without cooling chimneys or louvres. The space occupied by KERS and its ancillaries reduced the sidepod undercuts. Its suspension, gearbox housing and driveshaft were all modified to withstand the increased grip expected from slick tyres. The rear wing was centrally supported with large, simplified endplates, with a single diffuser under the beam wing and crash structure. Theissen again reiterated the aim of challenging for the World Championship, as had been stated every year since BMW's acquisition of Sauber. There was some promise at the start of the campaign, but the metronomic progress enjoyed since 2006 came to a sudden halt.

BMW Sauber split its KERS strategy at the start of the season and only Heidfeld raced with the system. In Australia, Kubica qualified fourth and, benefitting from being on the faster medium tyre at the time, closed to within five seconds of the leader with three laps to go, but when he went to pass the second-placed Red Bull of Sebastian Vettel around the outside of Turn 3 the two cars

Robert Kubica, BMW Sauber F1.09 (Bahrain GP)

collided. Both heavily crumpled machines continued only to crash again two corners later, Kubica's hefty shunt caused by his damaged front wing. His engine caught fire on lap two of the Malaysian GP. Heidfeld missed Q3 at both races despite using KERS. Slowed by damage caused in the first-corner incident in Australia, he was second when the Malaysian GP was red-flagged after staying out on worn intermediate tyres when others pitted. They finished outside the top ten in China, where Kubica crashed over Jarno Trulli's Toyota and Heidfeld picked up debris.

Both cars raced with KERS for the first time in Bahrain but remained off the pace. They were eliminated in Q2 and needed new front wings when involved in first-lap incidents. Kubica later collided

with Kazuki Nakajima's Williams-Toyota and spun as they finished at the back. With BMW Sauber's season in danger of unravelling and questions being asked at board level, the Spanish GP upgrade designed to redress the F1.09's lack of downforce included a lighter chassis, revised single diffuser, new wings, and more heavily undercut sidepods now that KERS had been dropped. There was some performance gain as Kubica qualified in the top ten and Heidfeld finished seventh thanks to a long opening stint. Kubica was slowed by an issue with his clutch.

However, they were eliminated in first qualifying in Monaco when unable to generate tyre temperature and did not figure in the race. BMW Sauber's version of the double diffuser was ready

Nick Heidfeld, BMW Sauber F1.09 (Malaysian GP)

for the Turkish GP although the existing gearbox design precluded full exploitation of the concept. Kubica finally scored his first points of 2009 with a hard-earned seventh. Heidfeld was 11th in Monte Carlo and at Istanbul Park, and both cars languished outside the points at the next three races. That mediocre run coincided with BMW's announcement on 29 July that it would withdraw from F1 at the end of the season.

Kubica snatched eighth at Valencia thanks to Mark Webber's slow final pitstop. The BMW Saubers featured in the shock qualifying order at Spa-Francorchamps with Heidfeld lining up third, two places ahead of Kubica. Kubica jumped into second at the start before Kimi Räikkönen passed him on the Kemmel straight and ran wide on the entry to Les Combes. There was contact as the Ferrari rejoined but Kubica survived to finish fourth despite losing out to Vettel at the final pitstops. Heidfeld also ran across the grass at Les Combes on that chaotic opening lap and finished fifth.

The low-downforce pace displayed in Belgium boded well for Monza, but engine problems during qualifying were subsequently blamed on a 'quality issue with the valve gear'. Heidfeld made a fast start from 15th and drove a steady race to seventh. Kubica had an eventful couple of opening laps. Having already clashed with Webber at the Roggia chicane, he passed Vettel into the first Lesmo despite being forced onto the grass as they approached the corner. Ordered to change his damaged front wing by race control, Kubica retired due to an oil leak.

Further revisions in Singapore delivered 0.7sec a lap. There were new front-wing endplates and a redesigned gearbox casing allowed the double diffuser to be optimised. Sent to the back of the grid due to an underweight car, Heidfeld started from the pitlane but was eliminated by Adrian Sutil's Force India, which hit him when rejoining into his path following a spin. That ended a run of 41 consecutive finishes. Heidfeld showed that the new package was finally working in Japan by starting fourth and finishing sixth following a slow pitstop. Eighth in Singapore and ninth in Japan, Kubica returned to form by finishing second in Brazil. Eliminated in first qualifying at Interlagos, Heidfeld ran out of fuel shortly after his pitstop due to a faulty rig. They filled row four in Abu Dhabi, where Heidfeld's fifth place was enough to snatch sixth in the constructors' championship from Williams-Toyota – a far cry from the title challenge that had been promised.

AT&T WILLIAMS

The Williams FW31-Toyota made its track debut at the Algarve test on 19 January when reserve driver Nico Hülkenberg completed 28 laps in mixed conditions. Sam Michael's technical department responded to the rule changes with a new concept in its attempt to reverse Williams's slide down the grid. The FW31 was one of only three new cars to incorporate a double diffuser from launch. It had a wide nose, undercut sidepods and pushrod suspension with a zero-keel at the front. The conventional wing package included a simple two-element front at the start of the season. Vertical 'skate' wings

Nico Rosberg, Williams FW31-Toyota (Monaco GP)

Kazuki Nakajima, Williams FW31-Toyota (Hungarian GP)

on either side of the driver's helmet were discarded after some winter evaluation. Williams Hybrid Technology developed a unique flywheel-based KERS and also investigated the battery route, but neither was raced.

Nico Rosberg and Kazuki Nakajima were confirmed in an unchanged line-up in October. Royal Bank of Scotland remained for the final year of its contract despite its bailout by the British taxpayer. Philips increased its sponsorship but the absence of Baugur Group (Hamley's), Petrobras and Lenovo logos was evidence of the credit crunch.

The Williams FW31-Toyota was quick in winter testing and showed impressive single-lap pace during free practice at several GPs. Rosberg qualified in the top ten at all but two races and scored points on 11 occasions, albeit without finishing on the podium. Seventh in the constructors' championship was a disappointing return given the FW31's potential.

The Australian GP saw protest and counter-protest as the diffuser row unfolded. This included a post-qualifying Williams challenge about the legality of Red Bull and Ferrari sidepods but this was later withdrawn. Rosberg was quickest in all three practice sessions and qualified fifth after making a mistake in Q3. After dropping a place at the start and a slow first pitstop, he set the fastest race lap and finished sixth on deteriorating super-soft tyres. In Malaysia, he made a demon start from fourth on the grid to lead the opening 15 laps only to lose out to Jenson Button at the pitstops. There was criticism of his pace on 'in' and 'out' laps, and he faded to eighth when rain arrived. Another wet race in China saw him finish only 15th and he came home ninth in Bahrain.

Rosberg then scored points at the next eight races, starting with eighth in Spain despite rear-end instability. His sixth place in Monaco included brave overtaking of Felipe Massa and Sebastian Vettel during an early dice. An aero upgrade for Turkey included a new triplane front wing with complicated endplates that redirected air around the wheels. Fifth at that race and the next (Silverstone), Rosberg recovered from poor qualifying in Germany to finish fourth. Williams kept up its aggressive development path as it tried to exploit its best car in years. There was a new front wing, engine cover and rear diffuser at the Nürburgring, and another iteration of both front and back wings in Hungary. Rosberg's scoring run

continued with fourth at the Hungaroring, where a stuck fuel nozzle at his first pitstop cost him a podium, and fifth in Valencia.

The FW31 lacked grip at Spa-Francorchamps, where Rosberg salvaged eighth, and all four Toyota-powered cars were down on straight-line speed at Monza. The FW31 was better suited to the low-speed and bumpy Singapore streets, where Rosberg qualified third and chased Lewis Hamilton's leading McLaren during the opening stint. However, a drive-through penalty for crossing the pit-exit line dropped him out of contention. Rosberg was eliminated in Q2 at Suzuka but started seventh due to grid penalties. He kept his fifth-place finish when his team successfully argued that his speeding behind the safety car was caused by a bug in the standard ECU, so he was unaware of the required delta time. He ran third in the early laps of the Brazilian GP only for his gearbox to fail. Abu Dhabi, his final appearance for Williams, brought a disappointing ninth.

Nakajima did not score a point during his chastening second full F1 season. Retirements from three of the first four races included crashing when running third in Australia. Front-wing damage on the opening lap of the Spanish GP ruined that race, having made Q3 for the first time, then he crashed on the last lap in Monaco. A strong showing in Turkey was not rewarded by the points finish it deserved due to a slow second pitstop when his front-left wheel nut stuck. Nakajima then used a light fuel load to start the British GP from a career-best fifth position and run fourth before fading. He tangled with Jarno Trulli at the start of the German GP, then qualified and finished ninth in Hungary.

Nakajima was quick on Friday at the European GP only for a Q1 engine issue to restrict him to the penultimate row of the grid. A puncture then dropped him to the back of the field and he parked his damaged car before the chequered flag. Last but one in Belgium, his was the leading Toyota-powered car when tenth in Italy. He celebrated the anniversary of his previous points score by finishing ninth in Singapore. Anonymous at his home race, Nakajima joined his team-mate in Q3 for the Brazilian GP, where he challenged for points. However, he had a sizable accident when he was forced onto the grass on the Reta Oposta during a feisty dice with compatriot Kamui Kobayashi's Toyota. Nakajima's F1 career petered out with 13th in Abu Dhabi.

Fernando Alonso, Renault R29 (Bahrain GP)

ING RENAULT F1 TEAM

Renault's victories in the autumn of 2008 were not the springboard back to title contention that had been hoped. Instead, the controversial repercussions of that's year Singapore GP enveloped the team as it sank to eighth overall, with every point scored by its lead driver. Informed before the season that ING would not renew its title partnership for 2010, the slump in global car sales and unfolding scandal placed Renault's future participation in doubt.

Fernando Alonso was disappointed when Ferrari extended Kimi Räikkönen's contract in September and Renault's hopes of retaining its star driver were boosted by his 2008 Singapore and Japanese GP wins. Lucas di Grassi impressed during a three-day test at Jerez, but Renault announced contract extensions for both of its existing drivers in November despite Nelson Piquet Jr's patchy debut campaign. Di Grassi relinquished his role as reserve in the hope of finding a race drive and was replaced by Romain Grosjean.

The Renault R29 initially failed its crash test but was ready to test as scheduled at Portimão on 19 January, with Piquet completing two days before handing over to Alonso. This was the first car under Dirk de Beer as head of aerodynamics, with technical directors Bob

Bell and Rob White responsible for chassis and engine respectively, and Tim Densham as chief designer. The new computational fluid dynamics centre in the basement at Enstone became operational in September 2008 and was instrumental in the later design stages.

The R29's blunt, wide nose, combined with dorsal fin on the engine cover and rudimentary wings, gave a bulky overall impression at launch. Vertical fins under the nose guided air to the sidepods, undertray and single diffuser. Renault had contacted the FIA's Charlie Whiting during the initial design of the R29 regarding its own interpretation of the double diffuser. The semantics of its enquiry proved crucial, for that concept was abandoned when the design team believed that it would be ruled illegal. The wheelbase was shortened to redistribute weight towards the front. Renault was given permission to unfreeze its engine specification over the winter to achieve parity with its rivals.

Developed with Magneti Marelli, the KERS was installed under the fuel cell, a location that raised the centre of gravity and spoiled the balance of the car. Unlike Ferrari, the tank could be lowered when KERS was disabled, giving better handling. It proved an expensive distraction at a time when cuts were being

Nelson Ângelo Piquet, Renault R29 (Monaco GP)

Romain Grosjean, Renault R29 (Singapore GP)

made elsewhere, especially in the aerodynamics department. A late decision was made to use the system in Australia, but it was dropped after the Bahrain GP and only adopted once more, at Monza. Alonso hauled the ungainly machine into the qualifying top ten for much of the campaign, but it lacked grip and aero stability, and Renault faded as development stalled.

Alonso had been bullish at launch: 'The intention is absolutely to win the championship, and from what I have seen so far I don't see any reason why we can't.' Rain affected its initial Portuguese test, where Renault was two seconds off the pace set by Nico Rosberg's Williams-Toyota. Mechanical gremlins restricted mileage and performance, while the final test at Jerez was interrupted when Alonso crashed on the first day after just four laps.

Neither driver made the top-ten qualifying shoot-out for the Australian GP, where Alonso used his KERS to keep more nimble cars at bay on the way to fifth. Laid low in Malaysia by an ear infection and battling his ill-handling machine, Alonso jumped from eighth to fifth at the start before fading to 11th when rain arrived. Needing a strong start to his campaign, Piquet was eliminated in Q1 at the first three races. He blamed brake failure for his crash in Australia, was 'anonymous' at Sepang and needed a new front wing when he spun in China. 'It's not going well for him,' was Edd Straw's understated comment in *Autosport*. The first iteration of Renault's double diffuser was flown to Shanghai and fitted to Alonso's car before qualifying. Alonso planned a short opening stint and used his low fuel load to claim a shock second on the grid only for rain to ruin his race strategy. He stopped early behind the safety car and recovered from a high-speed spin to finish ninth.

Dehydration from a broken drinks bottle caused Alonso to collapse after he was eighth in Bahrain. Piquet escaped Q1 for the first time at that race and finished tenth. Renault's upgrade in Spain only maintained its position in the midfield, although Alonso ran sixth after a great start and snatched fifth from Felipe Massa's fuel-starved Ferrari on the last lap. After finishing 12th in Spain, Piquet was punted out of the Monaco GP by Sébastien Buemi on the approach to Ste-Dévote; Alonso was seventh. They finished outside the points in Turkey and at Silverstone. The latest upgrade on Alonso's car at the Nürburgring included intricate new front-wing endplates and revised suspension. Piquet got through to final qualifying and started ahead of his team-mate for the first time, but made a bad getaway and never recovered. Alonso was eliminated in Q2 and spun on the warm-up lap, but then set the fastest race lap on his way to another seventh place.

Piquet's latest non-score triggered a performance clause in his contract stipulating that he had to be within 40 percent of Alonso's points total by this time. He was retained for Hungary where he continued to struggle in the midfield. Alonso's decision to qualify with a light fuel load once more was rewarded with his first pole position since 2007. He led the opening 11 laps while his fuel lasted, but emerged from his pitstop with the front-right wheel not properly secured. After losing the wheel in Turn 9, he three-wheeled back to the pits only to retire with low fuel pressure.

The fallout from the Hungarian GP was felt during the summer break. The FIA issued Renault with a one-race ban for Alonso's unsafe release, although this was reduced to a $50,000 fine on appeal. Piquet's sacking with immediate effect prompted an explosive pre-emptive statement on the Brazilian's website on 3 August and column inches in the specialist press thereafter.

With Renault cleared to race at the European GP, Alonso continued to shine by topping the FP2 timesheets, qualifying eighth and finishing sixth. Grosjean replaced Piquet, with di Grassi drafted in as reserve driver. The Frenchman was no more successful than his predecessor in his seven races with the team, finishing no higher than 13th. His debut included clashing with Luca Badoer's Ferrari at the second corner and a spin, after which he finished last of the unlapped runners. Raceday at the Belgian GP broke with news that Renault had been summoned by the World Motor Sport Council to answers questions regarding Piquet's crash at the 2008 Singapore GP. It was an unhappy race at Spa-Francorchamps as the R29s lacked downforce and retired, Grosjean having crashed into championship leader Jenson Button at Les Combes on the opening lap. At Monza, Renault used KERS for the first time since April as a one-off and it helped Alonso to claim fifth. Last after an altercation at the first corner, Grosjean was the penultimate finisher with intermittent use of his KERS.

Flavio Briatore and Pat Symonds left the team on 16 September, five days before a 90-minute hearing of the World Motor Sport Council found that Piquet had been instructed to crash deliberately. Those departures contributed to the suspension of Renault's exclusion from the championship, while Piquet was granted immunity when he alerted the FIA in July and was contrite: 'I bitterly regret my actions to follow the orders I was given.' ING accelerated its withdrawal and severed its association with immediate effect. In the wake of those revelations, Bob Bell became team principal with Jean-François Caubet promoted to managing director.

Confirmed by Ferrari for 2010, Alonso outperformed his car once more on the return to Singapore, where he qualified fifth, set the fastest race lap and finished third to claim Renault's only podium of 2009. Grosjean's recurring brake issues ended a miserable weekend. Both were eliminated in Q1 for the Japanese GP and made limited progress in the race. They lacked grip in Brazil, where Alonso was a first-lap victim of Adrian Sutil's spinning Force India and Grosjean finished a lacklustre 13th. A turbulent campaign ended with a downbeat Abu Dhabi GP where both cars were backmarkers.

FORCE INDIA FORMULA ONE TEAM

Force India signed a three-year technical partnership with McLaren-Mercedes on 10 November 2008. The team continued to design and build its own chassis with supply of engine, gearbox and hydraulics covered by the agreement. It was the first time Mercedes-Benz had supplied engines to a customer team since its official return in 1994. Force India also had access to the McLaren-Mercedes KERS but chose not to use it. A consequence of the deal was that Force India

Giancarlo Fisichella, Force India VJM02-Mercedes-Benz (Belgian GP)

dropped its own seven-speed seamless-shift gearbox, which had only been raced since August 2008.

McLaren operations director Simon Roberts joined as chief operating officer on a one-year secondment and team owner Vijay Mallya formally replaced Colin Kolles as team principal. Also leaving at that time, a year early, and heading for the law courts was chief technology officer Mike Gascoyne. An unchanged line-up of Giancarlo Fisichella and Adrian Sutil was confirmed before Christmas, with Vitantonio Liuzzi retained as reserve. Mallya's long-term commitment was emphasised by expansion of the Silverstone factory and investment in computational fluid dynamics.

The late completion of the McLaren-Mercedes tie-up delayed the launch of the Force India VJM02-Mercedes until 1 March. James Key (technical director), Mark Smith (design director), Ian Hall (design project manager) and Simon Phillips (head of aerodynamics) modified the back of the new monocoque, sidepods, cooling system and rear suspension, with the build completed in 108 days. Finished in the colours of the Indian flag, the VJM02 was a conventional single-diffuser design. The nose and front of the chassis were noticeably higher than before, so two tall struts supported the conventional triple front wing, which had turning vanes on the underside. Force India's was the only front wing not to have six-degree movable elements at the Australian GP but these were introduced in Spain; they were separated from the immovable central section by vertical fences as part of an impressive number of upgrades during the season. The sidepods were reduced in size due to the Mercedes FO108W engine's cooling requirements, with exhaust exit fairings ahead of the rear wheels. These had distinctive inlets that combined with side-mounted turning vanes and aerodynamic mirrors to control airflow from the front wheels.

Each driver had just four days in the new car at the end of pre-season testing, so Force India began on the back foot. That was enough time to identify a lack of downforce although straight-line speed and aero efficiency were good. Neither car negotiated Q1 at the first five races. Sutil lost his front wing at the first corner in Australia but recovered to finish ninth when just 0.037sec from snatching a point. Plagued by locking rear brakes, Fisichella's chances evaporated when he lost 20 seconds by overshooting his box at the first pitstop. They were the final classified finishers in

Malaysia, where Fisichella spun moments before the race was red-flagged. Sutil outperformed his team-mate in China but was denied sixth during the closing stages when he aquaplaned off at Turn 6.

Force India introduced its double diffuser in Bahrain. Key explained to *Autocourse*'s Mark Hughes how such a small team had been so quick with that development: 'We'd looked at it before but weren't convinced it would be allowed. That gave us a bit of a head start and we didn't wait for the ruling.' Still, it did not allow Force India to penetrate the top ten as Sutil had a three-place grid drop for impeding Mark Webber and Fisichella survived late contact with Felipe Massa in the race. They started from the last row at Barcelona, where the adjustable front wing was used for the first time. Sutil was caught up in the Turn 2 pile-up and Fisichella finished last after stopping four times due to a refuelling glitch.

Both cars escaped Q1 for the first time at Monaco and Fisichella finished ninth. Sutil repeated that qualifying improvement at Istanbul Park before fading in the race, with brake issues sidelining Fisichella after just four laps. Yet another aero upgrade for Silverstone included an intricate new front wing and undertray, although Sutil's Q1 crash at Becketts prevented either from progressing. Fisichella had a strong race into tenth while Sutil had to start from the pitlane in his newly assembled replacement chassis. Sutil starred at a wet Nürburgring by qualifying seventh despite a heavy fuel load. Briefly second during the first pitstops, a probable points finish was lost when he ran into Kimi Räikkönen's Ferrari when exiting the pits, forcing him to pit next time around for a replacement wing. The non-scoring continued in Hungary when Sutil retired after two laps and Fisichella again finished outside the top ten.

A major upgrade at the European GP was worth seven-tenths a lap. The latest front wing with complex channels underneath and revised movable upper element seemed to work for Sutil started 12th (having only just missed the Q3 cut-off) and finished tenth, two places ahead of his one-stopping team-mate. That improvement did little to prepare the watching public for incredible performances at the next two races. The VJM02's aero efficiency, strong engine and effective soft tyres helped Fisichella claim a shock pole position for the Belgian GP. He lost the lead when defenceless against Räikkönen's KERS on the Kemmel straight before shadowing the Ferrari throughout and finishing second, just 0.939sec behind at the

Vitantonio Liuzzi, Force India VJM02-Mercedes-Benz (Brazilian GP)

Adrian Sutil, Force India VJM02-Mercedes-Benz (Belgian GP)

chequered flag. Sutil narrowly missed Q3 and finished 11th.

Fisichella's performance at Spa-Francorchamps was rewarded with a Ferrari move, with Liuzzi promoted for the rest of 2009 despite stories linking the well-funded Vitaly Petrov to the drive. Pedro de la Rosa doubled as reserve for McLaren and Force India thereafter. Force India's excellent low-downforce set-up also suited Monza, where Sutil qualified second and Liuzzi started his first GP since 2007 from seventh. Sutil finished fourth and only lost a podium finish when he hit a mechanic at his second pitstop, while Liuzzi was on course to score points when a driveshaft failed. Unfortunately, that was his strongest performance for he finished the next four races outside the top ten.

Force India returned to Q1 backmarkers at Singapore's high-downforce Marina Bay street circuit. Sutil spun when he attempted to pass Jaime Alguersuari (Toro Rosso) and ran into Nick Heidfeld (BMW Sauber) as he rejoined, then retired with braking issues. Sutil qualified fourth at Suzuka although he started eighth when penalised for speeding through a yellow-flag zone. There was no reward in the race for he tangled with Heikki Kovalainen when attempting to take eighth as they exited the chicane, leaving both out of contention.

Simon Roberts returned to McLaren before the Brazilian GP and former Honda Racing vice president Otmar Szafnauer replaced him as chief operating officer. Sutil again excelled by qualifying third at a wet Interlagos but clashed with Jarno Trulli on the opening lap to prompt an angry trackside exchange between the drivers. Lacking grip in Abu Dhabi, neither driver got through Q1 and they finished among the backmarkers – a downbeat end to a mixed season.

Although Force India-Mercedes regularly threatened the top eight following the Valencia upgrade, the team scored points only twice, although those performances in Belgium and Italy did move it off the foot of the contructors' table.

SCUDERIA TORO ROSSO

Six months after its shock victory in the 2008 Italian GP, Scuderia Toro Rosso began a torrid campaign that ended with the Red Bull junior team last in the constructors' standings. The departure of Sebastian Vettel, the late arrival of its chassis, reliance on in-factory development (now that testing was curtailed) and restructuring caused an alarming slump.

Rather than sell his shares as had been mooted during 2008, Dietrich Mateschitz regained full ownership of Toro Rosso by acquiring Gerhard Berger's 50 percent stake in December 2008. The team continued to expand its workforce and facilities as it prepared to construct its own car in 2010. Franz Tost, Giorgio Ascanelli and Laurent Mekies remained as team principal, technical director and chief engineer respectively. Gianfranco Fantuzzi replaced Ferrari-bound Massimo Rivola as team manager.

Vettel was promoted to Red Bull Racing although there were some who questioned whether that was the right move given Ferrari's engine advantage over the Renault used by the senior team. Sébastien Buemi and Takuma Satō tested at Jerez on 17 and 18 September respectively as the team evaluated whether to

Sébastien Buemi, Toro Rosso STR04-Ferrari (German GP)

promote youth once more or hire an experienced driver. Buemi completed over 2,500 testing miles for Toro Rosso and Red Bull before being announced as Toro Rosso's first 2009 race driver on 9 January. Despite his inconsistent maiden campaign, Sébastien Bourdais was preferred to Satō as Buemi's team-mate. Brendon Hartley was named reserve driver for both Red Bull-owned teams after approval of his super licence by the FIA in May.

The conversion of the Red Bull Technology-designed Toro Rosso STR04-Ferrari was completed in 22 days, with fuel system, clutch, cooling ancillaries and hydraulics all modified at Faenza. The new car first ran in a private session at Adria in northern Italy on 3 March before joining the following week's Barcelona group test. Toro Rosso's Ferrari deal included the supply of a KERS although the team did not race it. The adaptations to the basic design shifted weight distribution rearwards, giving compromised high-speed aerodynamics and increased rear-tyre wear.

Already on the back foot following the late introduction of the STR04, pre-season mileage was limited by a suspension issue and teething troubles. Modest expectations appeared accurate when both cars were eliminated in first qualifying for the Australian GP. However, they adopted a long final stint and benefitted from a late crash to finish eighth (Buemi impressive on debut) and ninth (Bourdais). That became a double points score – seventh and eighth respectively – once the outcome of the Jarno Trulli/Lewis Hamilton yellow-flag incident was decided. A Q1 crash meant Buemi started last in Malaysia, and his spin as the monsoon hit was a contributing

factor to the race being abandoned, a decision rued by tenth-placed Bourdais. Buemi continue to impress by qualifying in the top ten in China. He survived running into the back of Vettel's Red Bull behind the safety car to finish eighth. That outshone his more experienced team-mate, who was eliminated in first qualifying and spun twice during his race into 11th. Q1 elimination followed for both drivers in Bahrain.

The first upgrade of the year at Barcelona included new wings and Red Bull's Malaysian-specification diffuser. Bourdais failed to negotiate first qualifying once more and the team-mates collided while trying to avoid Trulli's spinning Toyota at the second corner of the race. Bourdais eased mounting pressure with eighth in Monaco but Buemi rammed Nelson Piquet Jr's Renault at Ste-Dévote. Increasingly uncompetitive as they waited for much-needed upgrades, both cars were eliminated in Q1 at the next three races. Bourdais was last in Turkey, collided with Heikki Kovalainen at Silverstone and retired at the Nürburgring. Those performances took their toll for Bourdais was released four days after the German GP and did not race in F1 again.

In Hungary, Toro Rosso became the last team to introduce a double diffuser, to Red Bull's Silverstone specification. It required the hydraulics to be reworked and rear axle line moved back to increase space for the upper deck. Buemi used the revised STR04 to start from an improved tenth but made a poor start and finished last following a spin. Reserve driver at the German GP, Jaime Alguersuari replaced Bourdais in Hungary amid speculation that

Sébastien Bourdais, Toro Rosso STR04-Ferrari (Australian GP)

five-time World Rally Champion Sébastien Loeb would race at the season-closing Abu Dhabi GP. Loeb tested David Price Racing's GP2 car at Jerez on 8 October but that intriguing F1 one-off was cancelled when his super licence was denied. The youngest F1 driver to date when he started the Hungarian GP at 19 years and 125 days old, Alguersuari stayed out of trouble to finish that race and the next as he learnt the car and tracks without any testing. Buemi crashed out of the European GP when a brake disc failed.

In Belgium, Alguersuari was involved in the first-lap mêlée at Les Combes and Buemi finished 12th. A year after Vettel's Monza victory, the Toro Rosso duo qualified at the back and made no impression during the race. Both drivers retired on lap 48 in

Singapore and were accident-prone at Suzuka, where they crashed during second qualifying, Buemi (who was already quick enough to progress to Q3) exiting the Spoon Curve and Alguersuari at the first Degner. Given a five-place grid penalty for attempting to limp back to the pits after his shunt, Buemi was delayed on the grid by a clutch issue that terminated his race after 11 laps. A bruising weekend ended when Alguersuari lost control at 130R and crashed again.

Brazil saw Toro Rosso finally score points for the first time since Monaco when Buemi converted an excellent sixth on the grid into seventh at the finish. He backed that up in Abu Dhabi with another Q3 appearance and eighth place, although Toro Rosso-Ferrari still finished last in the constructors' standings.

Jaime Alguersuari, Toro Rosso STR04-Ferrari (Brazilian GP)

2009 RESULTS

DRIVER PERFORMANCE

DRIVER	CAR-ENGINE	AUS	MAL	PRC	BRN	E	MC	TR	GB	D	H	EU	B	I	SGP	J	BR	UAE
Jaime Alguersuari	Toro Rosso STR04-Ferrari	–	–	–	–	–	–	–	–	–	20 15	19 16	17 R	20 R	16 R	12 R	12 14	14 R
Fernando Alonso	Renault R29	10 5	8 11	2 9	7 8	8 5	9 7	8 10	10 14	12 7 FL	1 R	8 6	13 R	8 5	5 3 FL	16 10	10 R	15 14
Luca Badoer	Ferrari F60	–	–	–	–	–	–	–	–	–	20 17	20 14	–	–	–	–	–	–
Rubens Barrichello	Brawn BGP001-Mercedes-Benz	2 2	9 5	4 4 FL	6 5	3 2 FL	3 2	3 R	2 3	2 6	13 10	3 1	4 7	5 1	9 6	6 7	1 8	4 4
Sébastien Bourdais	Toro Rosso STR04-Ferrari	17 8	15 10	15 11	20 13	17 R	14 8	20 18	17 R	19 R	–	–	–	–	–	–	–	–
Sébastien Buemi	Toro Rosso STR04-Ferrari	13 7	20 16	10 8	16 17	15 R	11 R	18 15	19 18	17 16	11 16	15 R	16 12	19 13	13 R	13 R	6 7	10 8
Jenson Button	Brawn BGP001-Mercedes-Benz	1 1	1 1 FL	5 3	4 1	1 1	1 1	2 1 FL	6 6	3 5	8 7	5 7	14 R	6 2	11 5	10 8	14 5	5 3
Giancarlo Fisichella	Force India VJM02-Mercedes-Benz	15 11	18 18	20 14	17 15	20 14	13 9	19 R	16 10	18 11	17 14	16 12	1 2	–	–	–	–	–
	Ferrari F60	–	–	–	–	–	–	–	–	–	–	–	–	14 9	17 13	14 12	19 10	20 16
Timo Glock	Toyota TF109	19 4	3 3	19 7	2 7	6 10	20 10	13 8	8 9	20 9	14 6	13 14 FL	7 10	16 11	6 2	20 DNS	–	–
Romain Grosjean	Renault R29	–	–	–	–	–	–	–	–	–	–	14 15	19 R	12 15	18 R	17 16	13 13	19 18
Lewis Hamilton	McLaren MP4-24-Mercedes-Benz	18 DSQ	12 7	9 6	5 4	14 9	19 12	16 13	18 16	5 18	4 1	1 2	12 R	1 12	1 1	3 3	17 3	1 R
Nick Heidfeld	BMW Sauber F1.09	9 10	10 2	11 12	14 19	13 7	16 11	11 11	15 15	11 10	16 11	11 11	3 5	15 7	20 R	4 6	18 R	8 5
Kamui Kobayashi	Toyota TF109	–	–	–	–	–	–	–	–	–	–	–	–	–	NT DNP	11 9	12 6
Heikki Kovalainen	McLaren MP4-24-Mercedes-Benz	12 R	14 R	12 5	11 12	18 R	7 R	14 14	13 R	6 8	6 5	2 4	15 6	4 6	8 7	11 11	16 12	18 11
Robert Kubica	BMW Sauber F1.09	4 14	6 R	17 13	13 18	10 11	17 R	10 7	12 13	16 14	19 13	10 8	5 4	13 R	7 8	9 9	8 2	7 10
Vitantonio Liuzzi	Force India VJM02-Mercedes-Benz	–	–	–	–	–	–	–	–	–	–	–	–	7 R	19 14	18 14	20 11	16 15
Felipe Massa	Ferrari F60	6 R	16 9	13 R	8 14	4 6	5 4 FL	7 6	11 4	8 3	10 DNS	–	–	–	–	–	–	–
Kazuki Nakajima	Williams FW31-Toyota	11 R	11 12	14 R	12 R	11 13	10 15	12 12	5 11	13 12	9 9	17 18	18 13	17 10	10 9	15 15	9 R	13 13
Nelson Ângelo Piquet	Renault R29	14 R	17 13	16 16	15 10	12 12	12 R	17 16	14 12	10 13	15 12	–	–	–	–	–	–	–
Kimi Räikkönen	Ferrari F60	7 15	7 14	8 10	10 6	16 R	2 3	6 9	9 8	9 R	7 2	6 3	6 1	3 3	12 10	5 4	5 6	11 12
Nico Rosberg	Williams FW31-Toyota	5 6 FL	4 8	7 15	9 9	9 8	6 6	9 5	7 5	15 4	5 4	4 5	10 8	18 16	3 11	7 5	7 R	9 9
Adrian Sutil	Force India VJM02-Mercedes-Benz	16 9	19 17	18 17	19 16	19 R	15 14	15 17	20 17	7 15	18 R	12 10	11 11	2 4 FL	15 R	8 13	3 R	17 17
Jarno Trulli	Toyota TF109	20 3	2 4	6 R	1 3 FL	7 R	18 13	5 4	4 7	14 17	12 8	18 13	2 R	11 14	14 12	2 2	4 R	6 7
Sebastian Vettel	Red Bull RB5-Renault	3 13	13 15	1 1	3 2	2 4	4 R	1 3	1 1 FL	4 2	2 R	4 R	8 3 FL	9 8	2 4	1 1	15 4	2 1 FL
Mark Webber	Red Bull RB5-Renault	8 12	5 6	3 2	18 11	5 3	8 5	4 2	3 2	1 1	3 3 FL	9 9	9 9	10 R	4 R	19 17 FL	2 1 FL	3 2

FORMULA 1 RACE WINNERS

ROUND	RACE (CIRCUIT)	DATE	WINNER
1	ING Australian Grand Prix (Albert Park)	Mar 29	Jenson Button (Brawn BGP001-Mercedes-Benz)
2	Petronas Malaysian Grand Prix (Sepang)	Apr 5	Jenson Button (Brawn BGP001-Mercedes-Benz)
3	Chinese Grand Prix (Shanghai)	Apr 19	Sebastian Vettel (Red Bull RB5-Renault)
4	Gulf Air Bahrain Grand Prix (Sakhir)	Apr 26	Jenson Button (Brawn BGP001-Mercedes-Benz)
5	Gran Premio de España Telefónica (Catalunya)	May 10	Jenson Button (Brawn BGP001-Mercedes-Benz)
6	Grand Prix de Monaco (Monte Carlo)	May 24	Jenson Button (Brawn BGP001-Mercedes-Benz)
7	ING Turkish Grand Prix (Istanbul Park)	Jun 7	Jenson Button (Brawn BGP001-Mercedes-Benz)
8	Santander British Grand Prix (Silverstone)	Jun 21	Sebastian Vettel (Red Bull RB5-Renault)
9	Grosser Preis Santander von Deutschland (Nürburgring)	Jul 12	Mark Webber (Red Bull RB5-Renault)
10	ING Magyar Nagydíj (Hungaroring)	Jul 26	Lewis Hamilton (McLaren MP4-24-Mercedes-Benz)
11	Telefónica Grand Prix of Europe (Valencia)	Aug 23	Rubens Barrichello (Brawn BGP001-Mercedes-Benz)
12	ING Belgian Grand Prix (Spa-Francorchamps)	Aug 30	Kimi Räikkönen (Ferrari F60)
13	Gran Premio Santander d'Italia (Monza)	Sep 13	Rubens Barrichello (Brawn BGP001-Mercedes-Benz)
14	Singtel Singapore Grand Prix (Marina Bay)	Sep 27	Lewis Hamilton (McLaren MP4-24-Mercedes-Benz)
15	Fuji Television Japanese Grand Prix (Suzuka)	Oct 4	Sebastian Vettel (Red Bull RB5-Renault)
16	Grande Prêmio Petrobras do Brasil (Interlagos)	Oct 18	Mark Webber (Red Bull RB5-Renault)
17	Etihad Airways Abu Dhabi Grand Prix (Yas Marina)	Nov 1	Sebastian Vettel (Red Bull RB5-Renault)

DRIVERS' CHAMPIONSHIP

	DRIVERS	POINTS
1	Jenson Button	95
2	Sebastian Vettel	84
3	Rubens Barrichello	77
4	Mark Webber	69.5
5	Lewis Hamilton	49
6	Kimi Räikkönen	48
7	Nico Rosberg	34.5
8	Jarno Trulli	32.5
9	Fernando Alonso	26
10	Timo Glock	24
11	Felipe Massa	22
12	Heikki Kovalainen	22
13	Nick Heidfeld	19
14	Robert Kubica	17
15	Giancarlo Fisichella	8
16	Sébastien Buemi	6
17	Adrian Sutil	5
18	Kamui Kobayashi	3
19	Sébastien Bourdais	2
20	Kazuki Nakajima	0
21	Nelson Ângelo Piquet	0
22	Vitantonio Liuzzi	0
23	Romain Grosjean	0
24	Jaime Alguersuari	0
25	Luca Badoer	0

CONSTRUCTORS' CHAMPIONSHIP

	CONSTRUCTORS	POINTS
1	Brawn-Mercedes-Benz	172
2	Red Bull-Renault	153.5
3	McLaren-Mercedes-Benz	71
4	Ferrari	70
5	Toyota	59.5
6	BMW Sauber	36
7	Williams-Toyota	34.5
8	Renault	26
9	Force India-Mercedes-Benz	13
10	Toro Rosso-Ferrari	8

Lewis Hamilton leads into the first corner of the European Grand Prix at Valencia

INDEX

Ide, Yūji 211, 213, 214, 215
Iley, John 22, 72, 76, 126, 131, 161, 190, 252, 282
Illien, Mario 14, 99, 159
Ilmor 14, 41, 70, 84, 158
Irvine, Eddie 12, 17, 24, 27–29, 30, 42, 45, 49, 51–53, 56, 57, 78–80, 109, 114, 179

Jaguar 12, 16, 20, 24, 27–29, 38, 39, 40, 42, 45, 46, 48, 49, 51–53, 54, 55, 56, 64, 70, 78–80, 81, 83, 84, 86, 92, 93, 96, 97, 98, 101, 104, 107, 109–111, 116, 132, 133, 136, 138, 139, 140–142, 145, 147, 171, 173, 230, 231
  R1-Cosworth 27–29, 52
    R1B-Cosworth 52
  R2-Cosworth 51–53
  R3-Cosworth 78–80, 110
    R3B-Cosworth 79
    R3C-Cosworth 110
  R4 Cosworth 109, 110–111
    R4B-Cosworth 141
  R5-Cosworth 140–142, 171
    R5B-Cosworth 142
  R6-Cosworth 171, 208
Jani, Neel 107, 171, 208
Janiš, Jaroslav 54, 147
Jenkins, Alan 31
John Paul II, Pope 162
Jordan 15, 17, 19, 22–24, 27, 30, 38, 40, 42, 44, 45–47, 48, 49, 53, 55, 56, 64, 66, 69, 72, 74, 76–78, 80, 84, 92, 107, 113–116, 124, 126, 131, 134, 138, 139, 141, 142, 145–148, 149, 154, 160, 166, 171, 175–178, 181, 209, 267
  199-Mugen 23
  EJ10-Mugen 22–24
  EJ11-Honda 45–47
  EJ12-Honda 76–78
    EJ12-Cosworth 114
  EJ13-Ford 113–116
  EJ14-Ford 145–148, 176
  EJ15-Toyota 176–178
    EJ15B-Toyota 177, 178, 211
Jordan, Eddie 10, 22, 23, 24, 47, 76, 92, 113, 134, 145, 147, 175, 176
Juan Carlos I, King 189
Junqueira, Bruno 16, 17, 29, 42

Kalkhoven, Kevin 142, 171
Källenius, Otto 158
Kanaan, Tony 169
Karthikeyan, Narain 52, 114, 148, 175, 176, 178, 181, 205, 228, 233, 241, 264

Katayama, Ukyo 213
Kennedy, David 148
KERS (Kinetic Energy Recovery System) 274, 276, 277, 279, 280, 281, 282, 283, 284, 285, 286, 287, 288, 290, 291, 292, 293, 294, 296
Key, James 76, 176, 209, 239, 267, 294
Kiesa, Nicolas 119, 177, 178, 179
Kiuchi, Takeo 170, 195
Klien, Christian 132, 138, 140–142, 147, 149, 171, 172, 173, 191, 194, 202, 203, 204, 207, 235, 237, 241, 254, 265, 267, 287
Kobayashi, Kamui 231, 258, 278, 285, 287, 290
Kolles, Colin 176, 178, 208, 211, 238, 267, 269, 294
Kovalainen, Heikki 131, 148, 156, 188, 199, 226–227, 230, 232, 235, 250–252, 256, 263, 266, 278, 281–282, 295, 296
Krack, Mike 138, 198
Kreyer, Norbert 84, 111, 144
Kristensen, Tom 42
Kubica, Robert 179, 188, 192, 198, 199–200, 204, 221, 223, 224–226, 232, 242, 243, 246–247, 251, 254–256, 258, 264, 277, 278, 279, 280, 286, 287–289
Kurusu, Toshiro 111

Lacey, Simon 128, 235, 241, 250
Lainé, André 157
Lamborghini 213
Langford & Peck 58
Lasée, Marcel 76
Lauda, Niki 51, 53, 78, 79, 80, 109
Laurenz, Werner 16, 42, 97, 99, 136
Le Fleming, Andy 51
Leach, Martin 269
Lee, Marchy 179
Legge, Katherine 181
Leinders, Bas 147, 148
Lemarié, Patrick 20, 80
Leyton House 231
Ligier 48, 53, 213
Litjens, John 258
Liuzzi, Vitantonio 97, 138, 171, 172, 173, 174, 194, 200, 203, 204, 207, 208–209, 230, 233–235, 241, 267, 268, 294, 295
Loasby, Mark 167
Loeb, Sébastien 279, 297

Lola 51, 108, 117, 138, 180, 268
López, José Maria 131, 148, 188
Lotterer, André 27, 52, 53, 78, 79
Lotus 11, 228
Lowe, Paddy 158, 250, 280
Lyons, Richard 114, 148

Magneti Marelli (electronics) 44, 156, 252, 282, 291
Maik, Hans-Ulrich 99, 136
Maldonado, Pastor 179
Mallya, Vijay 241, 267, 268, 294
Manning, Darren 16, 20, 48, 80
Mansell, Nigel 14, 59
Manwaring, Rupert 59, 117
Marko, Helmut 171, 173
Marmorini, Luca 84, 111, 142, 164, 200, 282, 285
Marques, Tarso 58, 59, 64
Marshall, Rob 188, 202, 262
Martens, Jean-Claude 84
Martinelli, Paolo 66, 94, 161, 192, 222
Martinet, François 236
Martini, Pierluigi 16
Maserati 102
Massa, Felipe 74–76, 80, 87, 107, 114, 126, 129, 138–139, 141, 173, 174–175, 187, 190, 191–192, 198, 199, 222–223, 226, 243, 246–247, 248, 249, 251, 252–254, 261, 262, 268, 279, 282–284, 290, 292, 294
Matchin, Peter 79
Mateschitz, Dietrich 44, 74, 87, 171, 179, 204, 207, 209, 260, 295
Matsuura, Kosuke 105, 213
Mayer, Teddy 280
Mayländer, Bernd 10, 11
Mazzacane, Gastón 29–30, 54, 56, 64
McCool, Peter 238
McLaren 10, 13, 14–16, 17, 18, 21, 22, 24, 26, 27, 30, 31, 38, 39–41, 44, 45, 48, 49, 51, 53, 54, 58, 68, 69, 70–72, 74, 76, 78, 79, 87, 92, 95, 99–102, 110, 114, 126, 127, 128, 133, 135, 136–138, 141, 154, 157, 158–161, 162, 166, 167, 168, 187, 188, 191, 192–195, 199, 202, 205, 206, 209, 213, 218, 220, 221, 222, 223, 224, 225, 226, 227, 228, 230, 231, 235, 236, 241–243, 245, 249, 250–252, 253, 254, 256, 258, 260, 264, 267, 274, 276, 278, 279, 280–282, 290, 293, 294, 295
  MP4-14-Mercedes-Benz 27

MP4-15-Mercedes-Benz 14–16
MP4-15K-Mercedes-Benz 40
MP4-16-Mercedes-Benz 40–41
  MP4-16B-Mercedes-Benz 70
MP4-17-Mercedes-Benz 70–72, 99
  MP4-17D-Mercedes-Benz 99, 100–102, 136
MP4-18-Mercedes-Benz 93, 99–100, 101, 102, 136, 159
MP4-19-Mercedes-Benz 136–137, 159
  MP4-19B-Mercedes-Benz 136, 137–138, 158
MP4-20-Mercedes-Benz 158–161
  MP4-20B-Mercedes-Benz 193
MP4-21-Mercedes-Benz 192–195, 230, 241
MP4-22-Mercedes-Benz 241–243
MP4-23-Mercedes-Benz 248, 250–252
MP4-24-Mercedes-Benz 280–282
McLaren Electronic Systems 248, 250, 252
  Electronic Control Unit (ECU) 241, 248, 250, 252, 290
McLaren, Bruce 104, 280
McNish, Allan 79, 84–86, 102, 111, 132, 147
McQuilliam, John 22, 45, 114, 147, 176, 209, 268
Mekies, Laurent 208, 295
Mercedes-Benz 10, 14–16, 30, 37, 45, 53, 58, 64, 70–72, 93, 97, 99–102, 110, 114, 127, 127, 128, 135, 136–138, 145, 154, 157, 158–161, 167, 168, 188, 192–195, 199, 218, 220, 222, 223, 224, 226, 227, 241–243, 245, 248, 250–252, 253, 254, 256, 264, 274, 276–278, 279, 280–282, 284, 293–295
  FO110J (V10) 14
  FO110K (V10) 40
  FO110M (V10) 70
  FO110P (V10) 99
  FO110Q (V10) 136
  FO110R (V10) 159
  FO108S (V8) 193
    Phase 4 194

  FO108T (V8) 241
  FO108V (V8) 250
  FO108W (V8) 277, 294
Mercedes-Ilmor — see 'Ilmor'
Message, Gordon 49
Michael, Sam 42, 45, 97, 134, 167, 206, 207, 228, 264, 289
Michelin (tyres) 36, 42, 50, 52, 54, 58, 68, 69, 70, 71, 79, 80, 83, 84, 93, 96, 99, 102, 103, 104, 105, 107, 110, 117, 127, 128, 130, 133, 136, 138, 154, 155, 156, 157, 160, 161, 162, 164, 165, 170, 173, 174, 178, 186, 190, 191, 200, 201, 203, 205, 207, 208, 209, 220, 226, 229
Midland 175, 176, 178, 208, 209–211, 212, 215, 239
  M16 Toyota 209–211, 215, 239
Migeot, Jean-Claude 239
Minagawa, Saneyuki 276
Minardi 12, 18, 19, 29–30, 38, 42, 50, 51, 54, 56, 58–59, 72, 79, 81–84, 87, 92, 105, 109, 111, 113, 116–119, 124, 131, 138, 139, 147, 148–149, 154, 163, 173, 178, 179–181, 203, 207, 208, 211, 260
  M02-Fondmetal 29–30, 31
  PS01-European 58–59, 83
    PS01B-Cosworth 117
  PS02-Asiatech 81–83, 116
  PS03-Cosworth 116–119, 148
  PS04-Cosworth 119, 148
    PS04B-Cosworth 119, 148–149, 179
  PS05-Cosworth 180–181
Minardi, Giancarlo 58
Mitsusada, Hidetoshi 18
Mobil (fuel and oil) 250
Mol, Michiel 211, 241
Monaghan, Paul 171, 176, 279
Mondini, Giorgio 188, 210, 211
Montagny, Franck 102, 104, 131, 132, 156, 177, 178, 188, 214, 215, 231, 258, 267
Monteiro, Tiago 102, 160, 166, 175, 176, 177, 178, 179, 209, 211–212, 215, 233
Montin, Paolo 114
Montoya, Connie 135
Montoya, Juan Pablo 16, 17, 38, 39, 41, 42–43, 49, 55, 57, 65, 66, 68–70, 71, 73, 96, 97–99, 101, 127, 130, 132, 133–135, 136, 138, 157, 158, 159–161, 166, 168, 173, 178, 192, 194, 199, 207
Morbidelli, Gianni 58